INTERNATIONAL ORGANIZATIONS IN WTO DISPUTE SETTLEMENT

How Much Institutional Sensitivity?

This book analyses the role of international organizations in WTO dispute settlement as arising from a number of WTO disputes. In particular, the roles of the IMF, WIPO, the WCO and WHO are addressed. The use of the Vienna Convention rules of interpretation framework allows an evaluation of the weight attributed to this material by the WTO adjudicator. This allows specific conclusions to be drawn regarding the level of institutional sensitivity of the WTO adjudicator to each of the organizations. As well as being a valuable source of research, the analysis will appeal to international law scholars, civil servants and law practitioners interested in the WTO and dispute settlement.

MARINA FOLTEA is a researcher at the University of Bocconi, Milan, a senior research fellow at the World Trade Institute and a visiting lecturer for the LL M in intellectual property rights at the University of Turin.

CAMBRIDGE INTERNATIONAL TRADE AND ECONOMIC LAW

As the processes of regionalization and globalization have intensified, there have been accompanying increases in the regulation of international trade and economic law at the levels of international, regional and national laws.

The subject matter of this series is international economic law. Its core is the regulation of international trade and investment, and cognate areas such as intellectual property and competition policy. The series publishes books on related regulatory areas, in particular human rights, labour, environment and culture, as well as sustainable development. These areas are vertically linked at the international, regional and national level, and the series extends to the implementation of these rules at these different levels. The series also includes works on governance, dealing with the structure and operation of related international organizations in the field of international economic law, and the way they interact with other subjects of international and national law.

Series editors

Dr Lorand Bartels, *University of Cambridge*
Professor Thomas Cottier, *University of Berne*
Professor William Davey, *University of Illinois*

Books in the series

Trade Policy Flexibility and Enforcement in the WTO: A Law and Economics Analysis
Simon A. B. Schropp

The Multilaterization of International Investment Law
Stephan W. Schill

The Law, Economics and Politics of Retaliation in WTO Dispute Settlement
Edited by Chad P. Bown and Joost Pauwelyn

Non-discrimination in International Trade in Services: 'Likeness' in WTO/GATS
Nicolas Diebold

Processes and Production Methods (PPMs) in WTO Law: Interfacing Trade and Social Goals
Christiane R. Conrad

African Regional Trade Agreements as Legal Regimes
James Thuo Gathii

The Law and Politics of WTO Waivers: Stability and Flexibility in Public International Law
Isabel Feichtner

Public Services and International Trade Liberalization: Human Rights and Gender Implications
Barnali Choudhury

International Organizations in WTO Dispute Settlement: How Much Institutional Sensitivity?
Marina Foltea

INTERNATIONAL ORGANIZATIONS IN WTO DISPUTE SETTLEMENT

How Much Institutional Sensitivity?

MARINA FOLTEA

CAMBRIDGE
UNIVERSITY PRESS

CAMBRIDGE UNIVERSITY PRESS
Cambridge, New York, Melbourne, Madrid, Cape Town,
Singapore, São Paulo, Delhi, Mexico City

Cambridge University Press
The Edinburgh Building, Cambridge CB2 8RU, UK

Published in the United States of America by Cambridge University Press, New York

www.cambridge.org
Information on this title: www.cambridge.org/9781107028241

First published 2012

Printed and bound in the United Kingdom by the MPG Books Group

A catalogue record for this publication is available from the British Library

Library of Congress Cataloguing in Publication data
Foltea, Marina, 1977–
International organizations in WTO dispute settlement : how much
institutional sensitivity? / Marina Foltea.
pages cm. – (Cambridge international trade and economic law)
Includes bibliographical references and index.
ISBN 978-1-107-02824-1 (hardback)
1. World Trade Organization. 2. Foreign trade regulation. 3. International
agencies. 4. Arbitration (International law) I. Title.
K4610.5.F65 2012
382′.92 – dc23 2012030973

ISBN 978-1-107-02824-1 Hardback

CONTENTS

ABBREVIATIONS

AB	Appellate Body
ABR	Appellate Body Report
ACP	African, Caribbean and Pacific Countries
AD	Anti-dumping
BIRPI	United International Bureaux for the Protection of Intellectual Property
CBD	Convention on Biological Diversity
CITES	Convention on International Trade in Endangered Species of Wild Fauna and Flora
Codex	Codex Alimentarius Commission
CPM	Commission on Phytosanitary Measures
DSB	Dispute Settlement Body
DSU	Dispute Settlement Understanding
EC	European Commission
EFTA	European Free Trade Association
ESCAP	Economic and Social Commission for Asia and the Pacific
EU	European Union
FAO	Food and Agriculture Organization
FCTC	Framework Convention on Tobacco Control
GATS	General Agreement on Trade in Services
GATT	General Agreement on Tariffs and Trade
GPVD	Good Practice in the Use of Veterinary Drugs
HACCP	Hazard Analysis and Critical Control Points
HS	Harmonized Commodity Description and Coding System
IARC	International Agency for Research on Cancer
ICANN	Internet Corporation for Assigned Names and Numbers
ICAO	International Civil Aviation Organization
ICJ	International Court of Justice
IEC	International Electrotechnical Commission
IHR	International Health Regulations
IICA	Inter-American Institute for Cooperation on Agriculture
ILC	International Law Commission
ILO	International Labour Organization

IMF	International Monetary Fund
IMO	International Maritime Organization
IPCS	International Programme on Chemical Safety
IPPC	International Plant Protection Convention
ISO	International Organization for Standardization
ITC	International Trade Centre
ITLOS	International Tribunal for the Law of the Sea
ITO	International Trade Organization
ITU	International Telecommunication Union
JECFA	Joint FAO/WHO Expert Committee on Food Additives
NGO	non-governmental organization
OAU	Organization of African Unity
OECD	Organization for Economic Co-operation and Development
OIE	Office International des Epizooties/International Office of Epizootics, now World Organization for Animal Health
OIRSA	Organismo Internacional Regional de Sanidad Agropecuaria (Regional International Organization for Plant Protection and Animal Health)
PCIJ	Permanent Court of International Justice
PGE	Permanent Group of Experts
RFMO	Regional Fisheries Management Organizations
SCM	Subsidies and Countervailing Measures
SELA	Latin American Economic System
SPS	Sanitary and Phytosanitary Measures
TBT	Technical Barriers to Trade
TPRM	Trade Policy Review Mechanism
TRIPS	Trade-Related Aspects of Intellectual Property Rights
UNCLOS	United Nations Convention on the Law of the Sea
UNCTAD	United Nations Conference on Trade and Development
UNEP	United Nations Environment Programme
UNESCO	United Nations Educational, Scientific and Cultural Organization
UPOV	International Union for the Protection of New Varieties of Plants
VCLT	Vienna Convention on the Law of Treaties 1969
WCO	World Customs Organization
WHO	World Health Organization
WIPO	World Intellectual Property Organization
WTO	World Trade Organization
WWF	World Wildlife Fund

TABLE OF WTO REPORTS

Canada – Aircraft Panel Report, *Canada – Measures Affecting the Export of Civilian Aircraft*, WT/DS70/R, adopted 20 August 1999, as upheld by Appellate Body Report WT/DS70/AB/R, DSR 1999:IV, 1443, 70

Canada – Aircraft Credits and Guarantees Panel Report, *Canada – Export Credits and Loan Guarantees for Regional Aircraft*, WT/DS222/R and Corr.1, adopted 19 February 2002, DSR 2002:III, 849, 32, 71

Canada – Continued Suspension Appellate Body Report, *Canada – Continued Suspension of Obligations in the EC – Hormones Dispute*, WT/DS321/AB/R, adopted 14 November 2008, 245, 248–9, 264–5, 273–4

Canada – Continued Suspension Panel Report, *Canada – Continued Suspension of Obligations in the EC – Hormones Dispute*, WT/DS321/R, adopted 14 November 2008, as modified by Appellate Body Report WT/DS321/AB/R, 245, 248–9, 264–5, 273–4

Canada – Pharmaceutical Patents Panel Report, *Canada – Patent Protection of Pharmaceutical Products*, WT/DS114/R, adopted 7 April 2000, DSR 2000:V, 2289, 118

Chile – Price Band System Appellate Body Report, *Chile – Price Band System and Safeguard Measures Relating to Certain Agricultural Products*, WT/DS207/AB/R, adopted 23 October 2002, DSR 2002:VIII, 3045 (Corr.1, DSR 2006:XII, 5473), 109–10

Chile – Price Band System Panel Report, *Chile – Price Band System and Safeguard Measures Relating to Certain Agricultural Products*, WT/DS207/R, adopted 23 October 2002, as modified by Appellate Body Report WT/DS207AB/R, DSR 2002:VIII, 3127, 118

China – Auto Parts Appellate Body Reports, *China – Measures Affecting Imports of Automobile Parts*, WT/DS339/AB/R, WT/DS340/AB/R, WT/DS342/AB/R, adopted 12 January 2009, 104

China – Auto Parts Panel Reports, *China – Measures Affecting Imports of Automobile Parts*, WT/DS339/R, WT/DS340/R, WT/DS342/R and Add.1 and Add.2, adopted 12 January 2009, upheld (WT/DS339/R) and as modified (WT/DS340/R, WT/DS342/R) by Appellate Body Reports WT/DS339/AB/R, WT/DS340/AB/R, WT/DS342/AB/R, 227, 229–34, 236, 238–40, 244, 289

China – IP Rights Panel Report, *China – Measures Affecting the Protection and Enforcement of Intellectual Property Rights*, WT/DS362/R, adopted 26 January 2009, DSR 2009, 199, 201–2, 211–15, 217–18, 226

Dominican Republic – Import and Sale of Cigarettes Panel Report, *Dominican Republic – Measures Affecting the Importation and Internal Sale of Cigarettes*,

TABLE OF GATT 1947 REPORTS

Introduction

I. The phenomenon of fragmentation of international organizations

Today we witness numerous 'islands' in the general system of international law administered by various international organizations.[1] The origin of these international organizations can be traced back to the nineteenth century, when states realized the need to solve their problems on more than a bilateral basis.[2] The increasing interdependence of states led first to the rise of multilateral international conferences, initially on an ad hoc and later on a periodic basis (such as the Congress of Vienna of 1815).[3] More permanent modes of operation were evidenced in the creation of the Central Rhine Commission in 1804 and the European Danube Commission in 1856, which responded to commercial needs to regulate river traffic. Later, other international public administrative units emerged, such as the Universal Telegraphic Union (1865), the General Postal Union (1874), the International Bureau of Industrial Property (1883) and the International Union of Railway Freight Transportation (1890). The creation of these

1 See Henry G. Schermers and Niels M. Blokker, *International Institutional Law: Unity within Diversity*, 4th edn (The Hague and Boston, MA: Martinus Nijhoff, 2003), 26, defining international organizations as collections of sovereign states that have banded together as states to create, under a constitutive international agreement governed by international law usually known as a 'charter' or a 'constitution', an apparatus, more or less permanent, charged with the pursuit of certain defined common ends.

2 Although traces of modern international organizations already appear in the ancient Greek Achean League, through which city states sought to discourage conflict and generate co-operation. See Robert F. Riggs and Jack C. Plano, *The United Nations: International Organization and World Politics*, 2nd edn (Belmont, CA: Wadsworth Publishing, 1994), 1–15; Harold K. Jacobson, *Networks of Interdependence*, 2nd edn (New York: Knopf, 1984), 8; Philippe Sands and Pierre Klein, *Bowett's Law of International Institutions*, 5th edn (London: Sweet & Maxwell, 2001), 1.

3 Gerald J. Magnone, *A Short History of International Organizations* (New York: McGraw-Hill, 1954), at 98–123. See also Sands and Klein, above n. 2, at 1–13; Jacobson, above n. 2, at 7–10; Riggs and Plano, above n. 2, at 1–15; Federic L. Kirgis, *International Organizations in their Legal Setting* (St. Paul, MN: West Publishing Co., 1993), at 1–6.

organizations was driven by the need of states for common standards for commerce, communication and transportation.[4]

With the conclusion of the Versailles Treaty at the end of the First World War, the League of Nations – the forerunner of the United Nations – became the 'progenitor of the modern "universal" international organization'.[5] The League's system, designed to prevent war, failed, however, to do so, and the organization itself collapsed with the onset of the Second World War.[6] Correcting the League's perceived weaknesses provided, however, much of the inspiration for later institution builders, as in the context of drafting the UN Charter.[7] In response to the increasing need of states to co-operate, international organizations proliferated at a phenomenal rate after the Second World War.[8]

Today, with the continuing growth of states' interdependence, the problems of governments are increasingly international and, therefore, the international community has had to devise institutions which tackle these issues most effectively.[9] The proliferation of norm-creating

4 The functionalist historians explain the rise of these organizations also by the fact that states needed to co-operate in the wake of the new technical developments which emerged at the end of the nineteenth century. Thus it is not coincidental that the first international organizations were technical in nature, having to fulfil very specific functions relating to transnational communication and travel. On the relationship between technology development and functionalist theories, see generally Jacobson, above n. 2, at 62–7.

5 Magnone, above n. 3, at 128–56; Kirgis, above n. 3, at 6.

6 For an account of the failure of the League of Nations see Sands and Klein, above n. 2, at 13; D.W. Bowett, *The Law of International Institutions*, 4th edn (London: Stevens & Sons, 1981), at 17–18.

7 See José E. Alvarez, *International Organizations as Lawmakers* (Oxford University Press, 2005), at 22.

8 While in 1909 there were thirty-seven international organizations in the world, by 1956 there were 132 and by 1985 the number reached 378, with a decline to some 250 by the end of the century. See Charlotte Ku, *Global Governance and the Changing Face of International Law*, Acuns Reports and Papers 2 (New Haven, CT: ACUNS, 2001), available at www.reformwatch.net/fitxers/22.pdf.

9 See Evan Luard, *International Agencies: The Emerging Framework of Interdependence* (Dobbs Ferry, NY: Oceana, 1977), at 2–3. Leading works in the area of international organizations are those by international lawyers who give particular consideration to the constitution of international organizations, their legal personality and institutional problems. These often deal with several organizations and place particular emphasis on the League of Nations and the UN, sometimes on a single organization such as NATO, the OAU, or the EU. See, e.g., Alfred E. Zimmern, *The League of Nations and the Rule of Law* (London: Macmillan, 1939); Clarence W. Jenks, 'Some Constitutional Problems of International Organizations', (1945) 22 *British Yearbook of International Law* 11; Clarence W. Jenks, 'The Legal Personality of International Organizations', (1945) 28 *British Yearbook of International Law* 267; Clarence W. Jenks, *The Proper Law of International Organizations* (London: Stevens, 1962). Later, Professor Henry Schermers restricted himself to

and norm-influencing international organizations has determined the development of a large number of varied norms to regulate the conduct of both sovereign nations and individuals. The phenomenon was also attributed to other factors, including

> the increased emphasis on and prominence of regionalization, with international or intergovernmental institutions having immense norm-creating or norm-influencing power sprouting up in each region; fast-paced technology-driven global changes, which gave rise to new areas of regulation such as internet technology and biotechnology; climatic changes and increased stress on natural resource utilization and the need for common environment management policies; and greater prominence and recognition of individual rights by the international community and within regional and national legal systems.[10]

A consequence of this has been the fragmentation of international law incorporated in various regimes – an issue discussed by the International Law Commission (ILC).[11] The ILC Fragmentation Report reiterated that the problem with the fragmentation is that

international institutional law concerning the structure and functions of international organizations. See Henry G. Schermers, *International Institutional Law*, vols. 1 and 2 (Leiden: Sijthoff, 1972); see also Bowett, above n. 6. For a comprehensive summary of the legal literature in the field of international organizations see Clive Archer, *International Organizations*, 3rd edn (London: Routledge, 2001), at 128 et seq.

10 Victor Mosoti, 'Institutional Cooperation and Norm Creation in International Organizations', in Thomas Cottier, Joost Pauwelyn and Elisabeth Buergi Bonanomi (eds.), *Human Rights and International Trade* (Oxford University Press, 2005), 165–79.

11 International Law Commission (ILC), Report of the Study Group, 'Fragmentation of International Law: Difficulties Arising from the Diversification and Expansion of International Law: Conclusions', A/CN.4/L.702 (18 July 2006) (ILC Fragmentation Report); see the Analytical Study finalized by the Chairman, A/CN.4/L.682 and Corr.1 (13 April 2006). See also generally Bruno Simma, 'Self-Contained Regimes', (1985) 16 *Netherlands Yearbook of International Law* 111; Philippe Sands, 'Treaty, Custom and the Cross-Fertilization of International Law', (1998) 1 *Yale Human Rights and Development Law Journal* 85, at 88; Fiona Macmillan, 'International Economic Law and Public International Law: Strangers in the Night', (2004) 10 *International Trade Law and Regulation* 115, at 118; Georges Abi-Saab, 'Fragmentation or Unification: Some Concluding Remarks', (1999) 31 *New York University Journal of International Law and Policy* 919. For a discussion of the WTO and institutional fragmentation, see Pascal Lamy, 'The WTO in the Archipelago of *Global Governance*', speech at the Institute of International Studies, Geneva, 14 March 2006, www.WTO.org/english/news_e/sppl_e/sppl20_e.htm (visited June 2008). One final note here: Stephen Krasner defines 'regimes' as 'sets of implicit or explicit principles, norms, rules, and decision-making procedures around which actors' expectations converge in a given area of international relations'. Stephen Krasner, 'Structural Causes and Regime Consequences: Regimes as Intervening Variables', in Stephen D. Krasner (ed.), *International Regimes* (Ithaca, NY: Cornell University Press, 1983) 93–113, at 1.

> specialized law-making and institution-building tends to take place with relative ignorance of legislative and institutional activities in the adjoining fields and of the general principles and practices of international law. The result is conflicts between rules or rule-systems, deviating institutional practices and, possibly, the loss of an overall perspective of the law.[12]

Some commentators have shown their concern, perceiving that this erodes general international law, generating conflicting jurisprudence, forum-shopping[13] and loss of legal security.[14] The advent of this diversity of international specialized norms has sprouted an almost explosive expansion of independent and globally active, yet sectorally limited, courts, quasi-courts and other forms of conflict-resolving body.[15]

The concept of fragmentation is itself a fragmented concept. The problems associated with the fragmentation of international law can be seen as falling into two broad categories, reflecting two distinct points of entry. The first category refers to the fragmentation of substantive norms of international law which ensues from the complex interactions of a wide variety of substantive sources of international law, with a plethora of international treaties in addition to innumerable rules of customary international law. The difficulty posed by this type of fragmentation arises from what rule should be applicable to a given set of facts and, essentially, how to reconcile conflicts between such rules as they arise.[16] In the World Trade Organization, the 'trade and . . . ' debate is illustrative of this concern. While the WTO is preoccupied with disciplines promoting economic liberalization, other non-economic values stated in international legal conventions may in some cases seek to restrict these objectives.[17] In this context, it is necessary to have a clear regulatory framework addressing the

12 ILC Fragmentation Report, above n. 11, para. 8.

13 For an example of forum-shopping involving the WTO and ITLOS see below Chapter 4, section III.A.3.b.

14 ILC Fragmentation Report, above n. 11, para. 9.

15 Abi-Saab, above n. 11, at 923.

16 This issue has been authoritatively discussed by Joost Pauwelyn, *Conflict of Norms in Public International Law: How WTO Law Relates to Other Rules of International Law* (Cambridge University Press, 2003).

17 For example, the 'trade and . . . ' problem is expressed in conflicts between trade rules and environmental norms – see, e.g., Sabrina Shaw and Risa Schwartz, 'Trade and Environment in the WTO: State of Play', (2002) 36(1) *Journal of World Trade* 129 – or between trade rules and agreements relating to cultural diversity – see Tomer Broude, 'Taking "Trade and Culture" Seriously: Geographical Indications and Cultural Protection in WTO Law', 26 *University of Pennsylvania Journal of International Economic Law* 623 (2005); and Tania Voon, 'UNESCO and the WTO: A Clash of Cultures', (2006) 55 *International and Comparative Law Quarterly* 635. For the status of the discussion relating to environment and human rights see below Chapter 1, section IV.

proper relationship between these norms. Such conflicts are not peculiar to the WTO alone. Many other international regimes face the same structural problem (e.g. 'investment and . . .', the relationship between international humanitarian law and international human rights law, multilateral rules and regional rules, and treaty rules and international customary law).

But norm fragmentation does not only raise problems in the presence of overt normative conflicts. This also happens when different legal sources contain essentially the same substantive obligations and imperatives (or substantially similar ones), but produce different results. To give an example, the legality of the use of force in self-defence is based on both international customary law and treaty law – Article 51 of the UN Charter. Although the two norms are substantively similar, their fragmented independent existence gave rise to significant legal controversy before the International Court of Justice (ICJ) in the *Nicaragua* case.[18] The list can be completed with numerous other examples of multi-'sourced obligations' or 'parallel regimes' that raise problems due to norm fragmentation.

The second category of fragmentation relates to that of international authority. The main concern in this context is not the interaction of various rules and sources, but the distribution of authority and power among international, regional and national institutions which produce, interpret and apply international law. Here, the question is, rather, who has the authority to make a determination on a particular question arising under international law – whose determination should prevail if more than one body is found to have this authority. The question is highly relevant in the context of international dispute settlement, where, as illustrated above, numerous international tribunals operate. But this phenomenon also extends to political bodies. In fact, in contrast to the lawyer's perception of fragmentation as a problem generated by the lack of a clear norm and judicial hierarchy as evidenced in domestic law, the logic of politics locates the cause of fragmentation as being educed from the underlying conflicts between the 'policies' pursued by different international organizations and regulatory regimes.[19] The report of the International Law Commission (ILC) Study Group on Fragmentation of International Law dealt extensively with the difficulties created by fragmentation in substantive international law, but left the institutional

18 *Military and Paramilitary Activities (Nicaragua v. US)*, Merits, 1986 ICJ 14 (27 June).

19 Andreas Fisher-Lescano and Günther Teubner, 'Regime-Collisions: The Vain Search for Legal Unity in the Fragmentation of Global Law', (2004) 25 *Michigan Journal of International Law* 999, at 1003.

issues aside, stating that the 'issue of institutional competence is best dealt with by the institutions themselves'.[20] This signals the difficulty of lawyers having to deal with issues involving power and authority sharing – a topic which goes beyond the remit of this book.

This is explained by the fact that international organizations were conceived in a rather functionalist manner,[21] whereby each was assigned a specific task in its founding charter. Thus there are no clear models of how international organizations should interact in a system of shared international governance.[22] Despite the post-Second World War planners having devised an ambitious world system in which each area of international concern would be addressed by some international organization,[23] their tasks could not be neatly separated. They overlap considerably, for example in the fields of trade and environment, culture, agriculture, health, intellectual property (IP), development and monetary issues. As a result, only a few international problems can be placed squarely into one category, to be resolved by reference to a single regime.[24]

20 See Jan Klabbers, 'Constitutionalism Lite', 1 *International Organizations Law Review* 31 (2004), at 31. See also Tomer Broude, 'Principles of Normative Integration and the Allocation of International Authority: The WTO, the Vienna Convention on the Law of Treaties, and the Rio Declaration', (2008) 6 *Loyola University of Chicago School of Law Review* 173, at 176–7.

21 The functionalist approach to international organizations can be traced back to David Mitrany, *A Working Peace System* (London: Royal Institute of International Affairs, 1943). Later this was elaborated by Ernst B. Haas, *Beyond the Nation-State: Functionalism and International Organization* (Stanford University Press, 1964). Of all of the books produced by Haas, this contribution (in its most recent edition of 2009), contains the most complete and definitive statement of 'neo-functionalism' – the theory of transnational integration for which he is best known. Focusing on the International Labour Organization (ILO), his work is one of the first efforts to analyse systematically the dynamics and effects of a global international institution. See also Richard A. Falk et al., *The United Nations and a Just World Order* (Boulder, CO: Westview Press, 1991), at 138; Stephen Zamora, 'Economic Relations and Development', in Christopher C. Joyner (ed.), *The United Nations and International Law* (Cambridge: American Society of International Law and University of Cambridge, 1997) 232–86, at 233–4; Nigel D. White, *The Law of International Organizations* (Manchester University Press, 2005), at 2–7.

22 Other explanations for the fragmented nature of international law are the lack of centralized organs, the specialized nature of many areas of international law, the different structures of international legal norms and parallel regulation at the global and regional level. See Gerhard Hafner, 'Risks Ensuing from the Fragmentation of International Law', in Report of the International Law Commission on the Work of its Fifty-Second Session, 2000, UN Doc. no. A/55/10, at 321.

23 This impulse is revealed by the incorporation of pre-existing international organizations into the UN system.

24 Zamora, 'Economic Relations'.

Since there is no central government at the international level to rule over the activity of its different branches,[25] fragmentation may result in incoherence between different regulatory areas.[26] The international economic system is also ill-served by the UN system, in which a multiplicity of agencies operate in an unco-ordinated fashion. They deal separately with economic issues that are interrelated; consequently, global economic problems are ineffectively confronted.[27]

Constitutionalists have discussed this issue, proposing solutions which range from integrating existing international institutions to the extent they overlap or compete to less grand programmes which envision retaining the institutions but establishing some sort of hierarchy among them.[28] Nevertheless, nowadays it seems that there is no inclination to move towards taking any of these directions. The integration approach is undesirable from the effectiveness point of view, and it is not at all obvious that the results from a centralized organization would be better.[29] Although a hierarchical order would bring about more legal certainty, here, too, it is not evident that such an institutional framework would be effective in solving international problems; moreover, its creation would be fraught with difficulties. The co-ordination and reciprocal sensitivity between various regimes and their managing international organizations is therefore regarded in this study as essential in combating this problem. In this context, other scholars, too, have encouraged stronger institutional co-ordination.[30] While co-ordination of international organizations can

25 Devesh Kapur, 'Processes of Change in International Organizations', in Deepak Nayyar (ed.), *Governing Globalization: Issues and Institutions* (Oxford University Press, 2002), 334–55, at 354.

26 See Thomas Cottier and Panagiotis Delimatsis (eds.), *The Prospects of International Trade Regulation – From Fragmentation to Coherence* (Cambridge University Press, 2010).

27 See, e.g., David B. Steele, 'The Case for Global Economic Management and UN System Reform', (1985) 39 *International Organization* 561, at 561, calling for the establishment of a 'higher-level guiding body with an element of discretionary power, which would establish the major lines of short and medium-term global economic management'.

28 See Geir Ulfstein, 'Institutions and Competences', in Jan Klabbers, Anne Peters and Geir Ulfstein (eds.), *The Constitutionalization of International Law* (Oxford University Press, 2009), at 68–71.

29 Ibid., at 69.

30 For an account see generally Clarence W. Jenks, 'Coordination in International Organization: An Introductory Survey', (1951) 28 *British Year Book of International Law* 29. See also Mosoti, 'Institutional Cooperation'; Jeffrey Dunoff, 'Constitutional Conceits: The WTO's "Constitution" and the Discipline of International Law', (2006) 17(3) *European Journal of International Law* 647. See also Peter Passell, 'Loading the Trade Agenda with Diverse Issues Could Backfire', *New York Times*, 9 October 1997. See also World Commission on the Social Dimension of Globalization, 'A Fair Globalization: Creating Opportunities

be regarded as a deterrent to normative change,[31] most of the contributors argue that the absence of a proper interaction mechanism between these institutions may result in duplication of effort and the delivery of conflicting advice to member countries, particularly in relation to institutions with quasi-universal membership. This situation ultimately leads to increased transaction costs of governance.[32]

These concerns are valid for all intergovernmental international organizations alike, including the WTO and its dispute settlement system – the focus of this study. In the context of WTO dispute resolution, it is noted that the institutional sensitivity of the adjudicator – that is, the panel or the Appellate Body – vis-à-vis other international organizations is a factor which, apart from bringing about more uniformity in international law, adds to the legitimacy of the system.[33] Against this background, this study investigates the role of international organizations in WTO dispute settlement bearing in mind the desire to bring about more integration not only of substantive law but also of international authorities.

for All', March 2004, www.ilo.org/public/english/wcsdg/docs/report.pdf (visited December 2008), emphasizing the need for greater policy co-ordination among international organizations on issues on which their policies interact or mandates intersect. On the co-ordination between the WTO and WIPO see, e.g., Frederick Abbott, 'Distributed Governance at the WTO-WIPO: An Evolving Model for Open-Architecture Integrated Governance', (2000) 3(1) *Journal of International Economic Law* 63; Nikolai Khlestov, 'WTO–WIPO Co-operation: Does It Have a Future?', (1997) 10 *European Intellectual Property Review* 560; Ruth L. Okediji, 'WIPO–WTO Relations and the Future of Global Intellectual Property Norms', (2008) 39 *Netherlands Yearbook of International Law* 69.

31 Okediji, 'WIPO–WTO Relations', at 13, arguing that while contemporary arguments for inter-institutional co-operation have merit to them, it also is the case that such collaboration or co-ordination can be deployed to undermine prospects for normative change.

32 One good example is the IMF and the World Bank, which have expanded their activities throughout their existence in a manner that could have led to duplication of efforts. As argued by institutionalism (a version of functionalism that emerged in the 1980s in political science), the reduction of transaction costs is one of the features that enables international organizations to create 'conditions for orderly multilateral relations'. Robert O. Keohane, *After Hegemony: Cooperation and Discord in the World Political Economy* (Princeton University Press, 1984), at 244. See also Kenneth W. Abbott and Duncan Snidal, 'Why States Act through Formal International Organizations', (1998) 42 *Journal of Conflict Resolution* 3.

33 Robert Howse, 'Adjudicative Legitimacy and Treaty Interpretation in International Trade Law: The Early Years of WTO Jurisprudence', in Joseph H. H. Weiler (ed.), *The EU, the WTO, and the NAFTA: Towards a Common Law of Economic Integration?* (Oxford University Press, 2000), 35–69, at 62–8. See below Chapter 1, section II for a comprehensive account of institutional sensitivity as an ingredient for legitimacy in WTO dispute settlement.

II. International organizations in the WTO

For a better understanding of the issues addressed in this study, it is necessary to start with a historic illustration of the role of international organizations in the WTO. These interactions varied in intensity over time, as the WTO evolved from a quasi-institution into a fully fledged organization. Thus the dynamics of these interfaces were largely determined by the shift in the status of the organization, from a treaty – the General Agreement on Tariffs and Trade (GATT) – into an international intergovernmental organization – the WTO. But the picture would be incomplete without going back to the very origins of the system where attempts were made to create an International Trade Organization (ITO).

A. The International Trade Organization

The ill-fated ITO was conceived as a multifaceted organization which had aims other than liberalized trade, or at least reflected an awareness that other interests would have to be served if liberal trade was to prevail. It was an organization which was designed as a complement to the United Nations. Indeed, Article 86(1) of the Havana Charter contemplated that the ITO would become one of the 'specialized agencies' referred to in Article 57 of the Charter of the United Nations. It was therefore natural that the Havana Charter would have to regulate the relationship between the ITO and other UN specialized agencies. This interaction was set out in Article 86(3), which stipulated that the ITO 'should not attempt to take action which would involve passing judgment in any way on essentially political matters', which were the competence of the UN. Many Charter provisions refer to co-operation with the United Nations Economic and Social Organization (ECOSOC). Article 2(2) goes as far as to suggest 'concerted action under the sponsorship of [ECOSOC]' to supplement national measures to avoid unemployment. Moreover, the commercial provisions of the Havana Charter did not apply to measures taken under international commodity agreements (Art. 45(1)(a)(ix)), which were provided for in another part of the Charter, or under international agreements relating to the conservation of fishing resources or to the protection of migratory birds and wild animals (Art. 45(1)(a)(x)). Article 7 of the Charter also called for members to co-operate with the International Labour Organization (ILO) in taking 'whatever action may be appropriate and feasible to eliminate [unfair labour] conditions within its territory' and in resolving any disputes over labour standards that were referred to the dispute settlement mechanism of the ITO.

In the context of the par value exchange rate system established at Bretton Woods in 1944, the balance of payments exemption from the rule of elimination of quantitative restriction was also quite important. In this context, Article 24 of the Havana Charter set out a 'coordinated policy with regard to exchange rate questions' between the International Monetary Fund (IMF) and the ITO.[34] Essentially, the Charter prescribed deference to IMF judgement when the ITO was called upon to deal with exchange rate issues.[35] The records of the Havana Charter indicate that there were some fears among the negotiators that the ITO would be subservient to the IMF; these concerns, however, were dismissed on the grounds that the 'final decision as to whether restrictions would be instituted or maintained rested with the ITO, notwithstanding determinations made by the IMF'.[36]

Thus the ITO Charter was characterized as being quite ambitious in terms of members' obligations regarding some non-trade concerns and their responsible institutions.[37] It has even been claimed that the ITO never came into being in part because of controversy surrounding some of these obligations.[38] But since these provisions have never been tested in the dispute settlement process, it is difficult to assess how they would have played out in practice and to what extent the ITO would have taken into consideration these other organizations.

34 According to Eichengreen, the IMF and GATT were insufficiently co-ordinated in the critical early post-war years, when trade concessions by some countries might usefully have been 'traded' for elimination of exchange controls by others. Barry Eichengreen, *Globalizing Capital: A History of the International Monetary System* (Princeton University Press, 1996), at 101.

35 The ITO had essentially to accept the IMF's determination of 'all findings of statistical and other facts' relating to exchange issues, whether an ITO member had acted in accordance with the IMF Articles of Agreement in instituting trade restrictions for 'balance of payment purposes', what constituted a 'serious decline in . . . monetary reserves', what constituted 'a very low level' or 'reasonable rate of increase' in monetary reserves, and 'the financial aspects of other matters' covered in a case. See Havana Charter Art. 24(2).

36 UN Doc. E/CONF.2/C.3/SR.24, as cited in Daniel K. Tarullo, 'The Relationship of WTO Obligations to Other International Arrangements', in Marco Bronckers and Reinhard Quick (eds.), *New Directions in International Law: Essays in Honour of John H. Jackson* (The Hague, London and Boston, MA: Kluwer Law International, 2000), 155–73, at 159.

37 Tarullo, above n. 36, at 159.

38 Ibid., at 160. On the complicated relationship between GATT and ITO preparatory work see John H. Jackson, *World Trade and the Law of GATT* (Indianapolis: Bobbs-Merrill Company, 1969), at 42–9.

B. The GATT 1947

In contrast to the Havana Charter, the 1947 General Agreement on Tariffs and Trade (GATT) made fewer references to other international organizations.[39] Only the provisions relating to exchange rate arrangements and the International Monetary Fund (IMF) were included in the GATT in anything like the form they had assumed in the Charter. With the collapse of the par value exchange rate system in early 1979, the significance of these provisions had diminished, too, although it did not disappear.[40] Tarullo explains this shift through the fact that 'the GATT began life in institutional limbo. It was barely an organization at first, and except for the IMF, had little to do with other international organizations or, for that matter, with non-trade issues'.[41]

Besides the specific reference to the exchange rates and the IMF, the GATT positioned itself in a wider context of international law through the GATT Article XXI exception, which explicitly permits trade sanctions 'in pursuance of obligations under the United Nations Charter for the maintenance of international peace and security'.[42] An implicit linkage to other areas of regulation could be made through the 'general exceptions' provision enshrined in GATT Article XX, which justifies departures from the GATT obligations on various policy grounds, such as health and the environment.[43] The GATT soon withdrew itself to a more humble and isolated role arising from tariff reduction. These affairs took place far away from the political environment of the time.[44]

Interactions with international organizations were also mandated in GATT Article XXIII dealing with dispute settlement and, later, in the

39 Notwithstanding the legal separation and termination of GATT 1947, the GATT provisions and the legal instruments and decisions adopted by the GATT contracting parties were incorporated into 'GATT 1994' by reference to Annex 1A of the WTO Agreement. This legal continuity is reflected in many other WTO provisions. For instance, Art. IX of the WTO Agreement enjoins the WTO to 'continue the practice of decision-making by consensus followed under GATT 1947'. Art. 3 of the WTO's dispute settlement understanding affirms the members' 'adherence to the principles for the management of disputes heretofore applied under Articles XXII and XXIII of GATT 1947, and the rules and procedures as further elaborated and modified herein'.

40 See generally Michael J. Trebilcock and Robert Howse, *The Regulation of International Trade*, 3rd edn (London: Routledge, 2005), at 155–76.

41 Tarrullo, above n. 36, at 160.

42 GATT 1994, Art. XXI.

43 For an account of the types of linkage arising under WTO law see below Chapter 2.

44 Joost Pauwelyn, 'Unity and Fragmentation in International Law', Introductory Report on the World Trade Organization, Palma Workshop, 20–21 May 2005, http://eprints.law.duke.edu.

1979 Understanding Regarding Notification, Consultation, Dispute Settlement and Surveillance.[45] These rather general provisions mirror, to some extent, the modern WTO Dispute Settlement Understanding,[46] Article 13, which grants discretion to WTO panels to seek information from any source. While the ITO could not test the Havana Charter provisions referring to other international organizations, the GATT produced some judicial practice, which generally reveals that the GATT panels did not show particular sensitivity towards other international regimes and their administering authorities. An illustration of this comes, for example, from the *US – Tuna* case with the dismissal of some environmental information from other international organizations, including information on environmental law. Also, the *Thailand – Cigarettes* Panel rejected the attempt by the World Health Organization (WHO) to bring in its expertise in the field of health effects of tobacco trading in certain countries.[47]

C. The WTO

While the GATT generally saw less normative overlap with other regulatory areas, the situation changed in 1995 with the establishment of the WTO, which transformed the GATT into a membership organization forged solely on legal principles. It established a legal framework that brought together all the various pacts and codes and other arrangements that were negotiated under the GATT, while expanding significantly the traditional trade mandate. Today, members of the WTO must abide by the rules of all these agreements, as well as the rules of the GATT – as a 'single undertaking'. But the most important element of the WTO, the 'jewel in the crown', is the greatly strengthened dispute settlement mechanism.[48]

45 The Understanding on Notification, Consultation, Dispute Settlement and Surveillance, adopted 28 November 1979, BISD 26S/210. See for an overview on the evolution of dispute settlement under GATT 1947, Robert E. Hudec, *Enforcing International Trade Law: The Evolution of the Modern GATT Legal System* (Salem: Butterworth Legal Publishers, 1993); similarly, Robert E. Hudec, 'Free Trade, Sovereignty, Democracy: The Future of the World Trade Organization', (2002) 1 *World Trade Review* 211, at 330–9.

46 Understanding on Rules and Procedures Governing the Settlement of Disputes, Results of the Uruguay Round of Multilateral Trade Negotiations: The Legal Texts, WTO Legal Texts (Geneva: GATT Secretariat, 1994), 1869 UNTS 401, 33 ILM 1226 (1994).

47 For a detailed account of the role of WHO in *Thailand – Cigarettes*, see below Chapter 9.

48 Sylvia Ostry, 'Reinforcing the WTO', Occasional Paper 56, Group of Thirty, 1998, www.utoronto.ca/cis/ostry/, at 13.

It is a system which ensures adherence to the binding legal obligations of the WTO, treats all WTO members as equals, and gives force and meaning to an international agreement that is essential to achieving global economic prosperity.

With the advent of the WTO, a number of international organizations assumed a certain role in its decision making. Thus specific reference is made in WTO legal texts to the World Bank (GATS, Annex on Telecommunications, para. 6(a)); the Food and Agriculture Organization (FAO) (Agreement on Agriculture, Art. X(4)(b)); the Codex Alimentarius Commission (Codex) which implements the joint FAO/WHO Food Standards Programme (Sanitary and Phytosanitary Measures (SPS) Agreement, Arts. 3(4), 12(3),(5)); the International Office of Epizootics (Office International des Epizooties, OIE) and the International Plant Protection Convention (IPPC)[49] (SPS Agreement, Articles 3(4), 12(3),(5)); the Customs Co-operation Council (the current WCO) (Agreement on Implementation of Article VII, Art. 18(2) and Annex II; Annex I of the Agreement on Rules of Origin, Arts. 4(2), 9(1),(2)); the International Telecommunication Union (ITU) (GATS, Annex on Telecommunications); the World International Property Organization (WIPO) (TRIPS Agreement, Arts. 5, 63(2), 68).

This transition was determined by several factors. First, a number of highly technical agreements emerged in the WTO, basing the legality of trade measures on compliance with the standards of other international organizations (e.g. Codex standards for health and safety measures). Second, the WTO widened its mandate to include a number of non-trade issues by 'incorporating' non-WTO rules, for example the Trade-Related Aspects of Intellectual Property Rights Agreement (TRIPS), which assimilates, *inter alia*, provisions of the Berne, Paris, and Rome Conventions on intellectual property. As an organization which administers these treaties, WIPO is specifically referred to in the TRIPS Agreement. Third, the WTO dispute settlement process has been 'legalized': panels have compulsory jurisdiction, reports are virtually automatically adopted, and the legal aspects of a dispute are subject to review by the Appellate Body. This last process was also referred to as the *juridification* of the WTO system, which was mainly reflected in the increasing importance of

49 In May 2003 the OIE, created in 1924, became the World Organization for Animal Health but kept its historical acronym; 'OIE' is consistently used in this study to designate both. The IPPC is an international convention, not an international organization. However, for simplicity it will be designated as such in this study.

the rule of law.[50] This system stands in contrast to GATT 1947, where panels decided only issues of law to be applied to a 'cluster of undisputed facts'.[51]

The various references to international organizations in the WTO texts support interactions with these organizations in the day-to-day activities of the WTO, which emerge by virtue of their observership status, but also in informal settings. Given the diversity of the regulatory areas on the WTO negotiation table, the international organizations also make substantive contributions to the multilateral trade negotiations efforts, clarifying complex technical matters under discussion.[52] Many of the above provisions are important in understanding the role of international organizations in WTO dispute settlement, which is the focus of this study and will be illustrated in detail in Chapter 2.

III. International organizations in WTO dispute settlement

A role for international organizations in WTO dispute settlement arises explicitly or implicitly from a number of WTO legal provisions, in particular the Dispute Settlement Understanding (DSU). Notably, considering the important economic implications of the new WTO dispute resolution procedure for member states, Article 11 of the DSU specifically instructs that a panel should:

> make an *objective assessment* of the matter before it . . . and [an objective assessment of] the applicability of and conformity with the relevant covered agreements, and make such other findings as will assist the DSB [Dispute Settlement Body] in making the recommendations or in giving the rulings provided for in the covered agreements.[53]

50 For an account see Thomas Cottier, 'Dispute Settlement in the World Trade Organization: Characteristics and Structural Implications for the European Union', (1998) 35 *Common Market Law Review* 325, at 334–6; John H. Jackson, 'Dispute Settlement and the WTO: Emerging Problems', (1998) 1 *Journal of International Economic Law* 329, at 336; David Palmeter and Petros C. Mavroidis, *Dispute Settlement in the World Trade Organization: Practice and Procedure* (The Hague, London and Boston: Kluwer Law International, 1999), at 50; Ernst-Ulrich Petersmann, 'How to Promote the International Rule of Law? Contributions by the World Trade Organization Appellate Review System', (1998) 1 *Journal of International Economic Law* 25, at 33–6.

51 Joost Pauwelyn, 'The Use of Experts in WTO Dispute Settlement', (2002) 51 *International and Comparative Law Quarterly* 325, at 326.

52 For a more comprehensive overview of the WTO's co-operation with other international organizations see below Chapter 2, section IV.

53 DSU, Art. 11.

In order to fulfil this mandate, DSU Article 13(1) specifically authorizes a panel to 'seek information and technical advice from any individual or body which it deems appropriate'. These provisions affect the perceptions of how the dispute settlement mechanism should generally function, given in particular the highly technical issues with which the WTO adjudicator is entrusted.[54] Given that WTO dispute settlement (as international adjudication in general) does not acknowledge the principle of judicial restraint in highly technical cases,[55] it is difficult for the panels or the WTO Appellate Body to decide to whom to assign competence on specific technical issues. Thus the successful and legitimate resolution of disputes is determined by the ability to remain sensitive to those outside players that might be more knowledgeable in certain areas and help the adjudicator to make an objective assessment of the matter before it. This approach is also consistent with the early jurisprudence of the Appellate Body, which was 'concerned to make it very clear that the WTO is not a unique international organization that only need look at its own terminology and practices for guiding principles'.[56] For example, in the *US – Shrimp* decision, the Appellate Body acknowledged that the WTO could not and should not operate in isolation from non-trade institutions.[57]

Some WTO critics have argued, however, that the organization is closed to meaningful interaction with other international organizations, which raises legitimacy issues.[58] Moreover, other international arrangements and international organizations have frequently been perceived as being consigned to positions subordinate to that of the WTO and its adjudicating bodies.[59] This latter approach is overtly confirmed in the report

54 For example, in *EC – Asbestos* the Appellate Body refused to examine Canada's Technical Barriers to Trade (TBT) claims because the applicable law, the TBT Agreement, raised new issues. WT/DS135/AB/R, adopted 5 April 2001, paras. 81–2.

55 Pauwelyn, 'Use of Experts', at 361. See also generally Matthias Oesch, *Standards of Review in WTO Dispute Resolution* (Oxford University Press, 2003).

56 Jeffrey Waincymer, 'Reformulated Gasoline under Reformulated WTO Dispute Settlement Procedures: Pulling Pandora out of a Chapeau?', (1996) 18 *Michigan Journal of International Law* 141, at 165, who also notes extensive citation of decisions of the International Court of Justice by the Appellate Body in *US – Gasoline.*

57 *US – Shrimp*, ABR, para. 168.

58 Mosoti, 'Institutional Cooperation', at 177.

59 Tarullo, above n. 36, at 171. See also Okediji, 'WIPO–WTO Relations', at 3, arguing that the WTO, in a hierarchical division of labour with the World Intellectual Property Organization (WIPO), should be promoted as the future locus of substantive international intellectual property regulation, particularly with respect to the creation of intellectual property norms affecting the regulation and supply of global public goods such as health, education, scientific data and the environment.

produced by a consultative board to the Director General of the WTO (2004), which states in the relevant part that

> [t]he dispute settlement system of the WTO, due to its special characteristics and being self-contained in its jurisdictional responsibilities, offers no legal space for cooperation with other international organizations except on a case-by-case basis derived from the right of Panels to seek information. The Board endorses the maintenance of this policy.[60]

Indeed, interactions with international organizations in the dispute settlement process are in most cases limited to provision of factual information on the request of panels – a role which does not fully reflect their normative relevance.[61] Although the DSU does not prevent WTO panels from requesting 'legal advice' from other international organizations, they have repeatedly shied away from doing so.[62] Moreover, some WTO provisions that constitute the legal grounds for these interactions are not very clear, and they are frequently read by the adjudicator as assigning only a limited role to international organizations in the settlement of trade disputes. These problems are rooted partly in the WTO system itself, mainly in that trade should trump other societal values, but also in the architecture of other international organizations.[63]

IV. This study: task, method and structure

The task of this study is to investigate the type and nature of interactions between the WTO and other international organizations as arising in the narrow segment of the WTO dispute settlement. The study does not investigate WTO interfaces with international regimes in general, but focuses only on those which have a specific institutional backing and are administered by an international organization. Only a certain number of international organizations which have already emerged specifically in WTO dispute settlement with their proactive contribution (i.e. IMF, WIPO, WCO, WHO, Codex Alimentarius Commission) are analysed. This selection of international organizations is not accidental. Although the potential for

60 WTO, 'The Future of the WTO', Report by the Consultative Board to the Director-General Supachai Panitchpakdi (2004), www.WTO.org/english/thewto_e/10anniv_e/future_WTO_e.htm (visited March 2008).

61 See Part III for a thorough examination of the relevant WTO case law.

62 In *US – Section 110(5) Copyright Act* the Panel termed its request as 'factual' despite the fact that it was seeking legal interpretation. See below Chapter 7, section I.

63 See Chapter 4 for a detailed overview of these constraints.

linkages to international organizations through the WTO-covered subject matter is vast, specific interactions in WTO dispute settlement have been evidenced only with respect to several specialized international organizations, which are all part of this investigation. This is regarded as a proper method of taking stock of the current status of international organizations in WTO dispute settlement. This analysis can be drawn on for mapping out and forecasting the limits and nature of such interactions with other international organizations which are not part of this study.

It is also not the intention here to explore the question of normative fragmentation and jurisdictional overlaps of the WTO with other international tribunals. Both issues have already received great attention in scholarly contributions.[64] The objective of this study is to examinine interactions of the WTO judiciary with international organizations in the context of WTO dispute settlement. This has been made possible through placing the examination of such interactions within the framework of the rules of interpretation of the Vienna Convention on the Law of the Treaties 1969 (VCLT). This method allows for a systematic approach in exploring the proposed institutional interactions and assessing the weight that has been attributed by the WTO judiciary to the input of international organizations.

While the benefits of collaboration between the institutions are generally clear, the WTO does not have in place a structured mechanism for interactions with international organizations in the dispute settlement process. On the other hand, the contribution from international organizations during this process may potentially turn out to be essential to the discharge of the panel's duty to carry out an objective assessment of the matter. The extent to which the WTO panels make use of this contribution – be it in the form of law (hard or soft), information or expertise – is captured by the term 'institutional sensitivity' described in Chapter 1. These interactions will be analysed in detail in this study, which

64 See, e.g., Yuval Shany, *The Competing Jurisdictions of International Courts and Tribunals* (Oxford University Press, 2003); Chittharanjan F. Amerasinghe, *Jurisdiction of Specific International Tribunals* (Leiden: Brill, 2008); Andrew D. Mitchell and David Heaton, 'The Inherent Jurisdiction of WTO Tribunals: The Select Application of Public International Law Required by the Judicial Function', (2010) 31 *Michigan Journal of International Law* 561. For an account of the jurisdictional overlaps between the WTO and ITLOS, see Chuyang Liu, *Maritime Transport Services in the Law of the Sea and the World Trade Organization*, Studies in Global Economic Law (Berne etc.: Peter Lang, 2009). On the issue of normative fragmentation and how the WTO adjudicator has approached it, see below Chapter 1, section III.B and references therein.

argues that institutional sensitivity adds legitimacy to the WTO dispute settlement process and to the international trading system in general.

The issues covered by this study can be broken down into more specific questions, including the following: what type of output from the international organizations comes within the purview of the WTO adjudicator? to what extent and in what context is such output considered by the panels in their interpretation process? Do the types of interaction with and the level of sensitivity towards international organizations differ from one another, and what are the factors that determine these differences? How could the contribution of international organizations to WTO dispute settlement be enhanced, and, if so, in what manner?

In order to respond to these questions, the study will start by examining the foundations of the WTO adjudicator's concept of institutional sensitivity (Part I). Chapter 1 elaborates on the concept in general, followed by an illustration of the WTO's legal techniques supporting linkages with other international legal systems and their administering organizations. Chapter 2 expounds the main approaches in WTO law to defining the relationship to other international instruments. Given the reference in DSU Article 3(2) to the customary rules of interpretation, the relevant provisions from the VCLT are analysed in detail in Chapter 3 and are used as a framework for further analysis of the case studies in Part III. The aim of this exercise is to illustrate the interpretative techniques that the WTO adjudicator can use in order to show sensitivity to, and take account of, the relevant material ensuing from other international organizations. The analyses therefore inevitably link to the debate on the role of other international law in WTO dispute settlement, which is woven through the analyses of this study.

This is followed by an examination of the current constraints on the institutional sensitivity of the WTO adjudicator (Part II). These constraints stem from within the WTO (internal constraints) or from the relevant international organizations (outside constraints), and are examined in Chapter 4. As will be illustrated, the competence and credibility of international organizations are factors which need to be taken into account when deciding the level of judicial sensitivity vis-à-vis a specific international organization. Chapter 5 provides some guidance on how to evaluate these prerequisites, analysing the functioning of several WTO subsidiary bodies which are more suited to carrying out such assessment.

After having provided the theoretical framework, a sample of WTO cases which reveal interactions of the WTO panels or the Appellate Body with international organizations will be analysed (Part III). These cases reflect such interactions with the IMF (Chapter 6), WIPO (Chapter 7), the WCO (Chapter 8), WHO and the Codex Alimentarius Commission (Chapter 9). The factual background to and the findings in these cases will be outlined in brief. More attention will be given to the requests for advice addressed to other international organizations and the responses thereto, as well as the nature of the output provided or ensuing from a specific international organization. This will allow judgement on the extent to which the WTO adjudicator considered this material in their final deliberations. Each chapter in this part concludes with a brief evaluation of the relevant cases and conclusions. This is followed by a Concluding Summary, which provides a summary of the analysis in this study, policy recommendations prescribing how the judicial sensitivity of the WTO adjudicator can be enhanced and, finally, some suggestions as to the evolution of the relationship between the WTO adjudicator and the international organization under examination.

PART I

Foundations

1

The institutional sensitivity of the WTO adjudicator

I. Introduction

This chapter explains the rationale of this study, elaborating on the concept of institutional sensitivity and its legitimizing effect on the WTO dispute settlement system (section II). For sake of clarity, it is important to distinguish at the outset two dimensions of institutional sensitivity of the WTO adjudicator: *the vertical dimension*, addressing the interaction of the WTO adjudicator with the domestic regulators, and *the horizontal dimension*, concerned with the interplays with other international organizations in the settlement of trade disputes (section III). The horizontal dimension is at the heart of the analysis in this study. The horizontal dimension is perceived in wide and narrow terms. Wide terms refers to the way in which the panels/AB consider non-WTO law in general, whereas in the narrow sense they tackle the consideration and weight attributed to the various outputs ensuing from other international organizations. The current discussions and propositions regarding the institutional sensitivity of the WTO adjudicator are important in setting the scene for the investigation in this study and are therefore also examined (section IV). This examination is followed by the chapter conclusions (section V).

II. Institutional sensitivity as a legitimacy ingredient

The WTO's quest for legitimacy emerged with the increased interest in it on its establishment as a fully fledged organization, equipped with a strengthened system of dispute settlement. Consequently, the 'legitimacy of the WTO' – its rules, its institutions, its power – has become a byword in today's complex arena of international economic political relations.[1]

1 See Tomer Broude, *International Governance in the WTO: Judicial Boundaries and Political Capitulation* (London: Cameron May, 2004), at 57.

The legitimacy allegations levelled at the WTO can be categorized as relating to external and internal legitimacy.[2] The external challenges are those coming mostly from anti-globalist non-governmental organizations or non-state actors that are a priori deprived of an equal voice in the WTO system. They object to the perceived prioritization of free trade and the inability of the organization to reconcile this with other policy goals that impinge on the trading system. This, in their view, serves only the interests of transnational corporations and the economic elite – above important social and environmental values and interests.[3]

These claims have also focused on the perceived democratic deficit of the WTO relating to its processes of debating issues and forging rules. It has been argued that the WTO operates in a secretive, exclusionary manner that shuts out most developing country members and the public; in other words, it is perceived as lacking transparency.[4] This targets both political decision making and the dispute settlement mechanism, where the latter is regarded as undemocratic and unaccountable to the point of overruling the governments participating in the WTO.[5]

Such a criticism can be countered with the futility of stretching these legitimacy claims to international organizations in general, due to the absence of an effective direct link between international organizations and people of various member states. Another argument is that 'rather than comparing international organizations to idealized, ancient, Westminster-style, or imaginary political systems, the baseline should be the real-world practices of existing governments acting imperfectly under complex constraints'.[6] Moreover, the WTO is a member-driven organization and the democratic deficit claims and consequent proposals to redesign its decision-making process and/or structure (e.g. through increased transparency in deliberation) may hamper the performance of the organization or the so-called 'output legitimacy' by increasing the

2 Debra P. Steger, 'Book Review' (of C. E. Barfield, *Free Trade, Sovereignty, Democracy: The Future of the World Trade Organization*), (2002) 5 *Journal of International Economic Law* 565; Debra P. Steger, 'The Rule of Law or the Rule of Lawyers', (2002) 3(5) *Journal of World Investment* 769. See manifesto of the anti-globalist NGO Public Citizen, '"WTO – Shrink or Sink!" – The Turnaround Agenda International Civil Society Sign-on Letter', www.citizen.org/trade/article_redirect.cfm?ID=1569 (last visited April 2008).

3 Public Citizen, '"WTO – Shrink or Sink!"'. 4 Ibid.

5 Broude, *International Governance*, at 60.

6 Andrew Moravcsik, 'Is there a "Democratic Deficit" in World Politics?', (2004) 39(2) *Government and Opposition* 336, at 362.

pressure on negotiators from domestic rent-seekers.[7] Finally, the WTO is already engaging in serious efforts at some 'democratization' by improving its transparency and engaging national parliaments.[8]

The concept of output legitimacy (or substantive legitimacy) is concerned with the nature and content of WTO rules and their application. This category has erroneously received less attention. When substantive inputs, such as issues of security, welfare and identity, are missing, procedural democracy on the input side is often not sufficient.[9]

The concerns related to internal legitimacy arise from the WTO members who call into question the validity of basic aspects of the multilateral trading system, in particular with respect to developing countries. Since it is difficult for the members to challenge the validity of WTO norms to which they have acceded, the focus is on how these rules are interpreted and applied through the dispute settlement system. In this context the sentiments of some developing countries are that the Uruguay Round rules are 'asymmetrical' and that there is no consensus on many substantive aspects of WTO law, making it non-justiciable.[10] With the dispute settlement in focus, the challengers argue that the power exercised by the WTO dispute settlement system is far too great, resulting in the system producing new substantive rules that modify or extend given legal agreements defining the standards *ex post facto*.[11] The focus here is thus shifted from political decision making to the legitimacy of the dispute settlement system, which frequently is the ultimate target of the legitimacy assaults. In this context, it is claimed that the legitimacy

7 On possible effects of the democratic restructuring of the WTO see Joost Pauwelyn, 'The Sutherland Report: A Missed Opportunity for Genuine Debate on Trade, Globalization and Reforming the WTO', (2005) 8(2) *Journal of International Economic Law* 329.

8 Anne Peters, 'Compensatory Constitutionalism', (2006) 19 *Leiden Journal of International Law* 597, at 601.

9 Broude, *International Governance*, at 59, citing R. O. Keohane and J. S. Nye, 'The Club Model of Multilateral Cooperation and Problems of Democratic Legitimacy', in Roger B. Porter et al. (eds.), *Efficiency, Equity, Legitimacy: The Multilateral Trading System at the Millennium* (Washington, DC: Brookings Institute Press, 2001).

10 Broude, *International Governance*, at 63, referring to R. Ricuppero, (Secretary General, UNCTAD), 'Rebuilding Confidence in the Multilateral Trading System: Closing the "Legitimacy Gap"', in G. P. Sampson (ed.), *The Role of the World Trade Organization in Global Governance* (Tokyo: United Nations University Press, 2001), at 37; and C. E. Barfield, *Free Trade, Sovereignty, Democracy: The Future of the World Trade Organization* (Washington, DC: American Enterprise Institute Press, 2001).

11 Broude, *International Governance*, at 64, citing K. Raustiala, 'Sovereignty and Multilateralism', (2000) 1 *Chicago Journal of International Law* 401.

of the WTO dispute settlement process greatly influences the overall perception of the legitimacy of the WTO as a whole.[12]

It should be noted that this book does not place special emphasis on the distinction between the legitimacy of institutions and the legitimacy of their rules. After all, one set of rules creates institutions and those institutions create a secondary set of rules. Thus the legitimacy of an institution cannot or need not be separated from the legitimacy of the rules it creates, and vice versa. Both elements are agents of power, and it is power that is the main subject of the need for legitimation, be it the power of rules or the power of social institutions.[13] For the WTO dispute settlement system to be legitimate it should function according to legitimate rules. This alone, however, does not legitimate the rules made by the judiciary, nor does it legitimize the organization as a whole.

Although there are many factors which have a bearing on the assessment of the legitimacy of international organizations in general,[14] in this book the legitimacy of their judicial branch is regarded as an independent variable, which marks such perceptions of the rules and institutions as a whole.[15] The next subsections expand on the background to this view, examining the factors which are perceived to legitimize international adjudication in general, and WTO dispute settlement in particular.

A. *The legitimacy of international adjudication*

The legitimacy of an international tribunal relates to its ability 'to command acceptance and support from the community so as to render force unnecessary'.[16] While at the national level the legitimacy of the judiciary depends on its ability to maintain the proper boundaries between the judicial and other branches, or its regard for the relationship between the

12 See also Howse, 'Adjudicative Legitimacy', at 68.

13 See also D. Beetham, *The Legitimation of Power* (Basingstoke: MacMillan Education, 1991), at 56.

14 It should be noted that the legitimacy of the WTO system is a notoriously difficult concept to measure, as illustrated by the fact that various authors have sought to avoid this problem by relying on procedural alternatives. See, e.g., Deborah Z. Cass, 'The "Constitutionalization" of International Trade Law: Judicial Norm-Generation as the Engine of Constitutional Development in International Trade', (2001) 12 *European Journal of International Law* 39, at 45.

15 Laurence Helfer and Anne-Marie Slaughter, 'Toward a Theory of Effective Supranational Adjudication', (1997) 107 *Yale Law Journal* 273, at 273.

16 Ibid., at 284.

citizen and the state, at the international level the quest for legitimacy of the adjudicating bodies is far more complex. This is due to the fact that

> international tribunals lack a direct coercion mechanism to compel either appearance or compliance – they must rely instead on such factors as the immediate perceived interests of states involved in particular disputes in securing judicial settlements, their own legitimacy and that of any particular judgment reached, the strength and importance of the international legal rules governing a specific dispute, and the general force of normative obligation.[17]

While the legitimacy of international courts eludes precise definition, the sources of judicial legitimacy cover roughly a few elements, such as impartiality, principled decision making, reasoned decision making, continuity of court composition over time, consistency of judicial decisions over time, respect for the role of political institutions at the federal, state and local levels, and provision of a meaningful opportunity for litigants to be heard.[18] Three other factors have been found to affect judicial legitimacy: 'unanimity or near unanimity in decisions; professional civility in opinions; and continuity of the law over time'.[19] These definitions have had an overwhelming impact on attempts to define what would legitimize the WTO judiciary, as is illustrated below.

B. *The legitimacy of the WTO judiciary*

In the WTO context, after dividing its powers into legal, technocratic and judicial, three elements have been found to legitimize WTO judicial decisions. These factors are somewhat reflective of the elements listed above, and comprise fair procedures, coherence and integrity in legal interpretation, and institutional sensitivity.[20] In this equation, the power of the dispute settlement system in relation to WTO membership and political organs is not a critical part of its legitimacy. The legitimacy of WTO adjudication does not depend on filling the WTO legitimacy gap

17 Ibid., at 285.

18 For an overview of the literature on judicial legitimacy see Susan P. Sturm, 'A Normative Theory of Public Law Remedies', (1991) 79 *Georgetown Law Journal* 1357, at 1390–1411.

19 See Scott C. Idleman, 'A Prudential Theory of Judicial Candor', (1995) 73 *Texas Law Review* 1307, at 1388.

20 Robert Howse, 'The Legitimacy of the World Trade Organization', in Jean-Marc Coicaud and Veijo Heiskanen (eds.), *The Legitimacy of International Organizations* (Tokyo: United Nations, 2001), 355–408, at 376.

and is not concerned with the power discussion; it is, rather, focused on the procedures and provisions of the dispute settlement mechanism. In this constellation, the legitimacy of the judiciary is perceived as a factor adding to the overall legitimacy of the WTO system.[21]

These assertions should be contrasted with those authors who suggest that the deepest legitimacy problems in the WTO are actually rooted in a lack of broad approval of and support for the existing substantive rules and principles of the multilateral trading system.[22] Against this background, this book is concerned with the judicial legitimacy of the WTO as characterized by its institutional sensitivity towards other international organizations.

The WTO adjudicator's contact with international organizations does not alone necessarily legitimize the WTO dispute settlement system;[23] that effect is achieved when the WTO adjudicator considers the institutional strengths and weakness of these actors, who may have a particular expertise or stake in the disputed laws and policies.[24] Thus the proposal of this book regarding institutional sensitivity argues in favour of taking into account the output of the international organizations preoccupied with other legal regimes, be it in the form of the views of official organs responsible for the administration and development of the regime, opinions of the stakeholders and experts preoccupied with the regime in question or the values and interests that it puts to the front and centre.[25] All these could be expressed in various forms, as binding or non-binding acts ensuing under various internal procedures of those regimes. This will be illustrated in more detail in Chapter 3.

III. The dimensions of institutional sensitivity

A. The vertical dimension

The institutional sensitivity of the WTO adjudicator is not a new concept in academic discourse. It has traditionally been expressed through a call for judicial deference implying consideration by the panels of the findings of the domestic authorities in matters such as, for example, dumping determinations. In this study, this phenomenon is referred to as the vertical dimension of institutional sensitivity.

21 Ibid. 22 See, e.g., Broude, *International Governance*, at 66.
23 Howse, 'Legitimacy', at 391. 24 Ibid.
25 Howse, 'Adjudicative Legitimacy', at 67–8.

John Jackson – the father of the deference proposition – suggested that 'there should be some measure of deference in the dispute settlement process to national government decisions'.[26] Such an approach is considered essential in the adjudication of national health policies at the WTO – something that resulted in the emergence of an interpretative principle.[27] Jackson's formula of deference is not, however, very useful for three reasons: it gives little guidance as to how far this deference can go; it disregards the possibility that some other international regime might be the one with a claim to superior legitimacy (not the domestic authorities only); and, finally, this formula suggests yielding to the determination of another institution having some practical competence and credibility in dealing with factual or legal issues.[28] It tends to exclude other options, such as the panel giving special weight to aspects of that other institution's assessment which draws on its particular competency or legitimacy.[29]

An initial notion of vertical institutional sensitivity towards domestic institutions can be extracted from *EC – Hormones*. In this case, the Appellate Body did not support a crude deference to national authorities, but actually suggested a spectrum of deference which, with respect to fact-finding, lay somewhere between a *de novo* review of the facts at issue and total deference to national authorities. This standard represents an attempt to set out the limits of deference to domestic authorities, but it is imprecise; based on this statement it would be difficult for a WTO panel to know what point to choose on this spectrum.[30] The Appellate Body found it more appropriate to base such deference on the DSU imperative of 'making an objective assessment', as enshrined in Article 11,[31] noting that

26 Howse, 'Legitimacy', citing John H. Jackson, *The World Trade Organization: Constitution and Jurisprudence* (London: Pinder/RIIA, 1998), at 24.

27 Gregg M. Bloche, 'WTO Deference to National Health Policy: Toward an Interpretive Principle', (2002) 5 *Journal of International Economic Law* 825, arguing that the WTO system has come to treat protection of health as a de facto interpretive principle when disputes arise over members' treaty obligations.

28 Howse, 'Legitimacy', at 391. 29 Ibid.

30 *EC – Hormones*, ABR, para. 117, noting that panels are poorly suited to engage in *de novo* review, whereas total deference could not ensure an objective assessment as foreseen by Art. 11 of the DSU.

31 Ibid., para. 116. Note a certain inconsistency in the reasoning of the Appellate Body, as it held elsewhere that the DSU does not prescribe any particular standard of review (para. 114). See also Howse, 'Legitimacy', at 393.

> the weight to be given to *factual determinations* of other institutions will depend on some assessment of the relative competence and credibility of those institutions in the handling of the particular facts at issue. Similarly, with respect to *legal interpretation*, the AB suggested that the law 'directly on point' was the Article 11 duty to 'make an objective assessment of the matter before [the panel]'. This is really the notion of institutional sensitivity within the discharge of the panel's duty to 'make an objective assessment' – not the delegation of a part of that duty to some other institutions.[32]

This approach has been criticized, however, for lacking clarity and leaving the regulation of the institutional sensitivity to a WTO provision which actually does not determine any standard of review. In particular, it is argued that Article 11 of the DSU is somewhat limited, to providing due process guarantees with the WTO dispute settlement system[33] and no more.

Furthermore, even if this (vague) AB standard were to guide the interaction of the WTO adjudicator in relation to domestic authorities, this is certainly not easily transposable to the horizontal interactions – that is, with the international organizations. The latter interplays are actually outside the WTO domain. Here, we no longer speak of the power that the WTO members should retain in the dispute settlement process, but of the involvement of actors who pose quite different issues of democratic legitimacy. The horizontal interactions take place under conditions of an imperfect overlap between the WTO constituency and that of the relevant international organization, where different values and interests may prevail. Nonetheless, what can be retained and borrowed from the vertical sensitivity discourse is that it makes sense and would be natural for institutional sensitivity on the horizontal axis also to be dictated by the notion of objective assessment of the matter. Regardless of the importance of a relevant international organization in a given area of regulation, such interactions would not be unlimited and certainly do not presuppose total deference – something which would actually imply delegation of power.[34] This qualification remains nonetheless of little help in understanding what role international organizations should play in WTO dispute settlement and what specific weight panels should ascribe to the input of these actors in their fact-finding or interpretation process. This is something that this study intends to elucidate.

32 *EC – Hormones*, ABR, para. 118 (emphasis added).

33 See e.g. Trebilcock and Howse, *Regulation of International Trade*, at 70.

34 For a more detailed account of this topic see below Chapter 5, section III.A.

B. The horizontal dimension

While a simple transposition of the vertical standard of sensitivity to the sensitivity on the horizontal axis leaves a great number of questions unanswered, this study attempts to extract some guidance on this account from the practice of the WTO adjudicator in dealing with international organizations in the dispute settlement process. In order to define more accurately the scope of this investigation, two dimensions of institutional sensitivity on the horizontal axis are distinguished: broad and narrow terms. The *broad terms* are concerned with more general issues, such as how WTO law relates to other international law, which has received significant attention in the literature.[35] The emphasis is therefore placed on institutional sensitivity in *narrow terms* – being concerned with the specific contribution of international organizations to the resolution of WTO disputes. An introductory description of how WTO judicial sensitivity in broad terms is manifested would be useful here in order to make a better distinction between the two terms.

1. Sensitivity in broad terms

As noted by the Appellate Body in the famous *US – Gasoline* case, GATT 'is not to be read in clinical isolation from public international law'.[36] Against this background, sensitivity in broad terms refers to the receptivity of the WTO adjudicator to other public international law[37] and its classical sources, such as treaties, international customs and general principles of law.[38]

From the perspective of the WTO adjudicator, the scope of WTO law is set out in Article 1 of the DSU, which establishes the limits of their jurisdiction as covering adjudication of government measures or their consistency with the WTO agreements. These agreements are officially

35 See the subsequent subsection and references therein.

36 *US – Gasoline*, ABR, at 17.

37 Some WTO legal instruments, such as the WTO Charter and the TRIPS Agreement, specifically recognize other societal values such as economic growth (or development) as an overarching instrumental purpose underlying the international economic system. For an account see Friedl Weiss, 'The WTO and the Progressive Development of International Trade Law', (1998) 29 *Netherlands Yearbook of International Law* 71, at 78, briefly describing the history of socio-economic concerns in international economic regulation and identifying development, human rights and social justice as fundamental pillars of world order.

38 Art. 38(1) of the Statute of the Court of International Justice explicitly mentions the sources of public international law at the disposal of the ICJ judges.

recorded in annexes 1A, 1B and 1C of the WTO Agreement, following the conclusion of the Uruguay Round negotiations (with the exception of the Trade Policy Review Mechanism).

The WTO adjudicator can, however, refer to non-WTO law in the process of interpreting WTO law or can even apply those norms to a specific dispute.[39] Under the first method, the WTO treaty terms can be and have been interpreted with reference to other sources of international public law, such as international agreements (*US – Shrimp, EC – Tariff Preferences*), general principles of (international) law (*EC – Hormones, US – Shrimp* and *US – FSC*), and general customary international law (*US – Cotton Yarn*). For example, in *US – Tuna (Mexico)* and *US – Shrimp*, certain environmental treaties were used as references for the interpretation of 'exhaustible natural resources', such as the Montreal Protocol on Substances that Deplete the Ozone Layer and the Convention on International Trade in Endangered Species of Wild Fauna and Flora (CITES).[40] Moreover, in *US – Shrimp* the Appellate Body relied on international treaties that were not binding on all parties to the dispute in order to interpret WTO law.[41]

The application of non-WTO law is a far more complex issue. The notion of applicable law relates to the question of which law can be applied in disputes before WTO panels and the Appellate Body. Various approaches to this issue have been offered in scholarly literature,[42] ranging

39 Such a reading is widely supported in legal writings. See, e.g., Joost Pauwelyn, 'The Role of Public International Law in the WTO: How Far Can We Go?', (2001) 95 *American Journal of International Law* 535, at 559–65; Marco C. E. J. Bronckers, 'More Power to the WTO?', 4 *Journal of International Economic Law* 41 (2001), at 56–9; Thomas Cottier and Matthias Oesch, 'WTO Law, Precedents and Legal Change', (2001) 3 *Turku Law Journal* 27, at 38–41; Meinhard Hilf, 'The Role of National Courts in International Trade Relations', (1997) 18 *Michigan Journal of International Law* 321, at 116–25; Gabrielle Marceau, 'A Call for Coherence in International Law: Praises for the Prohibition Against "Clinical Isolation" in WTO Dispute Settlement', (1999) 33(5) *Journal of World Trade* 87, at 107–39.

40 E.g. the *US – Shrimp* Appellate Body decision applying the Vienna Convention on the Law of Treaties (VCLT) for the interpretation of GATT 1994 and other international agreements, such as UNCLOS and CITES (para. 130). For other examples, see the Panel and/or Appellate Body interpretations of the Lomé Convention in *EC – Bananas*; the Beme Convention in *US – Section 110(5) Copyright Act*; international Codex Alimentarius standards in *EC – Hormones*, and especially in *EC – Sardines*; the Organization for Economic Co-operation and Development (OECD) arrangement on export credits, in *Canada – Aircraft Credits and Guarantees*; environmental conventions and declarations in *US – Shrimp*; and the precautionary principle in *EC – Hormones*.

41 See below Chapter 3, section III.A for a more detailed account of *US – Shrimp*.

42 For an overview see Anja Lindroos and Michael Mehling, 'Dispelling the Chimera of "Self-Contained Regimes" International Law and the WTO', (2005) 16 *European Journal of International Law* 857; see also Michael Lennard, 'Navigating by the Stars: Interpreting the WTO Agreement', (2002) 5(1) *Journal of International Economic Law* 17, at 40 ff.

from the view that applicable WTO law includes all relevant international law to the view that it is limited just to the WTO domain.[43] The WTO texts are not too clear on this point, and a clarifying statement by the Appellate Body on this issue is still awaited. However, in WTO dispute settlement other international law has been commonly applied by the WTO panels and the Appellate Body in order to fill procedural gaps in the WTO Agreement. These gaps relate to questions such as burden of proof, standing, due process, good faith, representation before panels, the retroactive application of treaties, or error in treaty formation. As a result, reference has been made to rules of general international law addressing those questions, essentially on custom or general principles of law binding on all states.[44] The issue of making similar use of the substantive norms of international law remains sensitive, since it could provoke severe tension and conflicts between substantive provisions of WTO law and those of other systems of international law.

a. Discretion to refer to non-WTO law. DSU Article 3(2) is one of the most important provisions interfacing the WTO adjudicator with non-WTO law. Its second sentence reads as follows:

> The Members recognize that [the dispute settlement system of the WTO] serves to preserve the rights and obligations of Members under the covered agreements, and to clarify the existing provisions of those agreements in accordance with customary rules of interpretation of public international law.[45]

These rules are generally understood to refer to Articles 31–33 of the Vienna Convention on the Law of Treaties.[46] Article 31(3) of the VCLT

43 See Gabrielle Marceau, 'Dispute Settlement and Human Rights', (2002) 13 *European Journal of International Law* 753, at 776–7; Joel Trachtman, 'The Domain of WTO Dispute Resolution', (1999) 40 *Harvard International Law Journal* 333, at 342.

44 For an overview of relevant case law see James Cameron and Kevin R. Gray, 'Principles of International Law in the WTO Dispute Settlement Body', (2001) 50 *International and Comparative Law Quarterly* 248; Pauwelyn, 'Role of Public International Law', at 563. See also Meinhard Hilf, 'Power, Rules and Principles – Which Orientation for WTO/GATT Law?', (2001) 4 *Journal of International Economic Law* 111, at 111–30. For an increasingly isolated critique to this approach see John McGinnis, 'The Appropriate Hierarchy of Global Multilateralism and Customary International Law: The Example of the WTO', (2003) 44 *Virginia Journal of International Law* 229.

45 DSU, Art. 3(2). A similarly clear obligation to apply customary rules of interpretation of public international law can be found in Art. 17.6(ii) of the WTO Anti-Dumping Agreement.

46 There are, however, other non-codified rules of interpretation which are used in the context of WTO law. As noted by Lennard, the WTO adjudicator has relied on several

directs that, in interpreting a treaty, account must be taken not only of the treaty itself (*in casu*, the WTO treaty), but also of 'any subsequent agreement between the parties regarding the interpretation of the treaty or the application of its provisions' (para. a), 'any subsequent practice in the application of the treaty which establishes the agreement of the parties regarding its interpretation' (para. b), and 'any relevant rules of international law applicable in the relations between the parties' (para. c).[47] Thus this last paragraph is the only provision with explicit mention of international law. Given, however, that the WTO Agreement is part of public international law, even without the explicit confirmation found in DSU Article 3(2), the WTO Agreement cannot be applied in isolation from other rules of international law.

A second provision invoked in support of this discretion is DSU Article 7(2), mandating panels to 'make such findings as will assist the DSB in making the recommendations or in giving the rulings provided for in that/those agreement(s)'. This is read as an acknowledgement that WTO panels may need to resort to and apply rules of international law beyond WTO-covered agreements, as long as it assists the DSB in discharging its mandate.[48]

Finally, the discretion of the WTO adjudicator to refer to non-WTO law is implicit in the language of DSU Article 11, which requires panels to 'make an objective assessment of... the applicability of... the relevant covered agreements'. The outcomes of the WTO adjudication may not be objective if all the relevant rules, including those residing outside the trade regime, are not taken into account. This is not to suggest that Article 11 is the legal basis for application of non-WTO law by panels or the Appellate Body but rather that the reference to non-WTO law is implicit in its

interpretative 'maxims' or 'principles' in interpreting WTO obligations. These are not explicitly referred to in the Vienna Convention, but they have been treated in WTO forums as emerging naturally from the expressed principles in the Vienna Convention. (e.g. the principles of 'presumption of consistency', 'effectiveness', 'in dubio mitius', 'legitimate expectations', 'abus de droit' etc.). See Lennard, 'Navigating by the Stars', at 55–77.

47 VCLT, Art. 31(3).

48 Joost Pauwelyn, 'Dispute Settlement: How to Win a WTO Dispute Based on Non-WTO Law? Questions of Jurisdictions and Merits', (2003) 37(6) *Journal of World Trade* 997, at 999, arguing also that the question of whether a party can base its claim on non-WTO law has been avoided by the WTO judiciary, but it will not be held off much longer due to the ever-increasing interaction between WTO law and other branches of international law and because of the growing willingness of WTO members to rely on these other sources of law before WTO panels, inspired by the compulsory nature of the WTO dispute settlement.

language to the extent that an objective assessment of the matter cannot be carried out without consideration of this other law. The relationship to other international organizations in the WTO dispute settlement process is not characterized only by the interpretation or application of the formal law ensuing from these organizations. As is illustrated throughout the book, the widely employed 'international organizations' output' also covers non-binding instruments, information and expert advice provided or otherwise ensuing from these organizations. Thus the question is not only whether and how non-WTO law should be used in WTO adjudication but also how the output of international organizations can contribute to the objective assessment of the matter. Few would challenge the fact that the output of international organizations in the form of expert advice (technical, economic or scientific), information and negotiation records would play out in the panel's discharge of its duty to make an objective assessment of the matter. Article 11 is not the best provision for invoking application of non-WTO law as such. DSU Article 3(2) would have much greater relevance here, since it is the only DSU provision explicitly referring to international law. What, in this author's view, remains implicit in the language of DSU Article 11, read together with DSU Article 3(2), is that an objective assessment of the matter may require WTO panels also to consider relevant non-WTO law ensuing – in one form or another – from international organizations.

The effect of these non-WTO rules on the WTO obligations is diverse. Most notably, their use may affect the broadening or narrowing of the scope of WTO exceptions.[49] Therefore the degree to which other international law influences and applies in WTO law and its dispute settlement system continues to be the subject of intense debate.

b. The use of general international law in the WTO. The WTO is a specialized regime, and therefore the question arises as to its relationship to general international law.[50] The WTO dispute settlement system is a self-contained regime by virtue of Article 23 of the DSU, which excludes unilateral determinations of breach or countermeasures outside the specific rules enshrined in the WTO. Authors have argued that, given the peculiarity of the WTO system, general international law should not be applied in the administration of WTO treaties, as the latter differ fundamentally in

49 Ibid., at 997.

50 For an overview of the notion of self-contained or specialized regimes see ILC Fragmentation Report, at 65 et seq.

their general orientation from that of regular public international law. The principles of interpretation inferred from the two systems might contrast sharply with each other.[51] Nonetheless, as stated by the ILC Fragmentation Report, 'Few lawyers would persist to hold the WTO covered treaties, whatever their nature, as fully closed to public international law.'[52] This finds support also in the practice of international tribunals, including the WTO adjudicating bodies, which have made very wide use of international customary law and general principles to interpret WTO treaties.[53] This approach has been prompted by the Appellate Body's explicit recommendation in *US – Gasoline*, that WTO agreements 'should not be read in clinical isolation from public international law'.[54] Since then, the Appellate Body has frequently sought 'additional interpretative guidance, as appropriate, from the general principles of international law'.[55] The ILC Fragmentation Report concluded on the matter that 'there seems, thus, little reason of principle to depart from the view that general international law supplements WTO law unless it has been specifically excluded and that so do other treaties which should, preferably, be read in harmony with the WTO covered treaties'.[56]

As illustrated in the previous section, Article 31(3)(c) of the VCLT is the only codified principle of interpretation that explicitly refers to other rules of international law. This provision has received a great deal of attention from trade law scholars.[57] Some interpretative issues arising out of its application relate to whether the rules of international law need

51 See e.g. Jeffrey Dunoff, 'The WTO in Transition: Of Constituents, Competence and Coherence', (2001) 33 *George Washington International Law Review* 979, at 991–2.

52 ILC Fragmentation Report, para. 134. 53 Ibid. 54 *US – Gasoline*, ABR, at 16.

55 *US – Shrimp*, ABR, para. 151. For a detailed overview of the material referred to by the Appellate Body in this case see below Chapter 3, section III.A.

56 ILC Fragmentation Report, para. 169. See also generally Pauwelyn, *Conflict of Norms*.

57 See generally Pauwelyn, *Conflict of Norms*. Also, with some suggestions on how to overcome the entire membership requirement read into Art. 31(3)(c) VCLT, see Robert Howse, 'The Use and Abuse of Other "Relevant Rules of International Law" in Treaty Interpretation: Insight from WTO Trade/Environment Litigations', Institute for International Law and Justice Working Paper 2007/1, at 15; and Benn McGrady, 'Fragmentation of International Law or "Systemic Integration" of Treaty Regimes: *EC – Biotech* and the Proper Interpretation of Article 31(3)(c) of the Vienna Convention on the Law of Treaties', (2008) 42(4) *Journal of World Trade* 589, at 594; Jan Klabbers, 'Reluctant *Grundnormen*: Article 31(3)(c) and 42 of the Vienna Convention on the Law of Treaties and the Fragmentation of International Law', in M. Craven, M. Fitzmaurice and M. Vogiatzi, (eds.), *Time, History and International Law* (Leiden: Martinus Nijhoff, 2007), at 141; Campbell McLachlan, 'The Principle of Systemic Integration and Article 31(3)(c) of the Vienna Convention', (2005) 54(2) *International and Comparative Law Quarterly* 279; Richard K. Gardiner, *Treaty Interpretation* (Oxford University Press, 2008), at 260–78.

to be applicable between all disputants, all parties to the treaty under interpretation, or reflect the common intentions of the parties to the treaty under interpretation.[58] Other questions are raised with respect to the meaning of the term 'relevant' in Article 31(3)(c), the inter-temporality of rules, and the scope of the phrase 'rules of international law'. Although these questions remain largely unresolved, with respect to the issue of 'the parties' the ILC Fragmentation Report concludes:

> A better solution is to permit reference to another treaty provided that the parties in dispute are also parties to that other treaty. Although this creates the possibility of eventually divergent interpretations (depending on which State's parties are also parties to the dispute), that would simply reflect the need to respect (inherently divergent) party will as elucidated by reference to those other treaties as well as the bilateralist character of most treaties underpinned by the practices regarding reservations, *inter se* modification and successive treaties, for example.[59]

Despite this clarification which can be reasonably employed in dealing with other international law, the WTO judiciary has applied Article 31(3)(c) restrictively. One example emerges from *EC – Approval and Marketing of Biotech Products* (*EC – Biotech*), where the Panel applied a restrictive mode of treaty interpretation.[60] The EC argued that the 1992 Convention on Biological Diversity and the 2000 Cartagena Biosafety Protocol affected the scope of Article 5(7) of the SPS Agreement and that they should be considered by the Panel in the interpretation of WTO obligations enshrined therein. In this context, the Panel had to interpret

58 Art. 2(1)(g) VCLT defines, 'for purposes of the present Convention', a 'party' is 'a State which has consented to be bound by the treaty and for which the treaty is in force'.

59 ILC Fragmentation Report, Conclusions Nr. 21 and para. 472. For a criticism of the Study Group's focus on Art. 31(3)(c) without consideration of other principles of interpretation see Isabelle Van Damme, *Treaty Interpretation by the WTO Appellate Body* (Oxford University Press, 2009), at 365, noting: 'It follows that the Study Group's focus on Article 31(3)(c) VCLT without considering other principles of interpretation might have been a missed opportunity. A more comprehensive examination of the process of treaty interpretation by international courts and tribunals might have resulted in conclusions making superfluous the suggestion of an objective of "systemic integration" derived from Article 31(3)(c).'

60 See Robert Howse and Henrik Horn, 'European Communities – Measures Affecting the Approval and Marketing of Biotech Products', (2009) 8(1) *World Trade Review* 49; Margaret A. Young, 'The WTO's Use of Relevant Rules of International Law: An Analysis of the Biotech Case', 56 *International and Comparative Law Quarterly* 907 (2007). Also Matthias Oesch, 'The Jurisprudence of WTO Dispute Resolution', (2006) 16 *Revue suisse de droit international et de droit européen/Schweizerische zeitschrift fur internationales und europaischees recht* 501; Van Damme, *Treaty Interpretation*, at 372 and n. 75.

'the parties' set out in VCLT Article 31(3)(c). It rejected an evolutionary and effective interpretation of this term, contending that the various environmental treaty obligations could not be considered under 'any relevant rules of international law applicable in the relations between the parties' according to VCLT Article 31(3)(c), because they had not been agreed by the entire WTO membership. Such interpretation is perceived as undermining the intentions of the drafters of the VCLT and has been criticized in various academic writings.[61] An alternative, broader interpretation suggests that 'the parties' should be defined as 'the disputants', as suggested by the ILC Report.[62] Moreover, the restrictive mode of reading this provision would be inconsistent with WTO jurisprudence in general, proclaiming that trade law should not be read 'in clinical isolation from public international law'.[63]

Another constraint in the application of Article 31(3)(c) is that generally WTO jurisprudence has made infrequent use of non-WTO law.[64] With the exception of *EC – Biotech*, there has been very little discussion of this provision in WTO case law.[65] Some have argued that the reason for this is that, in most cases, the WTO adjudicator does not need other international law to understand the meaning of the treaty language.[66] The ILC Study Group, which examined the issue extensively, noted in this context that the underlying philosophy of Article 31(3)(c) is the principle of 'systemic integration', according to which treaties should be interpreted against the background of all rules and principles of international law, understood as a system.[67] In other words, the ILC Study Group recognized that VCLT Article 31(3)(c) reflects the principle of harmonization according to which a treaty should be read in harmony and consistently with the broader context of international customary and

61 Van Damme, *Treaty Interpretation*.
62 Ibid., at 372 and n. 75.
63 *US – Gasoline*, ABR, at 17.
64 For an overview of the case law, see ILC Fragmentation Report, paras. 433–460.
65 For an overview of the relevant WTO cases, see Van Damme, *Treaty Interpretation*, at 368–73.
66 Ibid., at 362. It has been argued that the role of this VCLT technique is not unique in its capacity to interface the WTO with other international law and that other principles enshrined therein might justify the same result. Thus the significance of VCLT Art. 31(3)(c) is frequently overstated. See Lennard, 'Navigating by the Stars', at 36. See also Donald McRae, 'Claus-Dieter Ehlermann's Presentation on "The Role and Record of Dispute Settlement and the Appellate Body of WTO"', (2003) 6(3) *Journal of International Economic Law* 709, at 713. For an example where an international treaty has been considered as context under Art. 31(1)(a) VCLT see below Chapter 3, section II.C.
67 ILC Fragmentation Report, paras. 413, 465.

treaty law.[68] The principle of systemic integration is clearly aimed at incorporating and conciliating through interpretation the relevant international law (both conventional and customary) as may apply between the parties. This finds confirmation in the strong advocation by the ILC Study Group of using VCLT Article 31(3)(c) to this effect.[69]

It has been claimed that VCLT Article 31(3)(c) does not display any overt or otherwise obvious institutional, authority-integrating aspects. This is not to say, however, that this provision does not have the indirect potential also to impact authority integration, which would be a spin-off of the substantive norm integration process. This, perhaps little visible, result can be achieved by considering the following characteristics and effects of this VCLT rule:

> [F]irst, it mandates norm integration via interpretative reference to pertinent ('relevant') rules from other systems (i.e. from outside the particular normative and institutional system associated with the treaty being interpreted) [footnote omitted]; second, in so doing it asserts the interpretative authority of the particular interpreter over these 'external' norms; third, it consequently introduces the problem of overlapping authority, insofar as the 'external' norm is subject to the concurrent interpretative authority of other jurisdictions (not an unforeseeable occurrence, given that these rules must be 'applicable' between the parties, somewhere in their legal relations); and fourth, this overlap agitates towards authority-integrating techniques, such as deference to 'external' interpretations of 'external' obligations.[70]

Thus not only can VCLT Article 31(3)(c) counter fragmentation of substantive law, it being a manifestation of the systemic integration approach, but the rules can also produce results that will affect authority integration. In other words, a harmonious reading of substantive law will integrate international authority. Although this study does not attempt to draw clear lines between the two categories, the above points once more to the acceptability of using the VCLT as a framework for the analysis of this study (see Chapter 3 below).

2. Sensitivity in narrow terms

Horizontal sensitivity in narrow terms, as described in this study, is preoccupied with the extent to which the WTO panels or the Appellate Body take into account the output of the international organizations in the

68 Ibid., paras. 37–43, also Conclusion Nr. 19. The ILC Study Group accepts that the principle of harmonization is 'a widely accepted principle of interpretation' (para. 38).

69 Ibid., at 8–10. 70 Ibid.

settlement of WTO disputes. While sensitivity in general terms refers to the consideration of public international law, when created by means of acts of the member states, this specific category ensues from the organs of the organization itself, even if those organs are composed of delegates of member states.[71] Thus the WTO adjudicator refers not only to the traditional categories of international law in their interpretation process but also to other rules, such as the acts emerging from international organizations.

a. Acts emerging from international organizations. As outlined, consideration of the acts of international organizations by the WTO adjudicator constitutes a first element of institutional sensitivity in the narrow sense. This accounts for their legislative power and normative influence within their administered regimes.[72] The legal impact of international organizations on the WTO is therefore of particular interest for a constitutional analysis of the world trading system.[73] Okediji notes that the role of the international organizations in the WTO stems largely from their perceived prominence and power, which has not been eclipsed by the 'de-centering of states in the international legal order and the recognition of multiple new actors'.[74] She contends that 'the influence and power wielded by international organizations has enhanced significantly both in absolute

71 Pauwelyn, *Conflict of Norms*, at 145.

72 For example, for an account of the BIRPI/WIPO normative influence see Ruth L. Okediji, 'Becoming WIPO', draft paper presented at the Fordham University Law School Symposium, 'When Worlds Collide: Intellectual Property at the Interface between Systems of Knowledge Creation', 31 October –1 November 2008.

73 Tarullo, 'Relationship of WTO Obligations', at 156. For an overview see Cass, '"Constitutionalization" of International Trade Law', at 56; Thomas Cottier, 'Limits to International Trade: The Constitutional Challenge', in American Society of International Law (ed.), *International Law in Ferment: A New Vision for Theory and Practice*, Proceedings of the 94th Annual Meeting of the American Society of International Law (Washington, DC: 2000), 220, at 221; Robert Howse and Kalypso Nicolaidis, 'Legitimacy through "Higher Law"? Why Constitutionalizing the WTO is a Step Too Far', in Thomas Cottier and Petros C. Mavroidis (eds.), *The Role of the Judge in International Trade Regulation: Experience and Lessons for the WTO*, vol. 4 (Ann Arbor: University of Michigan Press, 2003), 305–46, at 318–29.

74 Okediji, 'WIPO–WTO Relations', at 22. See also Scott Brewer, 'Scientific Expert Testimony and Intellectual Due Process', (1988) 107 *Yale Law Journal* 1535, in n. 104 referring to Michael Barnett and Martha Finnemore, *Rules for the World: International Organizations in Global Politics* (Ithaca: Cornell University Press, 2004), at 1–2, describing the pervasiveness and centrality of international organizations in addressing global problems; Alvarez, *International Organizations*, at 3, noting that '[b]ecause of their quasi-governmental status, [international organizations] are usually accorded "international legal personality" that approximates to that of the prime actors of state-centric international law'.

terms and by sheer virtue of their rapid proliferation'.[75] This accounts for the fact that scholars routinely recognize international organizations as significant *and* independent emergent sources of international law,[76] even though these norms do not fit neatly into any of the formal categories of Article 38 of the ICJ Charter.[77]

Stretching the scope of the orthodox sources to include the various acts of international organizations is not easy,[78] one reason for this being that the impact of international organizations on the generation of general principles of law is rather limited. Although the acts of the UN specialized agencies have generated general principles of law by influencing developments in the municipal law of member states, there are only a few examples, in practice, of the creation of such principles by international organizations. To give an example, the freedom of trade union associations, long espoused by the ILO, may arguably be considered a general principle of law due to its wide acceptance in municipal law.[79] In spite of this limited status, the WTO adjudicator has referred to the acts of international organizations on various occasions using the interpretation methods set out in Articles 31–32 of the VCLT.[80]

In order to distinguish this category of law from the formal sources, some of its features need to be singled out. The acts of international organizations possess at least three major characteristics:

> (a) they are adopted with some degree of formality by an authorized body of an organization, without the necessity of explicit consent by all members intended to be subject to it; (b) they are intended to provide a channel for the conduct of entities, usually states (and usually members of the organization), whether or not the act is formally binding by virtue of an antecedent or contemporaneous treaty obligation; and (c) they are of general application, either to the membership at large (occasionally, even beyond the membership) or to some sub-group having common characteristics to which the norm applies.[81]

75 Okediji, 'WIPO–WTO Relations', at 23.

76 See White, *Law of International Organizations*, at 158.

77 Ibid.

78 One of the best candidates for the list of the sources of international law are the resolutions of the UN General Assembly, given the representative value of this organ.

79 Zamora, 'Economic Relations', at 266, referring to Charles Alexandrowicz, *The Law-Making Functions of the Specialised Agencies of the United Nations* (Sydney: Angus & Robertson, in association with the Australian Institute of International Affairs, 1973), 11.

80 See Chapter 3 below for an overview.

81 Frederic L. Kirgis, 'Specialized Law-Making Processes', in Christopher C. Joyner (ed.), *The United Nations and International Law* (Cambridge University Press, 1997), 65–94, at 66.

The UN specialized agencies have devised an impressive variety of ways to promulgate norms to channel the conduct of their members.[82] The plethora of instruments ensuing from international organizations can be divided into a number of categories. These acts go far beyond the traditional sources of international law – principally custom and treaties that are subject to orthodox ratification procedures. The treaty law category is diverse and includes categories such as the so-called 'super-treaties' (treaties with strings attached, such as a duty to submit them to a ratification process and a duty to report periodically to the promulgating agency on compliance); provisional application of some treaties before they formally enter into force; and treaty-implementing standards that enter into force on tacit consent, subject to a limited opt-out privilege. Then we move on to other acts which are of more interest here, such as formally binding regulations, sometimes linked to an opt-out privilege, authoritative findings of legislative facts, to be implemented by regulatory regimes within or outside the agency; recommendations, often in the form of codes or guidelines, that clearly have more than hortatory design and effect; pronouncements, including formal pronouncements being developed as part of the dispute settlement proceedings or as reasoned interpretations by agency organs; and informal interpretations during contact with individual members.[83]

While the application of other international treaties in the WTO goes beyond the scope of the present investigation, this study examines the consideration by the WTO panels or the Appellate Body of the remaining categories, which include, but are not limited to, treaty-implementing standards, formally binding regulations, authoritative findings of legislative facts, recommendations, pronouncements, and informal interpretations. These categories illustrate the fact that international organizations are actively engaged in the process of lawmaking; the various categories resulting therefrom cannot be lightly discarded by the WTO adjudicator in their interpretation process. Against this background Chapter 3 will illustrate in more detail how, by use of the VCLT rules of interpretation, the WTO panels have made use of instruments covered by these categories and what weight they were attributed in the dispute settlement process.

82 Edward Yemin, *Legislative Powers in the United Nations and Specialized Agencies* (Leyden: A. W. Sijthoff, 1969), 6. See also Richard H. Lauwaars, 'The Interrelationship between United Nations Law and the Law of Other International Organizations', (1984) 82 *Michigan Law Review* 1604, at 1606 and 1611–17.

83 Kirgis, 'Specialized Law-Making Processes', 90.

One last point which needs emphasis is that the categories of international organizations' acts identified above entail rules of both hard and soft law. While the use of the latter category has been widely discussed in the literature, the role of the extra-WTO regime soft law in the WTO interpretation process is far from unequivocal. For that matter, the term 'soft law' generally covers two ideas. First, it refers to the *form*, where norms are not in the form recognized as a form of international law, so that they are not legally binding. Second, it refers to the *substance*, where even if a norm is expressed in a recognized legal form, its content is sufficiently vague as to make it difficult to recognize the legal obligation therein.[84] References to soft law emerging in other international regimes are evidenced in a number of WTO disputes.[85] An important number of such instruments came under the purview of the Appellate Body in *US – Shrimp*.[86] For interpreting the term 'natural resources' enshrined in GATT Article XX(g), the Appellate Body referred not only to conventions such as UNCLOS, the Convention on Biological Diversity, and CITES, but also to acts of international organizations, such as the Rio Declaration on Environment and Development[87] and Agenda 21,[88] Resolution on Assistance to Developing Countries, adopted in conjunction with the Convention on the Conservation of Migratory Species of Wild Animals.[89]

In *Mexico – Telecoms* the Panel's interpretation of 'anti-competitive practices' was informed also by the UN Set of Multilaterally Agreed Equitable Principles and Rules for the Control of Restrictive Business Practices and an OECD Recommendation. In using this latter instrument, the Panel added that both Mexico and the United States were OECD members.[90] None of these instruments have been considered, however, under VCLT Article 31(3)(c). Thus the 'other rules of international law'

84 See Olufemi A. Elias and Chin L. Lim, *The Paradox of Consensualism in International Law* (The Hague and Boston, MA: Kluwer Law International, 1998), 230. There is, however, disagreement in the existing literature as to the hard- and soft-law distinction. See Wolfgang Reininke and Jan Martin Witte, 'Interdependence, Globalization and Sovereignty: The Role of Non-binding International Legal Accords', in Dinah Shelton (ed.), *Commitment and Compliance: The Role of Non-binding Norms in the International Legal System* (New York: Oxford University Press, 2000).

85 For an account of the role of soft law norms in the WTO see Mary E. Footer, 'The (Re)turn to "Soft Law" in Reconciling the Antinomies of WTO Law', (2010) 11(2) *Melbourne Journal of International Law* 241.

86 For a more detailed account of the case see below Chapter 3, section II.C.

87 *US – Shrimp*, ABR, paras. 41, 73, 154, 168.

88 Ibid., paras. 130, 154, 168.

89 Ibid., para. 130.

90 *Mexico – Telecoms*, Panel Report, para. 7.236.

in VCLT Article 31(3)(c) has been read as referring only to the traditional sources of international law – most prominently treaties and custom. Against this background and given the complicated relationship of the WTO adjudicator with this VCLT rule,[91] it is difficult to imagine that acts of international organizations will be referred to under this VCLT provision.[92]

b. Information and expert advice. The second element of institutional sensitivity in the narrow sense relates to the consideration of information and expert advice of international organizations in the WTO dispute settlement process. This device is available to the WTO panels, as it arises from a number of legal provisions such as Article XV GATT, Article 13 DSU, and Article 11 SPS. The need of the adjudicators for information and expert advice can be explained by the fact that, in contrast to public participation, expert legitimacy is drawn from the superior knowledge of the expert in a specific area. Bodansky observes in this context that 'just as we rely on expertise rather than democratic decision making to build airplanes and to cure diseases, we might believe that, if economists were to make economic decisions and environmental experts environmental decisions, this would lead to best outcomes'.[93] Scott Brewer characterizes experts as 'epistemically superior beings' and rightly argues that 'the non-expert practical reasoner must defer epistemically to the theoretical expert to reach the practical judgment'.[94] Thus, the 'epistemic authority' of experts is what adds extra legitimacy to the expert-based WTO decisions. This expertise often lies with other international organizations that are specialized in specific areas. In fact, there have been prolific exchanges between the WTO panels and other international organizations in the process of adjudication on scientific-based disputes arising in the adjudication of health and environment issues. Part III below will examine in depth such interactions by providing concrete examples of relevant WTO case law.

91 See Van Damme, *Treaty Interpretation*, 370, with reference to the *EC – Chicken Cuts* Panel (the Appellate Body did not exclude the possibility of HS being considered under VCLT Art. 31(3)(c), but preferred not to take a position on this matter).

92 For a more detailed account of the use of VCLT Art. 31(3)(c) in WTO dispute settlement see below Chapter 3, section III.D.

93 Daniel Bodansky, 'The Legitimacy of International Governance: A Coming Challenge for International Environmental Law', (1999) 93 *American Journal of International Law* 596, at 620.

94 Brewer, 'Scientific Expert Testimony', at 1578 and 1589.

3. What can be drawn from the comity doctrine?

The similarity of institutional sensitivity on the horizontal axis with the so-called comity doctrine cannot pass unobserved in the context of this investigation. The term 'comity' eludes precise definition, but it has been suggested that it is a 'toothless abstraction, not a rule, invoked in an infinite variety of contexts to justify one governmental body's deference to another'.[95] As a concept which emerged in the context of domestic judicial review, the doctrine was tentatively proposed to stretch to international forums. This would allegedly 'capture the reciprocal deference' that organizations should have for one another.[96] The doctrine as applied in the international context envisions the 'organizations acting within their own self-interest' but 'voluntarily consenting to the law of another regime, except where that law offends the consenting organization's fundamental policies'.[97] The comity doctrine thus can be regarded as a tool which allows accommodation among various international regimes and is therefore close to the concept of institutional sensitivity.

The doctrine, however, has been criticized for its weakness and for reflecting only a notion of courtesy, not an obligation, as well as for posing some democratic legitimacy problems. Thus deference to the laws of other regimes requires consent of the governed members, because comity charges one actor with the application of the law of other actors with a different constituency.[98] Furthermore, it has been argued that the application of the doctrine leaves space for its ad hoc and opaque application. Against this background, there is a risk of undermining rather than increasing the legitimacy of decisions. It has also been noted that comity may obscure the existence of conflicts between regimes. Instead of discussing and negotiating these conflicts, comity may deter such meaningful solutions by avoiding the problem.[99] Another risk posed by the application of this doctrine is that, to the extent that comity excludes the participation of the international organization concerned from the

95 James C. Rehnquist, 'Taking Comity Seriously: How to Neutralize the Abstention Doctrine', (1994) 46 *Stanford Law Review* 1049, at 1066–7.

96 Claire R. Kelly, 'Power, Linkage and Accommodation: The WTO as an International Actor and its Influence on Other Actors and Regimes', (2006) 24 *Berkeley Journal of International Law* 79, at 93.

97 Ibid., at 94.

98 See the *pacta tertiis* principle concerned with state consent behind the decisions. As codified in Art. 34 of the VCLT, it enunciates that treaties do not 'create either obligations or rights for a third State without its consent'.

99 Rehnquist, 'Taking Comity Seriously', at 94.

assessment of whether their values should be taken into account, the application of the doctrine risks being viewed as self-serving.[100] Therefore a proper notion of comity would promote the participation of international organizations in their reciprocal decision making. This is very much in line with the proposal for greater institutional sensitivity. Yet given the undefined status of this doctrine in the international legal order and the criticism expounded above,[101] the comity doctrine remains an unelaborated normative accommodation technique among international regimes. With regard to the WTO, its application has been challenged on the grounds that even within the organization itself there might be a problem with comity, as it is not clear, for example, whether the panels or the Appellate Body would exercise comity with respect to the WTO subsidiary bodies.[102] Finally, what should be noted is that the only reason for having discussed this doctrine here is to illustrate the existence of legal notions similar to what in this study is referred to as institutional sensitivity.

IV. Other scholarly debate relating to institutional sensitivity

This opening chapter would be incomplete without presenting the current debates on the role of international organizations at the various stages of WTO decision making. Some useful insights on this are gained from the current WTO negotiations on fisheries subsidies under the SCM Agreement, where WTO members are discussing *inter alia* the role of some standards organizations in the dispute settlement process.[103] Other

100 José E. Alvarez and David W. Leebron, 'Symposium: The Boundaries of the WTO: Linkages', (2002) 96 *American Journal of International Law* 5, at 16, noting that 'autonomous linkages may result in increasing pressure for additional linkage structures'.

101 Kelly, 'Power, Linkage and Accommodation', at 95. The doctrine 'is elusive and difficult to define and therefore difficult to apply in a meaningful and coherent fashion.[footnote omitted] International regimes exercising comity subject themselves to the charge that they do so either as a convenient excuse when deciding an issue, or as a meaningless ploy to avoid deciding issues altogether.'

102 Ibid., referring to Ryan L. Winter, 'Reconciling the GATT and WTO with Multilateral Environmental Agreements: Can We Have Our Cake and Eat It Too?', (2000) 11 *Colorado Journal of International Environmental Law & Policy* 223, at 240, stating that the Committee's Report, 'at best, is merely a set of recommendations . . . Without subsequent action it becomes meaningless.'

103 For a comprehensive account see Margaret A. Young, 'Fragmentation or Interaction: The WTO, Fisheries Subsidies and International Law', (2009) 8(4) *World Trade Review* 477.

insights are gained from the literature addressing the linkage of trade and the environment.

A. *The SCM and the fisheries subsidies negotiations*

The WTO SCM Agreement generally relies on the dispute settlement rules of the DSU. However, the Agreement contains extensive special or additional dispute settlement rules and procedures providing, *inter alia*, for expedited procedures, particularly in the case of prohibited subsidy allegations. Unlike other consultation provisions in the WTO Agreements, Article 4(5) of the SCM Agreement offers a unique provision according to which the panel may request the assistance of the WTO Permanent Group of Experts (PGE) in examining whether the measure in question is a prohibited subsidy. It prescribes that

> If so requested, the PGE shall immediately review the evidence with regard to the existence and nature of the measure in question and shall provide an opportunity for the Member applying or maintaining the measure to demonstrate that the measure in question is not a prohibited subsidy. The PGE shall report its conclusions to the panel within a time-limit determined by the panel. The PGE's conclusions on the issue of whether or not the measure in question is a prohibited subsidy shall be accepted by the panel without modification.[104]

Furthermore, the SCM Agreement Articles 24(3) and 24(4) list three possible roles for the PGE in subsidy disputes: to provide, at the request of a dispute settlement panel, a binding ruling on whether a particular practice brought before it constitutes a prohibited subsidy; to provide, at the request of the Committee on Subsidies and Countervailing Measures (SCM Committee), an advisory opinion on the existence and nature of a subsidy; and, finally, at the request of a WTO member, to provide a confidential advisory opinion on the nature of any subsidy proposed to be introduced or currently maintained by that member. Thus the prerogatives of the PGE are greater compared with those of the expert review groups which could be appointed by the WTO Panels, and it is therefore unique.

The WTO Draft Consolidated Chair Texts of the Anti-Dumping and SCM Agreements (Chair's text) adopts two procedures for dispute settlement. For disputes about prohibited subsidies, panels are constituted

104 SCM Agreement, Art. 4(5).

according to the current procedure of the SCM Agreement, for other disputes according to the DSU. In both cases, if the dispute raises 'scientific or technical questions related to fisheries', the panel must seek advice from 'fisheries experts'. These experts are to be chosen by the panel in consultation with the disputing parties. The panel also has discretion to consult with international organizations.[105]

With respect to the consultations with international organizations, one reading of draft Article VIII(4) of the Chair's text gives the panel discretion to consult with an advisory fisheries expert group or relevant international organization on scientific or technical matters. According to another reading, however, the paragraph merely refers to the discretionary power of the panel to consult on the selection of fisheries experts. The latter reading is that preferred by the United States, which modified its initial proposal in order to avoid a situation where the FAO and other international organizations would be asked to provide assistance merely in *identifying* appropriate experts, and would not be called upon to provide expert opinions.[106] Thus the Chair's draft reveals reluctance from some negotiators to allow an expert role for other international organizations on scientific and technical matters.

A number of other interesting proposals can be noted in the context of these discussions. A World Wildlife Fund (WWF) proposal in the negotiations, for example, recommended that a permanent group comprising experts from the FAO, the United Nations Environment Programme (UNEP), regional fisheries management organizations (RFMOs) and non-governmental organizations (NGOs) sit at the WTO with the authority to make binding rulings on matters outside the traditional competence of the WTO.[107] This suggestion was not accepted by the WTO Rules Group entrusted with the negotiations, but the already existing WTO arrangements could, to some extent, promote authority-sharing with other regimes.[108] As the PGE has wide discretion to draw on a range of sources for assistance, including international organizations, scientific experts and NGOs, the WTO panels could consult this group for an assessment of whether subsidies were benefiting fishing activity. In addition,

105 Young, 'Fragmentation or Interaction', at 40, referring to Draft Consolidated Chair Texts of the AD and SCM Agreements, WTO Doc. TN/RL/W/213 (30 November 2007), Annex VIII to the SCM Agreement.

106 Young, 'Fragmentation or Interaction', at n. 191 and accompanying text.

107 David Schorr, 'Healthy Fisheries, Sustainable Trade: Crafting New Rules on Fishing Subsidies in the World Trade Organization', WWF Position Paper, 2004, at 39 and 105.

108 Young, 'Fragmentation or Interaction', at 42.

there are a number of other methods by which a WTO adjudicating body can seek information from other international organizations in resolving fisheries subsidies disputes, such as *amicus* briefs and submissions of the disputing parties themselves.[109]

B. *The trade and environment debate*

An interesting suggestion for the proposal for institutional sensitivity arises out of proposed shared adjudicative capacities between the WTO and other international organizations in the context of the trade and environment debate. In this context, Perez proposes extending the institutional space in which trade–environment disputes are deliberated through, *inter alia*, linking with environmental international intergovernmental organizations.[110] According to Perez, it is not enough to give an institution like the UNEP only observer status in the meetings of the WTO Committee on Trade and Environment or other subsidiary bodies. The linkage could be extended to giving the UNEP the right to intervene, as a formal party, in legal proceedings before the WTO and it could also be used to organize expert review groups under Article 13(2) of the DSU.[111] However, the mere incorporation of these international organizations into the legal process does not guarantee that the data they provide will be properly interpreted by the WTO panels. Perez therefore suggests that it is important to give the environmental international organizations a voice in the bodies that make the decisions, for example by appointing to the Appellate Body and to any panel deliberating a trade–environment dispute, a judge with environmental expertise, giving the UNEP the prerogative of the expert selection.[112]

Regrettably, the Doha Declaration reflects a rather modest approach towards granting such functions to other environmental international organizations in the WTO. Their role is limited to an agreement to negotiate on procedures for regular information exchange between multilateral environment agreement secretariats and the relevant WTO committees, and the criteria for granting observer status.[113] In this context it has been noted that sensitizing the WTO to other regulatory concerns (e.g. health, environment) cannot be achieved simply by changing the wording or interpretation of Article XX; novel institutional solutions have to be

109 Ibid.
110 Oren Perez, *Ecological Sensitivity and Global Legal Pluralism* (Oxford: Hart, 2004), at 96.
111 Ibid. 112 Ibid. 113 See the WTO Doha Declaration, Art. 31(ii).

designed which would facilitate this transformation.[114] This proposition is very much in line with what is suggested in this study.

V. Conclusions

This chapter has elaborated on the concept of the institutional sensitivity of the WTO adjudicator, perceived as a legitimacy ingredient in the WTO adjudication process. Two dimensions of the concept were identified, the vertical dimension characterizing the sensitivity of the WTO adjudicator vis-à-vis domestic regulatory authorities and the far less elaborated horizontal dimension, concerning the consideration by the WTO adjudication of the output of other international organizations. While the WTO adjudicator shows institutional sensitivity in wide terms when it refers to public international law in general, the narrow terms of this concept are concerned with the consideration of the acts of international organizations, their information and expert advice. This latter type of sensitivity is the focus of this study.

A few points should be noted at this stage. First, the sources of international law cannot be easily stretched to include the acts of international organizations, and it is therefore not a straightforward matter as to how the WTO adjudicating bodies can take them into account. The WTO panels have on some occasions relied on the acts of international organizations in their interpretative process, but have rarely assigned them a high normative value.[115] Moreover, the status of these acts in the WTO disputes is unclear, and this state of affairs is likely to be drawn on in order to counter arguments for their effective use in the WTO judicial interpretation process. One such argument, for example, is that relying on the decisions of other international institutions risks increasing uncertainty in the meaning of WTO obligations.[116] Therefore the issue needs some clarification, which is attempted in this study.

Second, the international organizations may play an essential role in the settlement of WTO disputes by providing direct input, such as information or expert advice. While the need for information may arise in a wide variety of WTO disputes, the role of the international organizations

114 See Perez, *Ecological Sensitivity*.

115 See e.g. the references to UN resolutions in *US – FSC (Article 22.6-US)* Arbitration report; ITU Recommendations and OECD Guidelines in *Mexico – Telecoms*. For an account see Petros C. Mavroidis, 'No Outsourcing of Law? WTO Law as Practiced by WTO Courts', (2008) 102(3) *American Journal of International Law* 421, at 437.

116 Howse and Horn, 'European Communities', at 36–7.

as an expert is narrower, as is primarily illustrated in Chapter 9 of this study. Such a role has been widely disputed in a number of WTO health disputes, and the analysis thereof will help in understanding the extent to which this function can be exercised by an international organization.

Lastly, the proposals made in the context of the WTO fisheries and environment-related negotiations on how best to make use of international organizations' contributions warrant attention and further elaboration. The WTO adjudicator should definitely be more direct in their approach to consideration of not only international organizations' acts but also their information and expertise. The analysis conducted in this study aims to provide some further insights into how this can be achieved.

2

The WTO linking techniques

I. Introduction

Under GATT 1947, an interface with other international regimes emerged from a number of legal provisions either directly, for example GATT Article XV, or indirectly, as under GATT Article XX.[1] With the advent of the WTO, its regulatory framework expanded substantially to include a number of new regulation areas. With that, the scope of the WTO linkages with other international regimes expanded, too. For example, with respect to the environmental regime, the Marrakesh Agreement establishing the WTO explicitly refers in its Preamble to the objectives of allowing the optimal use of the world's resources, sustainable development and the protection and preservation of the environment.[2]

The nature of WTO interactions with other international organizations in the dispute settlement process cannot be properly explored without providing an overview of the WTO law in point. Against this background, this chapter examines the WTO legal framework which links the WTO adjudicator to other regimes and their managing organizations. While it is true that the most explicit platform for such linkage is rooted in DSU Article 13 through the right of panels to seek information, other linkages are elicited from a number of WTO provisions. These rules entrench

1 See Tarullo, 'Relationship of WTO Obligations', at 162–71.

2 The Preamble of the Agreement Establishing the World Trade Organization illustrates the aspiration of the WTO to consider values other than trade. In its relevant part it reads,

> The parties to this Agreement,
>
> Recognizing that their relations in the field of trade and economic endeavour should be conducted with a view to raising standards of living, ensuring full employment and a large and steadily growing volume of real income and effective demand, and expanding the production of and trade in goods and services, while allowing for the optimal use of the world's resources in accordance with the objective of sustainable development, seeking both to protect and preserve the environment and to enhance the means for doing so in a manner consistent with their respective needs and concerns at different levels of economic development.

several devices by which the WTO permits (explicitly or implicitly) such linkages.[3] The difference between the WTO techniques of addressing other international organizations arises from substantive law, not from institutional ordering, and there is no claim here to the contrary.

The first type of linkage arises from a deference technique, for example one which is observed with respect to the IMF (section II). The second emanates from the incorporation of other international arrangements into WTO law, which links the WTO to WIPO and also to a number of standard-setting organizations (section III). The third linkage technique is contained in the co-operative arrangements of the WTO with other international organizations and in the exercise of their observer's rights.[4] Lastly, Article 13 of the DSU is regarded as a route which explicitly links the WTO adjudicator to other international organizations through its discretion to seek information from any source. A wide number of international organizations can be consulted by the WTO panels by reference to this provision alone.

II. Deference

The best example of WTO deference to another international regime is observed with respect to the international financial regime administered by the IMF.[5] The various, and at times repetitive, guidelines on mutual co-operation and assistance between the two leave no doubt that the interdependence of the monetary and trade systems has been very well understood by the international community.[6]

3 The intellectual project of mapping linkages between trade and other subjects is a subset of a larger enterprise to which much academic attention has been directed, namely the legal obligations of the WTO in the broader public international law system. See e.g. Pascal Lamy, 'The Place of the WTO and its Law in the International Legal Order', (2006) 17 *European Journal of International Law* 969, at 982; Pauwelyn, 'Use of Experts', at 535.

4 See Pauwelyn, 'Unity and Fragmentation', at 6–7, listing other devices making cross-references, such as the WTO waivers. See also Alvarez and Leebron, 'Symposium: Boundaries', at 16, categorizing the relational aspects of WTO linkages as deferential, collaborative or autonomous. According to them, the linkage is deferential if one regime defers to the determination of another regime, collaborative if the resolution of any issues relevant to the linkage must be resolved by some joint mechanism, and autonomous if the regime maintains its authority, without deference or collaboration, to make a decision.

5 See Steve Charnovitz, 'Triangulating the World Trade Organization', (2002) 96(1) *American Journal of International Law* 28, at 52.

6 See Claus D. Zimmermann, 'Jurisdictional Competition between the IMF and the WTO and its Impact on the Prevention of Monetary Protectionism', Society of International Economic Law (SIEL) Inaugural Conference Paper 16/08, 26 June 2008, at 23.

A. *References to the International Monetary Fund in the WTO law*

Apart from the reference in Article III of the WTO Agreement, the relationship with the IMF has been elaborated in a number of other instruments. The 1994 Final Act Embodying the Results of the Uruguay Round includes a Ministerial Declaration on the Relationship of the WTO with the IMF. According to this instrument, the relationship of the two institutions with regard to the areas covered by the Multilateral Trade Agreements is based on the provisions that governed the relationship of GATT 1947 with the IMF. Another document – the Ministerial Declaration on the Contribution of the WTO to Achieving Greater Coherence in Global Economic Policymaking – refers, *inter alia*, to 'the role of the World Bank and the IMF in supporting adjustment to trade liberalization'. A number of other provisions acknowledge the close interrelationship between monetary and trade policy instruments, such as Articles XII, XIV, XV and XVIII(B) of GATT 1994 and Article XII of the GATS. All these provisions call on the WTO to seek co-operation with the IMF with a view to pursuing a co-ordinated policy regarding exchange questions and to consult fully with the IMF when considering problems concerning monetary reserves, balances of payments or foreign-exchange arrangements.

B. *GATT Article XV*

Article XV of GATT 1947 is the cornerstone WTO provision aimed at avoiding inconsistent rights and obligations between the participants in the international trade and financial regimes.[7] It sets out rules attributing a concrete role to the IMF in WTO decision making through the consultation requirement. This intention arises clearly from GATT Article XV(1), which instructs contracting parties to seek co-operation with the IMF with a view to pursuing 'a co-ordinated policy with regard to exchange questions within the jurisdiction of the Fund and questions of quantitative restrictions and other trade measures within the jurisdiction of the Contracting Parties'. The provision sets out both the principle of WTO consultations with the Fund and the scope and effect of such

7 A role for the IMF in the WTO arises also from Arts. XII–XIV and XVIII, Section B of GATT. For a recent account of GATT Art. XV see Andrew D. Mitchell and Elizabeth Sheargold, 'GATT Article XV: Exchange Arrangements', in Rüdiger Wolfrum and Peter-Tobias Stoll (eds.), *Max Planck Commentaries on World Trade Law, WTO – Trade in Goods*, vol. 5 (Leiden: Koninklijke Brill NV, 2010), 353–65.

consultations, which includes monetary reserves, balance of payments and foreign exchange.[8] To illustrate this key provision, Article XV(2) reads:

> In all cases in which the Contracting Parties are called upon to consider or deal with problems concerning monetary reserves, balances of payments or foreign exchange arrangements, they shall consult fully with the International Monetary Fund. In such consultations, the Contracting Parties shall accept all findings of statistical and other facts presented by the Fund relating to foreign exchange, monetary reserves and balances of payments, and, shall accept the determination of the Fund as to whether action by a contracting party in exchange matters is in accordance with the Articles of Agreement of the International Monetary Fund, or with the terms of a special exchange agreement between that contracting party and the Contracting Parties. The Contracting Parties in reaching their final decision in cases involving the criteria set forth in paragraph 2(a) of Article XII or in paragraph 9 of Article XVIII, shall accept the determination of the Fund as to what constitutes a serious decline in the contracting party's monetary reserves, a very low level of its monetary reserves or a reasonable rate of increase in its monetary reserves, and as to the financial aspects of other matters covered in consultation in such cases.

There are a number of points which need to be singled out with respect to this provision, which help with understanding the nature of the WTO panels' interactions with the IMF. First, it should be stressed that the wording of GATT XV(2) on the IMF having to provide 'findings of statistical and other facts' seems to suggest submission of factual information on the three matters listed above by the IMF, not an interpretation of the relevant GATT articles.[9] However, given the language on the role of the IMF on exchange matters ('shall accept the determination of the Fund'), some authors have suggested that the IMF's contribution to WTO dispute settlement in this context entails a *legal* determination under its Articles of Agreement on exchange matters and a *factual* determination when it comes to assessments on monetary reserves and the balance of

8 Under GATT, the contracting parties made recourse to this provision on a few occasions through various mechanisms. See Tokyo Declaration of 1973 MIN (73)1, whereby the ministers recognized the dependence of trade liberalization on the monetary system; 1984 Decision on 'Exchange Rate Fluctuations and their Effect on Trade', L/5761; 1980 'Report of the Working Party on "Specific Duties"', L/5572; see also L/5721, 31S/52, 53–54, paras. 7–10; CG.18/W/74, 'The Relationship between the International Trading System and the International Financial System', dated 26 April 1983.

9 GATT, BISD (27th Supp., 1981).

payments.[10] Thus the former type of input would amount to a quasi-legislative fact, and the normative function of the IMF is apparently more pronounced in this case compared with the balance of payment issues.[11] That is why, in the case of the IMF, 'deference' is the proper term to capture the relationship with the WTO dispute settlement bodies. None of the other linking techniques portrayed below explicitly mandate consideration of legal determination by other international organizations in WTO dispute settlement.[12] This is primarily explained by the architecture of the relevant international organizations and the WTO legal base for the interface.[13]

1. The balance of payments assessments

Since the IMF offers factual analysis that becomes a component of the WTO's final ruling, the Fund's role in the balance of payments assessments has been characterized as a sort of service provided to the WTO.[14] The IMF balance of payments statement is prepared on specific request by the WTO, irrespective of whether such a request corresponds to the annual consultation cycle for the member or any current work with that member, such as provision of financing. As a result, updated analyses are provided which are considered by the Executive Board specifically for transmittal to the WTO by the Fund's representative in Geneva.[15] Thus

10 Deborah E. Siegel, 'Legal Aspects of the IMF/WTO Relationship: The Fund's Articles of Agreement and the WTO Agreements', (2002) 96(5) *American Journal of International Law* 569, at 570.

11 See ibid., at 571, arguing that this is construed on the basis of several provisions of GATT and the GATS. In GATT, this is found in Art. XV(9)(a), stating that 'Nothing in this Agreement shall preclude: the use by a [WTO member] of exchange controls and exchange restrictions in accordance with the Articles of Agreement of the International Monetary Fund or with that [WTO member's] special agreement.' Art. XII of the GATS contains an analogous statement.

12 This was also the case during GATT, when contracting parties were to accept a determination by the IMF as to whether a government's action in exchange matters accords with the IMF Articles of Agreement or with a special agreement between that government and GATT. This was regarded as allowing GATT's scope for deference to the IMF. See Charnovitz, 'Triangulating the World Trade Organization', at 52.

13 See Part II below for a detailed account of these limits.

14 Apart from this, Siegel notes that 'there is still space for discussions on the role of the IMF in the balance of payments matters and their linkage to trade regime. For example, the criteria justifying the use of the balance of payments safeguard are not linked in any way to an adjustment programme supported by Fund financing; this omission is not surprising, as the practice for such programmes evolved well after the GATT was drafted'. Siegel, 'Legal Aspects', at 584.

15 Ibid., at 580.

the role of the Fund in balance of payments assessments is to share such factual analysis with respect to a specific member, not to rule on whether the GATT balance of payments exception applies.[16] Nevertheless, a trend has developed whereby IMF statements in response to requests from the Balance of Payments Committee for consultation now often include its views on the appropriateness of the balance of payments measure, as well as the relevant factual determinations, blurring thereby the distinction between the IMF's factual contribution and the WTO's consideration of the case.[17] Moreover, the WTO also defends its turf when it turns to the IMF for a determination on what constitutes a 'serious decline . . . in monetary reserves' or what is a 'reasonable rate of increase in [a member's] monetary reserves', as set out in GATT Article XV. Although such a determination would 'feed directly' into one important component of the WTO's conclusion, the WTO must still consider whether other components of the balance of payments exception have been met.[18] This means that, irrespective of the IMF's data and views, such a decision remains with the WTO judiciary.

2. Exchange measures

Whereas in relation to the Fund's finding on balance of payments the WTO retains its scope for decision, it appears that this flexibility is qualified when it comes to determinations on consistency of exchange measures with the Fund's Articles. Thus the cases relating to exchange matters represent more deference to the Fund's regulatory authority than the balance of payments assessments. In this context, in the case of exchange matters the intervention of the Fund is more a legal determination than simply a factual finding.[19]

a. Exchange or trade measures. The interface of trade and exchange measures is a rather complex issue. A thorough investigation of this linkage needs to take account of how GATT Article XV(2) is to be read together with Article XV(4), which basically suggests that there are certain policy

16 Ibid., at 572. Given the legal consequences for WTO obligations of whether or not a measure is consistent with the Fund's Articles, the Fund agreed in the Co-operation Agreement 'to inform the WTO of any decisions approving restrictions on the making of payments or transfers for current international transactions, decisions approving discriminatory currency arrangements or multiple currency practices, and decisions requesting a Fund member to exercise controls to prevent a large or sustained outflow of capital' (WTO–IMF Co-operation Agreement).

17 Siegel, 'Legal Aspects', at 561 and 571–80. 18 Ibid. 19 Ibid., 571.

objectives that can be pursued either through exchange actions or through trade measures.[20]

As early as 1954 a special Sub-Group set up during the GATT Review Session recognized that the exchange and trade measures division is in some respects arbitrary. It is acknowledged that in many instances it is difficult or impossible to define clearly whether a government measure is financial or trade in character, and frequently it is both.[21] Whereas the GATT had never formally decided how to distinguish between the two, in 1960 the IMF established that such a measure would be regarded as an exchange action if it involved a direct government limitation on the availability or use of exchange as such, irrespective of its economic effect and underlying purpose.[22] This legislative vacuum of GATT/WTO is lessened, however, by the fact that the IMF itself, as a condition of financing the members, imposes a requirement that trade restrictions – not just exchange restrictions – be lifted.[23] So far, this conceptually different approach does not seem to have caused problems, but, for the sake of coherence, it is preferable just to defer to the IMF standard when need be.[24]

b. The use of IMF-consistent measures. Whereas Article XV(2) requires the WTO to accept the Fund's determination on the consistency of a measure with the Fund's Articles, Article XV(9)(a) calls for non-preclusion of the use of exchange controls or exchange restrictions that are consistent with the Fund's Articles.[25] An essential question arising in this

20 GATT 1994 Art. XV(4) reads: 'Contracting parties shall not, by exchange action, frustrate the intent of the provisions of this Agreement, nor, by trade action, the intent of the provisions of the Articles of Agreement of the International Monetary Fund.'

21 Siegel, 'Legal Aspects', at 586.

22 In 1960 the Executive Board evaluated different possibilities for defining exchange restrictions, and adopted a test based on 'whether it involves a direct governmental limitation on the availability or use of exchange as such' (Decision no. 1034-(60/27), para. 1, at 428 (1 June 1960)), Selected Decisions and Selected Documents of the International Monetary Fund (Twenty-fifth Issue, 2000), cited in Siegel, 'Legal Aspects'. For an account of this criterion see also Frieder Roessler, 'The Relationship between the World Trade Order and the International Monetary System', in Ernst-Ulrich Petersmann and Meinhard Hilf (eds.), *The New GATT Round of Multilateral Trade Negotiations: Legal and Economic Problems – Studies in Transnational Law*, 2nd edn (Deventer: Kluwer, 1991), at 363–86.

23 Trebilcock and Howse, *Regulation of International Trade*, at 168.

24 The trade and exchange measures distinction was taken up by the Panel in *Dominican Republic – Import and Sale of Cigarettes*. For an overview of how this issue has been dealt with in this case see below Chapter 6, section II.

25 See above n. 11.

context is what the consequences under GATT XV(9)(a) are when an exchange measure investigated under the WTO is found to be consistent with the Fund's Articles. Zimmermann has responded to this by making the following assessment:

> The meaning of 'nothing in this agreement shall preclude the use of' such measures is that they create an exception to the GATT obligations for a measure that the Fund determines is an exchange measure and is applied consistently with the Articles. However, this type of measure still can be actionable under the GATT provided the Fund did not approve it under the IMF Articles or found that the measure is not an exchange control measure falling within its jurisdiction. Yet, even if the exception would be justified under Article XV:9(a), it still could have been discussed under the GATT.[26]

The above interpretation of Article XV(9)(a) is qualified by Article XV(4) requesting the contracting parties not to frustrate the intent of either GATT or IMF provisions through their exchange or trade actions. The meaning of this provision is not entirely clear. The GATT 'Ad Note' attempting to describe circumstances that would frustrate the provisions of the GATT is not enlightening either, and the issue has not been further pursued by either organization. It might be improper to give precedence to paragraph 4 over paragraph 9, as such a situation would inevitably lead to jurisdictional overlap between the two institutions.[27] Moreover, such an approach is not supported by the negotiating history of the GATT, which indicates an affirmative intention that paragraph 9 of Article XV should not be limited by paragraph 4. The latter reading is also confirmed by John Jackson with reference to a discussion of the 1952 GATT case involving Greece.[28]

These analyses, which are only intended to give a flavour of IMF–WTO linkages, illustrate the complex constellations arising from the wording of GATT Article XV and the difficulty of elucidating the delicate balance between the WTO and the IMF. The case law analysed in Part III below reveals how the WTO panels or the Appellate Body have approached some of these issues and provides responses to some questions raised by the litigants with regard to the role of the IMF in WTO dispute settlement.

26 Claus D. Zimmermann, 'Fundamental Exchange Rate Misalignment and International Law', 10 November 2008, http://ssrn.com/abstract=1300542. Published as 'Exchange Rate Misalignment and International Law', (2011) 105 *American Journal of International Law*, 423–76. See also Siegel, 'Legal Aspects', at 590.

27 Siegel, 'Legal Aspects', at 591.

28 Jackson, *World Trade and the Law of GATT*, at 484.

III. Incorporation

The first and most evident example of incorporation in WTO law arises in relation to the WTO TRIPS Agreement which assimilated several intellectual property (IP) treaties – a novel feature in international treaty law.[29] The incorporation technique produces the most substantive linkage between the TRIPS and various treaties or conventions administered by WIPO, through what has been called 'common object'.[30] A second example which can be classified under this technique relates to the SPS Agreement and TBT Agreements. These, next to the TRIPS Agreement, are the most important cases of incorporation by reference to international standards into WTO law. This is followed by the OECD Arrangement on Guidelines for Officially Supported Export Credits (the OECD Arrangement). As illustrated below, it could be suggested that this linkage has also been carried out through incorporation. The Harmonized Commodity Description and Coding System (HS) Convention administered by the WCO might be also attributed to this category. While the WTO has not explicitly incorporated this treaty, all WTO members have used the HS in tariff negotiations and the resultant Schedules of Commitments, which are binding under the WTO.

The treaties and standards referenced above have been treated by the WTO adjudicator as autonomous sources of WTO law.[31] This is a natural effect of such incorporation. In the following, the most important examples of linkages by incorporation are illustrated in detail.

A. The TRIPS Agreement

While intellectual property was not at the forefront of the GATT, the subject was nonetheless prominent enough to be referenced in a number

29 Thomas Cottier, 'The Agreement on Trade-Related Aspects of Intellectual Property Rights', in P. F. J. Macrory, A. E. Appleton and M. G. Plummer (eds.), *The World Trade Organization: Legal and Political Analysis*, vol. 1 (New York: Springer, 2005) 1041–115, at 1063.

30 David Vivas-Eugui, 'What Agenda for the Review of TRIPS? A Sustainable Development Perspective', Center for International Environmental Law TEP 2–3 (Summer 2002), at www.ciel.org/Publications/AgendaTRIPS_Summer02.pdf (visited 20 March 2009). This incorporation of the rules of one's own kind has been described as a 'cannibalization of the WIPO conventions'. See Susan A. Mort, 'The WTO, the WIPO and the Internet: Confounding the Borders of Copyright and Neighbouring Rights', (1997) 8 *Fordham Intellectual Property, Media & Entertainment Law Journal* 184.

31 Mavroidis, 'No Outsourcing of Law?', at 427. Also Mitsuo Matsushita, Thomas H. Schoenbaum and Petros C. Mavroidis, *The World Trade Organization: Law, Practice, and Policy* (Oxford University Press, 2006), 55–6.

of its Articles – most notably GATT Article XX, Article XI relating to marks of origin, and a number of general provisions that apply to intellectual property to the extent that it is embodied in goods, such as the requirement of national treatment. This sporadic mention of intellectual property rights in the GATT is explained by the fact that, at the time, these rights were widely perceived as an acceptable obstacle to trade. This changed during the Uruguay Round, with the decision to expand the trade mandate to include intellectual property rights.[32]

Thus a traditionally separate regime was taken into the body of WTO law through the TRIPS Agreement, which incorporates by reference most, although not all, obligations of several intellectual property rights (IPR) treaties (the Paris Convention, the Berne Convention and the Treaty on Intellectual Property in Respect of Integrated Circuits).[33] This combination of the intellectual property rights treaties with the TRIPS Agreement has been attributed great significance due to the merger of detailed technical rules with effective dispute settlement resolution under the WTO.[34]

Footnote 2 to the TRIPS Agreement states that references to the intellectual property conventions are to specific versions of those conventions. In *US – Section 211 Appropriations Act*, the Appellate Body provided an explanation of the status of these agreements in WTO law, by confirming that these treaties had been incorporated into the WTO *acquis* by virtue of Article 2(1) of the TRIPS Agreement. Thus the obligations of countries of the Paris Union under the Paris Convention (1967) are also

32 The main proponents of the regime shift were the United States and the EC, due to the perceived weakness of WIPO in enforcing intellectual property rights. But see Ruth L. Okediji, 'TRIPS Dispute Settlement and the Sources of (International) Copyright Law', (2002) 49 *Journal of the Copyright Society* 585, at 594, noting that most commentators who criticize WIPO's lack of enforcement power have ignored the possible role the International Court of Justice could have played with respect to compliance with WIPO treaties. Other authors have noted the failure of WIPO to live up to the expectations of both industrialized and non-industrialized countries in respect of intellectual property norm development. See, e.g., Monique L. Cordray, 'GATT v. WIPO', (1994) 76 *Journal of the Patent and Trademark Office Society* 122, at 122; Marshall Leaffer, *Understanding Copyright Law*, 2nd edn (New York: Matthew Bender, 1995), at 372.

33 See TRIPS, Art. 1(3). The Rome Convention is also referenced in TRIPS but it has not been incorporated therein.

34 Some even suggest employing this technique in order to bring into the WTO other trade-related rules to the extent that they are clear. This is perceived as something which would serve to tighten the relationship between the WTO and the relevant international organization, while the latter would continue to develop further the detail of the respective area. See Veronika Hrbatá, 'No International Organization is an Island . . . The WTO's Relationship with the WIPO: A Model of Governance of Trade Linkage Areas?', (2010) 44 *Journal of World Trade* 1, at 35.

now obligations of all WTO members, whether they are parties to the Paris Union or not, and are enforceable under the DSU.[35] The selective incorporation of intellectual property norms into the trade regime has been characterized as a linkage fuelled by 'regime borrowing'.[36] With that, the TRIPS Agreement established a separate intellectual property regime.

The TRIPS Agreement was not limited, however, to the incorporation of the above treaties, but expanded the scope of intellectual property rights regulation. It embraced new subjects, such as the protection of geographical indications (Articles 22–24), protection of undisclosed information (Article 39), and enforcement obligations (Part III). While enhancing and expanding the existing norms,[37] it also specifically excluded some significant principles incorporated in those treaties (e.g. the moral rights under the Berne Convention Article 9). Thus, with the advent of the TRIPS Agreement, the protection of various forms of intellectual property rights became a mandatory part of the multilateral system, binding on all members alike and fully subject to WTO dispute settlement.[38]

It is clear that there is substantial overlap between the TRIPS Agreement and the categories of intellectual property covered by treaties administered by WIPO, an agency which should be given credit for the historical administration of these conventions. Despite the fact that a great deal of the intellectual property regime shifted to the WTO, today WIPO administers almost two dozen other treaties which are not incorporated into the TRIPS Agreement. As the administrator of the Madrid Arrangement, and especially the Berne and Paris Conventions, WIPO has a special claim to a role in articulating international intellectual property norms.[39] It has been claimed that WIPO's practice of appointing informal groups of experts to consider disputes under the treaties it administers provides, at

35 *US – Section 211 Appropriations Act*, ABR, para. 238.

36 See Alvarez and Leebron, 'Symposium: Boundaries', at 19–20.

37 See TRIPS Art. 1(3), binding all members to minimum standards at least equivalent to those embodied in existing conventions, Part III (enforcement obligations), Art. 27, defining patentable subject matter.

38 Thomas Cottier and Matthias Oesch, *International Trade Regulation: Law and Policy in the WTO, the European Union and Switzerland* (London: Cameron May, 2005), 916. For an overview of the TRIPS Agreement see also Cottier, 'Agreement on Trade-Related Aspects', 1041–120.

39 But see Okediji, 'WIPO–WTO Relations', at 43, suggesting that the WTO is capable of setting more nuanced intellectual property norms that account for differences in cultural, economic and political factors which are more likely to be consistently produced by the WTO than by WIPO.

least in theory, a mechanism for finding best rules.[40] Thus this institution emerges as a good example of an organization possessing superior legitimacy to that of the WTO on a specific subject matter. Against this background, the importance of the co-operation between WIPO and the WTO is indisputable.[41] This has been explicitly envisaged in several TRIPS Agreement provisions as well as in a separate Co-operation Agreement.[42]

The WTO panels have also turned to this agency on a few occasions. In their consideration of TRIPS-related claims, WTO panels asked for the advice of WIPO in a number of disputes, including *US – Section 211 Appropriations Act*, *US – Section 110(5) Copyright Act*, and *China – Intellectual Property Rights* and *EC – Trademarks and Geographical Indications*. Most of these disputes are analysed in depth in Chapter 7 below.

B. *The SPS and TBT Agreements*

The WTO SPS and TBT Agreements are two other instruments linking the WTO with other international organizations. These are organizations operating in the field of international standard setting. The essence of this interface is that compliance with these standards presumes the legality of the various measures covered by the relevant WTO Agreements. In the case of the SPS Agreement, this arises from the objective of the drafters of harmonizing the sanitary and phytosanitary measures of the members. Thus a first intersection of the WTO SPS Agreement and the Codex Alimentarius, the OIE and the IPPC emerges from the SPS Preamble, which expresses the desire of the members

40 Rochelle C. Dreyfuss and Andreas F. Lowenfeld, 'Two Achievements of the Uruguay Round: Putting TRIPS and Dispute Settlement Together', (1997) 37 *Virginia Journal of International Law* 275, at 293. But see Ernst-Ulrich Petersmann, 'Constitutionalism and International Organizations', (1997) 17 *Northwestern Journal of International Law & Business* 398, at 467, noting that 'the substantive standards, dispute settlement and enforcement mechanisms of the World Intellectual Property Organization have been criticized as inadequate by many countries. The proposals, made by the WIPO Secretariat after the conclusion of the Uruguay Round Agreements, to supplement the WTO dispute settlement system by a WIPO "Treaty on the Settlement of Disputes between States in the Field of Intellectual Property" have so far been opposed, notably by the United States.'

41 See Dreyfuss and Lowenfeld, 'Two Achievements', at 293, drawing on the fact that WIPO resonates well with the negotiating history of the TRIPS Agreement: the Uruguay Round would not have produced TRIPS had the administrators of WIPO not participated in the identification of generally accepted international norms.

42 See the TRIPS Agreement Preamble; TRIPS Art. 68. See Agreement between the World Intellectual Property Organization and the World Trade Organization, 22 December 1995, (1996) 35 ILM 754 (WIPO–WTO Agreement).

> to further the use of harmonized sanitary and phytosanitary measures between Members, on the basis of international standards, guidelines and recommendations developed by the relevant international organizations, including the Codex Alimentarius Commission, the International Office of Epizootics, and the relevant international and regional organizations operating within the framework of the International Plant Protection Convention.

This can be pursued without requiring members to change their appropriate level of protection of human, animal or plant life or health.[43]

A role for these organizations in the WTO, including in the dispute settlement process, arises from the risk assessment requirement set out in SPS Article 5. This provision entails consideration by WTO members of the risk assessment techniques developed by the 'relevant international organizations'. Furthermore, similar to DSU Article 13, SPS Agreement Article 11(2) explicitly refers to the possibility of the panel consulting with experts. 'To this end, the Panel may, when it deems it appropriate, establish an advisory technical expert group, or consult the relevant international organizations.'[44] The key element of SPS Article 11 is the reference to the 'relevant international organizations' to be consulted by panels. This term re-emerges several times in the SPS Agreement along

43 Other relevant provisions are found in SPS Art. 3(4), requiring members to 'play a full part, within the limits of their resources, in the relevant international organizations and their subsidiary bodies, in particular the Codex Alimentarius Commission . . . to promote within these organizations the development and periodic review of standards, guidelines and recommendations with respect to all aspects of sanitary and phytosanitary measures'; SPS Art. 12(3), instructing the SPS Committee to 'maintain close contact with the relevant international organizations in the field of sanitary and phytosanitary protection, especially with the Codex Alimentarius Commission . . . with the objective of securing the best available scientific and technical advice for the administration of this Agreement and in order to ensure that unnecessary duplication of effort is avoided'; and Annex A to the SPS Agreement (Definitions, para. 3), stating that international standards, guidelines and recommendations are '(a) for food safety, the standards, guidelines and recommendations established by the Codex Alimentarius Commission relating to food additives, veterinary drugs and pesticide residues, contaminants, methods of analysis and sampling, and codes and guidelines of hygienic practice'. See more on the relationship of the WTO with these organizations: Terence P. Stewart and David S. Johanson, 'The SPS Agreement of the World Trade Organization and International Organization: The Roles of the Codex Alimentarius Commission, the International Plant Protection Convention, and International Office of Epizootics', (1998) 26 *Syracuse Journal of International Law and Commerce* 27.

44 Note should be taken that the discretion to seek such information and advice is limited, however, by the fact that the panel is not in a position to make the case for a complaining party – the burden of proof lies with the litigants.

with the 'appropriate international organizations'.[45] While the terms refer to the three standard-setting organizations mentioned in the SPS Agreement (Codex, OIE, IPPC), this does not mean that the consultation in the context of Article 11(2) is limited to these three. Finally, an SPS interface with the relevant international organizations arises from the intention of the SPS negotiators to seek to balance the role of international standards. With that, they remind WTO members of their unimpaired rights to resort to the good offices or dispute settlement mechanisms of these international organizations (SPS Article 11(3)).

Despite the special status of their standards in the WTO, the advisory role of the standard-setting organizations in the WTO disputes settlement process is nebulous; it is mostly expressed through the suggestion of names of independent scientific experts to the panels.[46] Less frequently, they are approached for technical advice regarding the operation of their respective institutions. Their contribution to the settlement of relevant disputes could be further elaborated with a view to ensuring an 'objective assessment of the matter' by WTO panels. An important question that arises in relation to these international organizations is whether the prerogatives of these institutions should be expanded to the interpretation of their own standards, or whether their role should be limited to the elaboration and the furnishing of those standards in the WTO.

1. The 'relevant international organizations' under the SPS Agreement

As shown above, the SPS Agreement contains provisions specifically referring to the Codex, the OIE, and the IPPC. The Codex is responsible for food safety, while the OIE works in the field of animal health and safety. That list is supplemented with international standards, guidelines and recommendations developed under the auspices of the Secretariat of the IPPC, in co-operation with regional organizations. The IPPC standards relate to phytosanitary safety concerned with the life and health of plants.[47]

Prior to 1995, these organizations received limited attention from the international community, as they predominantly served as forums for

45 See above n. 43 for the relevant SPS Agreement references.

46 For a detailed overview of the role of the SPS standard-setting organizations in the WTO see Chapter 9 below.

47 Note that the IPPC is an international convention and not an international organization. For an overview on the functioning of these organizations see Chapter 5 below.

scientific and technical discussion between experts.[48] Their importance in the WTO was strengthened by the fact that members have an autonomous right to choose a given level of protection, which can be either the level contained in an international standard or a higher level. As noted by some authors, the presumption of conformity introduced by the SPS Agreement makes them 'satellite organizations'[49] of the WTO or 'quasi-legislators'.[50]

Although the Codex, the OIE and the IPPC are the only organizations mentioned in the SPS Agreement, the SPS Committee is authorized to identify other international organizations, open to membership of all members, which may promulgate standards, guidelines or recommendations for matters not covered by the three organizations.[51] Therefore, a number of other international agencies concerned with SPS issues are affiliated to the WTO; for instance, WHO, the FAO, the United Nations Conference on Trade and Development (UNCTAD) and the International Organization for Standardization (ISO) have regular observer status. Thus a broader range of standards are being called upon in practice than would be apparent on the basis of a simple reading of the SPS Agreement.[52]

2. International organizations under the TBT Agreement

The TBT Agreement elaborates the requirement of the Tokyo Round Standards Code for technical regulations and standards except for sanitary and phytosanitary measures, which are covered under the SPS Agreement. The Code was intended to minimize trade distortions that arose from disparate national regulatory requirements. It required the parties to the GATT to use multilaterally agreed standards, where they existed, as the basis for national measures (Art. 2(2)) and clearly established a requirement of non-discrimination in standards and their application.

48 Frode Veggeland and Svein O. Borgen, 'Negotiating International Food Standards: The World Trade Organization's Impact on the Codex Alimentarius Commission', (2005) 18 *Governance: An International Journal of Policy, Administration, and Institutions* 675, at 675 and 684, discussing the status of the Codex Alimentarius before 1995.

49 Sara Poli, 'The Adoption of International Food Safety Standards', (2004) 10 *European Law Journal* 615.

50 Gabrielle Marceau and Joel P. Trachtman, 'The Technical Barriers to Trade Agreement, the Sanitary and Phytosanitary Measures Agreement, and the General Agreement on Tariff and Trade, A Map of the World Trade Organization Law of Domestic Regulation of Goods', (2002) 35(5) *Journal of World Trade* 811, at 838.

51 SPS Agreement, Annex A.

52 Joanne Scott, 'Cooperative Regulation in the WTO: The SPS Committee', New York University, Global Law Working Paper 03/06 (2006), at 19–20, providing an example where the WHO advised the SPS Committee with regard to the risk of cholera posed by foodstuffs imported from Tanzania.

This applied with respect to imported products on the basis of their national origin and between foreign and domestic products (Art. 2(1)). The central criterion for determining the validity of a standard under the Code was whether the standard constituted an 'unnecessary obstacle to international trade' – a test that was not clearly articulated but has still been imported into the TBT Agreement. The Code also contained special dispute resolution procedures that anticipated the establishment of technical expert groups, which were to be created in order to advise the panels.

Under the WTO TBT Agreement, members' measures are exempt from the WTO disciplines if they are 'in accordance' with international standards set by an open list of international standard-setting bodies (TBT Art. 2).[53] While in the SPS context the relevant standards (at present) issue from the three sister organizations (Codex Alimentarius, OIE, IPPC), the scope of international standards is much broader in the TBT. For that matter, TBT Annex 1 clarifies that the term 'standard' is defined as a 'document approved by a recognized body that provides, for common and repeated use, rules, guidelines or characteristics for products or related processes and production methods, with which compliance is not mandatory'. The term 'international body' is defined in TBT Annex 1(4) as a 'body or system whose membership is open to the relevant bodies of at least all Members'.[54]

Thus a wide range of international organizations may fall under this definition, such as the ISO, the International Electrotechnical Commission (IEC), and the International Telecommunication Union (ITU).[55]

53 For an account of the TBT Agreement and standards see Robert Howse, 'A New Device for Creating International Normativity: The WTO Technical Barriers to Trade Agreement and "International Standards"', in Christian Joerges and Ernst-Ulrich Petersmann (eds.), *Constitutionalism, Multilevel Trade Governance and Social Regulation* (Oxford: Hart, 2006), 383–95.

54 In *EC – Sardines* the Panel found that, for TBT purposes, 'international standards are standards that are developed by international bodies'. But this does not provide a definition of the term 'standard' or 'international body'. See Panel Report, para. 7.63.

55 The ISO and the IEC are non-treaty international organizations, where membership consists of both non-government and government agencies. The ITU, on the other hand, is treaty-based and its members are limited to government agencies. These organizations have established tens of thousands of standards covering almost every conceivable topic. In addition to these, independent standards organizations such as ASTM International develop and publish technical standards for international use. Others set standards within some more specialized context, such as the SAE (Society of Automotive Engineers), the IETF (Internet Engineering Task Force), TAPPI (Technical Association of the Pulp and Paper Industry), W3C (World Wide Web Consortium),

One of the reasons why international organizations were not specified in the TBT lies in the disagreement between the EC and the United States over methods of standardization on a technical issue.[56] On these grounds, the United States did not take an active part in the ISO/IEC, which was founded and is largely managed by European countries. Only a small number of the standards issued by these agencies were proposed by the United States. On the other hand, in contrast to the SPS three sister organizations, the TBT standards-setting process is more privatized, with a number of private standardization bodies working in this field,[57] making it perhaps more difficult to provide a comprehensive list thereof in the TBT Agreement.

Similar to the SPS Agreement, the TBT contains a consultation provision in Article 14(2), providing that 'At the request of a party to a dispute, or at its own initiative, a Panel may establish a technical expert group to assist in questions of a technical nature, requiring detailed consideration by experts.' Unlike in the SPS however, under the TBT Agreement there is no mention of specific international organizations with relevance for this process.[58] Thus it is not clear if the WTO Panels or the Appellate

the IEEE (Institute of Electrical and Electronics Engineers), and the UPU (Universal Postal Union). Often, these international standards organizations are not based on the principle of one member per country. Rather, membership in such international organizations is open, having either organizational or corporate or individual technical expert members from around the globe. To exemplify, the UPU, by means of its Standards Board, defines, approves and maintains postal standards. The Standards Board's objectives are to provide strategic direction and to plan, develop and maintain technical and communications standards aimed at improving postal operational efficiency and quality of service, besides promoting inter-operability and compatibility of all UPU and international postal telematics initiatives. See http://en.wikipedia.org/wiki/Standard_setting_organisations#International_Standards_Organizations (visited 7 October 2009).

56 For an overview see Walter Mattli, 'International Governance for Voluntary Standards: A Game Theoretic Perspective', in George A. Bermann, Matthias Herdegen and Peter L. Lindseth (eds.), *Transatlantic Regulatory Cooperation: Legal Problems and Political Prospects* (Oxford University Press, 2000). See also Kenneth W. Abbott, 'US-EU Disputes over Technical Barriers to Trade and the "Hushkits" Dispute', in Ernst-Ulrich Petersmann and Mark A. Pollack (eds.), *Transatlantic Economic Disputes: The EU, the US, and the WTO* (Oxford University Press, 2004).

57 Harm Schepel, *The Constitution of Private Governance: Product Standards in the Regulation of Integrating Markets* (Oxford: Hart, 2005), 186–7.

58 One of the reasons for this is that most of the organizations concerned are not intergovernmental but private bodies. See Lukasz Gruszczynski, *Regulating Health and Environmental Risks under WTO Law: A Critical Analysis of the SPS Agreement* (Oxford University Press, 2010).

Body would invoke this provision to consult with other international organizations.

A few points should be outlined in relation to the status of international organizations under the TBT. First, it should be noted that there could be a wide range of organizations falling within the TBT definition of 'international body'. Second, the TBT, unlike the SPS, does not specifically require panels examining TBT measures to consult with other international organizations;[59] a panel can, however, resort to Article 13 of the DSU for this purpose. Third, the practice under the TBT Agreement disregards the distinction between non- and intergovernmental bodies, recognizing, for example, standards adopted by the Codex[60] – an intergovernmental body – and also the ISO – a non-intergovernmental body – as relevant.[61]

C. The SCM Agreement

Another mode of rules incorporation into the WTO arises from the reference to an 'international undertaking' in the SCM Agreement Annex I(k). In full, the second paragraph of item (k) reads:

> Provided, however, that if a Member is a party to an international undertaking on official export credits to which at least twelve original Members to this Agreement are parties as of 1 January 1979 (or a successor undertaking which has been adopted by those original Members), or if in practice a Member applies the interest rates provisions of the relevant undertaking, an export credit practice which is in conformity with those provisions shall not be considered an export subsidy prohibited by this Agreement.[62]

This reference has been understood to pass on the OECD Arrangement[63] concluded in 1978 and revised most recently in 2008.[64]

59 Collette Kinnon, 'World Trade: Bringing Health into the Picture', (1998) 19 *World Health Forum* 397, at 401.

60 Although both the Panel and the Appellate Body considered Codex standards as relevant for the purpose of the TBT Agreement; see *EC – Sardines*, Panel Report.

61 Gruszczynski, *Regulating Health*.

62 WTO SCM Agreement, Annex I(k).

63 For a relevant reference in WTO dispute settlement see *Brazil – Aircraft*, Panel Report, para. 5.79: 'we understand the essence of the second paragraph of item (k), at least at present to be that "an export credit practice" which is in "conformity" with "the interest rates provisions" of the OECD Arrangement "shall not be considered an export subsidy prohibited by" the SCM Agreement'.

64 See OECD, 'Arrangement on Officially Supported Export Credits' (2008 revision): OECD Trade and Agriculture Directorate TAD/PG(2007)28/FINAL, at www.oecd.org/ (visited September 2008). The arrangement is self-defined as a 'Gentlemen's Agreement among

Thus the WTO, next to the TRIPS incorporated treaties, has perceived this instrument as an independent source of WTO law.[65]

The term 'successor undertaking' enshrined in Annex I(k) of the SCM Agreement above allows the participants of the OECD Arrangement to update continually the terms of the exemption as it applies to them and to the rest of the WTO membership. A question raised in connection with this provision emerged during the proceedings in *Brazil – Aircraft (Article 21.5 – Canada II)*, where the Panel looked into the extent to which the relevant text of the OECD Arrangement was that of 1992, which is referred to in the SCM Agreement, or the successor instrument adopted in 1998.[66] The Panel decided that, because of the reference in Annex I(k) to the successor undertaking, it had to take into account the latest norms, that is, the 1998 Arrangement.[67] 'It is remarkable that the WTO membership agreed in 1994 that a sub-set of the WTO membership (the OECD members) had the legal right to modify not only their *inter se* legal relations, but the rights and obligations of the totality of the WTO Membership.'[68]

It may be argued that accepting that all subsequent modifications of the OECD Arrangement are covered as well, when it is not *ex ante* known which rights and obligations will be reflected therein, is tantamount to imposing new rights and obligations for all WTO members.[69] The Panel in *Brazil – Aircraft* considered that the acceptance of the latest agreement was justifiable in order for the OECD to share necessary expertise.[70] It noted, however, that if the participants in the OECD Arrangement 'were to abuse their power to modify the scope of the safe haven, the recourse of other WTO Members would be to renegotiate' the relevant provision of the SCM Agreement.[71] With this in mind, the current chair's text of the WTO Rules Group of negotiations contains a number of proposals regarding the operation of this provision, which essentially provides for

the Participants', in which the current participants are Australia, Canada, the EC, Japan, South Korea, New Zealand, Norway, Switzerland and the United States. For a detailed description of its operation, see Janet K. Levit, 'A Bottom-Up Approach to International Lawmaking: The Tale of Three Trade Finance Instruments', (2005) 30 *Yale Journal of International Law* 125, at 157–67.

65 Matsushita et al., *World Trade Organization.*

66 Note should be taken that the 1998 Agreement was negotiated only among OECD members, which constitute a small minority of WTO membership.

67 *Canada – Aircraft (Article 21.5 – Brazil)*, Panel Report, paras. 5.80–5.91. Note that the 1992 OECD Arrangement is no longer in effect.

68 Mavroidis, 'No Outsourcing of Law?', n. 35.

69 Matsushita et al., *World Trade Organization*, at 58.

70 *Brazil – Aircraft*, Panel Report, para. 5.88.

71 Ibid., para. 5.89, n. 86.

a notification requirement of the 'undertaking' to the SCM Committee and its eventual examination at the request of a member.[72]

This legal language, which practically incorporates an open-ended OECD Arrangement (namely its successor undertaking) into the WTO, reveals openness and sensitivity of the WTO towards the substantive law of another regime. The shortcomings in this context relate to the lack of involvement of the host institution in the process. There are a number of other WTO disputes involving Annex I(k) where neither the Permanent Group of Experts under the SCM nor the OECD had been consulted by the WTO adjudicator.[73] This does not satisfy the proposal for institutional sensitivity of the WTO adjudicator – a process which should also take into account the input of the responsible institutions.

IV. Co-operation and observership

Two other modes for interfacing the WTO with other international organizations arise from the option to conclude co-operative arrangements and the observership status of international organizations in the WTO. The Marrakesh Agreement Establishing the World Trade Organization (WTO Agreement) makes only one specific reference to other international organizations, in Article III, which sets out the functions of the WTO. One of these functions is to 'cooperate, as appropriate, with the International Monetary Fund and with the International Bank for Reconstruction and Development and its affiliated agencies'. On a more general note, Article V of the Marrakesh Agreement mandates the WTO General Council to conclude agreements with other international organizations. Thus WTO members, meeting through the General Council, are responsible for making 'appropriate arrangements' for effective co-operation and consultation with intergovernmental organizations and NGOs. By virtue of this mandate, Article V of the WTO Agreement has been considered as evidence that the WTO 'has treaty-making power and that in principle the General Council exercises it'.[74] Apart from that, there are other WTO Agreements which mandate explicitly the establishment of mechanisms

72 Draft Consolidated Chair Texts of the AD and SCM Agreements, WTO Doc. TN/RL/W/213 (31 November 2007), para. 76 (amendment to Annex I(k)).

73 See Young, 'Fragmentation or Interaction', at 39, n. 183, noting that the consultative power of the PGE or Panel does not appear to have been utilized in the following disputes involving Annex I(k): *Brazil – Aircraft*; *Canada – Aircraft Credits and Guarantees*.

74 Pieter J. Kuijper, 'Some Institutional Issues Presently before the WTO', in Daniel Kennedy and James Southwick (eds.), *The Political Economy of International Trade Law: Essays in Honor of Robert E Hudec* (Cambridge University Press, 2002), 81–110, at 108.

for co-operation with other international organizations. For example, the TRIPS Agreement instructs the TRIPS Council to establish such mechanisms with WIPO and suggests that the two organizations might work together in the establishment of a common register of members' intellectual property laws and regulations. The WTO co-operation with WIPO is specifically prescribed in the TRIPS Preamble and TRIPS Articles 63(2) and 68.[75]

A. *The WTO co-operation agreements and memoranda of understanding*

To date, the WTO has signed co-operation agreements with the IMF (1996),[76] the World Bank (1997),[77] WIPO (1996),[78] the OIE (1998)[79] and the ITU (2000).[80] These agreements normally take up such issues as participation in meetings, co-operation in the field of common competence, information sharing, exchange of statistical data and mutual technical assistance.

75 For a comprehensive account of the WTO provisions mandating co-operation with other international organizations see WTO, www.WTO.org/english/thewto_e/coher_e/coher_e.htm (last visited March 2010).

76 The agreement between the WTO and the IMF was signed as a Cooperation Agreement at the first WTO Ministerial Conference in Singapore. See WTO Doc. WTO/L/1995, 18 November 1996 (WTO–IMF Agreement).

77 A formal Co-operation Agreement was concluded between the WTO and the World Bank also at the Singapore Ministerial Conference in 1996 (signed 28 April 1997). The Agreement is not completely identical to the Agreement of the IMF with the WTO; there is no provision for written communication on matters of mutual interest to become part of the official records. It provides, however, a legal basis for a long-standing relationship, which during GATT times used to be largely informal. For an account of the conclusion of these agreements see Wolfgang Benedek, 'Relations of the WTO with other International Organizations and NGOs', in Friedl Weiss, Erik Denters and Paul de Waart, *International Economic Law with a Human Face* (The Hague, Dordrecht and London: Kluwer Law International, 1998) 479–96, at 489. Both agreements fulfil the mandate of the Marrakesh Declaration on Greater Coherence in Global Economic Policy Making and they are in line with the Agreement Establishing the WTO Art. III(5), the IMF Agreement Art. X and the World Bank Agreement Art. V(8).

78 The Agreement between the WTO and WIPO was adopted on 22 December 1995 and entered into force on 1 January 1996. See WTO, Decision of the Council for TRIPS, Doc. IP/C/6.

79 The Agreement between the WTO and the OIE was adopted on 4 May 1998. See WTO Doc. WT/L/272.

80 The Co-operation Agreement between the WTO and ITU was adopted on 26 May 2000 by the Council for Trade in Services and entered into force on 10 October 2000. See WTO Doc. S/C/9/Rev.1.

The WTO Co-operation Agreement with WIPO, for example, establishes a basic framework for co-operation in providing technical assistance relating to the TRIPS Agreement to developing country members of each organization. The WTO TRIPS Council and the WIPO Governing Bodies have taken additional steps with a view to strengthening the co-operation. The WIPO Co-ordination Committee has been designated by the WIPO Governing Bodies as the channel of communication between the two organizations. The TRIPS Council has decided that the WTO and WIPO should use a uniform system for notification by members of intellectual property rights laws which will be administered by WIPO. To put into practice the co-operation clauses of this Agreement, WIPO members have allocated additional resources for assisting countries in modernizing their intellectual property legislation and administrative infrastructure. Notably, by virtue of this WTO instrument, the TRIPS Council, at the request of its members, might seek guidance from WIPO in the context of dispute settlement and might consult WIPO concerning the evolution of multilateral intellectual property rights rules during periodic review of the TRIPS Agreement. These actions represent a significant step towards establishing a co-operative and mutually supportive relationship between the WTO and WIPO.[81]

Similar to co-operation agreements, the memoranda of understanding laid down the purposes and fields of co-operation between two organizations. They establish working relations and set up joint actions on assistance to the common member states in the achievement of the organizations' objectives. For this purpose, these instruments provide for exchange of necessary information, documents, statistics, mutual representations, joint research and technical co-operation. On the whole, the memoranda of understanding, seemingly simple in form and content, discharge an important function in the co-ordination between international economic organizations in the fields of their common competencies.[82]

81 Frederick Abbott, Thomas Cottier and Francis Gurry, *International Intellectual Property System, Commentary and Materials* (The Hague, London and Boston, MA: Kluwer Law International, 1999), 360–1. See also generally Frederick Abbott, 'The Future of the Multilateral Trading System in the Context of TRIPS', (1997) 20 *Hastings International and Comparative Law Review* 661.

82 See Sergei A. Voitovich, *International Economic Organizations in the International Legal Process* (Boston, MA: Martinus Nijhoff Publishers, 1995), 55–6.

An example is the Memorandum of Understanding between the WTO and the UNCTAD signed in April 2003. This instrument aims at deepening and giving 'practical effect to the strategic partnership for implementing the Doha Development Agenda, co-operating to ensure that trade serves development goals and for assisting in the beneficial integration of developing countries and least developed countries into the global economy'. The memorandum requires the two organizations to collaborate in technical co-operation, capacity building, training and research analysis.[83]

Against this background, it is natural to ask whether these instruments attribute any function to other international organizations in WTO dispute settlement. Given that most of the WTO co-operation agreements contain general co-operative clauses, this can be answered in the negative. At most, these agreements confer on the panels or the Appellate Body the right to seek information from these organizations, without delving into the nature and legal value of their contribution. The co-operation agreements with the Bretton Woods institutions, in particular with the IMF, are, however, more elaborated on this point. They set out the discretion of the IMF or the World Bank to participate as observers in the DSB meetings where matters of jurisdictional relevance to the Fund are to be considered. The WTO shall also invite the Fund to send a member of its staff to other meetings of the DSB, when the WTO, after consultation between the WTO Secretariat and the staff of the Fund, finds that such a presence would be of particular common interest to both organizations.[84] This suggests that in these specific DSB meetings the IMF and the World Bank are entitled to exercise their full observer rights.[85]

1. The need for further elaboration

While the coverage of panels by the GATT Article XV consultation requirement seems to be an open issue,[86] paragraph 8 of the mentioned agreement states that 'the Fund *shall* inform in writing the relevant WTO body (including dispute settlement Panels) considering exchange measures within the Fund's jurisdiction whether such measures are consistent

83 See the Memorandum of Understanding between the World Trade Organization (WTO) and the United Nations Conference on Trade and Development (UNCTAD), Geneva, 16 April 2003, Art. II. See also generally Mosoti, 'Institutional Cooperation', at 172.

84 WTO–IMF Agreement, above n. 76, para. 6.

85 See subsection B below for a comprehensive account of observer status in the WTO.

86 For a detailed account of this issue, see below Chapter 6, sections I and III.

with the Articles of Agreement of the Fund'. This obligation is, however, limited, as it seems to exclude the submission of information on the IMF decisions *approving* restrictions on payments and transfers or discriminatory currency arrangements.[87]

Thus the co-operation agreements concluded by the WTO with other international organizations reflect by and large the lowest common denominator between the two institutions; they certainly do not include all possible solutions. In relation to the Co-operation Agreement with the IMF, a series of issues could have been covered, such as the damaging effect of currency fluctuations on international trade, or the contradiction in working to solve the debt problems of developing countries through promoting export expansion, while advanced countries have in place trade measures that block this export expansion.[88]

In spite of this, it should be noted that a formalized relationship (although limited in scope) is an important step in the direction of greater sensitivity at the WTO towards these institutions, a co-operation model which will be sustainable in the long run. In the case of the Bretton Woods institutions, the agreements bring together the trade and finance communities, inducing a sense of common general commitment among the staff of the WTO, the World Bank and the IMF. Another advantage of having these instruments is that operating on a formal basis – even at the lowest common denominator – provides predictability in the relationship of these institutions. From this perspective, the co-operation agreements can serve as solid ground for expanding the scope of co-operation to include some of the issues that have been left out.

2. Their status in WTO dispute settlement

In the dispute settlement process, the WTO co-operation agreements and memoranda of understanding can be considered under 'subsequent agreements' in the sense attributed by VCLT Article 31(3). According to this provision, WTO adjudicating bodies must take account of subsequent agreements relating to the same subject matter.[89] The Appellate Body in

87 WTO–IMF Agreement, above n. 76, para. 3. This provision was invoked by Honduras in *Dominican Republic – Import and Sale of Cigarettes*. Honduras contended that since the IMF did not notify any measures with respect to the defendant, it could be argued that its measure was not approved by the IMF. See Panel Report, para. 7.148.

88 David Vines, 'The WTO in Relation to the Fund and the Bank: Competences, Agendas, and Linkages', in Anne O. Krueger (ed.), *The WTO as an International Organization* (Chicago: University of Chicago Press, 1998), 59–96, at 78.

89 Matsushita et al., *World Trade Organization*, at 54.

its report on *Argentina – Textiles and Apparel* implicitly acknowledged as much and held that the agreement between the WTO and the IMF was legally relevant, but that it did not modify, add to or diminish the rights and obligations of members under the WTO Agreement.[90] The same status would be valid for the memoranda of understanding. Although these clarifications are important, the status of these instruments as a matter of positive law remains, at this stage, unclear.[91]

B. The observer status

The WTO Agreement explicitly acknowledges the possibility of establishing subsidiary bodies in its various parts (Article IV(3)and (6)). Already by 2000, some forty councils, committees, subcommittees, and other standing groups and working parties had been officially established under the auspices of the WTO. The WTO Agreement does not, however, set out rules regarding these bodies' decision making, for example when a decision or a recommendation may be issued or their respective legal values.[92] Although such instruments are neither an amendment to nor an authentic interpretation of the WTO Agreements, various committees perform an important function in their implementation. This is frequently carried out through the interpretation of WTO rules, considering that a good number of provisions included in the covered Agreements are 'best endeavours', while others are new and technical in nature.[93] It has therefore been claimed as quite legitimate that these bodies can, in principle, through their actions affect the rights and obligations of the WTO members.[94]

Various international organizations come to play an important role in the work of these WTO bodies. This is exercised by virtue of their observer status and participation in the activity of these organs. As noted

90 *Argentina – Textiles and Apparel*, ABR, paras. 70–73.

91 Matsushita et al., *World Trade Organization*, at 54.

92 There is one exception however: the WTO Agreement Art. IX.4 refers to the decisions to grant a waiver.

93 For an account of the material issued by these bodies see Mary E. Footer, *An Institutional and Normative Analysis of the World Trade Organization* (Boston, MA: Martinus Nijhoff Publishers, 2006), 279. See also Yves Bonzon et al., 'Reflections on Modes of Decision-Making in the World Trade Organization', in Thomas Cottier and Panagiotis Delimatsis (eds.), *The Prospects of International Trade Regulation – From Fragmentation to Coherence* (Cambridge University Press, 2010).

94 See Mavroidis, 'No Outsourcing of Law?', at 432, referring to the activity of the WTO Anti-dumping Committee.

by Schermers, '[t]he word "observer" might give the impression that these entities with observer status fulfil a passive role. However, the opposite is often true. Observers often participate actively, transmitting their ideas to international organizations.'[95]

1. Granting observer status

When the WTO was established, the conditions for granting observer status were left open. Article V(1) of the Marrakesh Agreement provides that 'the General Council shall make appropriate arrangements for effective co-operation with other intergovernmental organizations that have responsibilities related to those of the WTO'. Thus the WTO has to limit its observer status to those organizations with a certain stake in the activities of the WTO.[96]

At the beginning, observer status within the WTO was granted on an ad hoc basis, a process devoid of precise rules. This is how some major intergovernmental economic organizations were granted status in the WTO, such as the UN, UNCTAD, the IMF, the World Bank, the FAO, WIPO and the OECD. Later, some guidelines were agreed by members to serve as a reference in this process.[97] Under the new guidelines, from July 1996, the basis for each request was considered case by case. The guidelines establish some criteria for the WTO to weight the observership request of one or another international organization. The guidelines require the international organization wishing to be granted observer status to demonstrate that matters discussed in WTO bodies are of direct interest to them, and that they have competence in trade policy matters or responsibilities related to those of the WTO. In making the decision, the WTO will take into account the nature of the work of the organization concerned, the number of WTO members in the organization, reciprocity with respect to access to proceedings, documents and other aspects and whether the organization has already been associated in the past with the work of the GATT.[98] Observer status has to be requested for each individual WTO body – the Ministerial Conference and the General Council, the Council for Trade in Goods or Trade in Services and so on.[99] This requirement was deemed necessary in order to take into account

95 Schermers and Blokker, *International Institutional Law*, para. 173.

96 Benedek, 'Relations of the WTO', at 490.

97 WTO, Decision of General Council of 25 July 1996, WT/L/161, Annex 3, 16–17: 'Guidelines on Observer Status for International Intergovernmental Organizations in the WTO'.

98 Ibid. 99 Ibid.

the new diversity of observership requests, which, besides the large international economic organizations, came from regional associations such as the Latin American Economic System (SELA), sectoral organizations (International Grains Council), and political organizations (Organization of the Islamic Conference).[100]

2. The rights of observers

Observers in the WTO can participate in all bodies except the Committee on Budget, Finance and Administration and the Dispute Settlement Body (DSB). However, the IMF and the World Bank are allowed to participate in the DSB on the basis of special co-operation agreements signed with the WTO in 1996. Although observer status is only granted within specific WTO bodies, international organizations may also attend meetings of WTO bodies at the specific invitation of a particular body, such as the Ministerial Conference. Invitations may also be extended to specific organizations to follow particular issues within a body. The observer with a specific WTO body may speak in meetings after members, but may circulate papers or make proposals only if specifically invited to do so. They cannot participate in the decision-making; however, they receive the main WTO documents as well as documents related to the work of the bodies in which they are participating. Observers are expected to attend the meetings on a regular basis. If an observer organization has not attended meetings of a body for more than a year, it automatically loses its status in that body. In the case of the Ministerial Conference, this period is two years.[101]

As noted by one commentator, the new WTO rules on observership demonstrate the concern of the WTO that its work might be hampered by the involvement of organizations which do not have a proper trade interest.[102] On the other hand, this attitude may also signal an attempt by the WTO to shut off the influence of other regulatory areas. The most prominent examples in this respect are the Convention on Biological Diversity (CBD) and the Cartagena Protocol, which applied for observer status with the SPS Committee without any success. Moreover, it should be stressed that most of the work of the WTO subsidiary bodies is carried out informally, which excludes other international organizations. Lastly, a restrictive approach towards participation of other international organizations in the work of WTO bodies is evidenced in the

100 Benedek, 'Relations of the WTO', at 490.
101 See above n. 97.
102 Benedek, 'Relations of the WTO', at 491.

Sutherland Report, which contends that WTO members 'would do well to benefit from the fact that the WTO is a *sui generis* international organization and to take positions on observers status based solely on the Organization's role as a forum for trade negotiations'.[103] This statement certainly comes into conflict with the proposal for greater institutional sensitivity, and has been criticized in a number of academic contributions.

V. The right to seek information

The right to seek information is the conventional mode by which the WTO adjudicator interacts with other international organizations. Originally, it was GATT Article XXIII(2) which provided the basis for the consultation of the contracting parties with other intergovernmental organizations in cases where they deemed such consultation necessary.[104] The consultation provision is elaborated more in DSU Article 13, which allows panels to seek outside information or advice in the dispute settlement system. This provision gives discretion to the panels to seek information from any source, including other international organizations, groups or individual experts, NGOs or other WTO bodies.

The operation of the WTO panels is governed by only a few procedural rules, and the right to seek information is among its few prerogatives. Robert Howse notes in this context that

> One of the fundamental differences between the two main kinds of domestic legal system (civil and common law) concerning the powers inherent in an adjudicator's fact-finding role is whether these extend to the 'inquisitorial' function of seeking information not brought to the attention of the adjudicator by the litigants, or through the briefs of intervenors. In civil law systems, crudely speaking, such an inquisitorial role is generally assumed as a normal judicial power, whereas in most kinds of litigation it would not be seen as appropriate in the common law world. In the presence of such divergent understandings of the appropriateness of an adjudicator 'seeking' information, an explicit authorization was clearly appropriate, given the choice of members of the WTO to opt for the inquisitorial model.[105]

103 WTO, 'Future of the WTO', para. 169.

104 This provision reads in the relevant part: 'The CONTRACTING PARTIES may consult with contracting parties, with the Economic and Social Council of the United Nations and with any appropriate inter-governmental organization in cases where they consider such consultation necessary.'

105 Howse, 'Legitimacy', at 382.

To illustrate, Article 13(1) of the DSU reads:

> Each Panel shall have the right to seek information and technical advice from any individual or body which it deems appropriate.

Article 13(2) of the DSU provides:

> Panels may seek information from any relevant source and may consult experts to obtain their opinion on certain aspects of the matter. With respect to a factual issue concerning a scientific or other technical matter raised by a party to a dispute, a Panel may request an advisory report in writing from an expert review group. Rules for the establishment of such a group and its procedures are set forth in Appendix 4.

The relationship between the two paragraphs of Article 13 is not very clear. Examining the WTO disputes where the provision has been applied, one commentator describes this liaison as follows:

> To date, there has been no unanimous opinion on the general relationship between the two paragraphs of Art. 13. The Panels' practice seems to indicate that the two paragraphs are not mutually exclusive. Panels frequently understood Art. 13.1 to be the principal norm, or referred to both paragraphs, when applying the provision. Similarly, Panels have not yet employed a consistent approach to the consultation of experts. According to the Panels in *EC – Asbestos*, there was no conflict between the two paragraphs, in a situation in which a Panel consults experts. In this context, the Panel considered Art. 13.2 to be complementary to Art. 13.1.[106]

Beyond that, it seems that it was contemplated that the two paragraphs of Article 13 DSU would differentiate the nature of the information sought by the Panel and the source of such information. As to the nature of the information, the provision introduces several categories: information (para. 1), technical advice (para. 1), expert advice (para. 2, first sentence), and scientific advice (para. 2, second sentence). Article 13 DSU does not define any of these terms or their interplay. Indeed, judging by the title of this provision ('The Right to Seek Information'), one may well contend that 'information' is the umbrella term for all the other categories. Irrespective of the relationship of the two paragraphs, it has been alleged that a categorization of this kind would not give rise to legal consequences concerning the rights of the Panel.[107]

106 Rüdiger Wolfrum, Peter-Tobias Stoll and Karen Kaiser, *WTO: Institutions and Dispute Settlement – Max Planck Commentaries on World Trade Law* (Boston, MA: Martinus Nijhoff Publishers, 2006), 417.

107 Ibid., at 418.

The term 'any relevant source' is ambiguous, too, but perhaps uncontentious, since it seems to give panels a very wide mandate regarding the actors it can approach for information. Since there are no definitions and there is a certain degree of ambiguity in the application of Article 13, the next subsection aims to shed some light on the nature and sources of information coming under the purview of WTO dispute settlement. This may give also a better idea of which source is more adequate in a specific circumstance and may even direct the WTO panels towards the entity in possession of this information.

A. *The nature of the information*

The terms 'information' and 'technical advice' may be used interchangeably. This is perhaps not so much the case for 'information' and 'expert advice', the latter being received through the consultation of experts. Scientific expertise is the expert advice provided with respect to issues relating to scientific or other technical matters and is more knowledge-intensive.

1. Information and expert advice

The first sentence in DSU Article 13(2) refers only to the consultation of an 'expert', whereas the second provides that on a 'factual issue concerning a scientific or other technical matter', an advisory report may be sought from 'an expert review group'. Thus the two sentences of DSU Article 13(2) distinguish between 'expert advice' as an umbrella term broken down into 'scientific and technical advice'. This distinction is supported also by the contention, made elsewhere, that the expert advice comprises scientific, technological and medical expert advice.[108] Pauwelyn makes the following suggestion on how to distinguish expert advice from information:

> Expert advice is information that the panel cannot normally provide itself. It comes from a source that is, in a particular field, more knowledgeable than the panel. For that reason, the panel must give deference to expert advice, even if it is not strictly speaking legally bound by it . . . A panel may also seek or acknowledge other non-expert information to complete

108 Roger Smith and Brian Wynne, *Expert Evidence: Interpreting Science in the Law* (London: Routledge, 1989), 9, providing that scientific expertise exists through acquaintance with bodies of knowledge developed systematically and having a high degree of certainty in their area of application; technical expertise exists by virtue of experience with situations in which knowledge is translated into practical activity, often with inherent uncertainties (thus resembling the circumstances in which management operates); and medical expertise is distinct because it depends on separate training and experience with individual people or bodies.

> its record, either because it is in the hands solely of one of the parties or because doing so more accurately reflects the interest at stake in a dispute (interests that are not necessarily reflected in the submissions of the disputing parties, as is often the case for amicus curie briefs).[109]

Thus while the term 'information' entails general information which is not in the hands of panels, 'expert advice' denotes possession of superior knowledge to that of the panel, which cannot be comprehended by it without the help of an expert. In WTO disputes, expert advice has been sought from individual experts, but also from international organizations. An example is the *Thailand – Cigarettes* case settled under the GATT dispute settlement system, where the Panel requested the WHO to provide its conclusion on the health effects of cigarette use and consumption.[110] Scientific advice is generally sought in WTO science-based disputes arising in relation to the adjudication of health and environmental disputes. The role of international organizations in these WTO disputes is analysed in detail in Chapter 9 below.

2. Factual and legal information

The explicit reference to 'factual issues' in Article 13(2) of the DSU denotes that the WTO panels may seek factual information from other sources. There is, however, a certain amount of ambiguity regarding their discretion to seek legal information under this provision. Despite some objections to the consideration of such points in WTO disputes, there are a number of authors who claim that legal information can be sought under DSU Article 13.[111] Following this view, it has been argued that

109 Pauwelyn, 'Use of Experts', at 330.

110 For a comprehensive analysis of *Thailand – Cigarettes* and WHO's contribution see below Chapter 9.

111 See Asif H. Qureshi, *Interpreting WTO Agreements: Problems and Perspectives* (Cambridge University Press, 2006), 40 ([Art. 13 of the DSU] has been interpreted thus to authorize the seeking of both factual and legal information and advice); Oesch, *Standards of Review*, 186 (DSU Art. 13 is not only relevant for the establishment of the relevant facts, but is equally applicable as regards issues of law); Pauwelyn, 'Unity and Fragmentation', 16 (WTO panels have broad authority under DSU Art. 13 to seek an opinion or expert advice from any source. Nothing limits this power so as to exclude legal questions. The *amicus curiae* procedures before certain cases at the Appellate Body, for example, were explicitly limited to legal questions, as the Appellate Body can, in principle, only examine legal, not factual, elements of the Panel report); Pauwelyn, 'Use of Experts', 332 (in *US – Section 110(5) Copyright Act* 'the Panel asking for advice from the WIPO seemed to go to great pains to portray its question as a factual one, repeating the word factual not less than three times in its one-page letter to the WIPO', although it was seeking legal information).

it is quite unlikely but still possible that the WTO adjudicator might – on its own – seek arguments as to possible interpretations in special circumstances.[112] According to Steger, 'in cases where there is a novel legal question or a question of significant public interest, Panels may find it pertinent and useful to hear opinions and legal arguments from persons and organizations which are non-parties to the dispute'.[113] Moreover, the panel's authority under Article 13 has been regarded as being comprehensive in order to enable it 'to make an objective assessment of the facts' and of the applicability and conformity of the relevant Agreements.[114] This authority has been interpreted as authorizing the seeking of both factual and legal information and advice[115] – a view which is shared by this author.

The approach of the WTO adjudicator on this point is contradictory. In *Japan – Agricultural Products II*,[116] the United States successfully argued that the 'information' that can be sought by panels under Article 13 includes clarification of legal points from any relevant sources.[117] In *US – Section 110(5) Copyright Act*, the EC argued that Article 13 of the DSU is limited to the seeking of factual information and technical advice and therefore does not include provision for legal arguments or legal interpretations received from non-members,[118] a contention that was not accepted by the Panel. On the other hand, in *US – Section 211 Appropriations Act* the Panel re-emphasized the words 'factual information' in its request for advice addressed to WIPO, while it was seeking to clarify the meaning of some provisions of the Paris Convention.[119] Although the negotiation records which were requested in this case would in all likelihood be considered as factual information, it would be more difficult to term as factual the understanding of the WIPO Secretariat of the legal terms of a convention, as occurred in this dispute. These examples

112 Oesch, *Standards of Review*, at 186.

113 Debra P. Steger, 'Amicus Curiae: Participant or Friend? The WTO and NAFTA Experience', in Armin von Bogdandy, Petros C. Mavroidis and Yves Mény (eds.), *European Integration and International Co-ordination: Studies in Transnational Economic Law in Honour of Claus-Dieter Ehlermann* (The Hague, London and New York: Kluwer Law International, 2002), 419–50, at 447.

114 *US – Shrimp*, ABR; *EC – Hormones*, ABR; *Japan – Agricultural Products II*, ABR.

115 Qureshi, *Interpreting WTO Agreements*.

116 *Japan – Agricultural Products II*, ABR, para. 30.

117 *US – Shrimp*, ABR, para. 106.

118 *US – Section 110(5) Copyright Act*, Panel Report, para. 6.6. The EC has proposed, however, that in the DSU reform under Art. 13 there should be authority to consider both factual and legal argumentation. See WTO Job [03] 69 Re 2, 29.

119 See below Chapter 7 for analysis of *US – Section 211 Appropriations Act*.

reveal that the WTO adjudicator does not have a clear approach to the issue and for reasons of consistency the Appellate Body should clarify the matter.

3. Issues of law and issues of fact

The question as to whether the panel can consider legal information under Article 13 DSU turns on the distinction between the information before the panel being considered an issue of law as opposed to an issue of fact. In jurisprudence, a question of law (also known as a point of law) is a question which must be answered by applying relevant legal principles, by an interpretation of the law. Such a question is distinct from a question of fact, which must be answered by reference to facts and evidence, and inferences arising from those facts. Answers to questions of law are generally expressed in terms of broad legal principles, and are capable of being applied to many situations, rather than being dependent on particular circumstances or factual situations.[120] This distinction is an institutional convention rooted in general legal theory and shaped by legal tradition.[121]

The practical dimension of this distinction relates chiefly to the necessity to divide competences between various judicial instances domestically (lay juries and expert lawyers in common law, for example).[122] For the purposes of international adjudication, the distinction is important for courts which comprise more than one entity empowered with judicial review,

120 See http://en.wikipedia.org/wiki/Issue_of_law (visited April 2008).

121 For the distinction as a general problem of legal theory, see John H. Farrar and Anthony M. Dugdale, *Introduction to Legal Method*, 2nd edn (London: Sweet & Maxwell, 1984); Herbert L. A. Hart, *The Concept of Law* (Oxford University Press, 1961), 47–58, 121; more specifically with regard to international law see Rudolf Bernhardt, 'Interpretation in International Law', in Rudolf Bernhardt (ed.), *Encyclopedia of Public International Law* (Amsterdam, New York and Oxford: North-Holland Publishing Company, 1981), Book 7 [Instalment 1], 318–27, at 319; with regard to GATT 1947/WTO proceedings see Marco C. E. J. Bronckers and Natalie McNelis, 'Fact and Law in Pleadings Before the WTO Appellate Body', in Friedl Weiss (ed.), *Improving WTO Dispute Settlement Procedures: Issues and Lessons from the Practice of Other International Courts and Tribunals* (London: Cameron May, 2000), 321–32; Pieter J. Kuijper, 'The Appellate Body and the Facts', in Marco Bronckers and Reinhard Quick (eds.), *New Directions in International Economic Law: Essays in Honour of John H. Jackson* (The Hague, London and Boston, MA: Kluwer Law International, 2000), 309–23; Jeff Waincymer, *WTO Litigation: Procedural Aspects of Formal Dispute Settlement* (London: Cameron May, 2002), 721–4, pointing to 'some comparative law tensions'.

122 Richard B. Bilder, 'The Fact/Law Distinction in International Adjudication', in Richard B. Lillich (ed.), *Fact-Finding Before International Tribunals* (Ardsley, NY: Transnational Publishers, 1992), 95–8, at 97.

and therefore applies to WTO adjudication, which is divided between ad hoc panels and the Appellate Body. One effect of the dichotomy turns on whether the Appellate Body will examine a specific issue. Its competence emerges from DSU Article 17(6), according to which Appellate Body review is 'limited to issues of law covered in the Panel report and legal interpretations developed by the Panel'.[123] Thus if the information considered by the Panel is factual, irrespective of its source, the Appellate Body will not re-examine the content of that piece of information. The AB should, however, examine claims relating to whether that information has been objectively assessed by the panel.

This distinction is also important because assessments of factual issues are inevitably linked to the collection and subsequent weighting of evidence. Accordingly, the issues of facts are subject to the rules on burden of proof applying to litigants.[124] Thus if the information received from an outside source is factual, this may result in a shift from one party to another of the burden of proof in the proceedings.[125] The effect of this is that the information submitted to the panel by an outside actor could be, in principle, rebutted in the proceedings by the parties. Conversely, if the input from this actor is legal, that point is generally not rebuttable. Thus the implications of the law and fact distinction should not be disregarded when the WTO adjudicator assesses the nature of the input received from outside actors, including international organizations.

123 See for an overview of Art. 17(6) of the DSU, Bronckers and McNelis, 'Fact and Law', at 321–33; Thomas Cottier, 'The WTO Dispute Settlement System: New Horizons', (1998) *Proceedings of the 92nd Annual Meeting of the American Society of International Law* 86, at 89–91; John P. Gaffney, 'Due Process in the World Trade Organization: The Need for Procedural Justice in the Dispute Settlement System', (1999) 14 *American University International Law Review* 1173, at 1216–21; Andreas F. Lowenfeld, *International Economic Law* (Oxford and New York: Oxford University Press, 2002), 169–71; Andreas Ziegler, 'Scope and Function of the WTO Appellate System: What Future after the Millennium Round?', (1999) 3 *Max Planck Yearbook of United Nations Law* 439, at 466–70.

124 The notion of burden of proof applies by definition only to issues of fact and not to issues of law; see Mojtaba Kazazi, *Burden of Proof and Related Issues: A Study on Evidence before International Tribunals* (The Hague, London and Boston, MA: Kluwer Law International, 1996), 44; Joost Pauwelyn, 'Evidence, Proof and Persuasion in WTO Dispute Settlement: Who Bears the Burden?', (1998) 1 *Journal of International Economic Law* 227, at 230. See also Michelle T. Grando, 'Allocating the Burden of Proof in WTO Disputes: A Critical Analysis', (2006) 9 *Journal of International Economic Law* 615, at 616, noting that the burden of proof is a concept that applies to issues of fact only. In other words, ambiguities in law must be resolved by the adjudicator through interpretation.

125 Comment made by Thomas Cottier, May 2008, World Trade Institute, Berne.

B. The source of information

With respect to the source of information, DSU Article 13(1) provides that the information or technical advice may be sought 'from any individual or body' which it deems appropriate, whereas the expert advice may be sought 'from any relevant source' (Art. 13(2), first sentence). For a scientific or other technical matter, a panel may request an advisory report from an expert review group. The rules for the establishment of such a group and its procedures are set forth in Appendix 4 to the DSU. In sum, DSU Article 13 indicates that information can be sought from (i) any individual or body, (ii) any relevant source, or (iii) an expert review group.

One problem arises in connection with the implementation of the expert review group provision. Starting with *EC – Hormones*, WTO panels have always preferred to seek information from experts directly – on an individual basis.[126] This practice has been criticized by some commentators.[127] One of the arguments against this approach is that the permissive 'may' enshrined in DSU Article 13(2) indicates that panels have discretion as to whether or not to request scientific expert advice. This discretion, however, does not apply with respect to the format in which such advice is to be sought once the decision to request it has been taken.[128] It has also been contended that, from a legal point of view, this approach of the panels conflicts with the rules of interpretation laid down in the VCLT, namely that interpretation must give meaning and effect to all the terms of the treaty. As the Appellate Body held in *US – Gasoline*, 'an interpreter is not free to adopt a reading that would result in reducing whole clauses or paragraphs of a treaty to redundancy or inutility'.[129] Against this background, it is claimed that the reading of Article 13(2) DSU as allowing for consultation with individual experts rather than groups would effect such redundancy.

VI. Conclusions

This chapter has examined the interactions between the WTO and other international organizations arising from a number of linkage techniques entrenched in the WTO legal text. The WTO interactions with the IMF

126 See Pauwelyn, 'Use of Experts', at 328–9, explaining the reasons for this. For a detailed overview of this issue, see below Chapter 9, section III.C.

127 See Theofanis Christoforou, 'Settlement of Science-Based Trade Disputes in the WTO: A Critical Review of the Developing Case Law in the Face of Scientific Uncertainty', (2000) 8 *New York University Environmental Law Journal* 622.

128 Ibid., at 637. 129 *US – Gasoline*, ABR, at 23.

emerge mainly from GATT Article XV, with its unique role in the WTO disputes. WIPO acquired relevancy for the WTO as a provider of factual information on intellectual property rights treaties incorporated into the TRIPS Agreement. Another type of linkage through incorporation arises from the legality of certain trade-restrictive measures in the WTO being explicitly related to the conformity of international standards set by international bodies. This links the WTO with such international organizations as the Codex, the OIE, and the IPPC, but also with a large number of other international organizations which set out standards for TBT purposes. Finally, a technique similar to incorporation is found in the WTO SCM Agreement, which refers to the Arrangement on Officially Supported Export Credits which interfaces the WTO with the OECD. DSU Article 13 is, however, one of the most solid platforms interfacing the WTO with other international organizations in the disputes settlement process.

The list is definitely not exhaustive, and a wide number of other references to international organizations are found in the WTO texts.[130] These provisions often appear in a highly technical context and set out rules which either instruct WTO members to co-operate with specific international organizations (e.g. the World Bank) or promote (or incorporate) their standards with their consultation on the implementation of relevant WTO legislation (e.g. WIPO, the ITU, the OIE).

Against this background, it may be concluded that the international organizations gained more ground in the international trade regime with the advent of the WTO as a fully fledged organization. The increased number of references to international organizations may also serve as an argument defeating the criticism levelled at this institution regarding its openness vis-à-vis outside actors. Not all the linkages and their supporting provisions ascribe a specific role to international organizations in WTO dispute settlement. Where this is not the case, as with the OECD as referred to in the SCM Agreement, the fact that these institutions should be ascribed weight in WTO dispute settlement should be read as implicit in the relevant norm. There would be little logic in incorporating an open-ended OECD instrument in the WTO without consulting this organization on the proper interpretation and application of the relevant provisions in WTO disputes. This is also the case for other international organizations discussed in this study.

130 For a comprehensive overview of these provisions see WTO, www.WTO.org/english/thewto_e/coher_e/coher_e.htm#igos_mandated_min_gc (last visited June 2009).

3

The VCLT rules of interpretation

I. Introduction

One dimension of institutional sensitivity investigated in this study concerns the extent to which the WTO adjudicator considers the output of international organizations in its interpretation process. This chapter seeks to assess the extent to which the WTO judiciary can best take account of these materials, thereby bringing more coherence and greater integration of legal systems.[1] Articles 31–32 of the Vienna Convention on the Law of Treaties, setting forth the basic rules of treaty interpretation, have been selected as a framework for this investigation.[2] This is explained by the fact that these rules were found, as the ILC Study Group did in the Fragmentation Report, to be the most relevant instrument for the proper exploration of how the various systems link to each other and to the general international law.[3] These VCLT rules seem to be one aspect that unites most of the new international regimes, including the WTO,

1 See above Introduction, section I, for a discussion of the phenomenon of fragmentation and the remedies therefor.

2 The choice of the VCLT rules of interpretation has been made in full acknowledgement of the fact that these codified principles of international customary law are not the only international norms which can promote the integration of international law and institutions. Other international legal sources, both conventional and customary, as well as general principles of international law, warrant examination along the same lines. The plethora of these other instruments may reveal their parallel or additional potential in integrating the WTO norms with other international legal regimes and their administering institutions. See e.g. Broude, 'Principles of Normative Integration', at 34–41, exploring the integrative effects of Paragraph 4 of the Rio Declaration on Environment and Development and the WTO as a softer model of integration than that entrenched in the somewhat more rigid language of VCLT Art. 31(3)(c). In contrast to the latter, the former is said to promote not only normative but also authority integration. See also John C. Dernbach, 'Achieving Sustainable Development: The Centrality and Multiple Facets of Integrated Decision-Making', (2003) 10 *Indiana Journal of Global Legal Studies* 247, stating that Paragraph 4 of the Rio Declaration 'asserts that environmental protection and development must be considered together, which would require integration of decision-making'.

3 ILC Fragmentation Report, para. 17.

in that they all claim binding force from, and are understood by their practitioners to be covered by, the law of the treaties.

The VCLT rules of interpretation prescribe consideration of the context, subsequent agreement and subsequent practice, supplementary means and special meanings, analysed in detail in section II below. The assessment of each technique and of how specifically it allows the WTO adjudicator to express more institutional sensitivity begins with a short illustration of the intended scope and purpose of the relevant provision as well as its general use by the WTO adjudicator. This is followed by the examination of specific material issued by international organizations as considered under each relevant VCLT rule in WTO dispute settlement. This helps with understanding how the VCLT interpretation rules allow proper consideration of this output in the WTO judicial interpretation process.

Since this last process poses a number of difficulties, a discussion is introduced on some of these challenges, in particular the one posed by the state consent procedure required to approve such material. Here some standards are suggested which may be validly employed by the panels or the Appellate Body in order to address the problems. The application of these standards will help the WTO adjudicator to apply effectively the VCLT interpretation rules and make wider use of material issuing from other international organizations (section III). Finally, this chapter provides some concluding remarks on the relevance and implications of the use of VCLT interpretative rules in support of the proposal of more institutional sensitivity by the WTO adjudicator (section IV).

II. The rules of interpretation of the Vienna Convention on the Law of Treaties as applied by the WTO adjudicator

While the authority to adopt authentic (or authoritative) and generally valid interpretations of WTO law lies exclusively within the Ministerial Conference and the General Council, panels and the Appellate Body are granted the competence to interpret WTO law in the course of disputes, with binding effect only for the parties and the matter involved.[4] Thus,

4 See DSU Art. 3(2); WTO Agreement, Art. IX(2). See for a definition of authentic interpretation Bernhardt, 'Interpretation in International Law', 325; Robert Jennings and Arthur Watts (eds.), *Oppenheim's International Law, Volume I: Peace*, 9th edn (Harlow: Longman Group, 1996), 1268.

due to its incompleteness, the WTO contract is consolidated through the interpretation process of the WTO adjudicating bodies. Such action is not only legitimate but, indeed, necessary.[5] What is important in this process is that the interpretative elements do not add to or diminish the rights and obligations set out by the WTO framers – an explicit condition provided in DSU Article 3(2).

In *US – Gasoline*, the Appellate Body stated for the first time that, under Article 3(2) of the DSU, reference to 'customary rules of interpretation of public international law' had to be understood as reference to the rules of interpretation as laid down in the Vienna Convention on the Law of Treaties.[6] Ever since, panels and the Appellate Body have constantly reiterated that Articles 31 and 32 of the Vienna Convention are customary international law and are part of the binding principles for the interpretation of WTO law.[7] They are binding on every WTO member regardless of whether they have ratified the Convention.[8]

One should also not disregard the rules of interpretation enshrined in the 1986 Vienna Convention on the Law of Treaties between States and International Organizations, or between International Organizations.[9] The Convention applies to treaties between one or more states and one or more international organizations, and to treaties between international

5 For a recent overview see Simon A. B. Schropp, *Trade Policy Flexibility and Enforcement in the WTO: A Law and Economics Analysis* (Cambridge University Press, 2009).

6 *US – Gasoline*, ABR, part III.B, 16–17. See Howse, 'Legitimacy', at 388, noting that the shift from the negotiation history widely deployed during the GATT to the various VCLT techniques had added to the social legitimacy of the WTO adjudicating bodies by privileging the interpretation of a broader community affected by interpretative decisions.

7 E.g. *Japan – Alcoholic Beverages II*, ABR, part D, 10; *India – Patents*, ABR, paras. 43–46; *US – Section 301 Trade Act*, Panel Report, paras. 7.21–22; *Turkey – Textiles*, Panel Report, para. 9.91; *US – Shrimp*, ABR, para. 114; *EC – Computer Equipment*, ABR, para. 84; *Argentina – Footwear (EC)*, ABR, para. 47; *US – Cotton Yarn*, Panel Report, paras. 7.16–20; *US – Hot-Rolled Steel*, ABR, paras. 57–62; *US – Section 110(5) Copyright Act*, Panel Report, paras. 6.43–46; *US – Section 211 Appropriations Act*, Panel Report, paras. 8.14–16.

8 See Lennard, 'Navigating by the Stars', 18; See also Pierre Pescatore, William J. Davey and Andreas F. Lowenfeld, *Handbook of the WTO/GATT Dispute Settlement* (Irvington-on-Hudson: Transnational Publishers Inc., 1998), 12. The International Court of Justice also held that VCLT Arts. 31 and 32 reflect customary international law. See *Territorial Dispute Case (Libya v. Chad)*, [1994] ICJ Rep. 6, para. 41.

9 See Official Records of the United Nations Conference on the Law of Treaties between States and International Organizations or between International Organizations, Vienna, 18 February–21 March 1986, vol. 2, Documents of the Conference (United Nations publication, Sales No. 94.V.5), Doc. No. A/CONF.129/15.

organizations. The Articles 1–72, including the customary rules of interpretation, retain *mutatis mutandis* the text of the relevant articles of the 1969 VCLT Convention on the Law of Treaties.[10] Thus, confronted with the need to interpret this type of instrument, the WTO adjudicator would be bound to use the same interpretative principles as enshrined in the former, on the entrance into force of the Convention.

According to VCLT Article 31, the interpretation is to be carried out in good faith (i) according to the ordinary meaning of terms taking into account (ii) the context and (iii) the object and purpose of the treaty. Further, there are listed in paragraphs 2 and 3 six matters which are either included in the context or are to be considered together with it: (i) the preamble and annexes; (ii) an agreement made in connection with the conclusion of the treaty; (iii) an instrument made by one or more parties and accepted by the others as related to the treaty; (iv) a subsequent agreement regarding the interpretation of the treaty or its application; (v) subsequent practice; and (vi) rules of international law applicable in relations between the parties.

The above suggests that the primary rule of natural meaning of the term is to be applied in the light of the context, the object and purpose of the treaty and the six other considerations referred to above. Furthermore, according to VCLT Article 31(4), 'A special meaning shall be given to a term if it is established that the parties so intended.' The preparatory work (not included in these considerations) and the circumstance of conclusion of the treaty enshrined in VCLT Article 32 are no more than supplementary means of interpretation. They are to be resorted to only when the application of the primary rules '(a) leaves the meaning ambiguous or obscure; or (b) leads to a result which is manifestly absurd or unreasonable'.[11]

Panels and the Appellate Body have utilized the VCLT methods and have generally followed them, looking for guidance in the case law of other judicial bodies and particularly of the International Court of Justice.[12]

10 Note should be taken that Art. 85 of the Convention provides that it enters into force after the ratification by thirty-five states (international organizations may ratify, but their ratification does not count towards the number required for entry into force). As at 8 August 2009, the UN Treaty Database listed forty-one parties to the Convention, of which only twenty-nine were states. As a result the Convention is not yet in force.

11 VCLT Art. 32.

12 On the rules of interpretation in the WTO see Cameron and Gray, 'Principles of International Law', at 254–63; Claus-Dieter Ehlermann, 'Some Personal Experiences as Member

These elements have been actively shaped by them, establishing over time interpretative principles of great significance to the resolution of the WTO disputes. To mention a few, these are the principle of effectiveness, of *in dubio mitius*, and, arguably, of good faith.[13]

The rules of interpretation enshrined in Articles 31–32 of the VCLT set out principles rather than rules, which accords some degree of flexibility to the WTO adjudicator in their application and interpretation. Thus the VCLT interpretation rules are not an exact science; depending on the weight one places on one (or more) of its elements, a different outcome is quite possible.[14] This implies that the VCLT may serve as a perfect vehicle for the WTO adjudicator in showing greater institutional sensitivity in their decision-making process. In fact, as illustrated in Chapter 1 above, the VCLT, in particular its Article 31(3)(c), has been regarded as a tool for achieving a harmonious interpretation – an exercise which would take account of the broader context of international customary and treaty law.[15]

of the Appellate Body of the WTO', Policy Paper RSC No. 02/9, Robert Schuman Centre's Policy Paper Series, 2002, paras. 40–52; Howse, 'Adjudicative Legitimacy', at 51–60; Lennard, 'Navigating by the Stars', at 17–89; Peter C. Maki, 'Interpreting GATT Using the Vienna Convention on the Law of Treaties: A Method to Increase the Legitimacy of the Dispute Settlement System', (2000) 9 *Minnesota Journal of Global Trade* 343, at 350–60; Donald M. McRae, 'The Emerging Appellate Jurisdiction in International Trade Law', in James Cameron and Karen Campbell (eds.), *Dispute Resolution in the World Trade Organization* (London: Cameron May, 1998), 98–110, at 107; David Palmeter and Petros C. Mavroidis, 'The WTO Legal System: Sources of Law', (1998) 92 *American Journal of International Law* 398, at 399; Pescatore, Davey and Lowenfeld, *Handbook*, 11–12; Frieder Roessler, 'The Institutional Balance Between the Judicial and the Political Organs of the WTO', in Marco Bronckers and Reinhard Quick (eds.), *New Directions in International Law: Essays in Honour of John H. Jackson* (The Hague, London and Boston, MA: Kluwer Law International, 2000), 325–45, at 339.

13 E.g. see *US – Gasoline*, ABR, part IV, at 23 for the principle of effectiveness; *EC – Hormones*, ABR, para. 165 for the principle of *in dubio mitius*; and *US – Sections 301–310*, Panel Report, para. 7.22 for the principle of *good faith*. For a comprehensive account of the last principle in WTO dispute settlement see Marion Panizzon, *Good Faith in the Jurisprudence of the WTO, The Protection of Legitimate Expectations, Good Faith Interpretation and Fair Dispute Settlement* (Oxford: Hart, 2006). See also Thomas Cottier and Krista Nadakavukaren Schefer, 'Good Faith and the Protection of Legitimate Expectations in the WTO', in Marco Bronckers and Reinhard Quick (eds.), *New Directions in International Law: Essays in Honour of John H. Jackson* (The Hague, London and Boston, MA: Kluwer Law International, 2000), 47–68.

14 Ian M. Sinclair, *The Vienna Convention on the Law of Treaties* (Manchester University Press, 1973), 118.

15 ILC Fragmentation Report, paras. 37–43, also Conclusion Nr. 19. The ILC Fragmentation Study Group accepts that the principle of harmonization is 'a widely accepted principle of interpretation', para. 38.

A. *Intrinsic and extrinsic interpretation techniques*

A distinction has to be made between what have been referred to as the 'intrinsic' and 'extrinsic' VCLT techniques of interpretation.[16] The intrinsic method is the one by which the adjudicator has to consider the elements contained in the treaty itself, whereas the extrinsic one allows them to leave the domain of the interpreted treaty and dwell on norms or elements external to it. The text of the treaty and also the context, as defined by VCLT Article 31(2), represent the main intrinsic elements.[17] But, as illustrated below, the WTO adjudicator routinely considers (and rightly so) extrinsic elements in their interpretation process. 'Subsequent agreement' or 'subsequent practice' in the application of the treaty, together with any 'relevant rules of international law applicable in the relations between the parties' are regarded as extrinsic elements, which have to be taken into account together with the context. The reference to the last category may be taken to include not only the general rules of international law but also treaty obligations existing for the parties.[18] VCLT Article 31(4), referring to the establishment of the special meaning of the term, can also be attributed to extrinsic elements. This is due to the fact that it may not be possible to extract the special meaning from the interpreted treaty but the special meaning may be found in another legal document.[19] By the same token, the preparatory work enshrined in VCLT Article 32 will, beyond doubt, be extrinsic to the WTO treaty. It is clear that all the extrinsic elements fall outside the interpreted treaty. Notably, some of these elements may reside outside the WTO regime. This state of affairs is valid not only for the 'other rules of international law' referred to in VCLT Article 31(3)(c). It applies also with respect to a number of other VCLT interpretation methods which link to a variety of external instruments comprising legal and factual information.

To give an example, the WTO has incorporated pre-existing intellectual property rights treaties. Given the emergence of those treaties elsewhere,

16 Sinclair, *Vienna Convention*, at 118–19.

17 VCLT Art. 31(2) defines the context of the treaty as comprising, in addition to the text, including its preamble and annexes: (a) any agreement relating to the treaty made between parties in connection with the conclusion of the treaty; (b) any instrument made by one or more parties in connection with the conclusion of the treaty and accepted by other parties as an instrument related to the treaty.

18 Sinclair, *Vienna Convention*.

19 See Henrik Horn and Robert Howse, 'European Communities – Customs Classification of Frozen Boneless Chicken Cuts', (2008) 7(1) *World Trade Review* 9, at 34. For a detailed account see below Chapter 3, section III.

the preparatory work remains within the hosting regimes, *in casu* WIPO. In such cases, to discharge their interpretative function effectively, panels would have to ask WIPO to provide them with the relevant negotiation history records. Thus, as illustrated, the external VCLT techniques are those with the potential to interface WTO law with other regimes and their responsible organizations, allowing for a greater manifestation of institutional sensitivity in WTO dispute settlement.

B. The legal value of interpretative material under the Vienna Convention on the Law of Treaties

Norms extraneous to the WTO may be valid interpretative elements for the WTO adjudicator.[20] These elements may take various forms, such as international treaties, international customary law, general principles of law or the acts and materials of other international organizations. The use in the process of these last elements is of major interest to this study. The materials of international organizations may fall under the purview of the WTO adjudicator by their employing a number of VCLT techniques, as illustrated in section III below.

The identification of this material through the use of the VCLT rules would inevitably lead to their classification.[21] This is important, as such a classification may point to a certain hierarchy across interpretative elements and, critically, define their legal value in the interpretation of WTO texts.[22] The interpretative techniques enshrined in the VCLT are not all of equal value: recourse to Article 32 elements for example, is to be made only after recourse to Article 31. A certain implicit hierarchy of the rules enshrined in VCLT Article 31 was acknowledged by the Appellate Body in *US – Shrimp*, when it stated that the *object* and *purpose* of the treaty have to be considered after the *context* of the words has been examined.[23] It has also been found that the instruments described in Article 31(2) VCLT were valued more highly than supplementary means of interpretation.[24]

As regards the legal effects of such classification under Articles 31–32 VCLT, if an international instrument is to be identified, for example, as 'subsequent practice', WTO panels are under an obligation always to

20 See above, Chapter 1, section III.B.1.

21 Mavroidis, 'No Outsourcing of Law?', at 448.

22 Ibid. Note, however, that there is no established hierarchy between these techniques and they are usually read *en ensemble* to establish the meaning of the interpreted term.

23 *US – Shrimp*, ABR, para. 114.

24 Van Damme, *Treaty Interpretation*, at 254.

review it, when relevant. This would not, however, be required of future panels if the instrument was attributed to the supplementary means of interpretation under Article 32.[25] It can be concluded that the value of material attributed to supplementary means of interpretation is somewhat lower than that considered under the primary rules enshrined in Article 31 of the VCLT. The recourse to the former is optional and to the latter, mandatory, as qualified by specific conditions.

C. The limited reference in WTO dispute settlement

Apart from the above, a number of constraints on the use of the VCLT rules of interpretation are found in the WTO judicial practice. The WTO adjudicator, although bound to use the VCLT interpretation techniques, only sparingly specifies the VCLT interpretative method which liaises with the relevant extraneous interpretative material. Moreover, they have relied heavily on what was understood to be 'the ordinary meaning of the terms, and much less on context, State practice, or subsequent practice. When in doubt, they preferred to attribute the interpretative elements to the supplementary means. Finally, the treatment of identical elements has, on occasion, been inconsistent across cases'.[26]

The Vienna Convention's rules of interpretation are not perceived as the only rules of interpretation by which the WTO adjudicator should abide. This is, perhaps, why the WTO adjudicator does not always provide a VCLT classification for the material used to interpret WTO obligations. There are a number of WTO cases pointing to this attitude. As described by Van Damme,

> [T]he Appellate Body appears increasingly torn between its formal attachment to Articles 31 to 33 VCLT and the recognition that the VCLT ultimately offers only a few basic principles. Incrementally and gradually, the Appellate Body explains its interpretations with less reference to the VCLT.[27]

This lax attitude towards specifying the specific VCLT interpretative rule employed is evidenced in a number of cases, such as *Japan – DRAMs*

25 Mavroidis, 'No Outsourcing of Law?', at 448–9.

26 Ibid., at 446. For the implications of these inconsistencies for the proposal for greater institutional sensitivity see below Chapter 4, section II.C.

27 Van Damme, *Treaty Interpretation*, at 273.

(Korea),[28] *US – Customs Bond Directive*[29] and, notably, *US – Shrimp*. Although this author recognizes the limitation of reliance on VCLT rules of interpretation alone, a first step towards consistency in interpretation is for the WTO adjudicator to state whether it intends to apply the rules, which should be followed by the sound legal theory behind its choice to classify interpretative material under one or another VCLT interpretative rule.

III. The classification of acts of international organizations in WTO dispute settlement

In order to establish how the WTO adjudicator regards the acts of international organizations in the interpretation process, this section examines how these instruments have been classified under the VCLT rules of interpretation. The case law analysis should allow a valid assessment to this effect, in particular with a view to outlining the legal value and weight attributed to these instruments in the interpretation process. Given that the acts of international organizations are an expression of their regulatory function, this will ultimately permit drawing conclusions about the level of the sensitivity of the WTO adjudicator towards other international organizations in general.

A. Ordinary meaning

Article 31(1) VCLT provides:

> A treaty shall be interpreted in good faith in accordance with the ordinary meaning to be given to the terms of the treaty in their context and in the light of its object and purpose.

The ordinary meaning is the starting point of the interpretation process which will elucidate the current and normal meaning of the interpreted term.[30] But the ordinary meaning of the term may change over time; moreover, the interpreted term may have several ordinary meanings. The relative character of the ordinary meaning is emphasized by the

28 *Japan – DRAMs (Korea)*, ABR, paras. 207–209, interpreting Art. 19.4 SCM Agreement, and paras. 237–242, interpreting Art. 12.9 SCM Agreement.

29 *US – Customs Bond Directive*, ABR, para. 226 interpreting ad note to Art. VI(2) and 3 GATT 1994.

30 Mark E. Villiger, *Commentary on the 1969 Vienna Convention on the Law of Treaties* (Leiden: Martinus Nijhoff Publishers, 2009), at 426.

reference to good faith in this provision. This relativity is confirmed by the existence of VCLT Article 31(4), which envisages the possibility of a 'special meaning'.[31]

In the practice of WTO adjudication the ordinary meaning has frequently been sought from dictionaries. Since the ordinary meaning has to be given to the terms in their context, treaty terms cannot be considered in isolation from the entire text of the hosting treaty. Generally, in the WTO, the interpreted terms have not been read in isolation from the broader context of the treaty language, the context of the dispute, the different uses of particular words or phrases, or the other interpretative elements mentioned in the VCLT.[32] There have, however, been occasions when the WTO adjudicator has relied on a non-contextual ordinary meaning, although these occasions have been rare.[33] Finally, to give effect to the object and purpose, the interpretative exercise would have to take account of a treaty's aims, its nature and its end. The consideration of the treaty's object and purpose together with the good faith principle will ensure the effectiveness of its terms.[34]

Many WTO cases could be chosen for an illustration of how the ordinary meaning of the interpreted term has been established. Given, however, the preoccupation of this study with the sensitivity of the WTO adjudicator and the extent to which the material of international organizations has been taken into account under the specific VCLT interpretation techniques, the choice stops with *US – Shrimp*, as supplemented by a few examples from *EC – Biotech*. In both disputes a large amount of extraneous legal material was cited, although its consideration in the clarification of the 'ordinary meaning' under VCLT indicates its somewhat limited effect on the interpretative exercise.

1. *US – Shrimp*

US – Shrimp is one of the best examples in the WTO jurisprudence of the diversity of extraneous legal material which has been taken into account in the interpretation process. In this case several countries filed a complaint with the WTO alleging that the United States had violated its WTO obligations by banning the importation of certain shrimps and

31 For a more detailed overview of 'special meaning' see below section III.F.

32 Van Damme, *Treaty Interpretation*, 222–3.

33 E.g. *Brazil – Aircraft (Article 21.5-Canada)*, ABR, para. 45; *EC – Bed Linen*, ABR, paras. 51–57; *EC – Tariff Preferences*, ABR, para. 90; *Korea – Dairy*, ABR, paras. 77–89; *US – Hot-Rolled Steel*, ABR, para. 99; *EC – Customs Matters*, ABR, paras. 224–227.

34 Villiger, *Commentary*, at 428.

shrimp products from WTO members that had no laws mandating certain methods of protecting endangered sea turtles during shrimp fishing. The Appellate Body concluded that the US ban was provisionally justified under GATT Article XX(g) as a measure necessary for the 'conservation of exhaustible natural resources'.[35]

a. 'Exhaustible natural resources'. Before arriving at this conclusion, the Appellate Body engaged extensively in the interpretation of the term 'exhaustible natural resources' to clarify whether the sea turtles would be covered by it. In this step, it did not share the claim advanced by the complainant that the sea turtles would not be covered by this term given that turtles were living natural resources which had the capacity to renew, hence could not qualify as exhaustible resources. In this context, the Appellate Body referred to a number of legal instruments but also modern biological sciences, which

> teach us that living species, though in principle, capable of reproduction and, in that sense, 'renewable', are in certain circumstances indeed susceptible of depletion, exhaustion and extinction, frequently because of human activities. Living resources are just as 'finite' as petroleum, iron ore and other non-living resources.[36]

In support of this reading, the Appellate Body referred to a statement by the World Commission for Environment and Development,[37] which the Appellate Body seemed to consider akin to the 'context' of interpreting 'exhaustible natural resources'.[38]

Essentially, the Appellate Body referred to a large number of rules of international law which helped it to derive international consensus on the interpreted term. In this step, it examined several international conventions that referred to 'natural resources', non-binding international documents, general principles of law, ICJ case law, academic literature and, as illustrated above, even modern biological science. For example, the Appellate Body employed references to the UNCLOS, the Convention on Biological Diversity, the CITES, acts of international organizations, such as the Rio Declaration on Environment and Development,[39] Agenda 21,[40] and the Resolution on Assistance to Developing Countries.

However, the decision of the Appellate Body to use this material in order to clarify the 'ordinary meaning', rather than resorting to Article 31(3)(c)

35 *US – Shrimp*, ABR, para. 145. 36 Ibid., para. 128. 37 Ibid., n. 106.
38 Van Damme, *Treaty Interpretation*, at 267.
39 *US – Shrimp*, ABR, paras. 41, 73, 154, 168. 40 Ibid., paras. 130, 154, 168.

or another Article 31 technique, did not send a strong signal as to its willingness to pursue a formal 'systemic integration' approach.[41] It regarded all these documents as evidentiary material rather than as normative rules. This implied that the WTO adjudicator preferred a less formal approach in considering material extraneous to WTO law, retaining some scope of discretion with regard to whether this material should impact the outcome of the interpretative exercise.[42] Since the case 'is prototypical of the trade and environment "interdisciplinary" nexus', the more formal approach resulting from the application of VCLT Article 31(3)(c) would have been more appropriate.[43]

This perception is fully shared by this author. One point, however, needs to be noted: the integrative effect of VCLT Article 31(3)(c) would work in the case of general international law, most frequently customs and principles of (international) law. The other acts referred to in *US – Shrimp*, which do not share this status, could not in any case be considered through the more formal technique of VCLT Article 31(3)(c) (see subsection E below).

b. The GATT Article XX chapeau. Multiple rules of environmental international law were also referenced in the second step of the interpretative exercise in *US – Shrimp*. The Appellate Body repeatedly cited a vast number of environmental hard and soft rules and explicitly recognized the objective of sustainable development to address whether the US ban was also consistent with the chapeau of Article XX. The chapeau provides that Article XX's exception may be invoked '[s]ubject to the requirement that such measures are not applied in a manner which would constitute a means of arbitrary or unjustifiable discrimination between countries where the same conditions prevail, or a disguised restriction on international trade'. In interpreting what constituted 'unjustifiable discrimination', the Appellate Body devised a test consisting of at least five different factors, ranging from whether the actions have an 'intended and actual coercive effect' on WTO members' policy decisions,[44] and whether prior to enacting the ban the respondent (the United States) had attempted to accomplish its objectives through bilateral or multilateral negotiations.[45] In this step, the Appellate Body even sought 'additional interpretative

41 Ibid. 42 Broude, 'Principles of Normative Integration', at 39.

43 Ibid. But see below the discussion in section III.E, which describes the restrictive approach towards international treaty law under VCLT Art. 31(3)(c) in the WTO judicial interpretation process.

44 *US – Shrimp*, ABR, para. 161. 45 Ibid., para. 166.

guidance, as appropriate, from the general principles of international law'.[46] Here, it explored the principle of *good faith* to make a finding on the doctrine of *abus de droit*.

Notably, in considering the compatibility of the US legislation under review with the chapeau of Article XX GATT, the Appellate Body turned to the WTO Ministerial Decision on Trade and Environment,[47] the preamble of which states that policy contradictions between the multilateral trading system and the objective of protecting the environment should be avoided. Significantly, in citing this reference, the Appellate Body noted two principles of the Rio Declaration: Principle 3, which is the formulation of the concept of sustainable development, and Principle 4 – the Rio formulation of the principle of integration.[48] The Appellate Body did not explicitly refer either to VCLT Article 31(3)(c) or to the supplementary means of interpretation of Article 32, as the phrase 'additional interpretative guidance' seems to have implied. It preferred to remain within the realm of VCLT Article 31(1), where the relevant material extraneous to the WTO was resorted to with the limited purpose of clarifying the 'ordinary meaning' of the interpreted terms.

What should be retained from this discussion is the fact that the cited extraneous material, irrespective of its form and character, had been taken into account to the extent that it was 'informative' – subject to the treaty interpreter's ultimate discretion. A more formal and mandatory basis prescribed in Article 31(3)(c), as applicable to treaties and principles of general international law, could have allowed a better integration of those norms into the WTO interpretation process. To the extent that such material is considered for the purposes of clarifying the 'ordinary meaning' of the terms, its value is certainly lower.[49]

Essential to this discussion, however, is that the material of other international organizations has been taken into account. The flaw of the Panel here arises from the fact that it did not dwell on the state consent requirement behind such material. The analysis of this aspect is, however, important, if those materials are to be given a weightier role in the WTO

46 Ibid., para. 158.

47 Adopted by ministers at the Meeting of the Trade Negotiations Committee at Marrakesh, 14 April 1994.

48 *US – Shrimp*, ABR, n. 147.

49 For a discussion see Broude, 'Principles of Normative Integration', 32–3 and 39–41, stating e.g. that 'reference to external sources through the "ordinary meaning" avenue of Article 31.1 can have (little or) no impact on the allocation of authority, at least no more than reference to *Webster's* dictionary terms'.

interpretation process. Some suggestions on how this assessment can be validly dealt with by the WTO judiciary is contained below in subsections C and D.

2. EC – Biotech

Another case which should be cited here (examined in detail in Chapter 1) is *EC – Biotech.*[50] In its analysis of Annex A of the SPS Agreement the Panel referred to terminological definitions used by the IPPC, the FAO, the OIE, WHO, and the Codex Alimentarius Commission.[51] While ultimately having rejected essentially all the interpretative implications of these sources, here, too, 'the Panel preferred the discretionary (and hence judicially avoidable) approach to norm integration presented by Article 31(1) VCLT, rather than the more constricting and binding principles of integration found in Article 31(3) (c) VCLT'.[52] As in *US – Shrimp*, the interpretative material which is not covered by the definition of the formal sources of international law could not have been attributed to Article 31(3)(c) VCLT in any case. Therefore the remaining VCLT techniques should be carefully explored, with a view to understanding their elasticity so as to embrace material issued by international organizations. This analysis is provided in the following subsections.

B. Context

Article 31(2) VCLT provides:

> The context for the purpose of the interpretation of a treaty shall comprise, in addition to the text, including its preamble and annexes:
>
> (a) any agreement relating to the treaty which was made between all the parties in connection with the conclusion of the treaty;
> (b) any instrument which was made by one or more parties in connection with the conclusion of the treaty and accepted by the other parties as an instrument related to the treaty.

From the above, the context includes the entire text of the interpreted treaty, its preamble, annexes and any connected agreement or other instrument. Thus the 'context' encompasses stand-alone instruments which

50 Given the wide discussion of this case in the context of the application of VCLT Art. 31(3)(c), the case is described in more detail below in section III.E.

51 For a more detailed account of the input of these organizations in *EC – Biotech* see below Chapter 9, section IV.C.1.

52 Broude, 'Principles of Normative Integration', at 33.

relate to the treaty under examination when their subject matter overlaps or is related. Context should have an exhaustive and narrow definition, covering only the instruments contemporary with the instrument being interpreted.[53] In practice, however, this limitation has not been applied so strictly, given that the VCLT rules at issue represent principles of interpretation and not rigid rules. This allows a more flexible approach in the application and interpretation of VCLT Articles 31 and 32.

At the time of the drafting of these VCLT provisions, the International Law Commission (ILC) showed concern over the state consent requirement behind the instruments which may fall under VCLT Article 31(2), mostly to do with their interpretative weight (rather than with the restrictive character of particular contextual elements).[54] Thus the ILC wanted to maintain the principle that all parties should consent to their treaty obligations, circumscribing situations where interpretative weight is attributed to unilateral acts as context.[55] Scholars have also clarified that the requirement that the instrument or agreement enshrined in Article 31(2) be related to the treaty under interpretation means that 'it must be concerned with the substance of the treaty and clarify certain concepts in the treaty or limit its field of application'.[56] The instrument or agreement under consideration also needs to be drafted at the time the treaty to which it relates is concluded.

Despite these important clarifications, apart from the immediate context of the treaty (the preamble, annexes and the rest of the agreement) and the *jus cogens*, which is relevant to the interpretation of any regime, it is not very clear what other instruments the WTO adjudicator can consider under this heading and, in particular, if the acts of international organizations may fall under this category.[57] A number of WTO cases

53 Lennard, 'Navigating by the Stars', at 24.

54 Van Damme, *Treaty Interpretation*, 215. See also Draft Articles on the Law of Treaties with commentaries 1966, ILC Yb. 1966, II, 177 as part of Report of the International Law Commission on the work of its eighteenth session (4 May–19 July 1966), Doc. A/6309/Rev.1, ILC Yb. 1966, II, 172, at 221 (ILC Draft Articles (1966)).

55 Van Damme, *Treaty Interpretation*.

56 Sinclair, *Vienna Convention*, at 129; Mustafa K. Yasseen, 'L'interprétation des traités d'après la convention de Vienne sur le droit des traités', (1976) 151/III *Recueil des Cours* 3, at 37; Lennard, 'Navigating by the Stars', at 26.

57 One good candidate, however, is the Marrakesh Declaration of 15 April 1994. It is considered to be an agreement between the WTO members that relates to the treaty and was reached in connection with the conclusion of the treaty. Its language is general and describes the object and purpose of the WTO. Other declarations adopted at the time of conclusion of the Uruguay Round serve a similar function. See, e.g., Ministerial

reveal the Appellate Body's approach towards this issue, which can be shown by examining the relevant judicial practice and the interpretation by the WTO adjudicator of this VCLT provision.

1. The Harmonized System

EC – Chicken Cuts offered the first substantial discussion of the interpretation of VCLT Article 31(2)(a).[58] Here, the Appellate Body considered the Harmonized System (HS) to be an 'agreement relating to the treaty which was made between all the parties in connection with the conclusion of the treaty'. Thus the fact that the HS was not a WTO-covered agreement did not prevent the Appellate Body from attributing it to the 'context'. The decision was grounded on the contention that Articles 31(2)(a), 31(2)(b), 31(3)(c) VCLT were 'not limited to treaty context', that is, the WTO treaty.[59] This was an atypical approach of the Appellate Body, as it had frequently classified international agreements under VCLT Article 32, that is, as supplementary means of interpretation.[60]

The perception that VCLT Articles 31(2)(a), 31(2)(b), 31(3)(c) are not limited to treaty context is consistent with the ILC's understanding that whether the agreements and instruments falling under Article 31(2)(a) and (b) are an integral part of the treaty depends on the intention of the parties. In *EC – Chicken Cuts* the Appellate Body spotted this intention from the language of Article 9 of the WTO Agreement on Rules of Origin, Article 27 SCM Agreement, and Article 2 Agreement on Textiles and Clothing, all of which refer to the HS for various purposes. In ascertaining these intentions, the Appellate Body also referred to the fact that GATT contracting parties previously adopted decisions that implicitly endorsed, and partially integrated, the HS in the GATT.[61]

Conference, Declaration on the Contribution of the World Trade Organization to Achieving Greater Coherence in Global Economic Policymaking, LT/UR/DEC-1/1 (15 April 1944); Decision on Notification Procedures, LT/UR/D-1/5 (15 April 1944); Decision on Measures Concerning Possible Negative Effects of the Reform Programme on Least-Developed and Net Food-Importing Developing Countries, LT/UR/D-1/2(15 April 1944).

58 For a detailed overview of this dispute and the role of the WCO in its adjudication at the WTO see below Chapter 8.

59 *EC – Chicken Cuts*, ABR, para. 195.

60 For example, this was the case in *US – Shrimp*, where the Appellate Body referred to various regional and multilateral environmental agreements to establish a wide agreement on certain facts, such as whether a species was endangered or whether certain resources were exhaustible. A similar situation was presented in *EC – Asbestos*, where the Appellate Body referred to some WHO Conventions as evidence of wide agreement on the toxicity of asbestos and its seriousness for public health.

61 *EC – Chicken Cuts*, ABR, paras. 197–198.

The problem with the classification of the HS as 'context' to the WTO treaties is the qualification for the requirement 'in connection with the conclusion of the treaty' enshrined in VCLT Article 31(2). The HS was already in force during the Uruguay Round negotiations, pre-dating the WTO treaty. According to Van Damme, it should have been clear that the HS did not fall under that provision because it was not concluded between *all* original WTO members.[62] Thus the Appellate Body report was criticized for its lack of precision and on the grounds that the aids to interpretation have been mostly disputed on the basis of their form rather than substance.[63]

The *China – Auto Parts* report also discussed the relevance of the HS for purposes of interpreting WTO-covered agreements. China argued that the HS constituted relevant context in interpreting the first sentence of Article II(1)(b) GATT 1994. This prompted the Appellate Body to clarify parts of the *EC – Chicken Cuts* report. Although it confirmed that the HS was context, the Appellate Body found that this instrument was not relevant for interpreting Article II(1)(b) in this case.[64] Thus the Appellate Body has not always been consistent with the ILC clarifications on the 'context' of treaty interpretation, in that it did not necessarily take a restrictive approach regarding the scope of the provision. This approach seems to be consistent with the history of VCLT Article 31(2)(a) and the ILC's Commentary, and is therefore also supported by this author.

2. The WTO Explanatory Notes and Scheduling Guidelines

US – Gambling elaborates on the role of the WTO Explanatory Notes and Scheduling Guidelines in the interpretation of the WTO obligations, in particular the GATS. In this case, the Appellate Body refused to consider several WTO documents, including the 1993 Scheduling Guidelines as 'context' under VCLT Article 31(2), on the grounds that they were drawn upon by the GATT Secretariat and not by the negotiating parties. Indeed, one of these documents (W/120) was circulated by the GATT Secretariat during Uruguay Round negotiations, but reflected, as far as possible, comments made by negotiating parties. The Explanatory Notes – another document circulated by the Secretariat – was produced in relation to the Scheduling Guidelines and was designed to assist in the preparation of

62 Van Damme, *Treaty Interpretation*, at 254–55.

63 Ibid., at 255; according to Van Damme, the interpretative relevance of HS does not diminish merely because it does not easily fit the precise language of Arts. 31(2)(a, b, c).

64 *China – Auto Parts*, ABR, para. 164.

offers, requests and national Schedules of Commitments in the GATS. These specified that the Explanatory Notes was not an authoritative interpretation of the GATS.[65]

According to the Appellate Body, instruments that were not drafted by the treaty negotiators could constitute 'context' only where there was sufficient evidence of their constituting an 'agreement between the parties' or their 'acceptance by the parties as an instrument related to the treaty'.[66] Examining the documents at issue, the Appellate Body concluded that they were more suitable for consideration under 'circumstances of... conclusion' of the treaty set out in Article 32 VCLT.[67] This classification has not been without criticism, since the Appellate Body failed to examine 'whether the two documents... constitute consensus among parties that had emerged during negotiations'.[68]

Thus the WTO case law analysis reveals that there was not explicit consideration of the international organizations' acts as context by the WTO adjudicator. It seems that there is little likelihood that the instruments will fall within the purview of the WTO panels or the Appellate Body under this VCLT rule. The acceptance only of treaty instruments under this heading, like the HS, has also been criticized. On the other hand, the application of the VCLT rule of interpretation does not entail a rigid and formal exercise; the contextualization has not been defined exhaustively, and nuances in the definition are possible.[69] Arguably, provided that the relevant international organizations' acts would meet the state consent, relevance and contemporaneity requirements elicited from VCLT Article 31(2), this leniency could be explored by the WTO adjudicator to attempt such identification. But, as illustrated below, there are a number of other VCLT interpretative methods which would allow for these acts to be taken into account more easily.

C. *Subsequent agreement*

Article 31(3)(a) VCLT requires that 'any subsequent agreement between the parties regarding the interpretation of the treaty or the application of its provisions' be taken into account in applying the general principle of interpretation. Three elements can be elicited from this definition:

65 *US – Gambling*, paras. 173–175 66 Ibid., para. 175.
67 Ibid., para. 196, n. 244. 68 Van Damme, *Treaty Interpretation*, at 326.
69 Arnold D. McNair, *The Law of Treaties*, 2nd edn (Oxford: Clarendon Press, 1961), at 365; Hans J. Morgenthau, 'Positivism, Functionalism, and International Law', (1940) 34 *American Journal of International Law* 260, at 269 and 271.

(i) that the documents constituting subsequent practice should be subject to agreement between 'the parties'; (ii) this agreement should have emerged subsequent to the conclusion of the treaty;[70] and (iii) the subsequent agreement can relate either to the interpretation or application of the treaty.

Subsequent agreement might cover an agreement on an interpretation proposed by a state or an international organization by another state or international organization in an interpretative declaration.[71] In this case there is no requirement for an agreement in a written form, nor that it should conform to the definition of a treaty enshrined in VCLT Article 2, although documentary evidence might be needed.[72] For the Appellate Body, Article 31(3) VCLT was intended to cover 'agreements bearing specifically upon the interpretation of a treaty', such as authoritative interpretations under Article IX(2) of the WTO Agreement, and agreements specifying how existing rules or obligations in force are to be 'applied'.[73]

1. The ITU instruments

One WTO case that comes to mind when investigating the identification of international organization material as 'subsequent agreement' is *Mexico – Telecoms*. Here the Panel referred to a series of regulations and recommendations by the International Telecommunication Union (ITU) to clarify its understanding of accounting rates. All these instruments were treated akin to subsequent agreement.[74] The Panel noted that the

70 As noted by Mavroidis with respect to the WTO, the subsequent agreement and subsequent practice provide the link with the WTO treaties to modernity; these elements cover exclusively instruments signed post-entry into force of the WTO Agreement. Mavroidis, 'No Outsourcing of Law?', at 449.

71 See Thirteenth Report on Reservation to Treaties, by Mr Alain Pellet, Special Rapporteur, Sixtieth Session (Geneva, 5 May–6 June and 7 July–8 August 2008), Doc. A/CN.4/60, para. 285.

72 See Gardiner, *Treaty Interpretation*, 207–208, 218, 220. VCLT Art. 2(a) provides that 'treaty' means an international agreement concluded between states in written form and governed by international law, whether embodied in a single instrument or in two or more related instruments and whatever its particular designation.

73 *EC – Bananas III (Article 21.5 – Ecuador II)/EC – Bananas III (Article 21.5 – US)*, paras. 390–391. On these grounds the Appellate Body had actually rejected in this case the qualification of 'subsequent agreement' to the Doha Article I Waiver agreed during the Doha Ministerial Conference in November 2001, which extended beyond 31 December 2002 the temporal scope of the banana-tariff quote concession enshrined in the EC schedule.

74 Mavroidis, 'No Outsourcing of Law?', at 452–3.

ITU regulations are binding instruments to which both Mexico and the United States had adhered; the ITU recommendations are relevant in the light of the fact that the parties to the dispute as well as a large number of other WTO members are also members of the ITU.[75] Although the above analysis seems to suggest that the Panel engaged in examining the appropriateness of identifying the ITU instrument as subsequent agreement, the discussion was placed under the heading of 'supplementary means' of interpretation. Had the Panel explicitly attributed the relevant acts to 'subsequent agreement', the status of these instruments would have been elevated, assigning them higher normative value. This, regrettably, would have been an atypical approach as, when confronted with similar situations, the Appellate Body has preferred to attribute this material to 'supplementary means of interpretation'.[76]

In spite of this missed opportunity to set out some practice on consideration of acts of international organizations under this VCLT rule, the clarifications provided by the Panel on this point are still valuable. It spelled out clearly that identification of material as 'subsequent agreement' would take place with regard to a binding instrument if both litigants adhered to the proposed instrument. Second, non-binding acts (such as recommendations) will be taken into account if disputants as well as a large number of the WTO members are also members of the relevant international organization. This clarification is particularly important as the Panel established some criteria for the consideration of binding and non-binding instruments under this VCLT rule.

2. The Berne Convention Report

Another important example of the application of the VCLT subsequent agreement rule arises from *US – Section 110(5) Copyright Act*.[77] The case is important for the discussion concerning the legal relevance of a Report adopted in connection with and subsequent to the conclusion of the Berne Convention, which is an instrument of direct relevance to the interpretation of the TRIPS Agreement. The Panel attributed this material to 'subsequent agreement' between the parties to the Berne Convention. The Report was not inserted as an amendment to the Berne Convention, but it was, however, adopted by the contracting parties. This occurrence

75 *Mexico – Telecoms*, Panel Report, paras. 7.129–7.136.

76 Mavroidis, 'No Outsourcing of Law?', at 452–3.

77 For a detailed overview of the case and the role of WIPO therein see below Chapter 7.

is quite interesting, considering that 'subsequent agreement' and 'subsequent practice' should cover instruments signed in the aftermath of the WTO Agreement. However, given the incorporation of the Berne Convention *acquis* into the TRIPS, the consideration of post-Berne material becomes relevant; it is as if the WTO adjudicator was itself interpreting the Berne Convention. Ignoring that material by invoking temporality would run afoul of the proposal for institutionally sensitive decision making at the WTO.

3. The OECD Arrangement

A slightly different aspect of temporality under VCLT Article 31(3) was discussed during the proceedings that led to the report on *Brazil – Aircraft (Article 21.5 – Canada II)*. This touched on the temporal link of the regimes incorporated into the WTO with their modern prolongations evolving outside the WTO. The Panel had to decide to what extent the relevant text of the OECD Arrangement was that of 1992 (which is referred to in the WTO SCM Agreement) or that of its successor – that is, the Arrangement of 1998 which was negotiated only among OECD members – a small minority of the WTO membership. The Panel decided that, because of the reference in item (k) of Annex I of the SCM Agreement to the 'successor undertaking', it had to take into account the 1998 Arrangement.[78]

Thus the Berne Convention and the OECD Arrangement examples reveal that it is not only WTO documents that can qualify as 'subsequent agreement' under VCLT Article 31(3)(a) but also material extraneous to the WTO regime. The remaining difficulty stems from the limited understanding on the relationship of the original treaty with its modern prolongations, which may affect the extent to which this material will be taken into account by the WTO adjudicator. It is partly in response to these difficulties that the ILC has now decided to include this topic on its agenda under the title 'Treaties over time'.[79] In this way, the ILC proposed to examine the role of subsequent practice and agreement in responding to the evolving context of long-standing treaties:

> with the resulting effect that treaties face the danger of either being 'frozen' into a state in which they are less capable of fulfilling their object and purpose, or of losing their foundation in the agreement of the parties. The

78 *Brazil – Aircraft (Article 21.5 – Canada II)*, Panel Report, paras. 5.80–5.91. See also above Chapter 2, section III.C.

79 Van Damme, *Treaty Interpretation*, at 349.

parties to a treaty normally wish to preserve their agreement, albeit in a manner which conforms to present-day exigencies.[80]

D. Subsequent practice

Subsequent practice is codified in Article 31(3)(b) VCLT as follows:

> 3. There shall be taken into account, together with the context:
>
> ...
>
> b) any subsequent practice in the application of the treaty which establishes the agreement of the parties regarding its interpretation; ...

The use of subsequent practice is regarded as an interpretative technique either to establish or to confirm the meaning of the treaty. Some authors, however, see a far more important role for it. According to one commentator, '[the subsequent practice] could potentially achieve the same substantive result as the amendment of the treaty'.[81] The AB in *EC – Chicken Cuts* observed that 'subsequent practice' in the application of a treaty may be an important element in treaty interpretation because 'it constitutes objective evidence of the understanding of the parties as to the meaning of the treaty'.[82]

In order to understand its value in WTO jurisprudence, it is useful to look at how the Appellate Body has defined 'subsequent practice'.[83] Thus in *Japan – Alcoholic Beverages II* the Appellate Body stated that subsequent practice within the meaning of VCLT 31(3)(b) entails:

> a 'concordant, common and consistent' sequence of acts or pronouncements which is sufficient to establish a discernible pattern implying the agreement of the parties [to a treaty] regarding its interpretation.[84]

80 Report on the work of its sixtieth session (5 May–6 June and 7 July–8 August 2008), Chapter XII, paras. 351–352, cited in Van Damme, *Treaty Interpretation.*

81 Alexander Orakhelashvili, *The Interpretation of Acts and Rules in Public International Law* (Oxford University Press, 2008), 358.

82 *EC – Chicken Cuts*, ABR, para. 255.

83 Subsequent practice was originally treated as supplementary means of interpretation, thus on an equal footing with preparatory work, and was intended to fill a similar function. See Third Report of the Special Rapporteur, Sir Humphrey Waldock (Sixteenth Session of the ILC (1964)), Doc. A/CN.4/167 and Add. 1–3, ILC Yb. 1964, II, 5, at 59 (Waldock Third Report (1964)).

84 *Japan – Alcoholic Beverages II*, ABR, at 106; and *Chile – Price Band System*, ABR, para. 214. See also *US – Gambling*, ABR, para. 192.

In *Chile – Price Band System* the Appellate Body established that it is insufficient merely to show the existence of a practice: the burden of proof includes giving evidence that the practice represents an *agreement* among WTO members regarding the interpretation of a particular provision.[85] Other clarifications on subsequent practice are sourced outside the WTO judicial context, namely in the ILC Draft Articles, which provide that it is not necessary that all parties to the treaty have participated in the practice; they need only to have accepted it,[86] through the possibility of taking note of the practice. This approach was also supported in *EC – Chicken Cuts*, where the issue received substantial attention.

1. The status of institutional practice in the WTO

Subsequent practice can emerge not only from the actions of members but also from committees or other bodies of the international institution concerned. Thus the phrase 'subsequent practice' is commonly interpreted to extend not merely to the practice of state parties to the treaty, but also to the practice of the organizations they have created. In the WTO for example, decisions of the Ministerial Conferences, the General Council, or other bodies and committees may qualify as 'subsequent practice' depending on their content, date of adoption and the members' intention. To date, it is still not very clear, however, if the practice of WTO committees and other WTO organs can be equated with subsequent practice of WTO members. The ICJ case law reveals that here, too, there is a lack of consensus on the status of institutional practice.[87] As the ILC has pointed out,

> The problem of the effect of practice of organs of international organization upon the interpretation of its constituent instrument raises the question how far individual Member States are bound by the practice. Although the practice of the organ as such may be consistent, it may have been opposed by individual Members or groups of Members which have been outvoted.[88]

This illustrates that the concerns posed by consideration of the acts of the organs of international organizations as subsequent practice relate to

85 *Chile – Price Band System.* 86 ILC Draft Articles (1966), above n. 54, at 222.

87 See, e.g., the ICJ *Expenses* case, where Judge Spender was against equating 'subsequent conduct of parties to a treaty' with 'the practice followed by an organ of United Nations'. *Certain Expenses of the United Nations (Article 17, paragraph 2, of the Charter)*, Advisory Opinion, [1962] ICJ Rep. 151. See also Leo Gross, *Essays on International Law and Organization*, vol. 2 (Leiden: Brill, 1984), 520–1.

88 ILC Report, 1964 (16th Session, Doc. A/5809, 8 October 1964), at 85, para. 14.

the state consent behind the decision – a requirement generally expressed through the principle *pacta tertiis nec nocent nec prosunt.* As codified in Article 34 of the VCLT, treaties do not 'create either obligations or rights for a third State without its consent' (Art. 34). Furthermore, Article 35 of the VCLT prescribes that '[a]n obligation arises for a third State from a provision of a treaty if the parties to the treaty intend the provision to be the means of establishing the obligation and the third State expressly accepts that obligation in writing.' This generally means that states cannot be bound by international obligations to which they have not subscribed.[89] Although the institutional practice was discussed during the negotiations of the VCLT, the discussions were limited to the effect of the practice of organs of an international organization on interpreting the constitutive agreements of international organizations – a problem which remained without a concrete solution.[90] The historical background of the negotiations of this provision does not clarify the status of the institutional practice in the interpretation process either.[91]

As regards the consideration of practice of other international organizations in the WTO, the Appellate Body in *EC – Computer Equipment* recommended attributing weight to WCO decisions in interpreting the tariff concessions in Schedule LXXX.[92] The Panel in *EC – Chicken Cuts* reconfirmed the validity of this approach with reference to the latter case.[93] Thus the Appellate Body found decisions of the HS Committee of the WCO as satisfying the requirements set out in VCLT Article 31(3)(b). Regrettably, neither this case nor subsequent WTO jurisprudence has elaborated on this essential point, which is a notable example of sensitivity towards the WCO's practice. The AB was relatively brief in explaining why relevant decisions of international organizations could constitute subsequent practice.[94]

2. *EC – Computer Equipment*

EC – Computer Equipment is important for having provided a few other important clarifications regarding the use of subsequent practice in WTO

89 For an account of the principle see Christine Chinkin, *Third Parties in International Law* (Oxford: Clarendon Press; New York: Oxford University Press, 1993), 52.

90 Waldock Third Report (1964), above n. 83, at 59–60.

91 For a detailed account of the status of institutional practice and the state consent requirement see Gross, *Essays*, at 520–3.

92 *EC – Computer Equipment*, ABR, para. 90.

93 *EC – Chicken Cuts*, Panel, para. 7.220.

94 For a more detailed analysis of the role of the WCO in WTO dispute settlement see below Chapter 8.

interpretation. The AB insisted that the material to be considered as such should be relevant and consistent.[95] Furthermore, it noted that 'subsequent practice' is valid if several WTO members (not just one) have established it; the Appellate Body therefore excluded reliance on the practice of just one or very few WTO members.[96] A further clarification was made with respect to the character of the 'agreement' between WTO members required for subsequent practice. Notably, the Appellate Body acknowledged that 'lack of reaction' is a possible form of establishing agreement, and that this might emerge when parties had been notified of the practice or had taken part in the forums establishing it.[97] Thus in order for the practice to be accepted as such a critical mass of WTO members would suffice. As stated in the Waldock Third Report, 'if all the Members of the international organization would have to engage in a consistent practice, it might become difficult to distinguish this factual reality from the result of an authoritative interpretation'.[98]

3. Limitations on use of institutional practice

The above clarifications are important, for they will come to bear on consideration not only of the WTO but also the practice of other international organizations in dispute settlement. One should not disregard, however, the limitations signalled above in relation to the use of institutional practice. Whereas there is a strong logic behind the assimilation of the WCO's practice to that of the WTO in a dispute over classification of goods (given the WTO's reliance on the HS Convention), the institutional practice is generally presumed to suffer from legitimacy flaws.[99] This is because it is not clear to what extent it should incorporate *express state consent* and whether this consent should be expressed by *all* the members of the organization concerned.[100] It may impose unwarranted obligations which may arise from the application by the WTO adjudicator of norms to which the WTO litigants have not adhered or the interpretation of the WTO obligations in the light of such instruments. In view of this, the WTO Appellate Body confirmed that the interpretative material drawn from public international law can only be referred to if it reflects the common intention of all WTO members.[101] In other words, 'the other

95 *EC – Computer Equipment*, ABR, para. 95.

96 *EC – Chicken Cuts*, ABR, para. 266.

97 Ibid., para. 272.

98 Waldock Third Report (1964), above n. 83.

99 Alvarez and Leebron, 'Symposium: Boundaries', at 118.

100 Ibid.

101 See *US – Gambling*, ABR, para. 159: 'Accordingly, the task of ascertaining the meaning of a concession in a Schedule, like the task of interpreting any other treaty text, involves identifying the common intention of Members.'

international law must be binding on all WTO members', as is the case for general custom, general principles and some treaties, or at least 'reflect their common intention', as may be the case for certain provisions in broadly supported multilateral agreements referred to by the Appellate Body.[102]

Some have suggested overcoming these concerns by simply accepting the practice as long as it is attributable to the organ concerned.[103] Thus the size of the majority in favour of the practice should not be relevant provided the conduct constitutes an act of the organ as a body.[104] Another example of how this issue can be approached arises from the *Texaco* case. This investment dispute between two oil companies and the Libyan government examined the relevance and legal value of some UN resolutions invoked by the litigants.[105] Essentially, the tribunal noted that

> Refusal to recognize any legal validity of United Nations Resolutions must . . . be qualified according to the various texts enacted by the United Nations. These are very different and have varying legal value . . . In appraising the legal validity of the above mentioned Resolutions, this Tribunal will take account of the criteria usually taken into consideration, i.e. the examination of voting conditions and of the provisions concerned.[106]

Following a meticulous investigation of the voting conditions behind the relevant UN legal instruments at issue, the Tribunal attributed legal value to and considered only those acts which were adopted by a *majority vote* distributed – quite evenly – among developing and developed countries. It contended that the said resolutions needed consideration because they were 'assented to by a great many States representing not only all geographical areas but also all economic systems'.[107] Moreover, it appeared essential to the Tribunal to 'distinguish between those provisions stating the existence of a right on which the generality of the States has expressed

102 Pauwelyn, 'Unity and Fragmentation', at 11. This latter category may be referred to, for example, when the WTO adjudicator needs to find out whether 'exhaustible natural resources' should be read to include living species or to decide whether something is part of the 'development, financial and trade needs' of developing countries by reference to other international treaties.

103 Chittharanjan F. Amerasinghe, *Principles of Institutional Law of International Organisations*, 2nd edn (Cambridge University Press, 2005), 51.

104 Ibid.

105 See Jörg P. Müller and Luzius Wildhaber, *Praxis des Völkerrechts*, 3rd edn (Berne: Stämfli Verlag AG, 2001), 90–3, referring to *Texaco Overseas Petroleum and California Asiatic Oil Company* v. *Government of the Libyan Arab Republic*, from 19 January 1977, (1978) ILM 17 (*Texaco* case).

106 Ibid., at 91. 107 Ibid.

agreement and those provisions producing new principles which were rejected by certain administrative groups and having nothing more than a *de lege ferenda* value in the eyes of the States which have adopted them'.[108]

Thus the state consent standard applied by the *Texaco* Tribunal with respect to the UN resolutions falls somewhere in the middle on the axis of the stringency of the state consent requirement – where at the one extreme the consent of *all* the members would be required, and at the other, the nature of consent is irrelevant as long as the act is attributable to an organ of the international organization. This standard can be validly employed by the WTO adjudicator when deciding whether to take account of the relevant institutional practice of other international organizations, provided all other requirements characterizing subsequent practice are met. Given its stringency, this standard would be more apposite for the WTO adjudicator, in dealing with extra-regime institutional practice. It is the view here that this would offer more assurance to the WTO adjudicator in considering institutional practice residing outside the WTO. Consequently, wider use of such practice would be expected in WTO dispute settlement.

E. Other rules of international law

The way in which WTO law relates to other international law and the limitations on the use of VCLT Article 31(3)(c) in WTO dispute settlement were discussed above in Chapter 1. The purpose of this subsection – as throughout the entire chapter – is to assess the extent to which Article 31(3)(c), which prescribes consideration of other rules of international law applicable in relations between the parties, could direct the WTO adjudicator to acts of other international organizations.

Note should be taken that the rules of international law correspond with the notion of the sources of international law as prescribed by Article 38(1) of the ICJ Statute.[109] These rules are applicable in relations between the parties – that is, binding on all the parties to the treaty at issue[110] – which means that non-binding rules of international law cannot be relied on under this VCLT rule. Thus the problem with the acts of international organizations is that they are not included in the list of traditional sources of international law. This fact would not pose any problem if such acts had evolved into customary international law or general principles of law.

108 Ibid., at 92. 109 See Villiger, *Commentary*, at 433. 110 Ibid.

This, however, is rarely the case.[111] While this issue can be diluted by the claim of the unclear status of sources of international law and the non-exhaustive character of the Article 38 list,[112] the acts of international organizations may not be validly considered in the interpretation of the treaty at issue if they are not binding rules. For that matter, binding rules have been defined as decisions which either change the law or oblige states to do so. In other words, they should change the pre-existing legal situation.[113]

The international organizations produce acts or 'decisions' of two general types. The first category is related to the internal operation of the organization, such as creation of subsidiary bodies, tribunals, adoption of rules of procedures for these bodies or courts. The second category has a prescriptive nature, for they directly create or affect rights or obligations of member states of the international organization. These are, for example, the decisions adopted by the UN Security Council (e.g. pursuant to Chapter VII of the UN Charter).[114]

F. Special meanings

Article 31(4) VCLT states:

> A special meaning shall be given to a term if it is established that the parties so intended.

The ILC Draft Articles (1966) describe special meaning as a 'technical or other special meaning'.[115] The provision itself does not explain how to find the special meaning and its application has more to do with the burden of proof that a special meaning should apply in a particular case by the litigant invoking it.[116] Thus Article 31(4) VCLT is an exception to Article 31(1) VCLT and to the application of other means of interpretation specified in the VCLT.

111 See Kirgis, 'Specialized Law-Making Processes', at 88–9, for some examples, the ILO most prominently.

112 See above Chapter 1, section III.B.2.a for a discussion. See also Pauwelyn, *Conflict of Norms*, 89–94.

113 Schermers and Blokker, *International Institutional Law*, para. 1318, citing J. Castañeda, 'Valeure Juridique des résolution des Nations Unies', 129 RdC (1970), at 22.

114 Art. 25 of the UN Charter provides that 'The Members of the United Nations agree to accept and carry out the decisions of the Security Council in accordance with the present Charter.'

115 ILC Draft Articles (1966), above n. 54, at 222.

116 Ibid., at 49.

The WTO adjudicator has rarely applied this provision explicitly in the interpretation process of WTO Agreements. Parties have claimed special meanings on several occasions but they have failed to meet the burden of proof to this effect. Only in *Mexico – Telecoms* did the Panel find that 'interconnection' in Section 2 of Mexico's Reference Paper had a special meaning. This, however, had been applied erroneously, since the Panel considered that it was sufficient that the 'provision is a technical one that appears in a specialized service sector' in order for it to establish the intention to give the term a special meaning.[117] In establishing this meaning the Panel consulted a number of documents elaborated outside the WTO system, such as the Telecom Glossary 2000, an ITU Report on Trends in Telecommunications Reform: Interconnection Regulation, and some national law and regulations.[118] The meaning offered by these documents did not, however, contradict the ordinary meaning of the interpreted term, so there was little value in this interpretative exercise in the elucidation of the status of the special meaning.

What is important to note is that the special meaning enshrined in VCLT Article 31(4) is an interpretation rule which provides scope for consideration of material ensuing from other international organizations, as illustrated in *Mexico – Telecoms*. However, given the difficulty of the burden of proof on the party invoking the special meaning, such documents will rarely be resorted to for presenting evidence of a special meaning.[119]

G. *Supplementary means*

Finally, Article 32 of the VCLT, entitled 'Supplementary means of interpretation', states:

> Recourse may be had to supplementary means of interpretation, including the preparatory work of the treaty and the circumstances of its conclusion, in order to confirm the meaning resulting from the application of article 31, or to determine the meaning when the interpretation according to article 31:
>
> (a) leaves the meaning ambiguous or obscure; or
> (b) leads to a result which is manifestly absurd or unreasonable.

117 *Mexico – Telecoms*, Panel Report, para. 7.108.
118 Ibid., paras. 7.108–7.110 and 7.175–7.177.
119 For an account of the use of special meanings in WTO disputes see Van Damme, *Treaty Interpretation*, 351–3.

Thus the supplementary means of interpretation can confirm an interpretation or determine the meaning of the term. This means that VCLT Article 32 is a strictly 'limited exception' to Article 31, not an alternative thereto.[120]

In WTO adjudication the supplementary means have been used as an umbrella, covering the longest list of interpretative elements, such as informal agreements between WTO members, domestic court decisions issued at the time of negotiation, reports by GATT/WTO adjudicating bodies, international treaties, acts of international organizations, decisions by international courts, domestic law and practice, and doctrine.[121] The acts of international organizations were attributed to the supplementary means of interpretation in, for example, the Arbitrator's Report on *US – FSC (Article 22.6 – US)*, containing an explicit reference to a report on state responsibility prepared by the ILC – voted as a UN resolution.[122] The Panel report on *Mexico – Telecoms* relied on OECD guidelines to confirm its understanding of the term 'anti-competitive practice'.[123] In *India – Patents*, the Appellate Body referred to the Permanent Court of International Justice (PCIJ) jurisprudence to support its findings that domestic law could be viewed as a factual matter.[124]

1. The preparatory work

The most common heading used by the WTO adjudicator under Article 32 VCLT is the preparatory work of the WTO Agreement and its annexes. Preparatory work has intentionally not been defined in Article 32 so as to avoid situations where the definition might exclude relevant evidence in a particular case.[125] Thus it includes all materials that are associated with the collective effort of negotiating the treaty which emerged prior to the conclusion of the treaty, including also unpublished but accessible material.[126] Accordingly, the interpreter should make sure that mere bilateral exchanges do not pass the standard of the collective effort. The

120 ILC Draft Articles (1966), above n. 54, at 223.

121 For an account see Mavroidis, 'No Outsourcing of Law?', at 462 ff.

122 *US – FSC (Article 22.6 – US)*, Panel Report, n. 52.

123 *Mexico – Telecoms*, Panel Report, para. 7.236.

124 *India – Patents*, ABR, para. 65.

125 Ibid., at 223. See also Gerald Fitzmaurice, 'The Law and Procedure of International Court of Justice: Treaty Interpretation and Certain Other Treaty Points', (1951) 28 *British Yearbook of International Law* 1, at 15–16; Hersch Lauterpacht, 'Some Observations on Preparatory Work in the Interpretation of Treaties', (1935) 48 *Harvard Law Review* 549, at 549, cited in Van Damme, *Treaty Interpretation*, at 309.

126 Lauterpacht, 'Observations'. See also Anthony Aust, *Modern Treaty Law and Practice* (Cambridge University Press, 2000), at 198 (emphasis added by author).

preparatory work covers for example, memoranda, minutes and drafts.[127] It is, however, often incomplete, unbalanced, even misleading, and is therefore mistrusted. It is not always documented in a material source; more often it is simply part of the institutional memory.[128]

Opinions in the literature regarding the weight attached to the preparatory work in the interpretation process vary from suggestions that it be assigned a high value to those advocating discarding it entirely.[129] In WTO jurisprudence the preparatory work has mostly been used to justify or confirm interpretations arrived at under VCLT Article 31. This was the case for example in *Argentina – Footwear*, *India – Quantitative Restrictions*, *Korea – Procurement*, *US – Section 211 Appropriations Act* and *US – Shrimp*. The reliance of the WTO adjudicator on preparatory work was quite substantial in *Chile – Price Band System* and *EC – Tariff Preferences*.[130] An atypical example of the use of preparatory work emerges from *Canada – Pharmaceutical Patents*. In this case, the Panel took into account the preparatory work of the Berne Convention to *clarify* (rather than confirming) the meaning of a condition laid down in a TRIPS provision. In justifying its choice, the Panel noted that the text of the condition it was examining was clearly drawn from the Berne Convention.[131] This example illustrates a departure from the general tendency to downplay the supplementary means of interpretation in WTO dispute settlement.[132]

2. Other supplementary means

In *EC – Chicken Cuts* the Appellate Body, recalling *EC – Computer Equipment*, confirmed the prevailing view in international law that Article 32 is non-exhaustive.[133] Apart from the preparatory work, other circumstances surrounding the conclusion of the treaty are relevant under this provision. Note should be taken that there is some overlap between this category and the preparatory work, since the former justifies ‘in appropriate cases, the

127 Van Damme, *Treaty Interpretation*, at 309. 128 Ibid.

129 See Hersch Lauterpacht, *The Development of International Law by the International Court*, revised edn (London: Stevens & Sons, 1958), 134, suggesting that preparatory work should be considered as ‘fundamental, and perhaps the most important, aspect of interpretation of treaties’; and Federico Ortino, ‘Treaty Interpretation and the WTO Appellate Body Report in *US – Gambling*: A Critique’, (2006) 9 *Journal of International Economic Law* 117, at 219, suggesting declaring an interpretative *non liquet* rather than considering the preparatory work in the interpretation process.

130 For a more detailed account see Van Damme, *Treaty Interpretation*, 315–20.

131 *Canada – Pharmaceutical Patents*, Panel Report, para. 7.70.

132 For a more detailed discussion on this point, see subsection G.3 below.

133 *EC – Chicken Cuts*, ABR, para. 283.

examination of the historical background against which the treaty was negotiated', along with the contemporary circumstances.[134] This was also confirmed by the Appellate Body in *EC – Computer Equipment*.[135]

In *EC – Chicken Cuts* the Appellate Body defined 'the circumstances' of the conclusion of the treaty as including:

> any event, act, or instrument not only if it has actually influenced a specific aspect of the treaty text in the sense of a relationship of cause and effect; it may also qualify . . . when it helps to discern what the common intentions of the parties were at the time of conclusion with respect to the text of a specific provision'.[136]

The circumstances of the conclusion of the treaty need to be relevant to the interpretation of the treaty provision, which should be assessed on the 'objective factors, and not subjective intent';[137] they should predate the point in time when the treaty is concluded, but continue to influence or reflect the common intentions of the parties at the time of conclusion.[138] The instrument identified as such has to be officially published, and should be publicly available so that any interested party can acquire knowledge of it.

3. Elucidation versus confirmation

EC – Computer Equipment should be singled out as a case where the Panel elaborated on the application of Article 32. It reasoned that consideration of the supplementary means of interpretation implied an obligation 'to assess the objective evidence of the mutual understanding of the negotiating parties' and not only of disputants.[139] The AB, however, applied a stricter standard: it reiterated that treaty interpretation is about finding the *common intentions* of the contracting parties.[140]

The requirement does not stand up, given that the preparatory work, by definition, cannot concern the common intentions of all contracting parties, which are generally formed once the treaty language has been drafted, and will develop over time and with the accession of new parties.[141] Furthermore, the treaty negotiation process reflects various perceptions of its participants which may significantly differ from each other. According to one commentator, a treaty 'is a result not only of meeting of minds,

134 Waldock Third Report (1964), above 83, at 59.

135 *EC – Computer Equipment*, ABR, para. 86.

136 Ibid., para. 289.

137 *EC – Chicken Cuts*, ABR, para. 291.

138 Ibid., para. 293.

139 *EC – Computer Equipment*, Panel Report, para. 7.75.

140 Ibid., ABR, para. 93.

141 McNair, *Law of Treaties*, 420; Van Damme, *Treaty Interpretation*, 313.

but meeting of various motives';[142] it is also about self-interest and strategy. That is why support for various perceptions of the litigants or even of the adjudicator itself can easily be found in the preparatory work. It is therefore difficult to speak of common intentions of the parties in this context. This is why it has been claimed that the role of the preparatory work and negotiation history should be one of justification and confirmation rather than elucidation:[143]

> [T]he history of the text cannot inform the meaning of the treaty text. It can be rebutted but the burden of proof is considerable. The larger the group of negotiators and signatories of a treaty the greater is that burden. It involves providing that there was a common intention among that group that the treaty text has a particular meaning, with written evidence.[144]

This means that since the common intentions standard will be almost impossible to meet,[145] the supplementary means of interpretation should be used only to confirm or support the meaning reached under VCLT Article 31. This approach is suggested in a number of academic contributions.[146] Its implications are twofold. First, it risks reducing to redundancy that part of Article 32 which prescribes use of supplementary means 'to determine the meaning' of the interpreted text. Second, the value of the material attributable to supplementary means will be reduced, since it would only serve to confirm a conclusion already reached; moreover, the WTO panels will not feel bound to cite this material in future cases.[147] These effects would also apply when the acts of international

142 Roy S. Lee, 'Multilateral Treaty-Making and Negotiation Techniques: An Appraisal', in Bin Cheng and Edward D. Brown, (eds.), *Contemporary Problems of International Law: Essays in Honour of Georg Schwarzenberger on his Eightieth Birthday* (London: Stevens & Sons, 1988) 157, 160–1.

143 Van Damme, *Treaty Interpretation*, 314. See also Stephen M. Schwebel, 'May Preparatory Work be Used to Correct Rather than Confirm the "Clear" Meaning of a Treaty Provision?', in Jerzy Makarczyk (ed.), *Theory of International Law at the Threshold of the 21st Century: Essays in Honour of Krzystof Skubiszewski* (London: Kluwer Law International, 1966); also Maurice Mendelson, 'Comment on "May Preparatory Work be Used to Correct Rather than Confirm the 'Clear' Meaning of a Treaty Provision?"', (2005) 2(5) *Transnational Dispute Management*, www.transnational-dispute-management.com.

144 Van Damme, *Treaty Interpretation*, at 315.

145 E.g. Fitzmaurice, 'Law and Procedure', at 14–15.

146 Aust, *Modern Treaty Law*, at 199; McNair, *Law of Treaties*, at 413; See also Waldock Third Report (1964), above n. 83, at 58. On a critical assessment of the use of preparatory work in the interpretation process see Christoph H. Schreuer,'Diversity and Harmonisation of Treaty Interpretation in Investment Arbitration', (2006) 3(2) *Transnational Dispute Management* 1, at 9; Lennard, 'Navigating by the Stars', at 49–54.

147 Mavroidis, 'No Outsourcing of Law?', at 50.

organizations come under the purview of the WTO adjudicator with reference to Article 32 VCLT. This will result in downplaying their legal value in the WTO judicial interpretation.

On the other hand, while it is true that the common intentions standard required for considering supplementary means for purposes of elucidation would be almost impossible to meet, this hurdle could be overcome by simply not applying the common intentions requirement with respect to the preparatory work, substituting it with a somewhat more lenient state consent requirement. Apart from avoiding the redundancy of the relevant part of VCLT Article 32, this would allow the WTO adjudicator to interpret legal obligations against the background of a wider scope of materials and acts ensuing from international organizations.

IV. Conclusions

This chapter has examined how the use of VCLT rules of interpretation by WTO panels or the Appellate Body interfaces the WTO with other international organizations. The level of judicial institutional sensitivity towards other international organizations can be judged by the frequency of use and legal value ascribed to this material. The legal value will be prejudged by the choice of the WTO adjudicator as to where to classify that material under VCLT rules of interpretation. The case law analyses reveal that the WTO adjudicator has attributed acts of other international organizations mostly to supplementary means of interpretation, with very few exceptions.

While the consideration of such material for the clarification of the 'ordinary meaning' is perceived as lacking normative value, and its use as 'context' is very unlikely to emerge, a number of standards have been elicited with regard to the remaining VCLT interpretative techniques, which could be used by the WTO panels or Appellate Body in order to make wider use of the acts of international organizations in the interpretation process. Thus the WTO *Mexico – Telecoms* standard seems apposite for dealing with the acts attributable to 'subsequent agreement'. Hopefully, the incipient analysis of state consent behind the material classifiable as such, provided by the Appellate Body in this case, will inspire future WTO panels to make wider use of this technique in order to take account of the relevant acts of international organizations. The unresolved issue of how subsequent agreements link to the original WTO treaty may, however, constitute a serious obstacle for the WTO panels in effectively using this option. The ILC mandate to clarify the issue is important, as it explicitly acknowledges the fact that treaties should be interpreted against present-day exigencies in order for them not to lose relevance.

The analysis of 'subsequent practice' elaborated on the significance of the institutional practice of treaty interpretation in WTO adjudication. Here also a number of challenges have been illustrated. First, the status of WTO institutional practice is not clear. In order to understand what role the practice of other international organizations may have in this process, the role of WTO practice in dispute settlement should first be elucidated. Second, institutional practice is perceived to suffer from legitimacy flaws. Here, the *Texaco* standard which prescribes examination of the decision making behind the act in question has been suggested as a plausible solution where all the other criteria of qualifying practice are met. One should not disregard for example the limitation of the temporality requirement which prescribes considering only practice that emerged in the aftermath of the conclusion of the WTO Agreement.

As noted, the acts of international organizations have mostly been attributed to supplementary means of interpretation in WTO dispute settlement. This definitely reduces the legal value of these acts in the WTO disputes. Some authors have warned that the WTO adjudicator should be careful not to turn this VCLT provision into a dumping ground for interpretative arguments and a vehicle for applying other rules of international law.[148] Indeed, the WTO panels or Appellate Body should try to better explore and make wider use of the other rules of interpretation enshrined in VCLT Article 31.

The role of the acts of international organizations in WTO judicial interpretation is further reduced by the fact that the instruments attributed to supplementary means are used mostly for confirmatory purposes. The legal value of the material considered under Article 32 VCLT would certainly be greater if the WTO adjudicator resorted to it not only for ascertaining the meaning already clarified under Article 31 VLCT, but also when this meaning could not have been clarified under the primary rules. This would be perfectly in line with the exigencies of VCLT Article 32.

What is important to note in conclusion is that the value of the acts of international organizations is not affected by their classification under

148 For an account see Van Damme, *Treaty Interpretation*, at 323–4. See e.g. the instances when the Appellate Body has classified non-codified principles of interpretation (e.g. *in dubio mitius*) under supplementary means (*EC – Hormones*, ABR, para. 165).

VCLT interpretation rules as long as panels remain in the realm of the primary rules of VCLT Article 31. One should cite here the pragmatic approach of the *EC – Chicken Cuts* Panel with regard to the consideration of the HS. The Panel contended in this case that the outcome of the interpretative exercise would not depend on the chosen classification.[149] While this may be so, the legitimacy of the decision may well depend on whether or not the WTO adjudicator has made use of all relevant material, including that residing outside the trade regime.

149 *EC – Chicken Cuts*, ABR, para. 194.

PART II

The constraints on institutional sensitivity

While Part I has set out the foundations of this study, elaborating on the concept of institutional sensitivity, the objective of Part II is to single out specific problems which would constrain the role of international organizations in the settlement of WTO disputes. Ostensibly, these limitations arise from a series of factors which stem either from the WTO system itself or are inherent in the architecture of the relevant international organizations, which are examined in Chapter 4. In Part I, the concept of institutional sensitivity of the WTO adjudicator was explored by drawing on some guidance from the Appellate Body's notion of deference to domestic regulatory authorities. This revealed that the relevant (outside) actors who make factual determinations that come within the purview of the WTO panels should display a certain degree of competence and credibility.

Observer status in the WTO is ascribed to international organizations according to specific rules on ascertaining that the international organization in question can make valid contributions to the WTO decision-making process.[1] Thus the quality of the observer of an international organization in the WTO should also induce the panels or Appellate Body to believe that they are dealing with a credible and competent international organization. The credibility of international organizations, however, is also determined, as outlined in this part, by a series of other factors. Against this background, Chapter 5 singles out factors which raise favourable presumption in support of the competence and credibility of an international organization.

1 See above Chapter 2, section IV.B for a comprehensive account of the observer's status in the WTO.

4

Internal and external constraints

I. Introduction

The WTO is unique among other international organizations for what it has to offer. As noted by Petersmann, its substantive guarantees of freedom, non-discriminatory competition and rule of law, as well as its institutional 'checks and balances' and compulsory dispute settlement system, are in many respects more developed and more ambitious than those of other worldwide organizations.[2] Nonetheless, some limits, or even deficiencies, can be spotted within the WTO system, which restrain if not overshadow the institutional sensitivity of the WTO adjudicator. These are referred to as internal constraints, which are examined in section II. Many of these constraints pertain to the functioning (or architecture) of other relevant international organizations. These are termed 'external constraints' and are explored in section III. Some concluding remarks follow a detailed analysis of these constraints (section IV).

II. Internal constraints

Several sources of internal constraints on the institutional sensitivity of the WTO adjudicator can be identified within the WTO system itself. These emerge from specific treaty text language (e.g. DSU Articles 2(1) and 3(2)) or imperfections in the relevant WTO positive law (e.g. DSU Article 13, some SPS and TBT provisions), from WTO political choices on how it should relate to other societal values, or from an inconsistent approach of the WTO adjudicator towards its jurisprudence.

A. The WTO legal framework

1. DSU Article 2(1)

DSU Article 2(1) is a provision dealing with the administration of the WTO dispute settlement rules and procedures, ascribing this function

2 Petersmann, 'Constitutionalism', at 460.

explicitly to the Dispute Settlement Body (DSB). In the relevant part the provision states:

> The Dispute Settlement Body is hereby established to administer these rules and procedures and, except as otherwise provided in a covered agreement, the consultation and dispute settlement provisions of the covered agreements. Accordingly, the DSB shall have the authority to establish panels, adopt panel and Appellate Body reports, maintain surveillance of implementation of rulings and recommendations, and authorize suspension of concessions and other obligations under the covered agreements.

Given this express language entrusting authority to a specific WTO body, this norm may be read in the light of the *delegatus non potest delegare* principle, or what is otherwise known as the non-delegation doctrine. The doctrine deals with the extent to which the exercise of a power entrusted to an authority may be delegated to another entity.[3] In domestic constitutional and administrative law the maxim has been used, for example, as a basis for invalidating delegations of government power, and as an element of statutory interpretation, leading – with other reasoning – to narrower constructions of statutory authority. Thus the object and purpose of the non-delegation principle is to ensure that powers are exercised by the entity to which those powers have been initially delegated, in the way that has been provided.[4]

There is great variation in the forms of delegation of power as applied to international organizations. One important characteristic of such delegation is that the delegator should expressly state its intention to delegate power, which means that a delegation of power can never be implied.[5]

3 Woolf et al. note in this context: 'A discretionary authority must, in general, be exercised only by the authority to which it has been committed. It is a well-known principle of law that when a power has been confided to a person in circumstances indicating that trust is being placed in his individual judgment and discretion, he must exercise that power personally unless he has been expressly empowered to delegate it to another . . . It applies to the delegation of all classes of powers.' Harry Woolf, Jeffrey L. Jowell, Stanley A. De Smith and Andrew P. Le Sueur, *De Smith, Woolf & Jowell's Principles of Judicial Review* (London: Sweet & Maxwell, 1999), 357–8.

4 Danesh Sarooshi, *The United Nations and the Development of Collective Security: The Delegation by the UN Security Council of its Chapter VII Powers* (Oxford University Press, 1999), 22, citing William Wade and Christopher Forsyth, *Administrative Law* (Oxford University Press, 1994), 347, who state that 'An element which is essential to the lawful exercise of power is that it should be exercised by the authority upon whom it is conferred, and by no one else.'

5 See European Court of Justice, *Meroni* v. *High Authority of the European Coal and Steel Community*, Case 9156, [1958] ECR 133. The ECJ, in dealing with the lawfulness of a delegation of powers by one of the organs of the EC, stated the following: 'A delegation

Furthermore, the lawfulness of a particular delegation of power will depend on whether the organ purporting to delegate has exceeded the limitations on their general competence to delegate. In international organizations, generally, this does not include authority to delegate powers of discretion to an entity that is external to that organization, unless otherwise specifically provided.[6]

As confirmed by DSU Article 2(1), within the WTO it is the DSB which is empowered to administer the dispute settlement rules and procedures. By virtue of this power, it has the authority to establish panels, adopt panel and Appellate Body reports, maintain surveillance of implementation of rulings and recommendations, and authorize suspension of concessions and other obligations under the covered agreements. There are no other WTO provisions specifying a further transfer of this authority to outside bodies. This found confirmation in *EC – Chicken Cuts.* Facing a request from a litigant to transfer the adjudication of the dispute to the WCO, the Panel noted that 'We understand that, once seized of a matter, Article 11 [DSU] prevents the Panel from abdicating its responsibility to the DSB. In other words, in the context of the present case, we lack the authority to refer the dispute before us to the WCO or to any other body.'[7]

What is of concern in the context of this study is whether the proposal for greater institutional sensitivity of the WTO adjudicator risks being regarded as an exercise of unauthorized delegation of power by the DSB to another international organization. It is claimed that the above provision, read in the light of the non-delegation doctrine, should not be perceived as preventing the WTO adjudicator from availing itself of the assistance of international organizations. This assistance may come in various forms, such as clarification on factual points, selection of scientific experts or even interpretion of highly technical documents, such as the Harmonized System developed under the WCO. An interpretative exercise of a kind at the WTO, without proper clarifications from the WCO, may just prove counterproductive and unobjective.[8] It is inevitable that interpretations of this instrument will emerge in the WCO, therefore producing a parallel

of powers cannot be presumed and even when empowered to delegate its powers the delegating authority must take an express decision transferring them', at 155.

6 Sarooshi, *United Nations*, at 18. 7 *EC – Chicken Cuts*, Panel Report, para. 7.56.

8 For an example of delegation of power by the WTO to outside actors see Abbott, 'Distributed Governance', at 67. He notes that several WTO TRIPS Council decisions have involved the delegation of functions to WIPO, particularly regarding the provision of assistance to developing countries and the collection and review of legislation.

interpretation in the WTO which may give rise to inconsistent obligations between the members of both organizations.[9] As suggested by Horn and Howse, who had examined the linkage of the two institutions, where there is no relevant WCO practice with respect to the adjudicated issue, in order to make their case before a WTO panel the complainants will need first to go to the WCO in order to establish that the defendant has interpreted the issue (e.g. on classification of goods under the HS) in a manner that is impermissible in the WCO system. As they point out, the question here is whether the adhesion of the parties to the WCO Convention and the arguably related absence of any code on customs classification in the WTO, indicate the expectation or assumption that problems of interpretation of the HS would be dealt with in the WCO.[10] Given that one of the features of the delegation doctrine is that the power can be delegated only explicitly, this would have to be answered in the negative. Pauwelyn notes this dilemma too, stating that 'for a Panel ... to suspend its work whilst the parties go back to another legal system ... may be borderline between, on the one hand transferring jurisdiction to another body without the agreement of the parties (something that a Panel cannot do) and, on the other hand, seeking advice from an epistemically superior institution (something that ought to enhance the legitimacy of the WTO process)'.[11]

What is important to retain from the above discourse is that it is the task of the WTO adjudicator to ensure that the sensitivity shown towards a specific international organization in the dispute settlement does not constitute a transfer of power (or jurisdiction), unless specifically provided for in the WTO Agreements. This provision is thus not seen as an impediment to the exercise of greater judicial sensitivity by the WTO adjudicator along the lines suggested in this study.

2. DSU Articles 3(2) and 19(2)

DSU Article 3(2) is one of the key provisions drawing the contours of the WTO jurisdiction by stating that

> recommendations and rulings of the DSB cannot add to or diminish the rights and obligations provided in the covered agreements.

9 For a detailed account of the contribution of the WCO to WTO dispute settlement, see the analysis of *EC – Chicken Cuts* in Chapter 8 below.

10 Howse and Horn, 'European Communities', at 35–6.

11 Pauwelyn, 'Unity and Fragmentation', at 17.

This is complemented by Article 19(2) DSU, which provides that

> In their findings and recommendations Panels and the Appellate Body cannot add to or diminish the rights and obligations provided in the covered agreements.

The provision basically says that in fulfilling its functions the DSB is constrained by the duty of showing full respect for the actual rights and obligations of the WTO members. This is also to say that it is for the WTO member governments to make political choices in negotiations, subject to democratic debate and parliamentary control in their respective countries. International judicial and other similar bodies are in charge of interpreting existing rules, not of laying down new ones. Thus the DSU clearly reflects the intention to limit and define the proper role of the dispute settlement system. This is also taken into account through the fact that although disputes are decided by independent and impartial bodies through application of the WTO rules, these bodies have not been defined as judicial organs, although this is, in reality, their function.[12]

These DSU provisions have sometimes been interpreted to mean that non-WTO law cannot be used in any way to effect whatever 'rights and obligations' are provided under WTO law. Joel Trachtman, for example, has argued that 'WTO dispute resolution panels and the Appellate Body are limited to the application of substantive WTO law and are not authorized to apply general substantive international law or other conventional law'.[13] He does not exclude, however, the application of the VCLT rules of interpretation as well as any other rules specifically incorporated.

The ILC Fragmentation Report pointed out that arguments like the one expressed above are countered by the language of DSU Article 3(2), according to which the panels and the Appellate Body are to apply the 'customary rules of interpretation of public international law' – a provision that incorporates not only the VCLT but, through its Articles 31 and 32, any other rules of treaty interpretation. This includes, for example, Article 31(3)(c) under which an interpretation should take into account 'any relevant rules of international law applicable in the relations between the parties'.[14]

12 See Giorgio Sacerdoti, 'The Dispute Settlement System of the WTO: Structure and Function in the Perspective of the First 10 Years', (2006) 5(1) *Law & Practice of International Courts and Tribunals* 49.

13 Trachtman, 'Domain of WTO Dispute Resolution', at 342.

14 ILC Fragmentation Report, para. 167. See also above Chapter 1, section III.B and Chapter 3, section III.E.

While the provision is of general importance in defining the relationship to other parts of international law, it is also of key importance in defining the scope of sensitivity towards the law and policy of other international organizations in dispute settlement. The somewhat constraining nature of the legal language in DSU Articles 3(2) and 19(2) has been manifested through the WTO adjudicator's limited use or restrictive approach towards other international law.[15]

3. DSU Article 13

While the WTO legal framework linking to other regimes has already been set out above, the objective of this chapter is to illustrate how some ambiguity in the relevant WTO legal provisions may affect the sensitivity of the WTO adjudicator towards other international organizations. For example, it is not clear if panels have the right to seek legal opinions and arguments pursuant to DSU Article 13 or if this is to be limited to factual points. Clarifications on legal points may be necessary in highly contentious WTO cases.[16] The relevant source in this case may be an outside actor, including an international organization.[17] The fact that the

15 See e.g. above Chapter 3, section III.A, with reference to the *US – Shrimp* and *EC – Biotech Products* cases.

16 Steger, 'Amicus Curiae'.

17 Note should be taken in this context of the *jura novit curia* – a principle of judicial procedure, according to which, courts are expected to know the law. This principle is recognized by the ICJ as generally applicable in international proceedings. See the statements by the ICJ in *Fisheries Jurisdiction (United Kingdom v. Iceland)*, Merits, Judgment of 25 July 1974, [1974] ICJ Rep. 3, at 9, para. 17; and *Military and Paramilitary Activities in and against Nicaragua (Nicaragua v. United States of America)*, Merits, Judgment of 27 June 1986, [1986] ICJ Rep. 14, at 24, para. 29. In general on the principle see Kazazi, *Burden of Proof*, 44; Hugh W. A. Thirlway, 'Evidence before International Courts and Tribunals', in Rudolf Bernhardt (ed.), *Encyclopedia of Public International Law* (Amsterdam, New York and Oxford: North-Holland Publishing Company, 1981), Book 1 [Instalment 1], at 58–60. As regards proceedings before WTO adjudicating bodies see Pauwelyn, 'Evidence, Proof and Persuasion', at 230–2; Waincymer, *WTO Litigation*, 537. The principles, however, should not be interpreted as preventing the panels from seeking outside help on points of law as long as the job of the panels and the Appellate Body is to make their own legal assessment, based on their own judgement, and to come up with the authoritative interpretative finding. The practical consequence of applying the principle is that, apart from factual claims, none of the parties bears the risk of non-persuasion. See for example, Kazazi, *Burden of Proof*, 48–9, contending that the principle of *jura novit curia* is not totally applicable, since international tribunals often benefit from the views of the parties on legal matters or even explicitly ask for the parties' opinion on the state of law in question. For an account of the implication of the principles on the burden of proof, see Yoshimichi Ishikawa, 'The Burden of Proof in WTO Dispute Settlement', draft doctoral thesis, 2010, World Trade Institute, Berne (on file with the author).

language of DSU Article 13 does not explicitly prescribe the option of seeking legal advice from these sources could be interpreted restrictively as not allowing panels to do so.[18] This may discourage them from using terminology suggesting that it tries to obtain legal information. Or, since there is no WTO legal provision expressly allowing this option, the panel may well just not solicit such information at all in cases where that would be necessary in order properly to elucidate the matter.

An analysis of the relevant case law reveals that when information has been provided by another international organization in the WTO dispute settlement, the panel has termed the information as factual even if there were grounds to believe that it was seeking legal opinions.[19] This diminishing of the importance of the international organizations not only reflects on perceptions of the degree of institutional sensitivity of the WTO adjudicator, but may also impair the fulfilment of the 'objective assessment of the matter' enshrined in DSU Article 11. Another important limitation arising in this connection is that the right to seek information is limited to the panels, being perceived as pertaining to their fact-finding mandate. If panels misinterpret the information received through this channel, the Appellate Body cannot re-examine it. Thus the objectivity of assessments in such cases is questionable, considering that unlike other international tribunals the Appellate Body cannot remand cases to panels for correction of factual errors.[20] Thus DSU Article 13 could usefully be amended to institutionalize the practice of allowing the Appellate Body to solicit the opinions of other international organizations, or allowing their opinions to be submitted on their own initiative. This would enhance the legitimacy of a system where both state and non-state actors were considered at the appellate stage, generating more institutionally sensitive WTO decisions.

4. The SPS Agreement

As illustrated in Chapter 2 above, SPS Article 11 prescribes consultation with other international organizations in the adjudication of complex scientific disputes arising under the SPS Agreement.[21] This provision is not a model of precision either. It is not entirely clear what the scope of this consultation is and whether the relevant international organizations could

18 See above Chapter 2, section V.A.2 for the distinction between factual and legal information.

19 See the example of *US – Section 211 Appropriations Act* described below in Chapter 7, section I ff.

20 Bronckers and McNelis, 'Fact and Law'. For an overview see above Chapter 2, section V.A.3.

21 See above Chapter 2, section III.B.

be ascribed wider prerogatives in dispute settlement, such as submission of scientific evaluations.[22]

The SPS Agreement explicitly refers to the three sister organizations empowered to issue standards (Codex, OIE and IPPC) in Annex A, para. 3(a–c).[23] The list of organizations is not exhaustive and the WTO SPS Committee is authorized to recognize standards of other international organizations (Annex A, para. 3(d)). Two requirements must be met for the SPS Committee to recognize a new international standard: first, the standard-setting organization must be 'open for membership to all [SPS] Members' and second, the standard must deal with 'matters not covered by [the Codex, OIE, or IPPC]'.[24]

The SPS Committee has not recognized standards from any other international organizations to date. Should, for example, the WHO International Health Regulations (IHR) 2005 be recognized as such a standard? One observer elaborates on the current constraints that would hinder such integration, remaining, however, of the view that a partial incorporation of the IHR 2005 into the list of WTO-recognized standards would benefit the enforcement of this new WHO legislation.[25] Another commentator asks an even a more specific question with regard to the enigmatic formulation in subparagraph 3(d) of Annex A of the SPS Agreement, which requires that international organizations are 'identified by the [SPS] Committee'. That is, does this phrase relate to the mandate of the particular organization or its current working agenda, or rather to (actually existing) standards?[26] It has been suggested that in order to avoid duplication, this phrase should be interpreted to refer to the working agenda which would avoid overlapping activity in the SPS area, without, however, introducing over-restrictive standards.[27] For the time being, the provision is lacking

22 See below Chapter 9, section III.C, for a comprehensive account of this point.

23 For an international relations perspective on the emergence of the three sister organizations in the WTO, see Tim Büthe, 'Agent Selection in International Delegation: The Delegation of Regulatory Authority in the SPS-Agreement of the WTO', paper prepared for presentation at the international conference on 'Trade-and-? The World Trade Organization's Fuzzy Borders', Graduate Institute of International and Development Studies, Geneva, 5–6 February 2009.

24 SPS Agreement, Annex A.

25 See Craig Murray, 'Implementing the New International Health Regulations: The Role of the WTO's Sanitary and Phytosanitary Agreement', (2009) 40 *Georgetown Journal of International Law* 625, at 640–1. See also Kelly, 'Power, Linkage and Accommodation', at 120, noting not only that there should be deference to the standards of the three sister organizations but that it is worth exploring the possibility of deferring to other standard-setting institutions (e.g. the Biosafety Convention).

26 Gruszczynski, *Regulating Health.* 27 Ibid.

in clarity and may slow down the process of the WTO bringing under purview the standards of other relevant international organizations.

5. The TBT Agreement

Another constraint arises from the TBT Agreement which covers a very broad range of products but does not specify the international standards to be taken as reference. To recall, TBT Annex 1 provides that the term 'standard' is defined as a 'document approved by a recognized body that provides, for common and repeated use, rules, guidelines or characteristics for products or related processes and production methods, with which compliance is not mandatory'.[28] But this formulation provides little guidance as to the relevant standards for specific products. Should a trade dispute involving biologicals emerge, for example, the WTO dispute settlement panels might have to take a decision regarding the standards which should apply to the case. They could be the WHO's guidelines and requirements – or the norms of another standardizing body. Thus there is some uncertainty as to what might happen in a dispute concerning, for example, vaccines, for which manufacturers have in some cases differing, yet equally valid, standards.[29]

Moreover, unlike the SPS, the TBT Agreement does not mention the international organizations which issue standards for TBT purposes, and a large number of agencies (government or private) may come under the purview of the WTO panels in a TBT case.[30] This means that the WTO adjudicator would have to understand who those bodies are, which are the 'systems' mentioned in TBT Annex 1(4) and whether their activity could be considered as standard-setting for TBT purposes. On the other hand, while referring specifically to international organizations in the TBT Agreement would have made things easier, the listing of the wide range of relevant government and private bodies in the TBT may have been simply impractical. For the time being this remains an open issue.

B. WTO political choices

The problem of institutional sensitivity of course goes deeper. The perception of the influences of other international organizations in the WTO dispute settlement system is by and large a matter of the extent to which the

28 For an overview of the international organizations relevant under the TBT Agreement see above Chapter 2, section III.B.

29 Kinnon, 'World Trade', at 401.

30 Above Chapter 3, section III.B.

WTO follows a philosophy of trade liberalization or of trade regulation. The type of approach followed will definitely reflect on how the panels or Appellate Body regard the output of other international organizations. By the same token, the level of involvement or the contribution of other international organizations in the WTO disputes will be determined by these WTO political choices. An agenda set on trade liberalization will make only restrictive recourse to other institutions and opt for limitations, as suggested in the Sutherland Report.[31] If trade regulation and balancing equally legitimate interests are at the centre, this will also positively affect the relationship of the WTO with other international organizations.

The topic has received a lot of attention in the literature discussing, *inter alia*, how the free trade objective should be reconciled with other values and interests, such as distributive justice, environmental concerns, the protection of human health and safety, and human rights.[32] One of the most ambitious proposals on how the WTO judiciary should position itself vis-à-vis other international organizations is found in the 'stakeholder model' of WTO dispute settlement propounded by Richard Shell. The model envisages opening up WTO dispute settlement to all interested stakeholders and the incorporation of various social and environmental norms within WTO law, such that the WTO members could use the system to enforce such norms.[33] All these proposals are, however, highly contested and no international consensus has yet emerged or is likely to emerge in the near future as to how these questions should be addressed.[34]

As noted, the various models on how best to balance these interests have implications for the interpretation of the WTO Agreements. For example, it has been pointed out that health and trade concerns can be largely reconciled through the interpretation process by the WTO panels or Appellate Body. Taking the *Dominican Republic – Import and Sale of Cigarettes* case as an example, one commentator finds that a narrow reading of the terms 'like product' and 'less favourable treatment' in the

31 See Introduction, n. 60.

32 For a comprehensive account of these debates and relevant literature see Cottier and Oesch, *International Trade Regulation*, 428–51, 513–32.

33 Richard Shell, 'Trade Legalism and International Relations Theory: An Analysis of World Trade Organisation', 44 *Duke Law Journal* 829 (1995), repr. in Robert Howse (ed.), *The World Trading System: Critical Perspectives on the World Economy*, vol. 2, *Dispute Settlement* (London and New York: Routledge, 1998), 333–416.

34 Stefan Zleptnig, *Non-Economic Objectives in WTO Law: Justification Provisions of GATT, GATS, SPS and TBT Agreements* (The Hague: Martinus Nijhoff Publishers, 2010), 15–53.

analysis of a national treatment violation (GATT Article III) may offer a safer harbour for assuring the consistency of health regulatory measures with the WTO.[35] This can also be achieved through a more balanced reading of the 'necessity' test under GATT Article XX.[36] Human rights, which have received a lot of scholarly attention from trade scholars, should be integrated into WTO law through interpretation of existing agreements, but also through the building of new common institutions.[37] The rights-based constitutionalist school submits that human rights have become guiding principles of international economic law and therefore endorse WTO interpretation in the light of human rights guarantees.[38]

Thus, depending on the political trend, the WTO judicial bodies either will attempt to reconcile trade with these other values, or, on the contrary, will fend off the influences from the relevant regimes. A reconciliatory interpretative approach by the panels and Appellate Body would definitely strengthen the relationship with the responsible international organizations. The taking into account of non-trade issues such as human rights or environmental protections displays a constitutional technique of balancing various values in order to determine which of the conflicting interests should prevail in the case in point. This has been called 'constitutionalism in a modest sense', an attitude and a framework capable of reasonably balancing and weighting different, equally legitimate and democratically defined basic values and policy goals.[39] This type of constitutionalism seeks to counter competing values entering into the picture only as narrow and carefully policed exceptions to trade rules. In that perspective these values are something more; they are provisions to protect legitimate policy goals, which form an integral part of a well-balanced multilateral trading system.[40]

35 Ibid., 316–26. For the merits and analysis of the case see below Chapter 6.

36 Tsai-yu Lin, 'Exploring a Modest Balance for Trade in Tobacco, Anti-tobacco Smuggling and Health Concerns in Light of the *Dominican Republic – Cigarettes* Case', (2008) 3 *Asian Journal of WTO & International Health Law and Policy* 308, at 329.

37 For a comprehensive literature review on the trade and human rights relationship see Cottier and Oesch, *International Trade Regulation*, 531.

38 See notably Ernst-Ulrich Petersmann, 'Time for a United Nations "Global Compact" for Integrating Human Rights into the Law of Worldwide Organizations: Lessons from European Integration', (2000) 13 *European Journal of International Law* 612, at 645–6.

39 Cottier, 'Limits to International Trade', at 221.

40 Anne Peters, 'Membership in the Global Constitutional Community', in Jan Klabbers, Anne Peters and Geir Ulfstein (eds.), *The Constitutionalization of International Law* (Oxford University Press, 2009), 216.

While it is agreed that a proper balancing test by the panels plays an important role in the sensitivity of the trading system in general, one of the central points of this study is that the WTO adjudicator should not exclude the relevant international organizations in the process of balancing these various interests.[41]

C. WTO judicial decision making

Before turning to the significance of consistent judicial decision making in the WTO, the significance regarding precedence of these decisions is briefly discussed.[42] The WTO panels and the Appellate Body regularly engage in interpretative exercises with a view to clarifying ambiguities and filling gaps in the GATT and WTO Agreements. This discretion is, however, constrained by the imperative that the WTO dispute settlement bodies should not change the rights and obligations agreed between the members. This concern is reflected in DSU Article 3(2), which states that the Appellate Body 'cannot add to or diminish the rights and obligations provided in the covered agreements'.

The only reports for which explicit provision can be found with regard to their value as precedents are adopted panel reports under GATT 1947. For that matter, Article XVI(1) of the WTO Agreement stipulates that 'the WTO shall be guided by the decisions, procedures and customary practices followed by the Contracting Parties to GATT 1947 and the bodies established in the framework of GATT 1947'.[43] However, it is now largely accepted that the WTO legal regime has effectively adopted the system of de facto precedential effect of prior decisions. Although the adopted panel and Appellate Body reports within the WTO system and

41 See also above Chapter 1, section IV.

42 The principle of *stare decisis et quieta non movere* ('to stand by and adhere to decisions and not disturb what is settled') is a very strong form of precedent prevalent in the common law world. Although the concepts of precedent and *stare decisis* are sometimes used interchangeably, it is wrong to talk of precedent as the presence or absence of *stare decisis*. See Raj Bhala, 'The Myth about Stare Decisis in International Trade Law (Part One of a Trilogy)', (1999) 14 *American University International Law Review* 845; Raj Bhala, 'The Precedent Setters: De Facto Stare Decisis in WTO Adjudication (Part Two of a Trilogy)', (1999) 9 *Florida State University Journal of Transnational Law and Policy* 1; Raj Bhala, 'The Power of the Past: Towards De Jure Stare Decisis in WTO Adjudication', (2001) *George Washington International Law Review* 873.

43 Although the Panel in *Japan – Alcoholic Beverages II* explicitly qualified adopted panel reports as 'judicial decisions' within the meaning of Art. XVI(1) of the WTO Agreement, the Appellate Body reversed this finding, cautiously stating that they were 'an important part of the GATT *acquis*'. See ABR, Section E, at 14.

the preceding GATT 1947 are short of being legally binding except for the particular dispute, they have nonetheless strong persuasive power.[44] These reports substantially contribute to the law-making process and the refinement of WTO law. In substance, 'Panels and the Appellate Body have developed a system of precedent under which they heavily rely on, but are not legally bound by, prior reports'.[45] Moreover, panels and the Appellate Body have an obligation to take into account prior unadopted panel reports too, and, in order to give due respect to the principle of legal certainty, they may be obliged to articulate particularly good and convincing reasons when departing from a previously developed line of argument and reasoning.

This de facto binding force of prior judicial reports came under challenge in the *US – Stainless Steel* decision, where the Panel consciously chose to stray from Appellate Body jurisprudence in a particularly contentious area of anti-dumping law as relating to 'zeroing'. This, however, was vindicated when the Appellate Body required panels to advance cogent reasons in order to justify departure from its previous decisions. This case represents a further step in WTO adjudication in a line of cases in which the Appellate Body has gradually sought to expand the binding force of its decisions. Bhala described the situation as 'de facto stare decisis' and forcefully argued to 'end the hypocrisy' and introduce a de jure stare decisis regime by amending the DSU.[46]

The following subsections examine why inconsistent judicial law-making constitutes a problem for the WTO in general and essentially how it overshadows the institutional sensitivity of the WTO judicial institutions.

1. Inconsistent interpretation as a legitimacy issue

Chapter 1 enunciated three factors which legitimize the WTO adjudication: fair procedures, integrity and coherence in legal interpretation, and institutional sensitivity. Incoherent legal interpretation generates inconsistent judicial decisions and, as a result, outcomes of disputes where similar conditions prevail will vary. Consistency in legal interpretation is thus perceived to legitimize the WTO adjudication for two main reasons.

44 Cottier and Oesch, *International Trade Regulation*, 28–30. See also Palmeter and Mavroidis, 'WTO Legal System', at 40; Rao Geping, 'The Law Applied by World Trade Organization Panels', (2003) 17 *Temple International and Comparative Law Journal* 137.

45 Cottier and Oesch, *International Trade Regulation*, at 111.

46 See Bhala, 'Precedent Setters', at 1 ff., and 'Power of the Past', at 873 ff.

First, by applying the law in a rational and coherent manner, the adjudicator rises above politics, proving its neutrality.[47] Second, integrity and coherence make the adjudication transparent, allowing public contestation of the manner in which the tribunal handles the legal material.[48]

Incoherent legal interpretation was more common under the old GATT dispute settlement procedure, when, unbound by previous decisions, panels used frequently to turn the GATT doctrine into a moving target. For example, in the *Tuna* cases the panel was inconsistent in the interpretation of the Article XX environmental exception.[49] The type of inconsistency at the heart of this discussion arises from the approach of panels towards the consultation of specific international organizations in dispute settlement. This is well illustrated in *Argentina – Textiles and Apparel*, where the Panel decided to consult the IMF pursuant to DSU Article 13, whereas in a previous similar case this had been done under GATT Article XV. As illustrated in more detail in Chapter 6 below, this was counterproductive, as consultation does not have the same effect under these two WTO provisions.[50]

The GATT practice was, however, streamlined with the advent of the WTO dispute settlement system, where the Appellate Body did much to bring about more consistency in legal interpretation. This was achieved with its insistence on moving away from the 'originalist' GATT approach towards a more 'textualist' interpretation, which took account of the ordinary meaning of the words in their context.[51] According to the Appellate Body, this was justified by the incorporation of the VCLT customary rule of interpretation into the DSU, which supports taking the words as the necessary starting point for an interpretative exercise.[52] The current dispute settlement system, however, is still far from perfection when it comes to integrity and consistency in interpretation.

2. Inconsistent interpretation as a problem for institutional sensitivity

While the institutional sensitivity of the WTO adjudicator is the main focus of this study, the integrity and coherence of legal interpretation

47 See Helfer and Slaughter, 'Toward a Theory', at 312–14.
48 See Philip M. Nichols, 'GATT Doctrine', (1966) 36 *Virginia Journal of International Law* 379, at 383–4.
49 For an account of these inconsistencies see Howse, 'Legitimacy', at 384–5.
50 See below Chapter 6, section III, for an evaluation of this issue.
51 Howse, 'Legitimacy', at 385.
52 See above Chapter 3 on the application of these rules in WTO dispute settlement.

also bear significantly on the realization of this proposition. This would be the case when, for example, in a WTO dispute the panel showed sensitivity towards an international organization, but the approach was departed from by subsequent panels in comparable circumstances. Furthermore, the level of institutional sensitivity may be impaired by an inconsistent interpretation of WTO provisions supporting linkages with other international organizations. One such example, which relates to the legal provision used for consulting the IMF, has been provided above in Chapter 2.[53] Another example arises from instances where the panel sought information from other international organizations, although not always citing DSU Article 13 or any other relevant provisions supporting such consultation. This was the case in *Thailand – Cigarettes*, where the Panel sought advice from WHO without reference to any specific provision, despite GATT containing provisions similar to those enshrined in the current DSU Article 13.[54]

Another inconsistency in the application of WTO provisions by the panels or Appellate Body which bears on the institutional sensitivity of the WTO adjudicator arises from its choice to appoint individual experts rather than expert review groups.[55] This formula is viewed as having less potential to garner interactions with intergovernmental organizations because the mandate of the individual experts is less precise and their authority is obviously less compared with that of expert review groups. As a result, the expert review groups would presumably have more prolific exchanges with international organizations in the dispute settlement process – an exercise which would contribute to the objective assessment of the matter by the WTO adjudicator as prescribed by DSU Article 11. Thus the latter option would offer a more institutionally sensitive approach.

Lastly, another example of such inconsistencies arises from how the WTO adjudicator has applied the VCLT rules of interpretation in considering material extraneous to the WTO. It was established above that the identification of acts of international organizations under various VCLT interpretation techniques qualifies their legal value in the interpretation process.[56] A study carried out by Mavroidis showed that the treatment of

53 See above Chapter 2, section II.B.

54 See GATT Art. XXIII(2) and the 1966 Decision of the Contracting Parties, as subsequently amended and codified in the 1979 Understanding Regarding Notification, Consultation, Dispute Settlement and Surveillance.

55 See below Chapter 9, section IV.C.3, for a comprehensive overview of the issue.

56 See above Chapter 3, section II.B.

identical elements has, on occasion, been inconsistent across cases.[57] This indicates clearly that an inconsistent approach in the application of VCLT rules may have the effect of reducing the legal value and significance of this material in WTO dispute settlement.

Thus situations may arise where the institutional sensitivity of the WTO adjudicator in a specific dispute may be regarded as adequate, but subsequent panels do not follow the approach, and do not provide an account of their departure therefrom. In order to make a general claim of institutional sensitivity on behalf of the WTO adjudicator vis-à-vis international organizations, a consistent approach is required.

III. External constraints

In addressing the current constraints on the institutional sensitivity of the WTO adjudicator it is instructive to look beyond the confines of the WTO, namely at the effects of the structure of international public law and its fragmented nature, as well as at the decision making of international organizations. These elements have been termed as external constraints on the institutional sensitivity of the WTO judiciary, and they are examined in detail in this section.

The first set of issues are perceived as originating in specific international regimes and are peculiar to their architecture. For example, in order for the WTO adjudicator legitimately to defer to the interpretations ensuing from international organizations, these would have to be approved authoritatively. This cannot be legitimately done if such structures are absent. Moreover, the lack of such workable systems within the international organizations is frequently accompanied by a weak or even absent dispute settlement mechanism for providing judicial interpretations. Given these limitations, it is natural for the WTO panels or Appellate Body to approach cautiously the interpretative efforts emerging from other international organizations. Finally, the issue of reciprocity with which other international organizations may consider the multilateral trade rules should not be overlooked by the proposal for greater institutional sensitivity on behalf of the WTO adjudicator. Sensitivity is not a one-way street, but is required equally on the part of other institutions vis-à-vis the WTO. In the following, these constraints are elaborated in more detail.

57 Mavroidis, 'No Outsourcing of Law?', at 446.

A. *Authoritative interpretation in international organizations*

The task for authoritative interpretations in international organizations is concerned almost exclusively with finding the meaning of rules set forth in constitutive acts of international organizations or various treaties.[58] There are several possible forums for such interpretation: international tribunals, especially the ICJ; the specialized agencies of the UN; national courts, which are occasionally called on to adjudicate cases in which the specialized agency has not issued an authoritative interpretation of one of its rules; and international arbitration panels.[59]

Authoritative interpretations fit into the category of 'determinations', which are an expression of the law-making function of the international organizations.[60] These determinations, which can also be termed pronouncements, may take the form of resolutions, declarations or decisions and so on, adopted by the competent bodies of the relevant international organizations. The accumulation of these determinations over time through their repetition can be characterized as evidence of the international customs referred to in Article 38(1)(b) of the ICJ Statute. Thus, by virtue of this function, the international organizations can be seen to have an important role in the development of international law.[61]

1. The role of the International Court of Justice

The authoritative interpretations which are of most interest to the WTO relate (although not exclusively) to the field of international economic law. For example the ICJ, which is regarded as the highest authority in international adjudication, has only occasionally been confronted with these issues. Interventions coming from its side were mostly limited to the adjudication of cases on the rights of foreign investors under national law. For the most part, however, the Court has not played an important role in generating rules of international economic law.[62] This is despite its designation in a number of related multilateral agreements as the appropriate authority for issuing authoritative interpretations. For example, several

58 Note that an authoritative interpretation would complement a provision of the primary law – it would determine the interpretation of the relevant provision.

59 See generally Ian Brownlie, *Principles of Public International Law*, 3rd edn (Oxford: Clarendon Press, 1979), at 20–5.

60 White, *Law of International Organizations*, at 178.

61 Müller and Wildhaber, *Praxis des Völkerrechts*, 90.

62 Zamora, 'Economic Relations', at 267, citing Georg Schwarzenberger, 'The Principles and Standards of International Economic Law', (1966/I) 117 *Receuil des Cours d'Academie de Droit International* 1, at 12.

treaties on intellectual property rights, such as the Paris Convention for the Protection of Intellectual Property (Art. 28), the Berne Convention for the Protection of Literary and Artistic Works (Art. 33), the Universal Copyright Convention (Art. XV), and the Patent Co-operation Treaty of June 19, 1970 (Art. 59), state that disputes concerning their interpretation may be brought before the ICJ.

The ICJ authoritative interpretation function stems also from the agreements setting out the relationship between the UN and its specialized agencies, which authorize certain organizations, such as the IMF and WIPO, to seek advisory opinions from the ICJ. Although the ICJ has issued a number of advisory opinions, it has never been asked to render a judgment involving one of the above-mentioned treaties on intellectual property rights.[63] This also holds true for the IMF.

Some reasons have been attributed to the unpopularity of the ICJ in interpreting economic-related subjects:

> First, economic conflicts are particularly adaptable to compromise solutions through negotiation, and networks for international negotiations over conflicting policies have long existed in the economic field . . . Second, the specialized agencies themselves have established enforcement mechanisms that, even if not exclusive, are considered more appropriate than the ICJ for enforcing the agencies' regimes. Finally, some states, especially those whose interests are well represented in the Bretton Woods regime, fear that political considerations may spill over into the adjudication of economic issues before the ICJ.[64]

Although, as correctly mentioned, many agencies have set out their own dispute settlement mechanisms, the problem is that they are not sufficiently efficient or are not as efficient as the WTO dispute settlement mechanism. Apart from serving as a pull for non-trade disputes towards the WTO, the absence of efficient judicial mechanisms in international organizations eclipses the WTO adjudicator's willingness to defer to such interpretative endeavours. The judicial decisions emanating from those systems (where they exist) can hardly be attributed authoritative value. Most dispute settlement provisions of those systems are incorporated

63 Note that Art. 34 of the ICJ Statute declares that only states can be parties to a contentious dispute before the courts. It follows that international organizations cannot be parties as plaintiffs or defendants in such proceedings. International organizations, however, if duly authorized, can request advisory opinions from the Court. See Elihu Lauterpacht, *Aspects of Administration of International Justice* (Cambridge University Press, 1991), at 60.

64 Zamora, 'Economic Relations', at 269.

into various multilateral treaties (e.g. treaties administered by WIPO), referring frequently to the ill-fittedness of the ICJ for this purpose. In the following subsections, a few examples of such systems are analysed in more detail.

2. The International Monetary Fund as a *sui generis* system

The authorization to request advisory opinions from the ICJ was granted to the IMF in the Agreement between the IMF and the UN which entered into force on 15 November 1947. This agreement was concluded pursuant to Article 63 of the UN Charter and Article X of the IMF's Articles. The relevant provision of this Agreement provides that

> The General Assembly of the United Nations hereby authorizes the Fund to request advisory opinions of the International Court of Justice on any legal questions within the scope of the Fund's activities other than questions relating to the relationship between the Fund and the United Nations or any specialized agency.[65]

Although the Fund has been given express authorization to request advisory opinions from the ICJ, it has never done so.[66] The reasons are not difficult to discover. First, although an advisory opinion would not be binding on the IMF, it would be highly embarrassing for the IMF to depart from, or even to qualify, an opinion of the ICJ. Parties can agree that an advisory opinion shall be binding, but the IMF could not make such an agreement or give such an undertaking because this would amount to an abdication of the IMF's function of authoritative interpretation. A second reason for such hesitation is that the ICJ might be less willing to follow a teleological approach to interpretation of the IMF Articles or might not be sufficiently familiar with the purposes and policies of the IMF in order for it to follow a sound teleological approach.[67] Lastly, the average interval between requests and opinions in the practice of the Court has been a substantial number of months, therefore this would not necessarily be a speedy procedure for matters regarded as urgent by international organizations. It is therefore difficult to imagine what type of incentive would induce the IMF to overcome its reservations vis-à-vis

65 Agreement between the IMF and the UN, 15 November 1947, www.imf.org/ external/ pubs/ft/sd/index.asp?decision=DN19 (visited June 2009).

66 See Joseph Gold, *Interpretation: The IMF and International Law* (London: Kluwer, 1996), 241. This authorization was granted in the agreement between the IMF and the UN which entered into force on 15 November 1947. It was concluded pursuant to Art. 63 of the UN Charter and Art. X of the IMF's Articles.

67 Gold, *Interpretation*, 244.

exposure to the ICJ judicial process. Thus the more elevated legalization of the ICJ proceedings apparently brings some degree of discomfort to specialized international organizations.

Notably, the IMF has its own well-functioning authoritative interpretation system binding on the members pursuant to Article XXIX of the Agreement.[68] In the IMF and some other financial organizations, such as the World Bank, interpretative issues are left to the Executive Directors and to the Board of Governors.[69] Article XXIX of the IMF Articles of Agreement explicitly provides that

> Any question of interpretation of the provisions of this Agreement arising between any member and the Fund or between any members of the Fund shall be submitted to the Executive Board for its decision. If the question particularly affects any member not entitled to appoint an Executive Director, it shall be entitled to representation in accordance with Article XII, Section 3(j).[70]

Thus any member may ask that an interpretation by the executive organ be referred to the respective Board of Governors, whose decision is final. Essentially, the IMF interpretative provisions set out rules regarding the terms which should be used in the interpretation process by the relevant bodies (Art. XXX IMF Articles). Given this well-functioning interpretative system, such formal IMF decisions are generally considered binding on national courts and on executive organs of the member states.[71]

Thus the IMF is an organization equipped with a system of internal interpretations that can be cited for its efforts to put in place a *sui generis* practice, which places the responsibility of interpreting the substantive Fund's commitments with the members (as compared with a Secretariat or another body). At first glance, the authoritative interpretation mechanism of the IMF seems to grant considerable power to its Executive Board. However, the mechanism is not all-encompassing as it does not cover all the decisions of the Executive Board; only a few of them have been designated as authoritative interpretations. This point has not always been recognized by courts, which tend to give authoritative recognition

68 White, *Law of International Organizations*, 182.

69 Given the political standing of the executive director of the IMF, as opposed to that of the WIPO Director General, for example, there is a presumption of legitimacy of these interpretations.

70 IMF Articles of Agreement, Art. XXIX(a).

71 Richard Edwards, *International Monetary Collaboration* (New York: Transnational, 1985), 37, n. 165, and authors cited therein.

to Executive Board decisions, and even to pronouncements of the Fund's staff, whether or not the full authority of Article XXIX is employed.[72] Despite this limitation in scope, the system should be commended for its outstanding effort to set out an efficient internal authoritative interpretation mechanism. This, in turn, can only affect positively the perception of this international organization by the WTO adjudicator as well as its sensitivity thereto.

3. Other workable systems

a. The UN specialized agencies. Apart from the IMF, a few other international organizations can be cited for their efforts to set out workable authoritative interpretation systems. A number of international organizations specifically provide in their charters for an authoritative interpretation mechanism which empowers them to interpret constitutional instruments, quasi-legislative acts and subsequent agreements that arise from such instruments. Most of the time, these agencies lack separate adjudicatory bodies for this purpose, and the principal decision-making organ of the agency therefore acts as an interpretative organ. This is the case, for example, with the plenary bodies in the Food and Agriculture Organization (FAO), the International Maritime Organization (IMO), the Organization of African Unity (OAU), and the International Civil Aviation Organization (ICAO). Similarly, some international organizations' charters elaborate internal alternative dispute-settlement or fact-finding mechanisms which permit interpretation of the charters or other treaties within their administration (e.g. the ILO).[73]

Thus the architectural superiority of these institutions should not be overlooked by the WTO judiciary, when their output may be brought to bear on the interpretation process of the WTO obligations. The more elaborate the authoritative interpretation system, the more legitimate the deference of the WTO adjudicator will be. This does not mean, however, that international organizations which do not enact such systems should be isolated. The weakness or absence of such mechanisms will certainly diminish the legal value of the relevant material coming from an international organization, but the WTO adjudicator still can take it into account when relevant.

72 Zamora, 'Economic Relations', at 270, n. 119, citing Joseph Gold, *The Fund Agreement in the Courts III* (Washington, DC: International Monetary Fund, 1986), 656–8.

73 See José E. Alvarez, 'Constitutional Interpretation in International Organizations', in Jean-Marc Coicaud and Veijo Heiskanen (eds.), *The Legitimacy of International Organizations* (New York: United Nations University Press, 2001), 104–49, at 111.

b. The International Tribunal for the Law of the Sea. The UN Convention on the Law of the Sea (UNCLOS) provided for the setting up of what was considered to be an innovative and far-reaching compulsory dispute settlement system – the International Tribunal for the Law of the Sea (ITLOS).[74] The system came under the purview of the international trade community in the context of the WTO *Chile – Swordfish* dispute between the European Union and Chile, and it is frequently cited as an example of the effects of the fragmented system of international law and judicial authorities.[75]

Chile had introduced conservation measures protecting swordfish fishing in the South Pacific, which had not been complied with by the EU. Since the EU believed that the Chilean measures violated Articles V and XI of GATT 1974 dealing with the commercial movement of goods, either in transit, or in access to the local Chilean market, it initiated dispute settlement proceedings before the WTO.[76] In a parallel proceeding, Chile brought a complaint against the EU before ITLOS, arguing that the EU had violated conservation-related obligations under Articles 64 and 116–119 UNCLOS, and also dispute settlement obligations under Articles 297 and 300 UNCLOS. The EU responded with a countercharge that Chile had itself violated these UNCLOS provisions by unilaterally applying its conservation regime. The decision did not take its judicial course, given that the litigants came to a mutual arrangement. The proceedings in both the WTO and ITLOS were not terminated but were continuously suspended through agreement of the parties.[77]

74 See Tommy T. B. Koh, 'A Constitution for the Oceans', Remarks made by the President of the Third United Nations Conference on the Law of the Sea, in Official Text of the United Nations Convention on the Law of the Sea with Annexes and Index (1983) E 83V5, xxxiii. But see Rosemary Rayfuse, 'The Future of Compulsory Dispute Settlement under the Law of the Sea Convention', (2005) 36 *Victoria University of Wellington Law Journal* 28, claiming that the system is not in fact a big success.

75 For a recent account of this dispute see Sabino Cassese, *When Legal Orders Collide: The Role of Courts* (Seville: Global Law Press – Editorial Derecho Global Seville, 2010). See also Marcos Orellana, 'The EU and Chile Suspend the Swordfish Case Proceedings at the WTO and the International Tribunal for the Law of the Sea', ASIL Insights (2001), www.asil.org/insights/insigh60.htm; Marcos Orellana, 'The Swordfish Dispute between the EU and Chile at the ITLOS and the WTO', (2002) 71(1) *Nordic Journal of International Law* 55; John Shamsey, 'ITLOS vs. Goliath: The International Tribunal for the Law of the Sea Stands Tall with the Appellate Body in the Chilean–EU Swordfish Dispute', (2002) 12 *Transnational Law and Contemporary Problems* 513.

76 See Chile – Measures Affecting the Transit and Importation of Swordfish – Request for Consultations by the EC,WT/DS193/1, G/L/367 (26 April 2000).

77 See *Chile – Measures Affecting the Transit and Importation of Swordfish*: Arrangement between the European Communities and Chile, Communication from the EC,

The above account points to the issue of the existence of two distinct international courts – the WTO and ITLOS – where parallel invocation of jurisdication is possible over disputes derived from what was essentially the same set of facts. This is troubling in this case, because the law that would have been applied by each tribunal would have been substantively different, which suggests that the likelihood of reaching substantially different decisions was very high.

This issue relates to a wider problem in international law – that of the proliferation of international tribunals,[78] which may lead to the hassles of forum-shopping as well as to a duplication of proceedings before various forums, involving a waste of judicial resources and contributing to a further fragmentation of international law.[79] These negative implications are evidenced not only in the context of the WTO–ITLOS parallel proceedings in the swordfish disputes but from a number of other high-profile cases, such as the *Tadić* case, the *MOX Plant* Arbitration and Cases, the *CME/Lauder* arbitration, and the *SGS* v. *Pakistan* and *SGS* v. *Philippines* cases.[80]

WT/DS193/3 (6 April 2001), and the approval of the Special Chamber of the ITLOS (see, most recently, ITLOS, *Case Concerning the Conservation and Sustainable Exploitation of Swordfish Stocks in the South-Eastern Pacific Ocean (Chile/European Community)*, Case No 7, Order 2007/3 (30 November 2007).

78 See, e.g, apart from the WTO dispute settlement mechanism, the establishment of specialized courts and tribunals such as the International Tribunal for the Law of The Sea (ITLOS), the International Criminal Court (ICC), the two ad hoc criminal tribunals – for the former Yugoslavia (International Criminal Tribunal for the former Yugoslavia (ICTY)) and for Rwanda (International Criminal Tribunal for Rwanda (ICTR)) – investment arbitration under the International Centre for Settlement of Investment Disputes (ICSID) and other institutionalized or ad hoc dispute settlement rules. At the same time these run in parallel with both the contentious and the advisory jurisdictions of the ICJ.

79 For an account see references in nn. 64 and 74 above. For an assiduously explored idea of 'regime shifting', which is relevant in this context, see Laurence Helfer, 'Regime Shifting: The TRIPS Agreement and New Dynamics of Intellectual Property Lawmaking', (2004) 29 *Yale Journal of International Law* 26.

80 ICTY–ICJ for *Prosecutor* v. *Duško Tadić* (ICTY), Case No. IT-94-1-A, Appeal Judgement, 15 July 1999; UNCLOS–ICJ for *MOX Plant Case (Ireland v. United Kingdom)*, (Order No 4) (Further Suspension of Proceedings on Jurisdiction and Merits) (2003) 42 ILM 1187; two ICSID arbitrations, *SGS Société Générale de Surveillance SA* v. *Islamic Republic of Pakistan* (Decision of the Tribunal on Objections to Jurisdiction), ICSID Case No. ARB/01/13, and *SGS Société Générale de Surveillance SA* v. *Republic of the Philippines* (Decision of the Tribunal on Objections to Jurisdiction), (2005) 8 ICSID Reports 515; UNCITRAL Arbitration Tribunal, *R. S.Lauder* v. *Czech Republic*, (2002) 14 [3] World Trade and Arbitration Materials 35, and UNCITRAL Arbitration Proceedings, *CME Czech Republic BV* v. *The Czech Republic*, Final Award, (2003) 15 [4] World Trade and Arbitration Materials 83.

This suggests that while a lack of authoritative interpretation mechanisms in other international forums casts doubt on the WTO adjudicator's readiness to defer to their interpretative efforts, the existence of other vigorous international tribunals which could validly interpret law brings up yet another concern. The existence of a parallel authority such as ITLOS may exacerbate the problem of non-integrated substantive norms of international law. As is claimed by Tomer Broude, 'had norm integration been standard practice, there would be little point in taking advantage of authority fragmentation through attempts at regime shifting in law-making, whose results would ultimately be integrated in substance'.[81]

B. Examples of weak dispute settlement mechanisms in international organizations

This section points to the fact that the weakness or absence of dispute settlement mechanisms in other international regimes may hamper the willingness of the WTO interpreter to defer to interpretative outcomes emerging therefrom. Many organizations do not have an all-inclusive dispute settlement mechanism comparable to the WTO two-tier judicial system where the Appellate Body streamlines and has the last word in the WTO jurisprudence. The presence of such systems in other international organizations would ascribe to them a certain legal value and determine a more open approach by the WTO adjudicator to deferring to these interpretative outcomes.

1. The World Intellectual Property Organization

As mentioned above, many treaties on intellectual property rights refer to the ICJ for authoritative interpretations. Given that this system is rarely used, there is no doubt that, for example, a WIPO-based authoritative interpretation mechanism for intellectual property obligations will be preferred.[82] There has, however, been little occasion for WIPO to issue authoritative interpretations of substantive rules of international intellectual property protection. One of the reasons for this is that WIPO-administered treaties tend to be procedural in nature (e.g. filing of applications, rights of priority, etc.) and leave the substantive rules of intellectual property rights to domestic law. Thus, it is noted, WIPO does

81 Broude, 'Principles of Normative Integration', at 15.
82 Zamora, 'Economic Relations', at 271, n. 119, citing Gold, *Fund Agreement*, 656–8.

not use the ICJ interpretative mechanism (for one reason or another) and does not provide a workable internal mechanism for this purpose either.

a. Dispute settlement with reference to the International Court of Justice. The above problem is compounded by somewhat weak dispute settlement procedures available within WIPO to provide valid judicial interpretations of the relevant treaties. Thus it offers several dispute settlement options, depending *inter alia* on the treaty under which the matter at issue falls.[83] A number of intellectual property treaties administered by WIPO provide for dispute resolution by resort to the ICJ mechanism. For example, the Berne Convention provides that

> [A]ny dispute between two or more countries of the Union concerning the interpretation or application of this Convention, not settled by negotiation, may, by any one of the countries concerned, be brought before the International Court of Justice by application in conformity with the Statute of the Court, unless the countries concerned agree on some other method of settlement.[84]

As mentioned above, however, states tend to show reluctance to bring their intellectual property disputes to the ICJ due to a number of limitations of the system. This generates some likelihood of introducing non-uniform application of the relevant rules due to the possibility of opting out of certain treaty obligations under the ICJ system. What adds to this is that the claims in these cases concern private parties that would generally be reluctant to have their complaint espoused by states at the ICJ.[85] In fact, at the time of the entry into force of the TRIPS Agreement, this extant channel had never been invoked.[86]

b. Independent dispute settlement systems. As early as 1997 WIPO had convened to examine the preparation of a Draft Treaty on the Settlement of Disputes between States in the Field of Intellectual Property. A most striking aspect of these negotiations within WIPO is that they were being pursued with considerable vigour by many of the same OECD

83 For an account see Hrbatá, 'No International Organization', at 14.

84 Berne Convention, Art. 33. See also Paris Convention, Art. 28, and Patent Co-operation Treaty, Art. 59, using identical language.

85 Edward Kwakwa, 'Some Comments on Rulemaking at the World Intellectual Property Organization', (2002) 12 *Duke Journal of Comparative & International Law* 179, n. 26. See also Hrbatá, 'No International Organization', at 14.

86 Abbott, 'Future of the Multilateral Trading System', at 358.

governments that had moved the centre of gravity of international property rights from WIPO to the WTO.[87] In spite of these efforts, this system was never agreed in WIPO, even on matters limited to registration of patent, trademark and design rights under the respective international co-operation agreements.[88] Thus Article 30 of the draft Patent Law Treaty, which provided for consultation, alternative dispute resolution and the possibility of a report being prepared by a panel, was clearly missing from the version which was finally adopted.[89]

One WIPO treaty does, however, incorporate a dispute settlement system similar to that of the WTO, and that is the Washington Treaty on Intellectual Property in Respect of Integrated Circuits. The treaty has not yet come into force, but, on this happening, indications are that it will nonetheless be of limited significance. The dispute settlement under this treaty resembles the GATT rather than the WTO, in that it requires consensus of the General Assembly for the adoption of panel reports and contains no follow-up in terms of the possibility of cross-retaliation in case of non-compliance.[90]

The above constraints do not hold true, however, for WIPO's alternative dispute settlement resolution, which has evolved into a well-functioning system for commercial disputes related to intellectual property. Thus any person or entity whose interests have been affected may resort to the procedures of arbitration or expedited arbitration, mediation, and expert determination rendered by the WIPO Arbitration and Mediation Centre. The Centre also takes on its roll disputes in the area of domain names relating to abusive registration and use of internet domain names ('cybersquatting').[91] This system has been characterized as a quick and efficient one which could be extended to other types of dispute resolution.[92] For the time being, however, the system is limited and cannot really compete with the WTO dispute settlement system, which is much wider in scope, adjudicating more categories of intellectual property rights. Thus, unlike the WTO, WIPO does not currently provide an efficient all-encompassing intergovernmental dispute settlement system covering all administered treaties.

87 Abbott et al., *International Intellectual Property System*, at 364–5.

88 Cottier, 'Agreement on Trade-Related Aspects', at 1110.

89 Cordray, 'GATT v. WIPO', at 132.

90 Hrbatá, 'No International Organization', at 14.

91 WIPO, *The WIPO Arbitration and Mediation Center: Dispute Resolution for the 21st Century*, WIPO Publication No. 779E, www.wipo.int/freepublications/en/arbitration/779/wipo_pub_779.pdf.

92 Hrbatá, 'No International Organization', at 15.

Apart from offering judicial interpretations which could be relied on by the WTO panels or Appellate Body, an independent WIPO adjudication system would certainly have a number of other advantages.[93] One of these relates to the fact that not all WIPO members are WTO members and not all intellectual property treaties are covered by the WTO dispute settlement mechanism. WIPO nowadays administers twenty-four treaties in the intellectual property area; the WTO TRIPS Agreement only incorporates the substantive provisions of a few of those WIPO Agreements. Similarly, not all intellectual property disputes are subject to resolution through the WTO dispute settlement system. For example, Article 9 of the TRIPS Agreement expressly excludes moral rights from its purview.[94] Lastly, and most importantly, the creation of a dispute settlement forum outside the WTO might permit states to resolve intellectual property rights-related disputes in an environment less politically charged than the WTO, where the stakes of dispute settlement are often amplified by intense media scrutiny and domestic political pressures on the litigants.[95]

As illustrated above, proposals on the creation of an independent WIPO dispute resolution system proved controversial, since they did not address the key issue – that is, the consequences for this system of the initiation of dispute settlement. One constraint was posed by the fact that many delegations sought to ensure that WTO dispute settlement was given priority within its sphere of application. Another reason why these negotiations did not bring results was due to the consolidation of the WTO enforcement mechanism covering substantive intellectual property obligations as incorporated into the TRIPS Agreement. The absence of such a system within WIPO and the non-use of the ICJ system indicate a lack of judicial norms which interpret the administered treaties by a competent body.[96]

93 See, e.g., a call for the strengthening of intellectual property right protection, including with regard to dispute resolution – United States General Accounting Office, Report to Selected Congressional Subcommittee, International Trade: Strengthening Worldwide Protection of Intellectual Property Rights, April 1987, GAO/NSIAD-87–65.

94 TRIPS Art. 9(1) provides: 'Members shall comply with Articles 1 through 21 of the Berne Convention (1971) and the Appendix thereto. However, Members shall not have rights or obligations under this Agreement in respect of the rights conferred under Art. 6bis of that Convention or of the rights derived therefrom.' Art. 6*bis* of the Berne Convention concerns the moral rights of authors, namely to claim authorship, to object to certain modifications and other derogatory actions, and means of redress.

95 Abbott et al., *International Intellectual Property System*, 365.

96 Although WIPO has failed to establish such a system, it has been quite successful in implementing the dispute settlement rules established for the enforcement of the Internet

This is believed to affect the credibility of this institution in the eyes of the WTO judiciary and their willingness to defer to such interpretative outcomes.[97]

2. The World Health Organization

WHO's architecture also reveals weaknesses on the enforcement side. Neither the WHO Constitution nor the International Health Regulations (IHR) attributes enforcement powers to WHO arising in connection with violations of binding rules of international health law.[98] As noted by one commentator, the widespread violation of IHR regulations without any enforcement mechanism has led to a situation where 'many legally binding Regulations tend to be treated in practice almost as recommendations',[99] that is, as non-binding instruments. As with WIPO, the ICJ advisory system is also available to WHO. Unlike WIPO, however, WHO has resorted to the system on several occasions. For example, WHO sought an advisory opinion from the ICJ, asking it to rule that any use of nuclear weapons would violate international law because of the adverse health consequences that would result from such use.[100]

On 23 May 2005, the World Health Assembly adopted the new IHR 2005 as an international treaty which entered into force in June 2007.[101] This step concluded the decade-long effort led by WHO to revise the old regulations (IHR 1969) in order to make them more effective against global disease threats. Originally adopted in 1951 and substantially changed in 1969, the IHR had lost their effectiveness and relevance by the mid 1990s,

domain names. But see Christopher May, *The World Intellectual Property Organization: Resurgence and the Development Agenda* (London: Routledge, 2007), 60–1, for a criticism of how WIPO implements this system.

97 For a detailed account of the role attributed to WIPO in WTO dispute settlement see below Chapter 7.

98 David P. Fidler, 'Return of the Fourth Horseman: *Emerging Infectious Diseases* and International Law', (1997) 81 *Minnesota Law Review* 771, at 847–9, discussing the problem of WHO's enforcement power.

99 David M. Leive, *International Regulatory Regimes: Case Studies in Health, Meteorology and Food*, vol. 1 (Lexington, MA: Lexington Books, 1976), 46.

100 ICJ, *Legality of the Threat or Use of Nuclear Weapons (Request of the UN General Assembly)*, Advisory Opinion, 8 July 1996, [1996] ICJ Rep. 679. For an analysis of the ICJ's ruling in this case, see generally Chittharanjan F. Amerasinghe, 'The Advisory Opinion of the International Court of Justice in the WHO Nuclear Weapons Case: A Critique', 10 *Leiden Journal of International Law* 525 (1997).

101 WHO, 'Application of the International Health Regulations (2005)', WHO Doc. WHA59.2, 26 May 2006 (Fifty-Ninth World Health Assembly), 2.

if not earlier.[102] The proposals put forward during the IHR negotiations had also taken up the idea of a WHO dispute settlement mechanism,[103] which saw the setting up of a Committee of Arbitration to settle disputes between WHO members over the interpretation or application of the IHR. This body is mandated to make international legal decisions and develop its own body of 'case law'. Thus the IHR 2005 eliminates the option for WHO members to submit disputes concerning the interpretation or application of the IHR to the ICJ; it replaces the ICJ procedure with arbitration in accordance with the Permanent Court of Arbitration Optional Rules for Arbitrating Disputes between States (IHR 2005 Art. 56(3)).

The amendment envisages WHO getting involved in interpreting IHR regulations. As a result, it would find itself in the realm of treaty interpretation under the rules embodied in the VCLT. These features are novel, as treaty interpretation is commonplace for the ICJ or for dispute settlement panels of the WTO, but historically not for any significant part of WHO's activities.[104]

The disadvantage of the new system is that IHR 2005 does not prescribe the establishment of a compulsory dispute settlement system at WHO. Non-compliance by a member state is not actionable unless that state volunteers to bind itself by a dispute settlement process.[105] Despite these limitations, the emergence of this system is a positive development, since the WTO adjudicator could count on an emerging body of health 'case law' and judicial norm interpretation, which could be validly relied on.

3. The World Customs Organization

The WCO also does not have an all-encompassing dispute settlement system. As with the intellectual property rights conventions under WIPO,

102 For an overview see Michael G. Baker and David P. Fidler, 'Global Public Health Surveillance under New International Health Regulations', (2005) 12 *Emerging Infectious Diseases* 1058.

103 See WHO, Revision of the International Health Regulations: Progress Report (Report by the Director-General), WHO Doc. A51/8, 10 March 1998, para. 7.

104 David P. Fidler, 'The Future of the World Health Organization: What Role for International Law?' (1998) 31 *Vanderbilt Journal of Transnational Law* 1078, at 1108.

105 David P. Fidler, 'From International Sanitary Conventions to Global Health Security: The New International Health Regulations', (2005) 4 *Chinese Journal of International Law* 325, at 333. See also Murray, 'Implementing', noting the weakness in the implementation of the new IHRs and suggesting enforcing them through the SPS Committee, interpreting parts of the new IHR as international standards within the SPS Agreement.

disputes are subject to specific provisions enshrined in the administered conventions. The WCO Convention on the Harmonized Commodity Description and Coding System (HS Convention) is the treaty with the greatest relevance to the WTO, given the decision of the WTO members to use the classification of goods provided therein.[106] Article 10(3) of the HS Convention prescribes that '[i]f the Harmonized System Committee is unable to settle the dispute, it shall refer the matter to the Council which shall make recommendations in conformity with Article III(e) of the Convention establishing the Council'. Furthermore, '[t]he Parties to the dispute may agree in advance to accept the recommendations of the Committee or the Council as binding' (Art. 10(4)).

One of the peculiarities of the system is its uniform application all over the world. The economic implications of this classification differ from country to country, as the same product may be subject to varying duty systems. For this reason, and given the technical nature of the Harmonized System, disputes in the HS Committee are settled purely from a classification point of view.[107] Due to reliance of the WTO on the HS Convention for scheduling the commitments in goods of its members, the HS dispute settlement decisions may have a significant impact on the decision of the WTO adjudicator. The mere existence of such a body of case law suggests that, where relevant, WTO panels should not hesitate in giving weight to these classification decisions.[108]

Apart from the HS system, the WCO administers about eighteen other treaties which also contain a dispute settlement system clause. These provisions are similar throughout all the conventions, and the dispute settlement provisions therein are non-binding; an express case-by-case agreement between the members would be required in order to make it binding. This suggests that members have the option not to comply with the final decisions on these disputes, something which certainly detracts from the value of these decisions as references for the WTO panels or Appellate Body. Nonetheless, the presence of such a practice may turn out to be useful to the panels when discussing issues falling within the scope of these conventions. Given the specific voting procedures provided

106 On the reference to the HS Convention in WTO dispute settlement see above Chapter 3, section III.A.1, and below Chapter 8, section III.A, for detailed analyses.

107 See WCO, www.wcoomd.org/home_wco_topics_hsoverviewboxes.htm (visited May 2009).

108 But see below Chapter 8, section IV.C, for the possible implication of the use of the HS dispute settlement by WTO members.

for in these WCO-administered conventions, the decisions arising from the settlement of these disputes acquire more legitimacy.[109]

4. The Codex Alimentarius Commission, the OIE and the International Plant Protection Convention

The WTO linkage with the SPS standard-setting organizations (Codex, OIE, IPPC) is premised on a different basis than that with other international organizations investigated above. As explained, these organizations emerged in the WTO through the SPS Agreement, which bases the legality of trade measures on compliance with the standards emerging from these organizations.[110] This means that in WTO disputes the panels may be confronted with the complex language of the standards, which may require further interpretation. While the WTO judiciary will apply the VCLT rules of interpretation to establish the meaning of the interpreted terms, it is important to understand whether these international organizations have internal interpretative or judicial mechanisms which can be referred to by the panels or Appellate Body.

Unlike the Codex, the OIE and the IPPC have an internal dispute settlement mechanism. The OIE process is initiated on mutual agreement of the parties and its outcome is legally binding only if both parties agree in advance to this effect.[111] The OIE system is perceived as offering a number of advantages[112] and it is certainly less costly than the WTO dispute settlement system. Moreover, it allows the settling of disputes of great technical complexity using a process which is less politically charged. The OIE's reports would not just condemn a specific measure; they would also propose alternative measures. Despite these advantages, the OIE's disputes system has hardly been used. Some explain this unpopularity by

109 See e.g. the Customs Convention on the ATA (Admission Temporaire/Temporary Admission) carnet for the temporary admission of goods, Art. 19.2: 'Any dispute which is not settled by negotiation shall be referred by the Contracting Parties in dispute to the Contracting Parties, meeting in conformity with Article 18 of the present Convention, which shall thereupon consider the dispute and make recommendations for its settlement.' To this end, Art. 18.3 therein prescribes: 'The Contracting Parties shall lay down the rules of procedure for their meetings. Decisions of the Contracting Parties shall be taken by a majority of not less than two-thirds of the Contracting Parties present at the meeting and voting.'

110 See above Chapter 2, section III, B. For suggestions on specific roles which can be assumed by these organizations in the WTO disputes see below Chapter 9.

111 OIE, Terrestrial Animal Health Code, Art. 1(2)(1)(3); OIE, Aquatic Animal Health Code (10th edn, 2007), Art. 1(4)(1)(3).

112 See WTO, SPS Committee, OIE Dispute Mediation Process, Communication from the World Organization for Animal Health (OIE) of 12 October 2006, G/SPS/GEN/731.

the existence of the competing WTO dispute settlement process, which has been very successful in adjudicating SPS disputes.[113]

The IPPC also provides a dispute settlement mechanism with respect to interpretation and application of the Convention.[114] Like the WTO dispute settlement system, the IPPC establishes a consultation mechanism between the parties to be resorted to as a first step in this process. If the consultation fails, the parties may request the Director General of the Food and Agriculture Organization (FAO) to designate a committee composed of five members, two of whom are appointed by the parties.[115] Their decisions are non-binding, however, and parties may choose whether to comply. While the report can be disclosed only to the parties of the dispute, the bodies of international organizations responsible for settling trade disputes (WTO panels and the Appellate Body) may request the report.[116] Despite these advantages, at the time of writing the IPPC system has never been used. However, the recent approval of the IPPC Dispute Settlement Manual illustrates the effort of this organization to popularize the system. The WTO adjudicator would benefit if this endeavour was successful. The body of case law and interpretations emerging from the IPPC adjudication would be very useful in the settlement of phytosanitary disputes brought to the WTO.

Despite their non-binding nature, the mere provision for a dispute settlement system mechanism by the OIE and the IPPC is an important achievement for these systems. This will give more weight to their pronouncements, which cannot pass unobserved by the WTO adjudicator. The Codex, regrettably, does not provide for such an option. This deficiency will most likely overshadow its significance as a source of judicial norm interpretation in the WTO adjudication process. This does not mean, however, that the Codex has no role to play in the WTO dispute settlement process.[117]

C. The issue of reciprocity

Lastly, the institutional sensitivity of the WTO adjudicator cannot be characterized without consideration of whether the WTO is being taken

113 Gruszczynski, *Regulating Health.* 114 IPPC, Art. XIII.

115 WTO, SPS Committee, IPPC Dispute Settlement Manual, Submission by the Secretariat of the International Plant Protection Convention, 22 June 2007, G/SPS/GEN/787, at 12.

116 Ibid., at 16.

117 See Chapter 9 below, illustrating the advantages from interactions with Codex in WTO dispute settlement.

into account by other international organizations. The idea of reciprocity has also been entrenched in the comity doctrine discussed in Chapter 1 above, which shares common elements with the concept of institutional sensitivity.[118] As illustrated, the comity doctrine captures the reciprocal deference that institutions should have for one another.[119] With the exclusion of the WTO from the assessment of whether its values such as free trade, open markets and tariff reductions should be accounted for in other forums, the concept of institutional sensitivity risks remaining one-dimensional. The principle of reciprocity is already to some extent being applied by WTO bodies in the examination of requests for observership by other international organizations. The consideration of this principle should be replicated at other stages of its decision making, such as in the dispute settlement, in deciding the extent to which the output of the relevant international organizations can be brought to bear on the WTO interpretation process.

Thus in the assessment of whether the international organizations concerned are sensitive to the WTO law and policies, one may look at the extent to which the WTO is present and invited to the relevant forums. Other factors to be considered are its prerogatives deriving from the observer or other status, the degree of consideration of trade policies in the international organization's decision making and, more generally, the extent to which the other international organization perceives the WTO as a legitimate organization. It is not always the case that international organizations have been supportive of WTO policies. The most prominent example that comes to mind is the rather critical approach evidenced in the human rights regime towards the WTO. The latter has been heavily criticized in a number of reports produced by the UN Sub-commission on the Promotion and Protection of Human Rights.[120] These documents

118 Above Chapter 1, section III.B.3.

119 Kelly, 'Power, Linkage and Accommodation', at 93.

120 See UN Sub-Commission on the Promotion and Protection of Human Rights, Globalization and its Impact on the Full Enjoyment of all Human Rights (Resolution 2001/5), 25th meeting, 15 August 2001, http://attac.org/nonewround/doc/doc08.htm; UN Sub-commission on the Promotion and Protection of Human Rights, Liberalization of Trade in Services, and Human Rights (Resolution 2001/4), 25th meeting, 15 August 2001, http://attac.org/nonewround/doc/doc07.htm; UN Sub-commission on the Promotion and Protection of Human Rights, Intellectual Property and Human Rights (Resolution 2001/21), 26th meeting, 16 August 2001, http://attac.org/nonewround/doc/doc06.htm. See also Joseph Oloka-Onyango and Deepika Udagama, 'The Realization of Economic, Social and Cultural Rights: Globalization and its Impact on the Full Enjoyment of Human Rights' (Preliminary Report), Sub-Commission on the Promotion and

raised concerns about several factors which allegedly have a negative impact on human rights. According to the rapporteurs,

> [T]he assumptions on which the rules of WTO are based are grossly unfair and even prejudiced. Those rules also reflect an agenda that serves only to promote dominant corporatist interests that already monopolize the arena of international trade.[footnote omitted] The rules assume an equality of bargaining power between all the countries that engage in trade. They are also designed on the basis of a premise that ignores the fact that the greater percentage of global trade is controlled by powerful multinational enterprises. Within such a context, the notion of free trade on which the rules are constructed is a fallacy.[121]

Since the WTO does not make reference to human rights principles, 'the WTO is a veritable nightmare' in their view.[122] The rapporteurs have faulted several aspects of the WTO Agreements, including their dispute settlement and patenting issues, particularly of life forms and plant varieties.[123] The report calls for a 'radical review of the whole system of trade liberalization' and critical procedures, the TRIPS Agreement and consideration of whether it is geared towards shared benefits 'for rich and poor countries alike'.[124]

This overly critical assessment by the UN Sub-commission on the Promotion and Protection of Human Rights did not remain without a response from the WTO. The head of the WTO expressed concern 'with the language, methodology and main conclusions of the report'.[125] He countered the allegations therein with solid arguments, noting *inter alia* 'that the WTO rules were negotiated and agreed by consensus by all WTO members, including developing countries who make up two-thirds of the membership', and that it would be difficult to understand why a large number of the WTO membership would engage in a process where they would have to abide by unfair rules.[126]

Protection of Human Rights, 15 June 2000, www.unhchr.ch/huridocda/huridoca.nsf/2848af408d01ec0ac1256609004e770b/21a92d3d0425a0cec125693500484d2f?OpenDocument&Highlight=2 ,Oloka-Onyango (last visited March 2010).

121 Oloka-Onyango and Udagama, 'Realization of Economic, Social and Cultural Rights', para. 14.

122 Consequently, the report became known as the 'Nightmare Report'. Marceau, 'Dispute Settlement', n. 2.

123 Oloka-Onyango and Udagama, 'Realization of Economic, Social and Cultural Rights', para. 18.

124 Ibid., para. 19. 125 Ibid.

126 Ibid. For a more detailed account of the exchanges between the two institutions on the above-mentioned report see Raghavan Chakravarthi, 'WTO Concerned over Human

IV. Conclusions

In this chapter the internal and external constraints on the proposal for greater institutional sensitivity by the WTO adjudicator were examined. Regarding the internal constraints, it has been established that a number of relevant WTO provisions need clarification and that there should be more consistency in the judicial decision making. Moreover, the level of institutional sensitivity of the WTO panels or the Appellate Body will be largely determined by the political orientation of the WTO as to whether it should follow the trade paradigm or also embrace other values and interests.

The external constraints pose far greater challenges, since they are beyond the control of the WTO. Apart from the alleged politicization of their decision-making process, most international organizations lack the architecture to enable them to provide authoritative interpretations of their charters, treaties or other instruments. Frequently, their founding charters do not formally assign this power to any entity, whether policy-making or judicial.[127] Even the resort to the ICJ in the UN system is hampered by its limited mandate to provide non-binding advisory opinions, not to mention the reluctance of international organizations to use the system. Therefore, interpretation endeavours in international organizations may end up with various institutional bodies or the secretariats – a process which does not fully withstand the legitimacy checks of the WTO. This in turn may affect the weight which will be ascribed to these interpretative outcomes by the WTO adjudicator, limiting their importance.

Thus some caution needs to be exercised by the WTO adjudicator when deferring to non-authoritative acts of international organizations, particularly in deciding on the legal value to be attributed to such material. This is not to say, however, that the international organizations' material should be completely disregarded on these grounds. The non-authoritative (or unofficial) interpretations may play an important part in the discharge of the panels' mandate on the objective assessment of the matter. Moreover, a vast range of the material could help panels to clarify purely factual matters. Interpretative issues in some of these

Rights Appraisal Report', TWN, Geneva, 27 August 2000, available at www.twnside.org.sg/title/appraisal.htm (last visited April 2010); see also Someshwar Singh, 'UN Human Rights Commissioner Responds to the WTO', Geneva, 29 August 2000, www.twnside.org.sg/title/responds.htm (last visited April 2010).

127 See Alvarez, 'Constitutional Interpretation', at 111.

international organizations are dealt with more formally through internal dispute settlement mechanisms arising under specific treaties (e.g. WHO, WCO, OIE, IPPC). Although these systems are generally characterized by weak enforcement, the decisions emerging from this process may be valuable and relevant for the WTO adjudicator. Finally, the degree of the WTO adjudicator's institutional sensitivity will also be affected by the reciprocity revealed by other international organizations in their perceptions and acceptance of the WTO system.

5

The competence and credibility of international organizations

I. Introduction

The lack of authoritative interpretation mechanisms within or reciprocity from international organizations is not however, the only external limitation which may affect the institutional sensitivity of the WTO judiciary. The vertical sensitivity standard defined in Chapter 1 above singles out prerequisites such as the competence and credibility of the external actors whose determinations may come within the purview of the WTO panels or Appellate Body.[1] There is no guidance, however, in the WTO on how compliance with these prerequisites is to be assessed, let alone on their application on the horizontal axis, which would apply to international organizations.

Against this background, this chapter points to some elements which may come to bear on the assessment of the credibility and competence of international organizations in WTO dispute settlement.[2] It starts by illustrating those factors which are assumed to raise positive presumption in favour of the competence and credibility of international organizations in the WTO (section II). Given the significance of the SPS standard-setting organizations in the WTO and the intensity with which they have been scrutinized, these have been selected for the examples. Selecting these examples will illustrate how some alleged imperfections

1 See above Chapter 1, section III.A.

2 It should be noted that the competence and credibility assessment of international organizations discussed in this chapter is somewhat similar to the theme of 'good governance' in international organizations. The latter concept is characterized by a number of attributes such as participation, transparency, responsibility, accountability and responsiveness. These can be validly drawn from in order to buttress the list of prerequisites analysed in this chapter. For an important contribution on this theme see Ngaire Woods, 'Good Governance in International Organizations', (1999) 5 *Global Governance* 39. See also the UN Economic and Social Commission for Asia and the Pacific (ESCAP), 'What is Good Governance?', www.unescap.org/pdd/prs/ProjectActivities/Ongoing/gg/governance.pdf (visited 22 May 2009).

in the decision making of the relevant international organizations may affect the perception of their competence and credibility in the eyes of the WTO adjudicator (section III). Although these factors give an idea of why the WTO panels or Appellate Body may be cautious in their consideration of the output of international organizations, it is essential to note that this type of assessment should not be carried out in the dispute settlement process. The WTO subsidiary bodies are more suitable for this purpose, and the judicial institutions should rely on their experience in dealing with various international organizations (section IV). This analysis is followed by some concluding remarks (section V).

II. Positive presumption in favour of an international organization

A. *Specific mention in the WTO legal texts*

The WTO linkages with other international organizations arise from explicit or implicit WTO treaty language in a variety of contexts.[3] These linkages arise, for example, from a number of non-trade values which have permeated the WTO treaty language – mostly through general and ambiguous terms. Thus the concerns for full employment, optimal use of the world's resources and preservation of the environment, enshrined in the Preamble of the WTO Agreement, link implicitly to a number of international regimes and their responsible institutions. Although these organizations may not be specifically mentioned in the WTO Agreements, they emerge in various WTO Ministerial Conferences where members proposed to examine these linkages. One example is the ILO, which is being discussed in the context of the debates on linkages between trade and labour standards.[4] This also holds true for environmental concerns, which although mentioned in the Preamble, are not actually cited in relation to specific administering organizations, such as UNEP. Despite this limitation, UNEP is widely present in WTO activity.[5]

3 See above Chapter 2. The WTO website provides that co-operation between the following organizations and the WTO is specifically mandated in WTO agreements, ministerial declarations or decisions, or General Council decisions: Codex Alimentarius, FAO, ILO, IMF, IPPC, ITU, ITC, OECD, UN, UNCTAD, UNEP, World Bank, WCO, WHO, OIE, WIPO. WTO, www.WTO.org/english/thewto_e/coher_e/coher_e.htm (visited August 2009).

4 This holds true for the Singapore (1996), Seattle (1999) and Doha (2000) Ministerial Conferences. WTO, www.WTO.org/english/thewto_e/coher_e/WTO_ilo_e.htm (visited August 2009).

5 Since 1995 UNEP has been an observer of the WTO Committee on Trade and Environment, and the two organizations have, in particular, worked closely in the context of

Thus the fact that some intergovernmental institutions (or treaty bodies) are not specifically mentioned in the WTO Agreements does not mean that they are not present in the WTO and are therefore underestimated. The absence of a specific mention may also relate to the fact that some international organizations built linkages with the WTO after the conclusion of the Uruguay Round, as the WTO members acknowledged the importance of taking account of values other than trade. Moreover, specific international organizations were mentioned not in the WTO Agreements but in subsequent Ministerial Declarations or Decisions. Another reason for non-reference to specific international organizations in the WTO treaty text might be that, at the time of the creation of the WTO, the architecture of some international organizations was too insubstantial and weak for them to gain specific recognition in the WTO Agreements. UNEP, for example, was historically perceived as 'weak, underfunded and ineffective',[6] bringing about a call to establish the World Environmental Organization.[7] Finally, those regimes might not have been preoccupied with burning issues when the WTO was created.

However, as a result of consolidation over time, either through structural reforms or successful appropriation of new and stringent regulation areas, some international organizations may now have a claim of competence and credibility in their field of regulation and relevance to the trade regime. The Convention on Biological Diversity (CBD) and its Cartagena Protocol on Biosafety are the best examples. Many are already actively participating in the WTO bodies as observers, while the applications of others are still pending approval.[8] The WTO should not neglect the importance

capacity-building activities to raise awareness on the linkages between trade, the environment and sustainable development, and to promote greater dialogue between trade and environment policymakers. The WTO has also participated in sessions of the UNEP Governing Council. WTO, www.WTO.org/english/thewto_e/coher_e/WTO_unep_e.htm (visited August 2009).

6 'Delivering as One', Report of the High-level Panel on United Nations System-wide Coherence, Doc. No. A/61/583, paras. 37, 39.

7 See Julie Ayling, 'Serving Many Voices: Progressing Calls for an International Environmental Organisation', (1997) 9 *Journal of Environmental Law* 243; Steve Charnovitz, 'A World Environment Organization', (2002) 27 *Columbia Journal of Environmental Law* 323; Sebastian Oberthür and Thomas Gehring, 'Reforming International Environmental Governance: An Institutionalist Critique of the Proposal for a World Environment Organisation', (2004) 4 *International Environmental Agreements: Politics Law and Economics* 359; Frank Biermann and Steffen Bauer (eds.), *A World Environment Organization: Solution or Threat for Effective International Environmental Governance?* (Aldershot: Ashgate, 2005).

8 See above Chapter 2, section IV.B.

and standing of these institutions in the WTO even if the Agreements do not refer to them.[9]

B. The universality of international organizations

It is further claimed that presumption in favour of the credibility and competence of international organizations is stronger in the case of universal international organizations, as opposed to closed or regional organizations.[10] It would be difficult to disregard the fact that the IMF, for example, through its universality acquires a special place in the politics of world economic relations, in particular with regard to financial and monetary aspects. This organization (as well as the World Bank) can claim a virtually universal membership and accountability to governments across the world. In this the IMF is different from most other international financial institutions, such as the Group of Seven (G-7), the Bank for International Settlements (BIS), the Group of Ten (G-10), and a host of other regulatory agencies. The IMF's claim to universal membership underpinned its recent insistence that deliberations on any reform of the global financial system should take place within the Fund's Interim Committee, as opposed to any ad hoc or US-selected groups of countries.[11] Moreover, the position of the IMF's Secretariat is stronger than that of other financial institutions.[12] This is also the case when the IMF is compared with many other international organizations, given that its members place greater reliance on the expert knowledge of staff. The World Bank is an even better example, considering the key role of its staff in the gathering and processing of economic data, and the negotiating

9 Positive presumption arises obviously with respect to international organizations which have concluded co-operation agreements or memoranda of understanding with the WTO. See above Chapter 2, section IV.A.

10 Henry G. Schermers, 'The International Organizations', in Mohammed Bedjaoui, *International Law: Achievements and Prospects* (Paris and Dordrecht: UNESCO, Martinus Nijhoff, 1991), 67–100, at 69, paras. 11–12, explaining that universal international organizations are those striving for universal membership, aiming at making rules for the entire world, and trying to expand their membership as widely as possible. The most important organizations in this category are the United Nations, the sixteen specialized agencies brought into relationship with the UN in accordance with the provisions of Art. 63 of the UN Charter and three other organizations related to the UN.

11 Ngaire Woods, 'The Challenge of Good Governance for the IMF and the World Bank Themselves', (2000) 28 *World Development* 823, at 823. She is of the view, however, that the Bretton Woods institutions need to reconsider the grounds on which they claim to be universal, representative and accountable organizations.

12 Schermers and Blokker, *International Institutional Law*, at 318–32.

of loan agreements, being instrumental in implementing development programmes.[13]

As regards WIPO, its universality and the wide coverage of various intellectual property rights allow for its claim of competence in articulating international intellectual property norms.[14] This role is also confirmed by the negotiating history of the TRIPS Agreement. The Uruguay Round could not have produced the TRIPS Agreement without WIPO's participation in the identification of generally accepted international norms.[15] The above applies also to WHO, which has a primary claim on international health regulation, and the WCO – the widest and best-adapted forum for discussing customs and goods classification issues.[16]

Finally, the universality of international organizations raises positive presumption for another reason, which is the likelihood of such international organizations having a membership largely overlapping with that of the WTO. This fact reduces the risks of emergence of non-uniform obligations applying to the same state, when WTO judicial institutions take account of the rules of these international organizations in their interpretation process.

13 Ibrahim F. I. Shihata, *The World Bank in a Changing World: Selected Essays* (The Hague: Nijhoff, 1991), at 171.

14 But see the criticism levelled at WIPO in May, p. 153 n. 96. See also Dreyfuss and Lowenfeld, 'Two Achievements', at 294–5, who point to WIPO's over-politicized deliberation which has interfered with its law-making functions. They claim that one principal reason that intellectual property wound up in the WTO was that WIPO had become unable to keep its treaties responsive to the needs of the innovation community.

15 International Bureau of WIPO, Existence Scope and Form of Generally Internationally Accepted and Applied Standards/Norms for the Protection of Intellectual Property, GATT, MTN.GNG/-NG11/W/24 Rev. 1; WIPO, WO/INF29, September 1988; see Gail E. Evans, 'Intellectual Property as a Trade Issue – The Making of the Agreement on Trade-Related Aspects of Intellectual Property Rights', (1994) 18 *World Competition, Law and Economics Review* 137, at 168.

16 On some criticism levelled at the WHO prior to the adoption of the IHR 2005 see Fidler, 'Future of the World Health Organization', at 1090. He notes that, regrettably, the WHO has achieved neither maximum protection against the international spread of diseases nor minimum interference with world traffic. He notes that the global surveillance system broke down because (i) WHO member states routinely failed to report required information to the WHO, and (ii) the focus on only three diseases proved inadequate to support a proper global surveillance system for infectious diseases. WHO member states also regularly violated the rules designed to ensure that disease control measures resulted in minimum interference with world traffic by applying excessive measures to the travellers and trade of member states suffering disease outbreaks.

III. The Codex Alimentarius Commission, the OIE and the International Plant Protection Convention

The SPS standard-setting organizations (Codex Alimentarius, OIE, IPPC) present special issues in the WTO, and their competence and credibility warrant a separate discussion. The status of these organizations in the WTO has been elevated by the SPS Agreement, which attributes to them authority to issue standards, compliance with which creates a presumptive exemption from WTO obligations. Some authors caution that 'even if these standards remain solely advisory, the stakes for the WTO Members in international SPS standards have become higher, and the potential exists for increased politicization of [these institutions'] processes when new standards are being set'.[17] These institutions are therefore different from other international organizations in that they have allegedly been delegated a regulatory function by the WTO.[18] While the incorporation of the relevant intellectual property rights conventions into the WTO has fully subjected these norms to the WTO, the rule-making process in these standard-setting organizations is an open-ended process, which continues to bear upon WTO decisions. The role of these international organizations in the WTO decision-making process triggers weighty scrutiny by the international community.[19] As a result, their internal procedures have been the focus of an important number of academic contributions.[20]

Against this background, a brief summary of the operation of the Codex Alimentarius, the OIE and the IPPC is given below, followed by an illustration of the main concerns raised in relation to their activity. It is

17 Stewart and Johanson, 'SPS Agreement', at 29.

18 For an overview of the principle of delegation and its implications in the WTO see above Chapter 4, section II.A.1.

19 See e.g. Tarullo, 'Relationship of WTO Obligations', at 166, referring to the reliability of decision making by the standard-setting organizations.

20 See Veggeland and Borgen, 'Negotiating International Food Standards', at 9, discussing the status of the Codex Alimentarius before 1995; David G. Victor, 'The Sanitary and Phytosanitary Agreement of the World Trade Organization: An Assessment after Five Years', (2000) 32 *New York University Journal of International Law & Politics* 874, at 890; Gruszczynski, *Regulating Health*. For an overview of the Codex see also Marsha A. Echols, *Food Safety and the WTO: The Interplay of Culture, Science and Technology* (London: Kluwer Law International, 2001); Marsha A. Echols, 'Institutional Cooperation and Norm Creation in International Organizations: The FAO–WHO Codex Alimentarius', Commentary on Victor Mosoti, in Thomas Cottier, Joost Pauwelyn and Elisabeth Buergi Bonanomi (eds.), *Human Rights and International Trade* (Oxford University Press, 2005), 192–8.

claimed that the identified issues may affect the perceptions by the WTO adjudicator of the competence and credibility of these organizations and qualify the weight attributed to their output in the dispute settlement process.

A. *The functioning of these international organizations*

1. The Codex Alimentarius Commission

The Codex Alimentarius Commission is an organization which was established in 1963 by the FAO and WHO.[21] The primary goal of the Codex is the protection of consumers' health, and ensuring fair practice in international food trade. This task is performed through the development of different documents, which include standards, codes of practice, principles, guidelines and recommendations (e.g. codes of conduct and recommended methods). The Codex standards (as well as other types of its documents) are adopted by simple majority voting.[22] In the case of regional standards, only member states belonging to the region or relevant group of countries have a right to vote.[23] In practice, Codex member states tend to adopt decisions by consensus. Its Rules of Procedure state this rule explicitly by requiring the Commission to 'make every effort to reach agreement on the adoption or amendment of standards by consensus'.[24] If consensus is not achieved, standards are adopted by simple majority voting (e.g. residue standards concerning five growth-promoting hormones and bovine somatotropin).[25]

The Codex implements eight distinct steps for the approval of its standards (guidelines and recommendations). The number of steps is fewer for the accelerated procedures deployed in cases where there is an immediate need for the envisaged standard or if there is broad consensus between the members with respect to the standard. Both procedures, however, give numerous opportunities to the members to comment on the proposed standard – a process which enhances their legitimacy.

21 See Codex Alimentarius Commission, *Understanding the Codex Alimentarius*, 3rd edn (Rome: FAO), www.fao.org/docrep/008/y7867e/y7867e00.htm (visited March 2009), which contains a chronology detailing the formation of this organization. See the Codex website for the Statutes and Rules of Procedure, www.fao.org/DOCREP/005/Y2200E/y2200e03.htm (visited March 2009).

22 Rule VIII(2) of the Rules of Procedures of the Codex Alimentarius Commission, in Codex Alimentarius Commission, Procedural Manual, at 6–18.

23 Ibid., Rule VIII(3). 24 Ibid., Rule XII(2). 25 *Understanding the Codex.*

2. The OIE

The OIE is an international organization first created in 1924 which currently has 174 members.[26] The objective of this organization is to provide a forum for the dissemination of information among its members on animal disease situations, and scientific information on disease controls, providing technical assistance to this end for its members. Its major purpose, however, is the development of sanitary standards. Notably, the development of these standards is highly inclusive due to the distribution of the drafts among the delegates and the opportunities for them to submit comments. Depending on these comments, there might be an additional review of the proposed standard or a recommendation may be passed to the OIE International Committee.[27] The OIE adopts standards by consensus. However, where there is no consensus the OIE standard will be adopted, provided that not more than ten members are against it. Thus the OIE does not provide for a positive voting procedure.

3. The International Plant Protection Convention

The IPPC is an international treaty (not a formal international organization) which was adopted in 1951 and with 173 contracting parties.[28] The main objective of the IPPC is to secure 'common and effective action to prevent the spread and introduction of pests of plants and plant products' while facilitating international trade.[29] The standard-setting in the IPPC is far simpler than in the Codex and the OIE.[30] Yet this simplified procedure still allows comments by all the IPPC parties on the proposed standards in the consultation stage. These comments are taken into account by the Standards Committee which revises the draft standard accordingly. The final approval of the standard rests with the Commission on Phytosanitary Measures (CPM), which, as a rule, works by consensus. If that is not possible, the CPM will adopt the standard with a qualified majority of

26 The number of members as at August 2009, www.oie.int/eng/OIE/PM/en_PM.htm?e1d1 (visited August 2009).

27 For a comprehensive description see OIE, www.oie.int/eng/OIE/en_objectifs.htm#2 (visited June 2009).

28 The number of parties as of 31 July 2009. See IPPC, https://www.ippc.int/IPP/En/default.jsp (visited September 2009).

29 IPPC, Art. I(1).

30 The IPPC adopts only phytosanitary standards and does not distinguish guidelines or recommendations as separate types of document. Nevertheless, standards as such appear under different names (e.g. Glossary of Phytosanitary Terms, Guidelines for Surveillance). Currently there are twenty-nine IPPC standards in force.

two-thirds of the votes cast. The adopted standards do not enjoy legally binding status.[31]

B. *Selected operational issues*

Although the latest evaluations of the activity of the three standard-setting organizations are positive, there is still scope for improvement in their operation.[32] An FAO/WHO report issued in 2002 took up various aspects of the functioning of the three organizations, suggesting some changes to their activities.[33] The analysis undertaken in this report pointed to a number of issues. One of the major problems revealed by the report concerned the under-inclusion of the developing countries and least-developed countries in the work of these organizations. There was some feeling from the developing countries that the developed members of these institutions drove both the scientific evaluation of risks connected with different products – reflective of the nutritional behaviour of the developed nations – as well as the agenda-setting in general. This problem stems largely from the lack of capacity on the part of the developing countries.[34]

A second category of issues arose in connection with the decision-making processes of these organizations, in particular relating to the use of the majority voting system. The main criticism was directed at the Codex, which provides the most liberal simple majority voting mechanism while operating in a highly sensitive area of regulation. A sensible compromise in this respect is observed within the OIE, which approves standards unless ten members or more are against them.[35] Furthermore, it has been claimed that the Codex decision-making is industry-driven.[36] This is explained by the fact that the majority of standards are of a very technical nature and the industry associations are those possessing

31 See IPPC Art. X(4), requiring that 'Contracting parties should take into account, as appropriate, international standards when undertaking activities related to this Convention'.

32 See Gruszczynski, *Regulating Health*.

33 FAO/WHO, Report of the Evaluation of the Codex Alimentarius and Other FAO and WHO Food Standards Work (2002).

34 Ibid., at 39.

35 See above section III.A.2.

36 Victor, 'Sanitary and Phytosanitary Agreement', at 886. As of 2002, of 151 NGOs with observer status at the Codex, around 71 per cent represented industry and 22 per cent were professional bodies, while only 8 per cent represented consumer/public interest. See FAO/WHO, Report of the Evaluation of the Codex Alimentarius and Other FAO and WHO Food Standards Work (2002), at 19.

the adequate expertise and financial resources to participate in the standard-setting.

The three sister organizations have addressed these concerns by improving the transparency and public participation of their decision making through NGOs, although, as noted by one commentator, the majority of participants are still industrial associations.[37] The involvement of consumer protection groups from developed countries poses another problem: they are seen as influencing the establishment of standards (e.g. acceptable daily intakes and maximum residues) at levels that are not achievable by the industries of developing WTO members.

The failure to introduce some improvements on the above points has thus resulted in these organizations losing credibility in the eyes of WTO members, who had put their trust in their respective systems by incorporating their standards into the WTO system. This in turn, is presumed to impact on the readiness of the WTO adjudicator to accord them a greater role in dispute settlement.

IV. The role of WTO subsidiary bodies

Although the competence and credibility of the international organizations may determine the extent to which the WTO adjudicator would defer to the acts, information or expertise of a specific international organization, the assessment of these prerequisites should certainly not be in the realm of the panels or the Appellate Body. This exercise is not suitable for a judicial context, as it risks undermining the principal functions of the judiciary.[38] Instead, this can be carried out more successfully by the WTO subsidiary bodies. The following sections illustrate how the prolific interactions of the WTO SPS and SCM Committees with other international organizations in their day-to-day activities make them better suited for such evaluations. For their part, the WTO panels or Appellate Body, when in doubt with regard to the competence and credibility of a relevant international organization, may rely on the evaluation of the relevant WTO subsidiary bodies rather than making such delicate assessments during the time-constrained dispute settlement process.

37 Joanne Scott, *The WTO Agreement on Sanitary and Phytosanitary Measures: A Commentary* (Oxford University Press, 2007), 247.

38 See also Yuval Shany, 'One Law to Rule Them All: Should International Courts be Viewed as Guardians of Procedural Order and Legal Uniformity?', paper presented at the Conference on Unity or Fragmentation of International Law – the Role of International and National Tribunals, Oslo, 14–15 May 2009 (on file with the author).

A. The SPS Committee

Although formulated in weak terms, the SPS Agreement grants power to the SPS Committee to exercise the overall supervision of health standards development within the standard-setting organizations (i.e. Codex, OIE, IPPC). In practice, the SPS Committee is perceived as a body performing something akin to a legislative function.[39] It is an important forum for the elaboration of the SPS standards, and its activities are aimed at avoiding disputes and enhancing compliance from the members. As noted by Scott,

> [I]n this setting, the committee is seen to operate as a contextualizing regime, whereby Members arrive at (provisionally) settled understandings of the standards laid down in the agreement, and of their implications for the boundaries of legitimate regulation by the Member States.[40]

Against this background, it is presumed that the emergence of a specific international organization in the activity of the SPS Committee suggests its relevance, competence and credibility in dealing with the relevant subject matter. Frequently, standard-setting organizations intervene with important guidance and expertise in the daily discussions of the SPS Committee, contributing to its effective operation. Naturally, the three sister organizations are around the table in these discussions, but they are not the only ones participating in the activity of the Committee (see below, subsection 2).

1. The peer-review function

Peer review is a crucial function exercised by the SPS Committee – at the heart of information exchange between the WTO members. In this process, the Committee operates as a multilateral forum where members are called upon to report, explain and justify their proposed SPS measures. The discussions within the Committee proceed by reference to binding standards laid down in the SPS Agreement, and non-binding standards such as those adopted by the three sister organizations.

If the credibility and competence assessment of these agencies is to be based on their ability to produce clear and unambiguous standards, it should be noted that the SPS Committee also stands as a guardian of this process, elaborating and clarifying these norms within the WTO system. To give an example, compliance with the Codex Hazard Analysis and Critical Control Points (HACCP) standard has been at the centre of discussion

39 Scott, 'Cooperative Regulation', at 13. 40 Ibid., at 11.

in the Committee. This is at least partly due to the fact that the Codex guidelines on this particular standard are rather ambiguous.[41] Following the various arguments presented by members in the SPS Committee, an understanding was reached on what could legitimately be required under an acceptable HACCP regime.[42]

2. Norm elaboration

Apart from peer review, the SPS Committee also issues norms which elaborate on the obligations laid down in the SPS Agreement or regulate its own activity.[43] In the exercise of this function, the SPS Committee approves internal rules and procedures and rules regarding the granting of observer status, and monitors the process of international harmonization, as prescribed by the SPS Agreement. The last two activities are of particular interest for this discussion and are elaborated in more detail below.

a. The granting of observer status in the SPS Committee. As specified above, the WTO General Council has developed guidelines on observer status for international intergovernmental bodies, but these are without prejudice to the decisions adopted by subsidiary bodies.[44] This means that the SPS Committee can independently examine and adopt requests for observership according to the 1996 Guidelines approved by the General Council.[45] By virtue of this status, apart from the three sister organizations, a number of other international organizations appear in the activity of the SPS Committee as regular observers.[46] Moreover, a number of other

41 Codex Alimentarius, HACCP Guidelines, www.who.int/foodsafety/fs_management/haccp/en/ (visited May 2009).

42 WTO, G/SPS/GEN/204/Rev.5, Part 4, paras. 96–98. Similarly, contesting the scope of HACCP, as applied to lower risk products such as confectionary and snacks, continues in the Committee. See WTO, G/SPS/36/R/Rev.2.

43 Scott, 'Cooperative Regulation', at 27.

44 For a detailed account of the granting of observer status in the WTO see above Chapter 2, section IV.B.

45 Para. 4 of the General Council Guidelines states: 'Requests for observer status shall be considered on a case-by-case basis by each WTO body to which such a request is addressed.'

46 These are the Food and Agriculture Organization (FAO), the International Plant Protection Convention (IPPC) (regional plant protection bodies join as part of the IPPC delegation), FAO/WHO Joint Codex Alimentarius Commission (Codex), International Organization for Standardization (ISO), International Trade Centre (ITC), Office international des epizooties (OIE), United Nations Conference on Trade and Development (UNCTAD), the World Health Organization (WHO), the World Bank, and the

organizations have been granted ad hoc (meeting by meeting) observer status.[47]

To date, the SPS Committee has not, however, succeeded in its long-term goal of adopting permanent criteria for observer status. Moreover, while applying preordained provisional criteria for observership, the decision on admitting new observers is taken by consensus. This means that even if an observer meets all the criteria, any WTO member may prevent an applicant from acquiring observer status. As a result of this flaw, a number of requests for observer status are still pending before the Committee. These include, most critically, a long-standing request by the Convention on Biological Diversity (CBD) and its Cartagena Protocol on Biosafety. The exclusion of these bodies from the SPS Committee process is regrettable, given the important objective promoted thereby. Although there can be little doubt that these bodies meet the provisional criteria for observer status with the Committee, their exclusion reflects broader political tensions in the WTO.[48]

The organizations which already enjoy observer status may turn out to be very useful to the activities of the Committee by providing important clarifications on regulation and standard-setting in their respective forums. One example is WHO – the host of the three standard-setting organizations – which has come to serve the SPS Committee with input and clarification regarding its own norms and activities. For example, the Committee had to discuss the imposition of a restrictive import measure by the EC on some Tanzanian food products on the grounds that they were posing the risk of cholera. WHO clarified in this context that the products at issue posed an almost 'non-existent risk' to the importing country. Following this observation, the EC removed the measure.[49] In this process, the SPS Committee had drawn on the WHO guidelines on this subject, which represented default standards, departure from which required justification.

International Monetary Fund (IMF). See above Chapter 2, section IV, for a more detailed account of observership status in the WTO.

47 These are the Organization for Economic Co-operation and Development (OECD), African, Caribbean and Pacific Countries (ACP), European Free Trade Association (EFTA), the Latin American Economic System (SELA), Inter-American Institute for Cooperation on Agriculture (IICA), Organismo Internacional Regional de Sanidad Agropecuaria (OIRSA).

48 See Scott, 'Cooperative Regulation', at 30. For an overview see also above Chapter 4, section II.B.

49 For a more detailed account of this case see the following WTO documents: G/SPS/R/10, G/SPS/204/Rev.5/Add. 3, G/SPS/R/11, and G/SPS/GEN/204/Rev. 5/Add.3.

b. Monitoring the process of international harmonization. The monitoring of the process of international harmonization is a task of the SPS Committee set out in Article 3(5) of the SPS Agreement. By virtue of this provision the SPS Committee should develop a procedure to monitor the process of international harmonization, and co-ordinate efforts in this regard with the relevant international organizations. Moreover, the SPS Agreement sets out that the Committee should, in conjunction with the relevant international organizations, establish a list of international standards relating to SPS measures, which the Committee determines as having major trade impact.[50] In order to implement this provision, the SPS Committee has elaborated some procedures whereby the members notify the Committee of difficulties encountered in relation to the use or non-use of the relevant standards.[51] Apart from identifying where there is a major impact on trade resulting from the non-use of international standards and the reasons thereof, this procedure sets out to identify, for the benefit of the relevant international organizations, where a standard is needed, or where it is not appropriate for its purpose or use. Against this background, the Committee may invite the relevant standard-setting organizations to consider a revision of the standards.[52]

The SPS Committee annual reports reveal that, so far, about fourteen issues have come up before it in monitoring the process of international harmonization. These cases were brought to the attention of the relevant international organizations, resulting in three instances of the adoption of new revised standards. With respect to the remaining cases, these agencies reported 'work in progress'. On several other occasions, the standard-setting organizations either rejected the need for a specific text, or issued a communication clarifying, as did the OIE, the 'apparent misunderstandings about the nature and purpose of the OIE international standards, their implementation and interpretation'.[53] Against this backdrop, Scott notes that

> [T]he peer-review in the SPS Committee is not confined to the vertical oversight of the measures imposed by Members. It operates also on a horizontal axis between the committee and the relevant international standard-setting bodies. This serves not only to encourage and facilitate coordination between the different bodies, but also to enhance the transparency of their activities, and critical oversight thereof.[54]

50 SPS Agreement, Art. 12.4.

51 For an overview of this procedure see the following WTO documents: G/SPS/11; G/SPS/14; G/SPS/17; G/SPS/25 and G/SPS/11/Rev.1.

52 See WTO, G/SPS/11/Rev.1, para. 1.

53 See WTO, G/SPS/16 and G/SPS/31.

54 Scott, 'Cooperative Regulation', at 35.

This oversight is limited for the time being to the three standard-setting organizations, but the Committee is specifically authorized to consider the standards of other international organizations. WHO standards, for example, may become a good candidate in this respect.

B. The SCM Committee

A peer-review function is also evidenced in the activity of the WTO SCM Committee. This is exercised with regard to the decision-making procedures behind the OECD Arrangement referred to in the SCM Agreement Annex I(k).[55] The peer review undertaken by the SCM Committee aims to ensure transparency in the activity of the OECD and information sharing with the WTO members. Margaret Young, who investigated the activity of the Committee, notes that

> [T]he existing and proposed collaborative practices of the WTO and OECD secretariats change the position of the OECD Export Credit Arrangement as a benchmark of conduct in the SCM Agreement. These practices require a level of transparency and openness in the OECD procedures to frame and update the benchmark, as scrutinized by the SCM Committee.[56]

1. Disciplining fisheries subsidies

In the context of WTO fisheries subsidies negotiations it was proposed that the peer-review function of the SCM Committee exercised in relation to the OECD Arrangement be extended to other international organizations. Various aspects of the fisheries disciplines are administered by a number of international regimes, such as the United Nations Convention on the Law of the Sea (UNCLOS) and some instruments of the Food and Agriculture Organization (FAO). The subsidies in the fishing sector have not only trade but also ecological consequences, especially for fisheries that are over-exploited.[57] Given the number of international organizations concerned, this state of affairs poses legal hurdles in negotiating, implementing and adjudicating matters of fisheries conservation and management.

As described in Chapter 1 above, the WTO members agreed to negotiate with the aim of clarifying and improving WTO disciplines on fisheries subsidies, as part of a more wide-scale reform of the SCM

55 See above Chapter 2, section III.C, for a detailed account of the reference to the OECD Arrangement in the SCM Agreement.

56 Young, 'Fragmentation or Interaction', at 39.

57 Ibid., at 1.

and Anti-dumping Agreements.[58] The negotiations were assigned to the Negotiating Group on Rules ('Rules Group'), which reports to the WTO Trade Negotiations Committee.[59] A Chair's text was issued in 2007, which consolidated the proposals of the participants regarding the SCM modification.[60] This text is proposed in the form of an annex ('Annex VIII') to the SCM Agreement. The draft WTO rules, as currently contained in the Chair's text, incorporate norms from other regimes as regards three main issues: the classification of subsidies, the benchmarks for fisheries management to which WTO members must adhere, and the settlement of subsidy disputes. These discussions frequently make reference to the standards of other international organizations which could help classify subsidies into 'good' and 'bad' or establish the proper fisheries management rules. The FAO was cited as one such organization by virtue of its international plan of action which defines illegal, unreported and unregulated fishing.[61] Moreover, on fisheries management, Argentina proposed, for example, that developing countries wishing to qualify for special and differential treatment should implement national fisheries management systems 'in keeping' with the FAO Code of Conduct.[62] Other international instruments were referred to for regulating the fisheries management national systems, such as the Fish Stocks Agreement, the Compliance Agreement, technical guidelines, and plans of action.[63]

2. The Food and Agriculture Organization

One particular proposal in the context of the above negotiations envisaged attributing authority to the FAO in the monitoring of the national

58 See above Chapter 1, section IV.A. For an account see also Peter Lloyd, 'When Should New Areas of Rules be Added to the WTO?', 4 *World Trade Review* 275 (2005).

59 Note also the Declaration at the Hong Kong Ministerial Meeting in 2005 which states '*recall* our commitment at Doha to enhancing the mutual supportiveness of trade and environment, *note* that there is broad agreement that the Group should strengthen disciplines on subsidies in the fisheries sector, including through the prohibition of certain forms of fisheries subsidies that contribute to overcapacity and over-fishing, and *call on* Participants promptly to undertake further detailed work to, *inter alia*, establish the nature and extent of those disciplines, including transparency and enforceability'. WTO, WT/MIN(05)/DEC (adopted on 18 December 2005), Annex D, para. 9.

60 WTO Draft, above Chapter 1, n. 105.

61 FAO, International Plan of Action to Prevent, Deter and Eliminate Illegal, Unreported and Unregulated Fishing (2001), www.fao.org/DOCREP/003/y1224e/y1224e00.HTM (visited May 2009).

62 WTO, TN/RL/GEN/138 (see draft Art. X.3).

63 WTO Draft, above Chapter 1, n. 105, Art. V.

fisheries management systems through an internal peer-review mechanism. It was proposed that the results of this procedure would be reported to the SCM Committee.[64] Some countries, however, have objected to the involvement of another international agency in the process of peer review, since not all WTO members may belong to that organization. Importantly, in addressing these concerns, the Chair's text has emphasized the continuing role of the SCM Committee in maintaining a dialogue with the FAO, and proposed that the peer-review process be considered as similar to the existing Trade Policy Review Mechanism (TPRM).[65]

Despite disapproval over the proposal to involve the FAO in peer review, a prominent role can be seen for the FAO in providing guidance on the conformity of the revised policies with the Fish Stocks Agreement, the Compliance Agreement, technical guidelines, and plans of action. The continued dialogue with this institution will bring about interactions of the type enunciated in the SPS Agreement with respect to the standard-setting organizations, whereby the SCM Committee will monitor the decision-making procedures of the FAO. This horizontal review process will definitely strengthen the role of the FAO in the WTO, and this close interaction will demonstrate recognition of the competence and credibility of this organization. Against this background, it can be concluded that the WTO subsidiary bodies are equipped with better mechanisms for assessing the competence and credibility of the relevant international organizations. Therefore this assessment should be left to their discretion and drawn on by the WTO adjudicator in relevant disputes when necessary.

V. Conclusions

The vertical institutional sensitivity standard set out by the Appellate Body establishes that there should be some assessment of the relative competence and credibility of the domestic regulatory authorities whose factual findings are relevant to the settlement of WTO trade disputes. In the absence of any comparable benchmarks applicable with respect to the international organizations, which also emerge as external actors in the WTO disputes, this chapter has transposed the vague standard of the Appellate Body on to the horizontal axis. In this context, a number of factors have been identified which may affect the perceptions of competence

64 Ibid., Arts. V(1) and VI(4).

65 *Bridges Digest*, 2 April 2008, cited in Young, 'Fragmentation or Interaction', at 37.

and credibility of international organizations in WTO dispute settlement. It is the view here that they may determine WTO panel or Appellate Body decisions regarding the role and importance to be attributed to one or other international organization.

It should be noted that this assessment is not just a theoretical exercise. It has practical implications when, for example, the WTO adjudicator, in its interpretation process, encounters legal matters falling within several legal regimes, at times with competing objectives.[66] The problems which may arise in this context are with balancing competing values and, similarly, with the role to be ascribed to the international organizations that claim competence in the relevant area. At this point, the panels might have to face the difficult task of identifying the competent and the credible organization which is able legitimately to provide information, expertise or other types of input as the need may arise.[67]

It has been established that there would be a stronger presumption in favour of universal international organizations which are specifically mentioned in the WTO legal texts or other subsequent legal documents. This also holds true with respect to those international organizations which were granted observer status in and/or have concluded co-operation agreements with the WTO. Essentially, apart from that, as presented in the analysis of the SPS standard-setting organizations, specific operational and decision-making constraints may affect the perceptions of competence and credibility of international organizations in the WTO.

Yet the emphasis on these factors is not intended to suggest that those international organizations which do not reveal any of the above attributes should be discounted. When they are relevant to the process, the consideration of their output may contribute to an objective assessment of the matter before the WTO panels, which ultimately will enhance the legitimacy of the system. The presence of the above qualifications will perhaps make referrals by the panels or the Appellate Body easier, but they should

66 One example which can be cited here is the regulation of biodiversity and biotechnology which is undertaken in various forums: the regulation of international trade aspects (WTO, UNCTAD); conservation of genetic resources (FAO, CBD); health (WHO); investment protection (UPOV); (agricultural) development (FAO, UNCTAD); access and benefit sharing (CBD); cultural and ethical values (UNESCO) and intellectual property rights and innovation (WTO, WIPO, UPOV). For a detailed account of this issue see Dirk De Bievre, 'Forum Shopping in the Global Intellectual Property Rights Regime', paper presented at the conference 'Trade-And-? The World Trade Organization's Fuzzy Borders', 5–6 February 2009, Geneva, http://graduateinstitute.ch/webdav/site/ctei/shared/CTEI/3413/Fuzzy-Borders-Bievre-Thomann.pdf.

67 Above Chapter 4, section II.B.

not work to the exclusion of other relevant international organizations. In the end, the WTO adjudicator will have to balance carefully the weight it ascribes to those international organizations which do not possess the above features and whose decision-making processes have received wide criticism.

Finally, a crucial point made in this chapter is that the competence and credibility assessment of international organizations is not the domain of the WTO adjudicatory bodies, as this function would detract from fulfilment of their main duties and delay the judicial process. The task is more suitable for the WTO subsidiary bodies, such as the SPS and SCM Committees, as illustrated in this chapter. The peer-review functions and the authority to grant observer status by these committees ensures far more intense interactions with the international organizations concerned. This state of affairs allows a more plausible assessment of their competence and credibility.[68] The WTO adjudicator should therefore look to the day-to-day experience of these bodies when in doubt about the competence or credibility of a specific international organization.

68 Above Chapter 2, section IV, outlining the criteria for obtaining observer status in the WTO.

PART III

International organizations in the WTO disputes settlement procedure

Part I of this study illustrated what is intended by the institutional sensitivity of the WTO adjudicator, how the WTO links to other international organizations and how the VCLT rules of interpretation can be effectively employed to take into account the material of international organizations in the WTO interpretation process. Part II provided an account of the constraints which are generally presumed to affect the WTO adjudicator's institutional sensitivity towards international organizations. These factors may, indeed, impact on the willingness of the WTO to consider these other international organizations.

The study now takes a bottom-up approach, where the interactions of the WTO with other international organizations are examined through a sample of relevant WTO case law. These cases have been singled out because they reveal direct and explicit interactions by WTO panels with specific international organizations, such as the IMF (Chapter 4), WIPO (Chapter 5), the WCO (Chapter 6), WHO and the Codex Alimentarius Commission (Chapter 7). The purpose of this analysis is to carry out an in-depth empirical investigation into the type and nature of their contributions to WTO disputes settlement, following the panels' or the Appellate Body's reasoning. Against the background of the two general preceding parts of this study, this analysis will identify specific constraints which prevent the assigning of greater weight to the international organizations in WTO dispute settlement. This will be accompanied by a general evaluation of the role of each international organization in the WTO dispute settlement process and some suggestions as to how to tackle the issues identified. The analysis will culminate in the provision of some prospects regarding future interactions with the investigated international organizations, essentially concluding that these models could be replicated to analyse interactions with other international organizations which are not part of this exercise.

6

The International Monetary Fund

I. Introduction

Given the strong linkage of trade and finance issues, the IMF is an international organization of great interest which has a strong impact on the WTO.[1] This chapter looks to investigate the role of the IMF in the settlement of WTO disputes by examining the relevant case law from four disputes: *Argentina – Textiles and Apparel*, *Korea – Beef*, *India – Quantitative Restrictions* and *Dominican Republic – Import and Sale of Cigarettes*. The analysis commences with an illustration of how the requirement for consultation with the IMF, enshrined in GATT Article XV, has been interpreted by the panels or the Appellate Body (section II). The role of the IMF in WTO disputes arises mainly in connection with evaluations of the balance of payments situation of its members and determinations on exchange restrictions or controls.[2] In this context, the case law analysis helps elucidate the status and weight of these determinations in WTO dispute settlement. In particular, its role in the exchange restrictions determinations is examined (section III). These analyses are followed by a thorough evaluation of the IMF's input in all four disputes, the weight attributed thereto in the WTO judicial decision making and some other issues identified in this analysis (section IV) culminating in conclusions (section V).

II. Consultation with the International Monetary Fund

The consultation of WTO panels with the IMF is at the heart of the interaction between the two actors in the WTO disputes. Although GATT Article XV appears clear on the face of it, in that it mandates contracting parties to seek co-operation with the IMF with a view to pursuing 'a co-ordinated policy with regard to exchange questions within the jurisdiction

1 For a more detailed overview see above Chapter 2. 2 Ibid.

of the Fund and questions of quantitative restrictions and other trade measures within the jurisdiction of the Contracting Parties',[3] the case law reveals some complexities in the application of this provision by the WTO judiciary. A restrictive reading of it may result in constraining the institutional sensitivity of the WTO adjudicator and not fully allowing the benefits of collaboration between the two institutions to be explored.

The first issue relating to the consultation of the IMF by WTO panels relates to whether the panels have such authority at all. While it is clear that, under DSU Article 13, the WTO can consult the IMF among other sources of information available to it, the issue has implications for the effect of such consultation under one or another provision.[4]

Korea – Beef was the first case where a GATT contracting party, namely South Korea, challenged the authority of the panels to consult the IMF by virtue of Article XV(2) (argument of South Korea). A drastic decrease in South Korean imports of beef was challenged by the United States on the grounds that South Korea's restriction was inconsistent with several GATT provisions. In its defence, South Korea invoked the balance of payments exception enshrined in GATT Article XVIII(B), arguing that the ordinary dispute settlement procedure under GATT Article XXIII could not be employed in this case due to the existence of special review procedures for balance of payments measures. It was of the view that the ultimate consultation authority of the Panel with the IMF had to be derived from the General Council's authorization.[5] Despite the disagreement regarding the legal entitlement of the panels to consult with the IMF, both litigants in *Korea – Beef* considered that the consultation of the Panel with the IMF was necessary in this case.

The Panel applied GATT Article XV(2) to request from the IMF an assessment of the balance of payments situation of South Korea. All available information, data provided by the IMF, had shown positive results from its balance of payments situation.[6] This was essential to the outcome of the Panel's decision, which resulted in South Korea losing the case. Despite the Panel making good use of this information, as explained below, the case would not adequately serve any future panels examining the question of the coverage by GATT Article XV(2).

3 Above Chapter 2, section II.B.

4 For a detailed account of DSU Art. 13 see above Chapter 2, section V.

5 *Korea – Beef*, Panel Report, para. 79.

6 The Panel found out also that the South Korean gross official reserves had increased by US$9 billion to US$12 billion by the end of 1988. *Korea – Beef*, Panel Report, para. 123.

The authority of the WTO panels to consult with the IMF under Article XV(2) was also discussed extensively in *India – Quantitative Restrictions.* This case arose out of Indian measures which imposed quantitative restrictions on imports of textiles using the balance of payments justification under GATT Article XVIII(B).[7] The measures were challenged in 1997 by the United States, which claimed regarding India's monetary reserves that they were no longer 'inadequate' and there was no 'threat of serious decline'.[8] Regarding the consultation with the IMF, the United States argued that the text of GATT Article XV(2) *required* the Panel to consult with the Fund; 'although [it] did not mention Panels, per se, an interpretation of WTO [Agreements] would include Panels'.[9] In India's view, however, this requirement did not extend to panels and was limited to the WTO General Council or the Balance of Payments Committee,[10] let alone that the consultation requirement did not apply in this case because of the specific considerations of Article XVIII(B) for developing countries.[11] According to India, these concerns gave rise to questions of distribution of competence among the organs of the WTO, which would be disrupted if the Panel consulted the Fund and adhered to its conclusions.[12]

The United States further noted that the Fund should be consulted as an 'expert' by the Panel under Article XVIII(B) and that any such determination was a 'factual finding' for the Panel's consideration.[13] In its view, the IMF's determination on the balance of payments situation

7 For a discussion of the case see Dukgeun Ahn, 'Linkages between International Financial and Trade Institutions: IMF, World Bank and WTO', (2000) 34(4) *Journal of World Trade* 1.

8 *India – Quantitative Restrictions*, Panel Report, para. 3.145.

9 Ibid., para. 3.305.

10 Ibid., para. 3.309.

11 Ibid., para. 3.315.

12 The same issue had also been brought up in *Korea – Beef*. The Panel did not have to deal with any contradictory decisions between the two bodies in these two cases, but an issue might arise in the future where the WTO Balance of Payments Committee does not share the IMF's view on balance of payments matters. In this context, Ahn states that the relationship between the IMF and the Balance of Payments Committee is not clear-cut. He notes that 'this relationship raises the question of the proper division and scope of works concerning balance-of-payments-related problems, particularly within the context of dispute settlement between Member countries. When the WTO dispute settlement deals with balance of payments matters of the Members, it faces a complicated question of how Panels should allocate the jurisdictional authority to the IMF and the Balance of Payments Committee'. Ahn, 'Linkages', at 17–18. See also Trebilcock and Howse, *Regulation of International Trade*, 163, contending that this discussion reveals that the competence of the DSB in balance of payments matters is still a contentious issue, which would need to be thoroughly reconsidered.

13 Ibid., para. 3.312.

should be factually dispositive, even if it was down to the WTO to make the final decision on the case. Any other reading would render meaningless the requirement that the WTO 'shall accept' the IMF's determination on the specific factual issues as set out in GATT Article XV(2).[14]

Although the parties had extensively argued on these points, the Panel did not find it necessary either to decide whether GATT Article XV(2) required it to consult with the IMF or whether to consider as dispositive specific determinations of the IMF. Instead, the Panel resorted to Article 13(1) of the DSU and consulted with the Fund in order to make an objective assessment of the facts as prescribed by Article 11 of the DSU.[15] It noted that the consultation was necessary for two reasons. First, the Balance of Payments Committee itself had not made a determination on the issue following its consultation with the IMF on this matter. Second, India's balance of payments situation might have changed since it was last taken up in the Balance of Payments Committee.[16]

The Fund's statement was prepared by its staff and approved by the Executive Board in accordance with the usual procedures,[17] following which India's balance of payments situation was found to be positive. On appeal, the Appellate Body concluded that the Panel had critically assessed the data of the IMF and compared it with the data provided by other sources (such as the report of the Reserve Bank of India).[18]

The consultation requirement with the IMF was also discussed in *Argentina – Textiles and Apparel*. The case concerned an import surcharge imposed by Argentina on imports of footwear, textiles and apparel, which was designed to cover the costs of the statistical services rendered to foreign trade operators. As the United States challenged the consistency of the measure with the GATT, Argentina argued that the import surcharge was a 'commitment' to the IMF, undertaken by it while receiving funding under the Memorandum of Understanding signed with the IMF in 1995. Therefore, action under the WTO was precluded in the interests of consistency between the two institutions. Argentina further contended that the surcharge was required by the IMF as a condition for funding, hence falling under the IMF conditionality policies. These allegations turned on the question whether the WTO Agreements provide an exception for policies applied by a member when receiving financing from the Fund.

14 Ibid. 15 Ibid., para. 5.13. 16 Ibid., para. 5.12.

17 See above Chapter 2, section II.B.1, for a more detailed account of balance of payments assessment procedures in the IMF.

18 *India – Quantitative Restrictions*, ABR, para. 149.

Despite having a clear premise for consultation with the IMF in this case, the Panel decided not to consult. In support of its decision, the Panel stated that under Article XV(2) it was required to consult the Fund on matters regarding 'monetary reserves, balance of payments or foreign exchange arrangements', and measures that were part of an IMF-supported programme were not part of the list.[19] Neither did the Panel use its discretionary right to seek information from the IMF under DSU Article 13. Moreover, confirming the finding of the Panel that it was not required to consult the IMF, the Appellate Body noted that Panels had full discretion to determine whether to seek information at all.[20] The Appellate Body nonetheless recognized that it might have been useful for the Panel to have consulted with the IMF on the arrangement between Argentina and the IMF in this case.[21]

III. Determinations on exchange matters

The Panel consulted the IMF in *Dominican Republic – Import and Sale of Cigarettes* in connection with the Dominican Republic's application of charges and fees on the import and sale of cigarettes, which was challenged by Honduras. One of these fees was ostensibly a foreign exchange fee calculated on the value of imports at the selling exchange rate for foreign currency.[22] The phasing-out of this (transitional) fee by the Dominican Republic would have depended on the reform of the tax system, which was under consideration, and the economic stabilization negotiations with the IMF. Honduras complained that the measure was therefore inconsistent with GATT Article II(1)(b), second sentence,[23] in the light of the Understanding on the interpretation of this provision.

One of the questions the Panel had to clarify in this context was whether the foreign exchange fee constituted an 'exchange control' or an 'exchange restriction' under GATT Article XV(9)(a).[24] A positive finding in this respect would have justified the application of the measure by

19 Ibid. 20 Ibid., para. 84. 21 Ibid., para. 86.

22 *Dominican Republic – Import and Sale of Cigarettes*, Panel Report, para. 2.

23 GATT Art. II(1)(b) reads in full: 'Such products shall also be exempt from all other duties or charges of any kind imposed on or in connection with the importation in excess of those imposed on the date of this Agreement or those directly and mandatorily required to be imposed thereafter by legislation in force in the importing territory on that date.'

24 GATT Art. XV(9)(a) reads in full: 'Nothing in this Agreement shall preclude: (a) the use by a contracting party of exchange controls or exchange restrictions in accordance with the Articles of Agreement of the International Monetary Fund or with that contracting party's special exchange agreement with the CONTRACTING PARTIES, or . . . .'

the Dominican Republic. The Panel decided to consult the Fund, which in turn provided that the foreign exchange fee in question did not fall within the categories listed in Article XV(9)(a) – that is, it was not an exchange control or exchange restriction.

Notably, having agreed with the IMF, the Panel decided, however, to apply autonomously the IMF's criterion in making a determination to this effect, arriving at the same conclusion. In this exercise, the Panel examined whether there was a 'direct limitation on availability or use of exchange as such' – a rule set out by the IMF's Executive Board in a 1960 Decision.[25] This IMF instrument clarified that the distinctive feature of a restriction on payments and transfers for current transactions is 'whether it involves a direct governmental limitation on availability or use of exchange as such'.[26] This guiding principle is also used to discern exchange measures from trade measures and to define the border between the Fund's and the WTO's jurisdiction. In this context, the Panel noted that

> [T]he ordinary meaning of the 'direct limitation on availability or use of exchange . . . as such' means a limitation directly on the use of exchange itself, which means the use of exchange for all purposes. It cannot be interpreted in a way so as to permit the transactions on the use of exchanges that only affects importation . . . to conclude otherwise would logically lead to the situation whereby any WTO Member could easily circumvent obligations under Article II:1(b) by imposing a foreign currency fee or charge on imports at the customs and then conveniently characterize it as an 'exchange restriction'. Such types of measures would seriously discriminate against imports while not necessarily being effective in achieving the legitimate goals under the Articles of Agreement of the IMF.[27]

It is worth noting that, after having found that the measure at issue was not an exchange restriction, the Panel decided to assess its conformity with the second requirement enshrined in GATT Article XV(9)(a) – that is, whether the fee was imposed 'in accordance with' the Article of the IMF Agreement.[28] In taking this step the Panel contended that, assuming the foreign exchange fee was an 'exchange restriction', GATT Article XV(9)(a) required exchange measures to be applied 'in accordance with' the Articles of Agreement of the IMF.[29] The need for this determination emerged from the defendant's claim that the exchange fee at issue was permitted under the IMF by virtue of a waiver from the non-observance of performance

25 IMF Art. VIII and Art. XIV, Executive Board Decision No. 1034-(60/27), 1 June 1960. See *Dominican Republic – Import and Sale of Cigarettes*, Panel Report, para. 5.52.

26 Ibid., para. 5.53.

27 Ibid., para. 7.137.

28 Ibid., paras. 7.150–7.154.

29 Ibid., para. 7.151.

criteria set out in a standby arrangement with the IMF.[30] The Panel thus examined whether the Dominican Republic discharged its burden of proof in demonstrating that its foreign exchange fee was 'in accordance with' the Articles of Agreement of the IMF. Given that the only evidence put forward by the Dominican Republic in support of this claim was a reference to an IMF press release mentioning the approval of such a waiver, the Panel concluded that the defendant had not discharged its burden of proof on this point.

IV. Evaluation

Although the Panel in *Argentina – Textiles and Apparel* correctly found that the tax applied by the defendant was not justified on the grounds that it involved an adjustment measure under a Fund-supported programme,[31] the Panel's decision not to consult the IMF amounted to a missed opportunity to clarify the legal nature of this instrument. In an academic contribution on the IMF relationship with the WTO, Siegel clarifies that a member's overall programme for adjustment measures taken in connection with Fund financing should be distinguished from the measures that the Fund identifies as conditions for the continuation of such financing (known as 'Fund conditionality').[32] Thus the conditions of receipt of Fund financing, which are usually set out in an arrangement, do not constitute obligations to the Fund and 'the failure to complete those measures results solely in the non-fulfilment of a condition for the use of Fund resources'.[33] This explanation is consistent with that provided by Joseph Gold in his contribution on the 'Interpretation of the IMF Agreement'. As an IMF legal officer with extensive experience on the subject, he noted that 'the IMF has decided that an arrangement and the annexed letter of

30 Ibid., paras. 7.146–7.147: 'The Dominican Republic argues that Art. XV(9)(a) does not oblige that a measure be "required" under the terms of a stand-by arrangement. In its view, to the extent that this fee is "permitted" under the terms of the stand-by arrangement, this fee is "in accordance with" the Articles of Agreement of the International Monetary Fund as provided by Art. XV:9(a).'

31 The Appellate Body stated that Art. XV(2) identifies certain circumstances under which a member is 'excused from certain of its obligations under the GATT 1994', but the case did not involve those matters (ABR, para. 73). The Panel also ruled that there was insufficient evidence to support Argentina's argument that a Memorandum of Understanding with the Fund is a 'simplified agreement' which includes an 'undertaking' or an 'obligation' on (Argentina's) part to collect a specified amount in the form of a statistical tax (Panel Report, para. 65).

32 Siegel, 'Legal Aspects', at 573–4.

33 Ibid.

intent and other documents do not constitute an international agreement or a contract between the IMF and the member'.[34] This distinction has been further elaborated as follows:

> In seeking financing from the Fund, the government sends a 'letter of intent' that states the member's intended policy for a program of adjustment measures. The Executive Board of the Fund decides whether to support the member's program, usually through a decision called an 'arrangement', which is the instrument that will identify specific conditions for the member to continue receiving Fund resources. Thus while this letter of intent is a necessary step in obtaining Fund financing, the member's program is legally distinct from, and broader than, Fund conditionality. Although measures identified as conditions are drawn from the policy intentions stated in the letter of intent, they must be limited to those that are consistent with the Fund's Articles. Thus not all of the adjustment measures that a member decides to undertake while receiving Fund financing constitute Fund conditionality; this broader set of policies is properly referred to as a 'Fund-supported program'.[35]

The clarifications made above are significant when addressing coherence concerns between the two institutions as they help define the IMF obligations and distinguish them from WTO obligations. Argentina's argument that the alleged GATT inconsistency should be excused under the principle of 'coherence in global economic policy making' and co-operation stated in the Ministerial Declaration, has logical appeal, but this reading finds no support in the WTO Agreements.[36] There were proposals to grant WTO waivers to member countries that committed to WTO-inconsistent measures under IMF programmes; this, however, may not be necessary, given the fact that the 'Fund's approach is to help members avoid planning adjustment measures that would violate WTO obligations or, for that matter, trade taxes or subsidies even if they were WTO-consistent'.[37] Moreover, there are important informal exchanges between the staff of the IMF and the WTO for the purpose of checking eventual inconsistencies with Fund-supported programmes which can achieve avoidance of such conflicts. All these important clarifications could have emerged in the context of the WTO judicial practice, had the Panel decided to consult the IMF in this case.

34 See Gold, *Interpretation*, at 61. But some lawyers still seem to have difficulty with this proposition. See, e.g., Ileana De Giovan Battista, 'Acuerdos entre el gablerno argentine y el Fondo Monetario Internacional (Aspectos Juridicos)', *La Ley* (Buenos Aires), 13 February 1990, 1–2. Also, Thomas Cottier expressed disapproval of this claim during a presentation at the World Trade Institute, Berne, February 2008.

35 Siegel, 'Legal Aspects', at 573. 36 Ibid., at 575. 37 Ibid.

By deciding not to consult the Panel showed lack of institutional sensitivity towards this institution. The Panel's main argument justifying non-consultation rested on its assertion that the question at issue was not among the matters falling within the scope of the GATT Article XV(2) consultation requirement. But the Panel also did not exercise its discretionary right to seek clarifications from the IMF under DSU Article 13, which encroached on the fulfilment of the objective assessment of the matter set out in DSU Article 11. An institutionally sensitive approach would have certainly entailed consultation by the Panel with the IMF in these circumstances.

Korea – Beef and *India – Quantitative Restrictions* reveal an inconsistent approach by panels towards the interpretation of the WTO legal provision prescribing consultation with the IMF on balance of payments issues.[38] In both cases the Panel requested the IMF to present an assessment of the balance of payments situation of the two countries involved. In *Korea – Beef* the Panel consulted the IMF by virtue of GATT Article XV(2), whereas in *India – Quantitative Restrictions* Article 13 DSU was used. It should be noted in this context that the latter entails only a discretionary right of the Panels to consult; therefore the implications of this inconsistent approach by the two panels are quite obvious.[39] The setting out of a discretionary judicial practice on the consultation with the IMF does not find support in the negotiation history of the GATT, and proper consideration should be accorded to Article XV(2) under the newly established DSU. Moreover, the hesitance of the WTO adjudicator to consult the IMF would also not be justified by its concerns over the alleged weak architecture of this organization, as might be the case with respect to other international organizations investigated in this study. As presented above, in Chapter 5, the IMF is *sui generis* in the sense that it is one of the few organizations to offer a well-functioning authoritative interpretation system, let alone its uncontested competence and credibility.[40]

38 See above Chapter 4 for a discussion on the effects of the inconsistent WTO interpretation on the institutional sensitivity of the WTO adjudicator.

39 For a description of the GATT's balance of payments exception and its applicability to this case see Thomas Chantal, 'Balance-of-Payments Crises in the Developing World: Balancing Trade, Finance and Development in the New Economic Order', (2000) 15 *American University International Law Review* 1249.

40 See above Chapter 6, section II. But see Hector R. Torres, 'Reforming the International Monetary Fund – Why Its Legitimacy Is at Stake', (2007) 14(1) *Journal of International Economic Law* 237, who criticizes the IMF.

Finally, another point of inconsistency between the two similar cases relates to the fact that according to the Panel, the IMF was not the sole source of information on India's balance of payments situation; it also approached the Reserve Bank of India. The Appellate Body seems to have commended this choice in spite of its inconsistency with *Korea – Beef*, where the IMF alone had been consulted. The latter approach is hardly commendable in the context of this study. It only serves to downplay the authoritative effect of the IMF's contribution which can, as the Panel's approach in *India – Quantitative Restrictions* seems to suggest, be regarded as rebuttable evidentiary material. The judicial inconsistency between the two cases can be viewed as undermining the objective of adding clarity to the WTO provisions in the judicial interpretation process. By deciding to change its approach to what can be presented as the same or quasi-identical factual situation, the *India – Quantitative Restrictions* Panel missed the opportunity to reinforce the approach of a previous panel with regard to a similar factual issue, without good reason for such a derogation.[41]

In addition, the outcomes in both *Korea – Beef* and *India – Quantitative Restrictions* are also unsatisfactory because the Panel did not clarify whether the consultation requirement enshrined in GATT Article XV(2) as applicable to the GATT contracting parties extended to panels. Elsewhere, the following assessment has been made of this outcome:

> [T]he case cannot be cited for the proposition that the consultation requirement either does or does not extend to the panels. The panel chose to consult the Fund under its authority to seek information from outside experts, which is a positive result for both institutions. However, the rationale is troubling, because the panel treated consultation as discretionary, which therefore leaves open the question whether a future panel faced with issues covered by GATT Article XV would decline either to consult the Fund or to accept its determinations as *dispositive* of the issues on which it is consulted.[42]

The above evaluation brings up the third issue which relates to whether the panels should accord dispositive effect to the IMF's assessments in balance of payments matters under GATT Article XV(2).[43] It is claimed that

41 For the impact of the inconsistent interpretation on the institutional sensitivity proposition see above Chapter 4, section II.C.

42 Siegel, 'Legal Aspects', at 576–7 (emphasis added).

43 For a general discussion on the role of the IMF on balance of payments issues see above Chapter 2, section II.B.1.

such consultation should indeed be dispositive on the panels.[44] Otherwise a determination by the Fund would be treated as a rebuttable presumption, meaning that the litigants could introduce other factual evidence or call in other 'experts' to convince the Panel.[45] In support of the dispositive character of such assessments, Siegel also argues that the language of GATT Article XV 'not only reflects the plain meaning of the text, but also is supported by the drafting history of the GATT, which, as noted by the United States, records a considered decision of drafters to reject a proposal (by Australia) to change "shall accept the determination" to "shall give special weight to the opinions of" the Fund'.[46]

Some may argue that according dispositive effect to the IMF findings may impair the objective assessment of the facts by the panel established in DSU Article 11. Yet '[g]iven the rule in DSU 3.2, the clause on objective analysis of the facts should yield to the special requirements on consultation with the Fund . . . the inclusion of the Dispute Settlement Understanding in the WTO Agreements should not be interpreted in a way that changes the relationship between the Fund and the WTO.'[47] The significance of the IMF in matters relating to balance of payments cannot just be simply compared to submissions from any other expert in the field. The IMF is an international organization where a large number of states are represented, with a well-established reputation, which makes decisions according to special voting procedures. As noted in Chapter 4 above, the balance of payments statement is provided by the Executive Board, an authority to which the international community has explicitly assigned a role in making these determinations. In its proceedings, the IMF members can express their views and engage in debates over the factual description and evaluation of the balance of payments problem. This state of affairs only adds to the legitimacy of such evaluations and buttresses the conviction that the balance of payments determinations should have a dispositive effect in the WTO dispute settlement process.

In *Dominican Republic – Import and Sale of Cigarettes* the Panel engaged in the interpretation of the IMF criteria in determining whether the measure was an exchange control or exchange restriction. What the Panel actually did in this case was to apply the relevant IMF decision enunciating these criteria to the measure at issue. As Viterbo rightly notes in this context,

44 Siegel, 'Legal Aspects', at 580.

45 Ahn, 'Linkages', at 25, suggesting this approach.

46 Siegel, 'Legal Aspects', at 582.

47 See also ibid., at 582–3.

> the Panel declared itself able to analyse the nature of the Dominican Republic's measure (applying the IMF standard) and, in the absence of an IMF assessment of the fee compatibility with the Articles, established that it was on the [responding state] to prove that the measure fell within the [GATT Art. XV(9)(a)] exception.[48]

According to this Decision, one of the criteria for establishing that the measure is an exchange control or an exchange restriction is its introduction by a monetary authority. The information presented by the IMF on the mechanism of implementation of the measure revealed that it was not implemented by the monetary authorities, hence was not an 'exchange restriction' or an 'exchange action' and therefore did not fall under IMF jurisdiction. This should actually have sufficed for the Panel not to engage in testing the second requirement of GATT Article XV(9)(a) – that is, whether the fee was 'consistent with the Articles of the Agreement'. If the measure is not under IMF jurisdiction checking its legality under the IMF Agreement is redundant. Although the Panel's decision to apply the IMF criterion in this case reveals institutional sensitivity in the broad sense towards this regime,[49] directly deferring to the IMF for this purpose would have been more appropriate, evidencing an explicit recognition of its institutional expertise in the field. This would have been consistent with the notion of institutional sensitivity, which encourages not only consideration of the other international regimes but also the input of the relevant international organization.[50]

V. Conclusions

The analyses of WTO case law with contributions from the IMF reveal a unique role of this institution in the international trading system and the WTO dispute settlement. This is in line with the perceptions of this organization as one entailing a well-functioning and authoritative decision-making system.[51] This is also so given its special place in the politics of world economic relations, in particular with regard to financial and monetary aspects.[52] Finally, this approach is also elicited from the intentions of

48 Annamaria Viterbo, 'Monetary Measures Affecting Trade and Investments: The Overlapping Jurisdictions of the IMF, WTO and the ICSID', SIEL Online Proceedings Working Paper No. 34/08 (2008), 14, published by *Transnational Dispute Management*, January 2009.

49 Above Chapter 1, section III.B.1.

50 Above Chapter 1, section III.A.

51 Above Chapter 4, section III.A.

52 Above Chapter 5, section II.A.

the GATT contracting parties, who perceived strong subject-matter linkage between the two regimes – something which was reflected in GATT Article XV through the requirement of consultation with the IMF.[53] Evidence is also presented by the formalization of the relationship through a large number of GATT/WTO documents. There is no other intergovernmental institution which has been attributed this much authority in the GATT/WTO. There are also only a few WTO provisions like GATT Article XV, which would pencil in express provisions purporting to avoid inconsistencies between the WTO and another international regime.[54]

In spite of this, the case law reveals a number of issues in the relations between the two institutions which may impair the institutional sensitivity of the WTO towards this institution. Thus special regard should be given to exploring fully the prerogative of the panels for consultation with this institution in order not to miss the opportunity to seek clarifications from it. It is important that the WTO panels do not read GATT Article XV(2), which prescribes mandatory consultation, as limiting their discretion to consult the IMF under DSU Article 13 on issues going beyond those enunciated in this GATT provision.[55] GATT Article XV(2) could not envisage all the situations where the IMF's expertise would be relevant in the dispute settlement process. Article 13 was introduced, as was the entire DSU, to strengthen further and elaborate the dispute settlement procedures in the newly established system, without, however, overriding, *in casu*, the more specific legal language on consultation prescribed by GATT Article XV(2).

The WTO High-Level Working Group on Coherence,[56] which was set up to discuss overlapping issues between the two institutions, could

53 Jackson, *World Trade Organization*, ch. 2. See also Richard N. Gardner, 'The Bretton Woods–GATT System after Fifty Years: A Balance Sheet of Success and Failure', in Orin Kirshner (ed.), *The Bretton Woods–GATT System: Retrospect and Prospect After 50 Years* (New York: M.E. Sharpe, 1996), 181–209.

54 Another example of such a provision is GATT Art. XXI.

55 Above Chapter 2, section II.B.

56 The High-Level Working Group on Coherence created by virtue of the WTO Co-operation Agreement with the IMF is the only inter-institutional forum where coherence is discussed and is created at the staff level. It consists of senior staff from the IMF, World Bank and the WTO. In 1999, the activity of the Group focused mainly on trade developments in the wake of the emerging markets' financial crisis, efforts to address the economic problems faced by small states, regionalism, credit for autonomous trade liberalization. Later, it streamlined its activity to preparations and participations in WTO Ministerial Conferences, as well as preparations for, and analysis of the results of, the IMF/WB Development Committee Meetings. WT/TF/COH/S/3 of 21 October 1999, 3, and WT/TF/COH/S/4 of 14 December 2000, 5.

also serve as a vehicle for fostering institutional sensitivity on behalf of both actors with respect to each other. This option should be fully explored with a view to clarifying the remaining issues. While the judicial process in specific WTO cases is more apposite for testing the viability of WTO norms, it is certainly more appropriate to look for a solution and clarification on the above issues outside the litigious context.[57]

57 See also Siegel, 'Legal Aspects', at 588, suggesting that these issues should not be solved by panels: 'To the extent that there are ambiguities or varying views on the meaning of the governing provisions, these issues should be resolved in consultations between the organs of the institutions that represent the trade and finance community of members of the two organizations rather than in the WTO dispute settlement process.'

7

The World Intellectual Property Organization

I. Introduction

The World Intellectual Property Organization is an international organization whose links to the WTO were relatively weak under the GATT. This changed with the emergence of the WTO TRIPS Agreement. Due to the incorporation of a number of intellectual property rights treaties into the WTO *corpus juris*, this organization on the one hand lost some regulatory space but, on the other, gained more authority in the WTO due to its expertise in the field of intellectual property.

The need for co-operation between the WTO and WIPO arises from several TRIPS provisions and essentially from the Co-operation Agreement signed in 1996.[1] Unlike with the IMF, none of these, however, prescribes a role for WIPO in WTO dispute settlement. Therefore some guidance on this issue is sought in WTO case law where the panels requested information from this institution, in particular *US – Section 110(5) Copyright Act*, *US – Section 211 Appropriations Act* and *China – IP Rights*.

The analyses start by illustrating in brief the merits and requests for factual information from WIPO by the panels (section II). This is followed by an examination of how various WIPO output, such as treaties, interpretations by the contracting parties, documents prepared by the WIPO Secretariat and its opinions have been considered by the WTO panels in the interpretation process (sections III–VI). The chapter culminates in an evaluation of the role of WIPO in WTO dispute settlement and the level of sensitivity accorded to it by the WTO adjudicator (section VIII), and ends in chapter conclusions (section VIII).

II. The request for factual information by panels

The *US – Section 110(5) Copyright Act* dispute between the EC and the United States originated when the latter amended its copyright law in 1998

1 Above Chapter 2, section IV.A.

to expand the exemption enjoyed by certain of its establishments from the obligation to pay royalties on some copyright music.[2] Specifically, the EC objected to the *homestyle exemption* applying to US establishments using one receiver, and to the *business exemption* applying to all retail, drinking and eating establishments.[3] The Panel upheld the EC's claim with respect to the US business exemption, while ruling that the homestyle exemption did not violate any WTO Agreement. Neither side appealed against the ruling.

The second dispute in which the Panel sought information from WIPO was *US – Section 211 Appropriations Act*.[4] The dispute arose when the US Bacardi company acquired the 'Havana Club' trademark in 1997. Subsequently, the approval of Section 211 of the 1988 Omnibus Appropriations Act by the United States prohibited the enforcement of, and transactions related to, the registration and renewal of trademarks that were the same or substantially similar to those used in connection with a business that

2 For an account of issues arising in this dispute see David J. Brennan, 'The Three-Step Test Frenzy – Why the TRIPS Panel Decision Might be Considered Per Incuriam', (2002) 2 *Intellectual Property Quarterly* 212; Helen A. Christakos, 'WTO Panel Report on Section 110(5) of the US Copyright Act', (2002) 17 *Berkeley Technology Law Journal* 595; Laurence Helfer, 'World Music on a US Stage: A Berne/TRIPS and Economic Analysis of the Fairness in Music Licensing Act', (2000) 80 *Boston University Law Review* 93; Laurence Helfer, 'World Music on a US Stage: An Analysis of the Section 110(5) WTO Dispute', (2001) 6 *International Intellectual Property Law and Policy*; Laura McCluggage, 'Section 110(5) and The Fairness in Music Licensing Act: Will the WTO Decide the United States Must Pay to Play?', (2000) 40 *IDEA: The Journal of Law and Technology* 1; Gene Grossman and Petros Mavroidis, 'Dispute Settlement Corner: United States – Section 110(5) of the US Copyright Act, Recourse to Arbitration under Art. 25 of the DSU: Would've or Should've? Impaired Benefits due to Copyright Infringement', (2003) 2 *World Trade Review* 233.

3 *US – Section 110(5) Copyright Act*, Panel Report, para. 3.1.

4 For an account of this dispute see Robert Howse and Damien Neven, 'United States–Section 211 Omnibus Appropriation Act of 1998 (WT/DS176/AB/R; DSR 2002:II, 589, DSR 2002:II, 683): A Comment', in Henrik Horn and Petros C. Mavroidis, *The WTO Case Law of 2002: The American Law Institute Reporters' Studies* (Cambridge University Press, 2005), 482–522; Stephen J. Kimmerling, 'Havana Club: A Case Summary and an Analysis of Selected Legal Issues', *Cuba in Transition*: Volume 9: Papers and Proceedings of the Ninth Annual Meeting of the Association for the Study of the Cuban Economy (ASCE), 12–14 August 1999, http://lanic.utexas.edu/la/cb/cuba/asce/cuba9/kimmerlg.pdf, visited April 2008; Frederik Abbott and Thomas Cottier, 'Dispute Prevention and Dispute Settlement in the Field of Intellectual Property Rights and Electronic Commerce: US – Section 211 Omnibus Appropriations Act 1998 ("Havana Club")', in Ernst-Ulrich Petersmann and Mark A. Pollack, *Transatlantic Economic Disputes – The EU, the US, and the WTO* (Oxford University Press, 2003); Alan Swan, 'Havana Club in the WTO: Herein of International Law and American Power', *Cuba in Transition*: Volume 12, Papers and Proceedings of the Twelfth Annual Meeting of the Association for the Study of the Cuban Economy (ASCE), 1–3 August 2002.

was confiscated by the Cuban government, as was the case for the 'Havana Club'. Since this provision was allegedly affecting the economic interests of the French company Pernod Ricard which was seeking registration of the trademark in the United States,[5] the EC launched a complaint to the WTO, arguing that US Section 211 violated certain provisions of the TRIPS Agreement, including those providing protection for trademarks, trade names or commercial names.[6] The case resulted in victory for the United States.

In *China – IP Rights*, the United States challenged several separate matters in the WTO dispute settlement system. These related to the threshold requirements for criminal procedures and penalties in Chinese law, the disposal of goods confiscated by Chinese customs authorities that infringe intellectual property rights, the issue of copyright and related rights protection for works that have not been authorized for publication or distribution within China, and the unavailability of criminal procedures and penalties for persons engaged in unauthorized reproduction or unauthorized distribution of copyright works.[7] With respect to the issue of the thresholds, the Panel found that the United States had not established that they were inconsistent with China's obligations under the TRIPS. However, China's rules on disposal of goods and those on copyright protection for works whose publication or dissemination had been prohibited by law were found to be inconsistent with the TRIPS Agreement.[8]

In all three cases the Panel requested advice from WIPO. In *US – Section 110(5) Copyright Act* it asked for 'factual information' available to it on Articles 11 and 11*bis* of the Berne Convention and the negotiating history and subsequent developments and practice concerning the relevant provisions, and sought clarification on the so-called 'minor exceptions' doctrine.[9] WIPO noted that some of the material requested was vast in scope, and unavailable in a systematic form, expressing concern that any selection of material for the dispute would imply risks of interpretations

5 This was due to their participation in a joint venture with a Cuban liquor company.

6 *US – Section 211 Appropriations Act*, Panel Report, paras. 3.1–3.4.

7 *China – IP Rights*, Panel Report, Annex A: United States' first written submission, paras. 3–12.

8 Ibid., Panel Report, paras. 8.1–8.2. For an account of the case see ICTSD, 'Mixed Ruling on China IP Enforcement', (2009) 13 (1) *ICTSD News and Analysis*, http://ictsd.net/i/news/bridges/44213/ (visited June 2009); James Mendenhall, 'WTO Panel Report on Consistency of Chinese Intellectual Property Standards', (2009) 13 *ASIL Insight* 4.

9 *China – IP Rights*, Panel Report, Attachment 4, at 245.

thereof, which would be incompatible with the neutral status of WIPO in WTO dispute settlement.[10]

In *US – Section 211 Appropriations Act*, the Panel requested 'any factual information available to WIPO on the provisions of the Paris Convention relevant to the dispute, in particular, the negotiating history and subsequent developments concerning those provisions',[11] and on the way in which the regulation of the determination of the trademark owner had been addressed in the negotiating history of the Paris Convention or in its subsequent developments.

WIPO provided the Panel with excerpts from the records of the conferences for the conclusion and revision of the Paris Convention.[12] To give one example, in its response WIPO clarified that according to the drafters of the Paris Convention, Article 6 therein intended to solve the problems arising from the differences relating to trademark application formalities in different states. Its aim was to state a principle, then existing in certain states through bilateral agreements known as '*telles quelles*', according to which, the trademark duly registered in one country had to be protected *as is* in other countries.[13]

In *China – IP Rights*, too, WIPO submitted factual information relevant to the resolution of the dispute.[14] It was requested to present any factual information available to it on the relevant provisions of the Paris Act of

10 Ibid., Letter from the Director General of WIPO to the Chair of the Panel, 22 December 1999, para. 18 stating as follows:

> This request covers a vast amount of material which is not available in a systematic and detailed indexed form. Any selection of material considered relevant for the dispute will invariably imply risks of interpretations of the material which would be incompatible with the neutral status of WIPO in relation to the dispute. In order to fulfil the request neutrally, it would be necessary to carry through a complete review of major parts of the copyright and related rights activities of WIPO during the period of so–called 'guided development' from 1967 to 1991 and a general review of the implementation of the treaty provisions in all national laws of Berne Union Member States. Such research would take a long time, and it has therefore not been undertaken. The International Bureau is, however, prepared to furnish any non–confidential material in its possession which is specified in such a way that it can be identified without the need for the International Bureau to make any interpretations of the substantive provisions of the Berne Convention.

11 *US – Section 211 Appropriations Act*, Panel Report, para. 6.1. These referred to the following Paris Convention provisions: Arts. 2.1, Art. 6, Art. 6*bis*, Art. 6*quinquies*, and Art. 8. As regards Art. 6*quinquies*, the Panel requested any factual information on its intended scope. Note should be taken that *EC – Trademarks and Geographical Indications* is another case where the Panel sought information from WIPO on issues relevant for the interpretation of the Paris Convention. See Panel Report (Australia), paras. 2.16–2.18.

12 *US – Section 211 Appropriations Act*, Panel Report, paras. 6.2–6.3.

13 Ibid., para. 6.14.

14 Ibid., paras. 2.7–2.9.

1971 of the Berne Convention and their relationship.[15] Following this request, WIPO presented all the information, which was considered by the Panel as outlined in subsequent sections.

Two points warrant emphasis at this stage. The first is that in all three cases the Panel limited itself to asking WIPO for factual information (not legal) which it intended to use for the interpretation of TRIPS provisions. The second point arises from *US – Section 110(5) Copyright Act*, where WIPO invoked its neutrality. Such neutrality of WIPO does not specifically arise from any legal instruments setting out the relationship of the two institutions (like the TRIPS Agreement or the WTO–WIPO Co-operation Agreement). In this case, it is rather for the WTO panels to be concerned with a possible delegation of power to other institutions in their interpretation process, to which they would not be entitled under WTO law.[16] Moreover, the statement that WIPO could not provide full information on specific provisions due to time constraints should have raised some doubt on the Panel's ability to make an objective assessment of the matter as set out in DSU Article 11. This in turn should have led to additional arrangements relating to the gathering of the missing information. For example, WIPO could have been asked to provide its opinion on the points of interest for the missing part of the information, if other solutions were not available.

III. Non-incorporated WIPO treaties: *US – Section 110(5) Copyright Act*

US – Section 110(5) Copyright Act has to be singled out as an important case revealing how WTO panels or the Appellate Body can approach intellectual property rights treaties emerging in WIPO after the advent of the WTO. Moreover, this is one of the cases where there was an extensive discussion by the Panel of the VCLT as it relates to the interaction of the WTO and WIPO, as illustrated in the following sections.

In this case, the Panel examined the relevance of the WIPO Copyright Treaty (WCT) to its interpretative exercise. Despite the WCT not being incorporated into TRIPS, the Panel approached this instrument as if it were incorporated. The Panel noted that, along with the Berne Convention, the WCT formed 'the overall framework for multilateral

15 Ibid., Annex D, Letter Dated 21 April 2008 from the Panel to the International Bureau of WIPO, p. D-8.

16 For an account of the delegation doctrine see above Chapter 4, section II.A.1.

copyright protection'.[17] Since most of the countries that participated in the diplomatic conference at which the WCT was concluded were also WTO members and hence parties to (and in most cases negotiators of) TRIPS, the WCT 'is designed to be compatible with this framework'.[18] In the Panel's view, it should therefore also be interpreted together with TRIPS in such a way as to avoid conflict between them.[19]

This reading has significant implications for the way in which the WTO panels and the Appellate Body should deal with non-incorporated treaties negotiated under the auspices of WIPO. The approach in *US – Section 110(5) Copyright Act* is commended and should certainly be followed by future panels. It reveals significant institutional sensitivity on behalf of the WTO adjudicator towards another international regime with high relevance to the interpretation of WTO law. The following sections of this chapter address the core issues examined in this study – that is, how the WTO panels or the Appellate Body have taken account of all the other interpretative material emerging from WIPO in the relevant disputes.

IV. Interpretations by the contracting parties

A. The General Report to the 1948 Berne Revision Conference

In *US – Section 110(5) Copyright Act*, the Panel had to interpret the 'minor exceptions doctrine' to decide whether it could be read into the WTO TRIPS Agreement.[20] This doctrine consists of certain limited and inconsequential exceptions to the exclusive rights recognized under the Berne Convention that are permissible in national legislation which are not expressed therein; rather, they exist by implication and are understood as such by the members of the Berne Union.[21]

17 *US – Section 110(5) Copyright Act*, Panel Report, para. 6.70. 18 Ibid. 19 Ibid.

20 This is key to understanding the reasoning of the Panel in *US – Section 110(5) Copyright Act* in choosing to apply the 'three-step test'.

21 According to Sam Ricketson, the doctrine is based on the *de minimus* principle of interpretation, namely that the law is not concerned with trifles; this means that exceptions to the rights granted in the relevant articles of the Convention must be concerned with uses of minimal, or no, significance to the author. Thus, while not part of the wording of Berne, the minor exceptions doctrine is said to be part of its 'spirit'. See Sam Ricketson, *The Berne Convention for the Protection of Literary and Artistic Works: 1886–1986* (London: Queen Mary College – University of London, 1987), para. 9.63(1). See also the European Commission, Report to the Committee Established under Art. 7 of Council Regulation (EC) No. 3286/94 (Trade Barriers Regulation), Examination Procedure Regarding the Licensing of Music Works in the United States of America, LE.3/JVE D(98), Brussels 23 February 1996, 13.

After having noted the principal rule of interpretation in the VCLT, the Panel stated that 'in accord with Article 31(2)(a) the context for the purpose of the interpretation of a treaty shall comprise, in addition to the text, including its preamble and annexes, any agreement relating to the treaty which was made between all the parties in connection with the conclusion of the treaty'.[22] The Panel took special note of the reference to the minor exceptions doctrine in the General Report to the 1948 Berne Revision Conference as expressing such agreement.[23]

This statement was taken by the Panel to indicate that an agreement 'was made between all the parties in connection with the conclusion of the treaty', under which minor exceptions could apply to the rights contained in those articles. Thus, having established the applicability of the minor exceptions doctrine under the Berne Convention to the rights involved in the dispute, the Panel determined that TRIPS Article 9(1) incorporated not only the legal language of this Convention, but also its *acquis*, that is, the context of each provision's enactment and their prevailing interpretations.

B. *Other conference documents*

In interpreting the trademark-related obligations enshrined in the Paris Convention Article 6*quinquies*,[24] the *US – Section 211 Appropriations Act* Panel found that the US measure was not inconsistent with it, inasmuch as the restrictions it placed on registration were not related to the form of the trademark. The broad sense of Article 6*quinquies* of the Paris Convention, which was asserted by the EC, implied that the country was obliged to register this trademark and, not only that, it had to register it 'as is' unless one of the exceptions applied. The narrow meaning, asserted by the United States, suggested that if the domestic law of a country otherwise permitted

22 *US – Section 110(5) Copyright Act*, Panel Report, para. 6.44.

23 The statement of the Rapporteur-General read: 'Your Rapporteur-General has been entrusted with making an express mention of the possibility available to national legislation to make what are commonly called minor reservations. The Delegates of Norway, Sweden, Denmark, and Finland, the Delegate of Switzerland and the Delegate of Hungary, have all mentioned these limited exceptions allowed for religious ceremonies, military bands and the needs of the child and adult education. These exceptional measures apply to Articles 11bis, 11ter, 13 and 14. You will understand that these references are just lightly pencilled in here, in order to avoid damaging the principle of the right.' Ibid., para. 6.48.

24 This provision reads in part: 'Every trademark duly registered in the country of origin shall be accepted for filing and protected *as is* in the other countries of the union, subject to the reservations indicated in this article' (emphasis added).

the registration of this trademark, that country was obliged to register it in exactly the form that it was presented, subject to some exceptions.

To support the narrow (US) reading of this provision, the Panel referred to the documents concerning the Lisbon Conference of 1958 provided by WIPO, namely to an *agreed interpretation* of contracting parties on the provision predating Article 6*quinquies* of the Paris Convention.[25] But since this agreed interpretation was set aside later on, the Panels contended that it had a reduced value as a possible interpretative tool under subsequent agreement set out in Article 31(3)(a) of the Vienna Convention.[26] Therefore, it was attributed to and considered as historical record. Due to the omission of this agreed interpretation in the subsequent versions of the Paris Convention, the Appellate Body, too, was unsure about relying on it and stated solely that 'we simply observe that our interpretation . . . is not inconsistent with this interpretation [of the Panel]'.[27]

C. Evaluation

It is noteworthy that in *US – Section 110(5) Copyright Act*, the statement made by the Rapporteur-General of the Conference on the interpretation of the minor exceptions doctrine was considered by the Panel as establishing an 'agreement' between Berne Union members in the sense of Vienna Convention Article 31(2)(a). The Panel thus attributed significant weight to this statement, using it to buttress its conclusion on the existence of the doctrine and its incorporation into the TRIPS Agreement.[28]

Some criticism, however, has been levelled at the Panel's application of the 'three-step test' enshrined in TRIPS Article 13, which sets out some limits on departures from the exclusive rights of the authors.[29] This TRIPS

25 *US – Section 211 Appropriations Act*, Panel Report, para. 8.82. Para. 4 of that Final Protocol in 1883 explained that Art. 6*quinquies* A(1) 'should be understood in the sense that no trademark may be excluded from protection in one of the States of the Union for the sole reason that it does not comply, with regard to the signs of which it is composed, with the conditions of the laws of that State, provided it complies on this point with the laws of the country of origin and that it has been properly filed there. Subject to this exception, which only concerns the form of the mark, and subject to the provision of the other Articles of the Convention, each State shall apply its domestic law'.

26 VCLT Art. 31(3)(a) reads: 'There shall be taken into account, together with the context: any subsequent agreement between the parties regarding the interpretation of the treaty or the application of its provisions.'

27 *US – Section 211 Appropriations* Act, ABR, para. 146.

28 But see Brennan, 'Three-Step Test Frenzy'.

29 For an account of the three-step test see Brennan, ibid. See also Kamiel J. Koelman, 'Fixing the Three-Step Test', (2006) 28 *European Intellectual Property Review* 407; Jane

provision, entitled 'Limitations and Exceptions', provides that 'Members shall confine limitations or exceptions to exclusive rights to certain special cases [step 1] which do not conflict with a normal exploitation of the work [step 2] and do not unreasonably prejudice the legitimate interests of the right holder [step 3].' The criticism in point was aimed at the alleged disregard by the Panel of some parts of the Rapporteur-General's report qualifying the status of the minor exceptions doctrine.[30] This, according to an observer, reveals the ad hoc character of the WTO panels' decision-making, with important issues being left according to their whim.[31]

Conversely, in *US – Section 211 Appropriations Act* there is no clear attribution of the agreed interpretation of the Paris Convention to the 'context'. Howse and Neven note in this context that reading the agreed interpretation into the 'context' would have been a correct approach. This is because, according to them, Vienna Convention Article 31(2)(a) applies not only to agreement, which is explicitly made an integral part of the main treaty, but to any agreement connected with the conclusion of the treaty.[32] Thus 'the fact that the instrument incorporating the agreed interpretation was not made an integral part of subsequent versions of the treaty, does not as such defeat its status as an "agreement . . . made in connection with the conclusion of the treaty"'.[33] These authors conclude with an important statement: 'the Vienna Convention would have allowed the Appellate Body to rely to a greater extent than it did on the agreed interpretation, which it appeared to treat almost as supplementary means, like *travaux*, which could normally be used to confirm an interpretation based on primary sources'.[34] Thus the attribution of the agreed interpretation to the primary rules of interpretation would have ascribed it a higher normative value. This would have made the Panel decision more compatible with the proposal for greater institutional sensitivity of the WTO adjudicator towards the material ensuing from another international organization.

C. Ginsburg, 'Toward Supranational Copyright Law? The WTO Panel Decision and the "Three-Step Test" for Copyright Exceptions', (2001) 187 *Revue Internationale du Droit d'Auteur*; Daniel J. Gervais, 'Towards a New Core International Copyright Norm: The Reverse Three-Step Test', (2005) 9 *Marquette Intellectual Property Law Review* 1.

30 Brennan, 'Three-Step Test Frenzy', at 19.

31 Ibid., noting that 'Perhaps the Panel in the home-style decision found the allure of the three-step test so mesmerising, that in its rush to apply the test broadly, the Panel allowed itself to overlook the very material which would have properly tempered the test's application.'

32 Howse and Neven, 'United States–Section 211', at 498.

33 Ibid.

34 Ibid.

The WTO adjudicator in this case not only took account of the WIPO's *acquis* on implicit or explicit agreement of the members; it made numerous references to other WIPO documents with relevance to the interpretation process. These documents are commonly generated in the exercise of the regulatory-administrative functions of WIPO.[35] The nature and weight attributed to these instruments in the WTO dispute settlement is illustrated in the following section.[36]

V. Documents prepared by WIPO

A. *Uruguay Round documents in* US – Section 110(5) Copyright Act

In support of its positive finding in *US – Section 110(5) Copyright Act* on the incorporation of the minor exceptions doctrine into the TRIPS Agreement, the Panel referred to a briefing document produced by WIPO in the context of the 1988 Uruguay Round TRIPS negotiations. Entitled 'Existence, Scope and Form of Generally Internationally Accepted and Applied Standards/Norms for the Protection of Intellectual Property', the document described the operation and nature of the various treaties administered by WIPO – including the Berne Convention.[37] This was produced by the International Bureau following a decision taken by the GATT Negotiating Group on Trade-Related Aspects of Intellectual Property Rights, inviting WIPO 'to prepare a factual document to facilitate an understanding of the existence, scope and form of generally internationally accepted and applied standards/norms for the protection of intellectual property'.[38] The use of this material in the Panel's

35 For example, to express their understanding of the matter, WIPO used statements such as 'it is generally believed'.

36 For a more general account of the material from international organizations see above Chapter 1, section III.B.2.a.

37 See WTO document MTN.GNG/NG11/W/24/Rev.1, 15 September 1988.

38 *US – Section 110(5) Copyright Act*, Panel Report, para. 6.64, referring to WTO document MTN.GNG/NG11/6, and para. 6.65, referring to MTN.GNG/NG11/W/32/Rev.2, 2 February 1990. This last document 'contains the first specific proposals on the rights to be conferred and on the permissible limitations, exceptions and compulsory licensing in the area of copyright. The first column in each table sets out the provisions of the international treaties existing at that time corresponding to the proposals made. The Secretariat prepared the content of this column drawing on the above-mentioned document prepared by the International Bureau of WIPO. In the first column of paragraph 5 on limitations, the Secretariat reproduced, in its rendering of the existing international standards, the above-mentioned information provided by WIPO on minor exceptions

interpretation process lead ultimately to finding that the Berne Convention 'minor exception' doctrine was incorporated into the TRIPS Agreement.

The reference of the Panel to these instruments reveals sensitivity towards the Berne *acquis* but also acknowledges the historical role of WIPO in the administration of these core intellectual property rights treaties, as well as a role in the negotiations of the TRIPS Agreement.[39] The Panel did not specifically classify this material under the Vienna Convention interpretation rules, but given the explicit statement of the Panel that the material was confirmatory of a conclusion reached, it is obvious that the documents were considered as a supplementary means of interpretation.

B. Guides and reports

1. The three-step test in *US – Section 110(5) Copyright Act*

According to the defendant in *US – Section 110(5) Copyright Act*, TRIPS Article 13 justified the exemptions from the payment of royalties as introduced with *US – Section 110(5)*. As noted above, TRIPS Article 13 (as well as the related provision in Article 9(2) of the Berne Convention) imposes a 'three-step test' to evaluate the legitimacy of exceptions and limitations on copyright exclusive rights. The substantive difference between the TRIPS Article 13 obligation and Article 9(2) of the Berne Convention is that the latter covers only the *right of reproduction*, while the former condones possible limitations and exceptions to 'exclusive rights' in general (i.e. the right of reproduction, the right of communication to the public and the right of rental).[40] In this context, the EU contended that TRIPS Article 13 should apply only to the rights newly introduced into TRIPS; it should not provide an additional or broader defence to a violation of pre-existing Berne Convention rights.[41] In the light of this argument, the Panel set its task as addressing the relationship between the mentioned exceptions set forth in the Berne Convention as incorporated

doctrine.' See also Evans, 'Intellectual Property', at 168–9. See also generally on the negotiation of the TRIPS Agreement, Daniel Gervais, *The TRIPS Agreement, Drafting History and Analysis*, 2nd edn (London: Sweet & Maxwell, 2003).

39 Gervais, *TRIPS Agreement*, n. 73, noting that WIPO played an important role throughout the TRIPS negotiations.

40 Mihaly Ficsor, *The Law of Copyright and the Internet* (Oxford University Press, 2002), 301–2.

41 *US – Section 110(5) Copyright Act*, Panel Report, paras. 6.34 and 6.47–6.66.

in TRIPS, and the general TRIPS Article 13 exception. Having equated the performance rights' 'minor exceptions' with exceptions permitted under the three-step test, the Panel analysed each of the steps, in order to assess whether the US exemption could be justified under this latter provision.[42]

While the Panel did not refer to any WIPO material in the assessment of whether the US exemption qualified as a 'certain special measure' (step one of three), a number of such important references emerged in the application of the remaining two steps – 'that [limitations or exceptions] do not conflict with the normal exploitation' of the work and that they do not 'unreasonably prejudice the legitimate interests of the right holder'.[43]

a. 'Do not conflict with the normal exploitation'. In examining this second step of the test, the Panel turned to the 'normative' connotation of the term 'normal exploitation'. It is in this context that it examined WIPO documents prepared for the 1967 Stockholm Revision Conference that drafted Article 9(2) of the Berne Convention. Citing a Report of the Swedish government and the United International Bureaux for the Protection of Intellectual Property (BIRPI),[44] the Panel indicated that the disputed exception 'should not enter into economic competition' with the right-holder. According to the Report, 'all forms of exploiting a work, which have, or are likely to acquire, considerable economic or practical importance, must be reserved to the authors'.[45] Applying the 'economic competition' standard, the Panel ruled that the US Section 110(5)(B) business exemption was impermissible, whereas the homestyle exemption did not 'conflict with a normal exploitation of the work', as the latter appeared to be of little economic or practical importance.[46]

b. 'Do not unreasonably prejudice the legitimate interests of the copyright holder'. On the interpretation of the third step – with regard to the tolerable levels of 'prejudice' – the Panel noted that the formulation 'not unreasonably prejudice' 'connotes a slightly stricter standard' than

42 See Mihaly Ficsor, 'Copyright in the Digital Era: the WIPO "Internet" Treaties', (1997) 21 *Columbia Journal of Law and the Arts* 8, at 22–3, stating that 'generally and normally, there is no conflict between the Berne Convention and TRIPS Agreement as far as exceptions and limitations to the exclusive rights are concerned', citing WIPO Publication No. 464(E).

43 TRIPS, Art. 13.

44 Bureaux for the Protection of Intellectual Property, the predecessor organization to WIPO.

45 *US – Section 110(5) Copyright Act*, Panel Report, para. 6.179, quoting Document S/1: Berne Convention; proposals for Revising the Substantive Copyright Provisions (Arts. 1–20), prepared by the Government of Sweden with the assistance of the BIRPI, at 42.

46 Ibid., paras. 6.209–6.219.

'reasonable'.[47] In this specific context, the Panel referred to the WIPO Guide to the Berne Convention.[48] Citing the 'persuasive value' of this document, the Panel noted that the prejudice might be brought back to tolerable levels. Thus 'in cases where there would be a serious loss of profit for the copyright owner, the law should provide him with some compensation (a system of compulsory licensing with equitable remuneration)'.[49] The US exception, however, imposed an outright exemption; it did not offer any compensation. Thus the reference to the WIPO Guide backed the Panel's finding that the US exemptions caused unreasonable prejudice to the copyright holder.

2. Interpretation of Article 17 of the Berne Convention in *China – IP Rights*

Article 17 of the Berne Convention, as incorporated into TRIPS Article 9(1), establishes that governments have certain rights to control the exploitation of works.[50] Invoking a defence under this provision, the defendant in *China – IP Rights* referred to the WIPO Guide to the Berne Convention in response to the US claim that Chinese legislation was denying copyright protection as conferred under Article 5(1) of the Berne Convention. The reference was made to support China's view that Article 17 of the Berne Convention 'relates mainly to censorship and public order'.[51]

Although the Panel agreed with this interpretation, it argued that there was no reason to suppose that censorship would eliminate those rights entirely with respect to a particular work. According to the Panel, China was unable to explain why censorship interfered with copyright owners' rights to prevent third parties from exploiting prohibited works. It therefore found China's legislation at issue to be inconsistent with Berne Convention Article 5(1).[52]

C. *Model provisions in* China – IP Rights

Another reference in *China – IP Rights* is made to WIPO material in the interpretation of the obligations set out in Article 61 of the TRIPS

47 Ibid., para. 6.225. 48 Ibid. 49 Ibid., n. 205.

50 In full, Art. 17 of the Berne Convention reads: 'The provisions of this Convention cannot in any way affect the right of the Government of each country of the Union to permit, to control, or to prohibit, by legislation or regulation, the circulation, presentation, or exhibition of any work or production in regard to which the competent authority may find it necessary to exercise that right'.

51 *China – IP Rights*, Panel Report, para. 7.131. 52 Ibid., para. 7.132.

Agreement.[53] The exercise involved the first sentence of this provision, requiring members to 'provide for criminal procedures and penalties to be applied at least in cases of wilful trademark counterfeiting or copyright piracy on a commercial scale'.

1. The explanatory observation as 'context'

With a view to clarifying the meaning of the phrase 'on a commercial scale' set out in TRIPS Article 61, the Panel took note of China's reference to the activity of the WIPO Committee of Experts on Measures against Counterfeiting and Piracy in 1988, which took place in parallel with the early negotiations of the TRIPS Agreement. In order to guide the activity of this WIPO Committee at the time, the International Bureau issued a 'Draft Model Provisions for National Laws' in a Memorandum. This document contained a proviso referring to the term 'on a commercial scale' which was accompanied by an explanatory observation reading as follows:

> 'Commercial scale' is a notion which will have to be applied taking into consideration the circumstances accompanying the manufacture. The quantity of the goods manufactured, the way in which they were, are, or are intended to be used and the will to make profit are among the factors that the courts will have to take into consideration.[54]

The *China – IP Rights* Panel did not give weight to this explanation, arguing that 'the explanatory observation did not purport to be a definition but was prepared by the International Bureau of WIPO for the specific purpose of accompanying a provision on manufacturing in the draft Model Provisions'.[55] Moreover, the Panel believed that the Report issued by the above Committee showed that the concept of 'commercial scale' was controversial and therefore it was not an example of ordinary usage of this term.[56] Finally, to argue against the possible consideration of this material as 'context', the Panel submitted that the draft Model Provisions was never agreed, as the Committee's work was not completed; therefore it did not find it appropriate 'to elevate it to the status of the proper interpretation of a treaty text that was negotiated in another forum and that *was* finally agreed'.[57]

53 Ibid., paras. 7.503–7.669. 54 Ibid., para. 7.562 and n. 539. 55 Ibid., para. 567.
56 Ibid. 57 Ibid. (emphasis added).

2. The explanatory observation as supplementary means

The reference to the explanatory observation re-emerged in *China – IP Rights* during the consideration by the Panel of the supplementary means of interpretation.[58] The Panel also discarded this material from the interpretative exercise on rather dubious grounds. Reasserting that the explanatory observation did not represent the *common intentions* of the WIPO Committee participants, the Panel noted that this was also true with respect to the participants in the negotiations of the TRIPS Agreement. Specifically, the Panel considered that the fact that

> 'Documents of the WIPO Committee of Experts, including the draft Model Provisions, were *communicated* to the TRIPS negotiating group and *made available* in the GATT Secretariat for consultation by interested delegations, *but not circulated*, in June 1988 [emphasis added]', evidenced only that the negotiators were aware of this material but were not indicating that the 'content of that explanatory observation represented their common intentions'.[59]

Furthermore, despite the use of the term 'commercial scale' in the TRIPS negotiation group, the Panel referred to the EC argument, which noted that the interpreted term was not sourced from another instrument; not from the explanatory observation to the Model Provisions of WIPO.[60] In support of its decision to discard this instrument from its consideration, the Panel contended that, in any event, there were differences between the draft Model Provisions of WIPO, the EC proposal during negotiations and the terms of the interpreted Article 61 of TRIPS.[61] Against this background, the interpretation of the term 'commercial scale' as found in the draft Model Provisions was not considered by the Panel under the supplementary means either.

D. Evaluation

In spite of its alleged attribution to the supplementary means of interpretation under the Vienna Convention rules, the references to the BIRPI

58 Ibid., paras. 7.582 -7.590. 59 Ibid., para. 7.586. 60 Ibid., para. 7.587 and n. 564.

61 Ibid., para. 7.588. In particular, the draft Model Provisions incorporated the phrase 'on a commercial scale' into the concepts of 'counterfeiting' and 'piracy', while Art. 61 used the phrase 'on a commercial scale' to qualify the concepts of 'wilful trademark counterfeiting or copyright piracy'. Further, the explanatory observation that accompanied the draft Model Provisions was limited to the act of manufacturing, while Art. 61 encompassed the range of acts of counterfeiting and piracy.

Report and WIPO's Guide to the Berne Convention were essential for the outcome of *US – Section 110(5) Copyright Act*. It is clear that the consideration of these elements under the VCLT primary rules of interpretation would have ascribed them higher value,[62] but the reliance of the Panel thereon is to be praised in any case, as it evidences reliance on the customary international rules of interpretation for the purpose of its exercise and an endeavour to make an objective assessment of the matter.[63]

China – IP Rights reveals that the Panel did not consider the WIPO explanatory observation on the draft Model Provisions presented during the TRIPS Agreement negotiations. Despite the repeated mention of this document in the records of the TRIPS negotiations, the Panel rejected considering it as preparatory work, with the argument that it did not reflect the common intentions of the negotiators. It is believed, however, that the standard prescribed by this instrument is clearer, and a more helpful statement of the meaning of 'commercial scale'.[64] It sets out general guidance that the circumstances relating to the manufacturing at issue should be taken into account. Then it refers to more concrete factors such as the 'quantity of goods', the intended use, and the 'will' to make a profit. This explanation offers a far more precise explanation than the Panel's interpretation, and could have been used in the interpretation of the text of TRIPS Article 61.[65]

Moreover, there is no doubt that the preparatory work may turn out to be very heterogeneous and devoid of a clear definition.[66] It seems, however, that the common intentions requirement applied to the Model Provisions by the Panel is akin to the proposition that the preparatory work should be limited to include only representations which establish a concordance of the parties on the material at issue.[67] Linderfalk, for example, defines preparatory work as 'any representation, whether textual or non-textual, produced during the drafting of a treaty'.[68] He ignores

62 See above Chapter 3 for an account.

63 For a detailed account of VCLT rules of interpretation see above Chapter 3.

64 Commentary to *China – IP Rights*, Panel Report, at 23, available at www.worldtradelaw.net (visited July 2009).

65 Ibid.

66 Ulf Linderfalk, *On the Interpretation of Treaties: The Modern International Law as Expressed in the 1969 Vienna Convention on the Law of Treaties* (New York: Springer Verlag AG, 2007), 241, citing Gyoergy Haraszti, *Some Fundamental Problems of the Law of Treaties* (Budapest: Akademiai Kiado, 1973), 120.

67 See e.g. Daniel P. O'Connell, *International Law*, 2nd edn, vol.1 (London: Stevens & Sons, 1970), 262; see also Haraszti, *Some Fundamental Problems*, at 122.

68 Linderfalk, *On the Interpretation of Treaties*, 241.

the concordance requirement on the grounds that it deviates from this definition.[69]

The view here is that the preparatory work should not be constrained by the common intentions requirement. If this is to be read as such, it would be difficult to make a distinction between the preparatory work and the context of the conclusion of the treaty, where agreement is explicitly required under Vienna Convention Article 31(2).[70] What is more, the absence of common intention should certainly not be inferred from the non-circulation of the material to every party to the treaty. It seems that the material in question was brought to the attention of the TRIPS negotiating group twice, and this should have sufficed for it to qualify as preparatory work, even if the discussion on the scope of trade in counterfeit goods was never concluded.[71]

The issues arising from this decision of the Panel are twofold. First, the Panel seemed to approach the non-circulation of the material as akin to non-acquaintance, which according to some authors should prevent the consideration of the material as preparatory work.[72] Second, the non-conclusion of the discussion seems to be equated with the suggestion that preparatory work does not cover representation that did not mark the final text of the negotiated treaty.[73] While the second approach does not find clear support in the definition of the preparatory work provided above, the issue of acquaintance has been widely disputed in the literature after the PCIJ *River Oder* case.[74] In this regard, the International Law Commission stated in its 1966 Commentary that 'it does not stand to reason that we should treat a representation as not forming part of the preparatory work of a treaty, just because all treaty parties were not involved in its production – especially so if we consider the many important multilateral

69 Ibid. 70 For a comprehensive discussion see above Chapter 3, section III.G.3.

71 *China – IP Rights*, Panel Report, para. 7.586.

72 But see Linderfalk, *On the Interpretation of Treaties*, 243, discussing (and actually disapproving of) this requirement, which prescribes that 'In order for a representation to be considered part of the "preparatory work" of a treaty, each and every party which itself was not a negotiating state must have had at least an opportunity to acquaint itself with the contents of the representation; that opportunity must have existed prior to the moment when a party in question expressed its consent to be bound.'

73 For this view see O'Connell, *International Law*, at 262; Linderfalk, *On the Interpretation of Treaties*, 241, citing Haraszti, *Some Fundamental Problems*, 125.

74 *Case Relating to the Territorial Jurisdiction of the International Commission of the River Oder (UK v. Poland)*, 1929 PCIJ (ser. A) No. 23 (Sept. 10). The author who first made clear his rejection of this approach was Hersch Lauterpacht. See Linderfalk, *On the Interpretation of Treaties*, at 273; and Sinclair, *Vienna Convention*, at 142.

treaties that are open to general accession'.[75] Against this background it can be concluded that the *China – IP Rights* Panel applied the acquaintance requirement too restrictively, which led to the exclusion of the explanatory observation to the WIPO Model Provisions from its consideration.

VI. The opinion of the WIPO Secretariat: *US – Section 211 Appropriations Act*

An important testimony to the WTO judicial sensitivity towards WIPO arises in *US – Section 211 Appropriations Act* in relation to the EC's claim that the US legislation was inconsistent with TRIPS Article 16 (corresponding to Article 6*bis* of the Paris Convention).[76] To apply this provision, the Panel had to understand whether the Paris Convention prescribed *how* the trademark owner has to be determined under the domestic law of Paris Union members.[77] Thus the Panel asked WIPO to provide any factual information on the way in which this issue might have been addressed in the negotiating history of the Convention or in subsequent developments.

The Director General of WIPO explained in response that even though some provisions of the Paris Convention referred to the concept of trademark ownership, no provisions addressed the question of *how* the owner of a trademark had to be determined under the domestic law of states party to the Paris Convention.[78] On appeal, the Appellate Body noted that the Panel had not discussed this issue; however, it seems that the Panel implicitly accepted WIPO's determination that the definition of the conditions of ownership had been left to the legislative discretion of individual countries of the Paris Union by Article 6(1) of the Paris Convention (1967).[79] WIPO's input was allegedly a legal evaluation, as it turned on

75 See ILC Draft Articles (1966), above Chapter 3 n. 54, at 223.

76 The provision confers a substantive right to exclude third parties from using the mark for identical or similar goods or services such that there is a likelihood of consumer confusion.

77 *US – Section 211 Appropriations Act*, Panel Report, para. 6.2.

78 Ibid., para. 6.41. The letter from the Director General of the International Bureau of WIPO, dated 2 March 2001, states: 'Even though some provisions of the Paris Convention refer to the concept of trademark ownership (Art. 5C(2) and (3), and Art. 6*septies*: "proprietor", Article 6*ter*(1)(c): "owner", Article 6*bis*(1) "being already the mark of a person entitled to the benefits of this Convention"), no provision addresses the question how the owner of a trademark has to be determined under the domestic law of States party to the Paris Convention.'

79 Ibid., ABR, para. 189.

its understanding of the legal provisions of the Paris Convention.[80] Considering this fact, the Panel certainly showed considerable sensitivity to an opinion which ensued from the WIPO Secretariat, in contrast to a decision approved by the WIPO members. As explained above, there are some limits to the level of such sensitivity, dictated by a number of WTO internal and external factors.[81] In this particular case, it could easily be argued that the Panel and the Appellate Body went beyond those limits, making their decision a clearer target for criticism. In spite of this, the approach is commended in the context of this study, provided the Panel weighs carefully this type of information.

VII. General evaluation

The case law analysis has revealed that WIPO's input considered in the WTO disputes was not, like the WIPO Copyright Treaty, limited to the conventional law but included other material as well, such as guides to the WIPO-administered conventions, reports on issues arising thereof and publications or Model Provisions for national law. This reveals that a large number of WIPO instruments can be relevant to the interpretation process of the panels or the Appellate Body in TRIPS-related disputes.

It should be recalled that the attribution by the WTO adjudicator of these secondary instruments to primary as opposed to secondary VCLT rules of interpretation is key to the judgement of the degree of sensitivity of the WTO panels towards this organization. For example, the approach of the Panel in *China – IP Rights* could hardly be regarded as showing such sensitivity. As stressed above, the draft Model Provisions invoked by China was not considered under either heading – context or supplementary means of the VCLT rules of interpretation.

While the large number of references to these instruments shows a positive development for the institutional sensitivity proposition advocated here, this account does not present the entire picture. To complete the analysis, one needs to look at the nature of this material and mostly at the weight it brings to bear on the outcome of the interpretative exercise.[82]

80 For a more detailed account of this issue see section VII.A below presenting arguments in favour and against this deference.

81 For a discussion of these limits see above Chapter 4, in particular section III discussing 'External constraints'.

82 For an account of the classification of interpretative material under VCLT rules of interpretation and its impact on establishing the level of institutional sensitivity of the WTO adjudicator, see above Chapter 3.

A. *The nature and weight of WIPO's input*

Unlike with the IMF, where the WTO panels explicitly used the term 'consultation', WIPO was approached with a request for *factual information* in all examined cases. WIPO duly complied with all these requests which were relied on by the panels.[83] The predominant argument in the literature relating to the nature of this information is that WIPO has never interpreted a relevant provision of an intellectual property convention on behalf of WTO panels; it has mostly delivered factual information on matters such as the historical record of a certain provision or the existence and contents of subsequent treaties in a specific field of interest.[84]

The case law analysed in this study indeed reveals that the panel requests addressed to WIPO usually emphasized the word 'factual'. However, at least with respect to *US – Section 211 Appropriations Act*, it has been claimed that the information submitted by WIPO to the Panel was a legal interpretation of the Paris Convention.[85] This sensitivity of the Appellate Body has been praised by Howse and Neven, who note that 'the adjudicator's deference to the WIPO's opinion in this case is an example of the kind of "institutional sensitivity" that [was] recommended in dispute settlement'.[86] This approach serves to enhance the legitimacy of the WTO dispute settlement institutions.[87] What is striking here, according to these authors,

83 With the exception of *US – Section 110(5) Copyright Act* and *China – IP Rights*, where WIPO tried to limit its contribution to the Panel on the grounds that it risked engaging in an interpretative exercise, which would allegedly run contrary to its neutral status in relation to the WTO. See above section I in this chapter.

84 Oesch, *Standards of Review*, 211–12; Cottier and Oesch, *International Trade Regulation*, 118. Okediji, 'WIPO–WTO Relations', at 47, for example, summarizes the role of WIPO in WTO disputes as follows:

> [I]n the majority of the twelve reports issued, TRIPS dispute panels or the Appellate Body either have not referenced WIPO at all in their legal analyses or have only referenced factual information about WIPO, such as noting WIPO's administrative oversight of the Berne and Paris Conventions. [footnote omitted] In several disputes, the panel/Appellate Body has requested factual information from WIPO, [footnote omitted] and a few decisions reflect reliance on WIPO publications and documentation in interpreting the TRIPS obligations at issue. [footnote omitted] It is interesting that it is predominantly in this latter sense that WIPO's activities have penetrated the WTO regime, illustrating yet again the normative power of WIPO's historical technical obligation to issue publications in the field of IP. [footnote omitted]

85 See above section VI.

86 Howse and Neven, 'United States–Section 211', at 503.

87 See above Chapter 1, section II.B.

is the Appellate Body's endorsement of such deference not just with respect to factual matters, but also in legal interpretation; this qualifies what seemed in some earlier cases the Appellate Body's tendency to consider itself competent to interpret the relevant law of other regimes, including municipal law, as if it were interpreting WTO law itself (provided of course that the other law was properly before it as relevant to the application of a WTO Agreement; India – Patents, EC – Bananas).[88]

On the other hand, one wonders whether in this case the Appellate Body could have attempted a contextual definition of the relevant TRIPS obligation. This interpretation would have implied that the owner of a trademark was the undertaking that had originally used or registered the mark (the EC argument). The Panel instead deferred to WIPO, which suggested that the matter was at the discretion of domestic authorities.[89]

An issue thus may also arise at the opposite extreme – that is, having too much deference – which might discourage the WTO adjudicator from properly exploring the interpretative elements residing in the WTO. It has been argued that the Appellate Body's conclusion that the silence of the TRIPS Agreement on ownership implies that it is the home authority that gets to decide the bona fide owner is perverse; this may imply that, through ownership measures, a government can impose a wide range of responsibilities on an entity that wishes to have the status of the 'owner' of a mark, including social responsibility.[90]

This view is also shared by Alan Swan, who notes that 'By turning the issue of trademark ownership over to national law, rather than keeping it

88 Howse and Neven, 'United States–Section 211', at 503.

89 See also Laurence R. Helfer, 'Adjudicating Copyright Claims Under The TRIPS Agreement: The Case for a European Human Rights Analogy', (1998) 39 *Harvard International Law Journal* 357, at 437, who is of the view that this approach respects the TRIPS drafters' decision to impose a single limitations clause with a distinctive three-part test while preserving much of the national discretion that governments enjoyed when applying that same test under Berne Art. 9(2). It is also consistent with TRIPS Art. 13's drafting history, an interpretation given by WIPO, the new WIPO Copyright Treaty, and the views of most commentators that the bulk of Art. 9(2)'s deferential practices have been preserved in TRIPS. He admits, however, that WIPO's reading of Art. 13 can be criticized as non-committal and opaque, but that it is consistent with the approach advocated above. See also WIPO International Bureau, 'Implication of the TRIPS Agreement on Treaties Administered by WIPO', *International Review of Industrial Property & Copyright Law* (May 1996) 164, at 171, providing that the limitations and exceptions permitted under Berne, 'if correctly applied' are consistent with Art. 13.

90 Howse and Neven, 'United States–Section 211', at 504. They argue on this point that 'the very nature of 16.1 [TRIPS] is that of an obligation that rights established in one jurisdiction (the home jurisdiction) be recognized by the authorities of other WTO jurisdictions; thus, there is arguably no need to define ownership'.

strictly within the confines of TRIPS and the other treaties, the Appellate Body knew it was opening the matter up for genuine abuse as nations would undoubtedly be tempted to craft many and novel discriminatory limitations on the recognition of foreign trademarks.'[91] Along the same lines, Oesch also notes that the reference of this Panel to the 'correct interpretation' implies the existence of only one (correct) interpretation, something which is incompatible with a 'certain degree of deference' towards interpretations presented by the defending member or WIPO.[92]

The concerns over the level of deference to WIPO in this matter are tenable, but the fact that the WTO adjudicator looks for material and advice beyond the trade system should not be regarded as something which would discourage it from primarily exploring the WTO sources. A counter-argument to the above concern is that the need to go beyond the system actually arises because, pursuant to the VCLT rules of interpretation, an examination of the WTO sources alone does not elucidate the interpreted term. As a result, the point at issue might not be assessed objectively just by reference to the WTO system alone – disregarding the expertise and the decennial experience in the field of another international agency. In this context, the panels or Appellate Body will have to balance properly the exploration of WTO sources with those residing elsewhere. This in fact is the primary preoccupation of the 'objective assessment of the matter' dictum enshrined in DSU Article 11, which guides the activity of the WTO judiciary.

B. *The future*

An assessment of the institutional sensitivity of the WTO adjudicator vis-à-vis WIPO is not independent of perceptions of its role in the international governance of the intellectual property regime. It should be recalled that, as it is a UN specialized agency, WIPO's central objective is to provide a forum for international co-operation in the development of rules to define intellectual property rights, to administer the rules agreed on, and to provide technical assistance to those contracting states that need it. These objectives have been carried out through negotiations of multilateral intellectual property rights conventions, establishment of a

91 Alan C. Swan and John F. Murphy, *Cases and Materials on the Regulation of International Business and Economic Relations: Documents Supplement* (New York: Matthew Bender, 2001), 224.

92 Oesch, *Standards of Review*, at 213.

Secretariat capable of administration at international level and the creation of a staff of intellectual property rights specialists competent in rendering technical assistance.

Following the incorporation of a number of key intellectual property rights treaties into the WTO regime, one might wonder, however, whether WIPO is still relevant in general, and in particular for WTO dispute settlement. Opinions are divided on this question. Some downplay its role, suggesting the centralization of intellectual property rights norm-setting at the WTO with no need to resort to WIPO. Okediji observes in this context that

> [N]othing in the Dispute Settlement Understanding (DSU) or TRIPS Agreement obligates the WTO dispute panels or the Appellate Body to refer to WIPO for interpretive guidance, nor are they necessarily bound by the information WIPO provides. Further, the decision whether to request information from WIPO in the first place appears to be wholly at the discretion of the panels and the Appellate Body. In short, WIPO's role in the authoritative IP norm-setting role of the WTO is subject entirely to the discretion of the WTO. And while considerations of prudence might demand that a panel or the Appellate Body look to WIPO for some support, the credibility with which the TRIPS dispute decisions are generally viewed suggests that resort to WIPO by the WTO is not required, and certainly not inevitable in implementing global IP norms.[93]

Others perceive WIPO as an actor in a distributed governance model with the WTO,[94] although there are no clear ideas on how actually to distribute their respective functions in order to achieve this parity.

Despite the intellectual property regime shift to the WTO, WIPO has a continued role in intellectual property rights norm-setting. Important legislative initiatives have emerged and have been successfully concluded under its auspices. In the aftermath of the Uruguay Round, two important treaties emerged related to copyright protection in the digital environment.[95] Thus WIPO proves to be an ideal laboratory which experiments with soft law in the various fields of intellectual property.[96] In this context, WIPO has gained more intellectual property rights terrain which it may not be possible for the WTO Panels to explore objectively without WIPO's input, which has gained specialization with these new

93 Okediji, 'WIPO–WTO Relations', at 47–8. 94 Abbott, 'Distributed Governance'.

95 The WIPO Copyright Treaty and the WIPO Performances and Phonograms Treaty, also collectively referred to as the 'Internet Treaties'.

96 For an overview see D. K. Dass, 'Intellectual Property Rights and the Doha Round', (2005) 8 *Journal of World Intellectual Property* 33.

treaties with relevance to the TRIPS interpretation. The specific role of this institution in the WTO dispute settlement is outlined further below, arising out of two categories of norms: incorporated and non-incorporated intellectual property regimes.

1. Incorporated regimes

The case law overview has revealed that the interactions of the WTO adjudicator with WIPO emerge out of the need of the former to interpret relevant TRIPS provisions, which incorporate treaties formerly administered by WIPO. The Berne and Paris regimes were shown to be those with the highest record of inquiries from the WTO. These regimes had been incorporated in the WTO in a static form; this does not mean, however, that these norms stopped their evolution in WIPO. One of WIPO's objectives is to ensure administrative co-operation among the unions which formed around specific treaties. Accordingly, its functions include performing 'the administrative tasks of the Paris Union, the Special Unions established in relation to that Union, and the Berne Union'.[97] Thus WIPO remains a source of state practice as related to these conventions – now incorporated into the WTO TRIPS Agreement. The WTO adjudicator needs to show sensitivity towards this practice if it proposes to make an objective assessment of the matter and provide a fair interpretation of the terms enshrined in the TRIPS Agreement. This can be achieved by seeking information and expert advice, and by giving proper weight to the relevant instruments emerging under its auspices, preferably by use of the VCLT primary rules of interpretation.[98]

2. Non-incorporated regimes

There are about two dozen WIPO-administered treaties whose independent operation is not suspended by the TRIPS Agreement. New intellectual property rights conventions are under negotiation in WIPO as well as amendments being introduced into the existing treaties, including those incorporated by reference to the TRIPS Agreement. As mentioned above, after the conclusion of the Uruguay Round, two important treaties emerged under the auspices of WIPO related to copyright protection in

97 WIPO Convention, Art. 4.

98 Helfer, 'Adjudicating Copyright Claims', at 421, suggesting this approach for WTO Panels, drawing from the ECHR experience. He considers that the ECHR practice suggests that member states will be more willing to accept state practice as a justification for achieving such interpretive advances. For an overview on why VCLT primary rules of interpretation are to be preferred over the secondary rules, see above Chapter 3.

the digital environment (the so-called 'Internet Treaties') which introduced new concepts into the previously familiar architecture of WIPO's normative orientation.

The WIPO Secretariat has also taken the lead in promoting multilateral rule-making processes. The most famous example is the establishment of the Internet Corporation for Assigned Names and Numbers (ICANN) which has in part acted on the basis of WIPO Final Report recommendations.[99] One of the issues that may arise in the context of these initiatives is whether the WTO members will take account of these treaties. Abbott suggests that one way to reflect these new norms is to amend the TRIPS Agreement through either the ordinary or the expedited amendment procedure.[100] The most difficult question with respect to this latter option, which requires a consensus vote of the TRIPS Council, is whether all members of the WTO would accept a multilateral agreement negotiated under WIPO auspices.[101] It would be unusual for all WTO members to be parties to a WIPO agreement and they might not maintain the same perspective on desirable rules in each forum. Thus additional treaties or protocols might be adopted by WIPO that were not contemporaneously approved or adopted by the WTO. These developments could lead to situations in which states may be in compliance with TRIPS and in derogation of rules of WIPO-administered treaties, and vice versa.

Although WIPO does not manage the entire intellectual property rights regime,[102] it can nonetheless claim authority on the administered treaties which are at the heart of intellectual property rights regulation.[103] With

99 Abbott, 'Distributed Governance', at 72. Under the ordinary amendment procedure, the approval of a two-thirds majority of the WTO Ministerial Conference is required to submit an amending proposal to the members for acceptance. Such an amendment becomes effective for members that have accepted it following their two-thirds acceptance. The expedited amendment procedure envisaged in the WTO and the TRIPS Agreements is used for cases in which the purpose of the amendment is to 'adjust . . . to higher levels of protection of intellectual property rights achieved, and in force, in other multilateral agreements and accepted under those agreements by all Members of the WTO'. This proposal requires a consensus vote of the TRIPS Council and it may thereafter be adopted by the WTO Ministerial Conference 'without further acceptance process'.

100 Abbott et al., *International Intellectual Property System*, at 362.

101 Ibid.

102 The intellectual property norm-setting today is shared between WIPO and a number of other international organizations such as the FAO, WHO, UPOV and UNESCO. Although the other organizations may not necessarily set intellectual property rights norms, they frequently regulate matters which bear on intellectual property rights. On various intellectual property rights and related forums see De Bievre, above p. 180 n. 66.

103 Zamora, 'Economic Relations', at 251.

a view to avoiding tensions between these two systems, the consideration of non-incorporated regimes by the WTO adjudicator will turn on consideration of these new norms. They may be pertinent, indeed necessary, for the interpretation of the WTO TRIPS-related obligations. As rightly pointed out by Okediji,

> When a WTO panel is called upon to determine whether compliance by a state is satisfactory under existing international IP rules, the panel's task requires evaluation and interpretation not only of the extant obligations of the TRIPS Agreement but, pursuant to the Vienna Convention on the Law of Treaties, any subsequent treaty developments. [footnote omitted] Such developments clearly will encompass new treaties developed by WIPO, but also treaties or other soft-law actions evolving from regimes in which IP issues bear relevance to organizational mandates.[104]

An example of such considerations arises from *US – Section 110(5) Copyright Act*, where the Panel considered the WIPO Copyright Treaty (WCT) as *contextual* guidance in the interpretation of the TRIPS obligation.[105] The WCT was used as interpretative material in spite of the fact that not all WTO members had accepted it.[106] Moreover, given their content, it has been suggested that a conflict between a WIPO new treaty and an existing WTO obligation in the field of intellectual property, including the new Internet Treaties, would be unlikely.[107] In a document prepared by WIPO to encourage countries to sign up to these instruments, it is stated that countries 'whose laws are already in compliance with TRIPS would not need to make any amendments in order to satisfy these provisions'.[108]

As to the possible consideration of soft-law developments by the WTO panels,[109] an example can be found in the field of traditional knowledge and traditional cultural expressions where WIPO elaborated the so-called 'draft provisions'. Interest in regulating through soft law might be greater from the countries which show reluctance to agree on hard law that

104 Okediji, 'WIPO–WTO Relations', at 44.

105 See above section II of this Chapter.

106 For a discussion on the relevance of the all parties requirement see the *EC – Biotech* analysis in Chapter 1, section III.B. It is interesting to note that some authors perceived the approach of the *US – Section 110(5) Copyright Act* Panel as rather an exception from the established rule, not a renegation of the *EC – Biotech* all parties requirement. See Hrbatá, 'No International Organization', at 29.

107 Hrbatá, 'No International Organization', at 28.

108 Ibid., n. 121.

109 For some examples of how the WTO adjudicator has taken into account soft-law developments in other international regimes see above Chapter 1, section III.B.2.a, and Chapter 3, section III.A.

entails burdensome obligations. The failure, up to the time of writing, of the conclusion of the Patent Law Treaty may serve as an example. Moreover, the soft law may help pave the way for members to subscribe to harder obligations; thus it is not inconceivable that the provisions on traditional knowledge will evolve into hard law.[110]

Another point in favour of a greater consideration of WIPO in the WTO is not only that it runs the negotiations of the new intellectual property rules but that this process is now closer to balancing the interests of the intellectual property rights right-holders on the one hand and the users on the other. WIPO has been criticized in the past for failing to achieve such a balance, but recent developments have been more successful in meeting this challenge. This trend has been reflected, for example, in a set of authoritative Agreed Statements on the WIPO Internet Treaties, explicitly acknowledging limitations on the proprietary rights of copyright owners.[111] These Statements recognize that states could exercise the necessary discretion to create additional limitations and exceptions at the domestic level in order to maintain an appropriate balance between the interests of owners and users. Thus the interpretation of TRIPS in the light of this policy shift at WIPO 'may establish an evolving international norm of access that should surely, even if slowly, permeate the approach of TRIPS dispute panels with respect to how intellectual property norms should be governed in a multilateral setting'.[112] Finally, WIPO may keep its norm-setting relevance due to the exemption of the new treaties from the 'most favoured nation' obligation set out in TRIPS. This will supposedly encourage participation in WIPO by the parties to the WTO Agreements.[113]

VIII. Conclusions

This chapter has examined the differing input provided by WIPO in the settlement of the three key TRIPS disputes at the WTO and the weight attributed to it in the interpretation process. While a large number of WIPO documents have come within the purview in the WTO dispute settlement process, the organization's input has been commonly referred

110 Hrbatá, 'No International Organization', at 22.

111 Okediji, 'WIPO–WTO Relations', at 46. For a contribution illustrating this change in WIPO see also Andréa K. Menescal, 'Changing the WIPO's Ways? The 2004 Development Agenda in Historical Perspective', (2005) 8 *Journal of World Intellectual Property* 761.

112 Okediji, 'WIPO–WTO Relations'.

113 Alvarez and Leebron, 'Symposium: Boundaries', n. 47.

to as factual and treated accordingly. This can be explained mostly by the perception of this organization as one playing a historical role in the oversight of a regime which was shifted to the WTO. But, as illustrated in Chapter 4 above, such an approach is not just determined by perceptions; more objective impediments to WIPO being given a wider role are entrenched in its decision-making process. Thus WIPO is an international organization which lacks a mechanism by which authoritative decisions could be taken which could be considered by the WTO panels as a matter of law. Moreover, the institution lacks an all-encompassing solid dispute settlement mechanism which would provide a valid judicial interpretation of its own regime. The ICJ system referred to in the WIPO-administered treaties has proven inefficient in providing such authoritative guidance.[114] The input of the WIPO Secretariat is certainly helpful for factual purposes, but one cannot validly sustain the claim of considering this input as normative, with its legitimacy being derived solely from the contribution of a few of the WIPO staff. This probably explains the somewhat restrictive approach of the WTO adjudicator towards giving a greater weight to WIPO's material which came under purview in the cases analysed in this study. One of the best examples of such manifestation arises from the approach in *China – IP Rights*, where the Panel applied the acquaintance requirement too restrictively, leading to the exclusion of the explanatory observation to the WIPO Model Provision from its consideration.

On the other hand, WIPO remains a regime which can hardly be disregarded in the interpretation of the TRIPS obligations. It offers complementarity to the WTO's approach, which could mean getting the best of both worlds. The interpretation of the current WTO TRIPS obligations would be biased without consideration of the subsequent developments in this field, which by and large emerge in WIPO. Thus while not being without shortcomings, the relationship between the two organizations may offer many benefits to the WTO system.

114 See above Chapter 4, section III.A.1.

8

The World Customs Organization

I. Introduction

Interactions of the WTO adjudicator with the WCO emerge, as a rule, in the context of WTO disputes examining the classification of goods. This is explained by the fact that the WTO members have scheduled their WTO concessions in goods following the Harmonized Commodity Description and Coding System (Harmonized System, or HS) Convention administered by the WCO.[1] In pursuit of its administrative functions relating to the HS Convention, the WCO set up the HS Committee with its Review Sub-Committee and a Working Party, responsible for the revision and amendment of the HS Nomenclature, Explanatory Notes and Compendium of Classification Opinions before their final adoption by the HS Committee.[2]

Thus the relevant WCO documents relating to the application of the HS Convention came within the purview in several WTO disputes, helping the panels to elucidate the interpretative issue. *EC – Chicken Cuts* and *China – Auto Parts* are the most prominent cases in this context. They reveal not only reference by the Panel to the WCO documents but also the submission of information by the WCO at the explicit request of the Panel. These cases have been selected for more detailed examination below.[3]

1 *EC – Chicken Cuts*, Panel Report, para. 187.0: 'Further, the HS was used as a basis for the preparation of the Uruguay Round GATT schedules. This is apparent from the Modalities Agreement, which provides that agricultural products in respect of which tariff commitments are to be established are based on the HS and from the fact that the HS has been used to define product coverage under the Agreement on Agriculture'. Apart from that, reference to the WCO is found in several WTO Agreements, such as Art. 18(2) and Annex II of the Agreement on Implementation of Article VII; Arts. 4(2), 9(1,2) and Annex I of the Agreement on Rules of Origin.

2 See WCO, www.wcoomd.org/home_wco_topics_hsoverviewboxes_committees_committstructhsworkpart.htm (visited April 2009).

3 *EC – Computer Equipment* is not omitted from the analysis, but since it has been followed by the other two panels on the points of interest to this study, the references thereto will be made when relevant.

In order to assess the role and weight attributed to this organization in WTO dispute settlement, this chapter opens with a brief description of the merits of the cases and an examination of the request for information by the Panel from the WCO (section I). This leads into an examination of how, in its interpretation process, the Panel has considered the various documents and the information submitted by the WCO (section II). As in the previous chapters, this is followed by a general evaluation of the role of the WCO in WTO dispute settlement and the level of sensitivity of the panels or the Appellate Body revealed in this process, culminating in conclusions (sections III and IV respectively).

II. The request for factual information

EC – Chicken Cuts concerned an EC measure which reclassified from one tariff heading to another frozen chicken cuts imported from Thailand and Brazil. As a result, chicken cuts previously subject to an *ad valorem* tariff of 15.4 per cent (under subheading 0210.90.20), were now (under subheading 0207.41.10) subject to a higher tariff,[4] which claimants argued was resulting in a tariff treatment less favourable than provided for in the EC's Schedule of Concessions.[5] The Panel examined whether the measures at issue had resulted in the imposition of duties and conditions on the products in excess of those provided for in the EC's Schedule of Concessions, and concluded that it was clear that the products classified under the new heading were granted less favourable treatment. These findings were upheld by the Appellate Body, resulting in victory for the claimants.

The Panel sought information from the WCO pursuant to DSU Article 13(1). The response was provided by the Secretary-General of the WCO with a view to clarifying the meaning of the term 'salted', the classification practices and the relationship between different headings in the Harmonized System (HS). The WCO provided the requested information,[6] and by way of general comment, stated that the parties to the dispute should follow the HS Convention dispute settlement procedures before the WTO Panel made its decision.[7]

4 *EC – Chicken Cuts*, Panel Report, para. 7.3.
5 Ibid., para. 3.2.
6 The responses to the questions of the Panel are contained in Annex C-12 and C-13 to the Panel Report.
7 *EC – Chicken Cuts*, Panel Report, para. 53.0.

In *China – Auto Parts* the claim, which was brought by Canada, the EC and the United States, was slightly more complicated as it did not involve only a classification question. The issue was whether certain imported auto parts in China could be characterized, for customs purposes, as completed motor vehicles, and would thus be subject to a higher tariff (on average the tariff for motor vehicles was 25 per cent, whereas the tariff on auto parts was 10 per cent). The determination that auto parts would be subject to the higher rates applicable to motor vehicles would not be made by China until after the parts were used to make an automobile. In other words, if a complete motor vehicle was made with a substantial portion of imported parts the tariff rate charged for those parts would be raised from the 10 per cent initially collected to the 25 per cent that applied to imported motor vehicles. As in *EC – Chicken Cuts* the Panel report in this case was appealed.[8]

The Panel asked for the assistance of the WCO in the form of any factual information available to it with respect to the relevance and application of General Interpretative Rule 2(a) and the Harmonized System Committee Decision on the Interpretation of General Interpretative Rule 2(a) in interpreting China's tariff headings in question.[9] The parties were given the opportunity to comment on the information provided by the WCO which was important during the Panel's examination of GATT Article II claims.[10]

III. Consideration of the WCO instruments

The main task of the Panels in *EC – Chicken Cuts* was to interpret the term 'salted' appearing in the EC Schedule.[11] In examining the 'context' and the 'subsequent practice', the Panel referred to a number of WCO instruments such as the Harmonized System and its Explanatory Notes, decisions of the HS Committee, and some WCO letters of advice provided to customs

8 For a detailed legal and economic analysis of the case see Jasper Wauters and Hylke Vandenbus Sche, 'China – Measures Affecting Imports of Automobile Parts', (2010) 9 *World Trade Review* 201.

9 *China – Auto Parts*, Panel Report Annex C-1, page C-2 and Annex C-3. The responses from the WCO are contained in Annex C-2 and Annex C-4.

10 Ibid., Panel Report, paras. 7.369–7.612.

11 The Panel began by examining the ordinary meaning of the term as contained in heading 02.10 of the EC Schedule ('Meat and edible meat offal, *salted*, in brine, dried, smoked; edible flours and meals of meat or meat offal . . . '). *EC – Chicken Cuts*, Panel Report, para. 104.0.

authorities. The WCO information was important in the interpretation of the term, in the light of the object and purpose of the treaty as prescribed by the VCLT.

In *China – Auto Parts*, the WCO material was relevant for shedding light on treatment of auto parts under China's challenged measures and its compliance with China's Schedule of Concessions. This turned on whether the imported auto parts were subject to an ordinary customs duty in excess of China's concessions, consequently according less favourable treatment to imported auto parts. In this exercise, the term 'motor vehicles' in China's Schedule of Concessions had to be interpreted.

A. *The Harmonized System*

The Panel showed significant reliance on the HS Convention in its interpretation process, since this instrument constitutes the basis of the EC Combined Nomenclature which is the foundation of the EC Schedule of Concessions in the WTO.[12] The Appellate Body noted that although the HS is not formally part of the WTO Agreement, the concept of 'context' under Article 31 of the Vienna Convention would not be limited to the WTO Agreement but may also extend to other instruments as set out in paragraphs 2 (a) and (b) therein. Recalling some decisions of the GATT contracting parties,[13] the Appellate Body ruled that the HS Convention was context for the purpose of interpreting the WTO Agreements including the Schedules of Concessions of trade in goods, as established under

12 The Harmonized Commodity Description and Coding System (Harmonized System Convention, Brussels, 14 June 1983; in short, Harmonized System or HS) for the customs classification of goods into the tariff scheme of the HS Nomenclature, has resulted in the worldwide strengthening of tariff nomenclatures since its first usage in 1988. It is in use in more than 200 countries and economic regions (however, only 135 countries are contracting parties as at January 2009), and more than 98 per cent of all trans-border trade is statistically and economically classified by help of the HS Nomenclature. See www.wco.org (visited May 2009). According to the EC Combined Nomenclature (CN) Regulation Art. 1(2), the CN includes: '(a) the harmonized system nomenclature; (b) Community subdivisions to that nomenclature, referred to as "CN subheadings" in those cases where a corresponding rate of duty is specified; (c) preliminary provisions, additional section or chapter notes and footnotes relating to the CN subheadings.' For an overview see Izaak Wind, 'HS 2007: What's It All About?', (2007) 2 *Global Trade and Customs Journal* 79, at 82.

13 GATT Concessions under the Harmonized Commodity Description and Coding System, Decision of 12 July 1983, L/5470/Rev 1, BISD 30S/17; GATT Concessions under the Harmonized Commodity Description and Coding System, Procedures to Implement Changes in the Harmonized System, Decision of 8 October 1991, L/6905, BISD 39S/300.

Article 31(2)(a) of the Vienna Convention. The attribution of the HS Convention to 'context' under the Vienna Convention rules of interpretation is unique, since at the time of writing it is one of the very few times that an international agreement has been accepted as such by the WTO adjudicator.[14] This approach towards the HS Convention found confirmation in *China – Auto Parts*.[15]

The role of the WCO was seen through provision of factual clarifications to the Panel regarding the historical developments of the HS headings at issue. Essentially, in *EC – Chicken Cuts* the WCO presented the Panel with the rationale behind separate identification of goods included in the HS. It gave a few details about earlier nomenclatures that affected the structure of the HS and some information that answered more directly the classification question.

Commentators have noted, however, that the Panel in *EC – Chicken Cuts* did not rely heavily on the WCO advice on this point.[16] The Panel had asked the WCO only a limited number of not very well formulated questions on the classification practices.[17] Moreover, the WCO apparently had not exhausted the issue of classification before the Panel.

In contrast, the reliance on HS in *China – Auto Parts* is more nuanced in the sense that the Panel gave substantial consideration to the General Rules of Interpretation for HS (GIR) and Explanatory Notes for the clarification of the interpreted term. The use of these two instruments in the analysed law is illustrated further below.

B. *General Rules for Interpretation of the Harmonized System*

In *EC – Chicken Cuts* the Panel also addressed the question of applicability of certain WCO rules dealing with certain problems of the application and interpretation of HS classification. These are referred to as the General Rules for Interpretation of the Harmonized System (General Rules, GIR). The Panel noted that Article 1(a) of the HS Convention provides clearly that the HS comprises the General Rules and therefore they were considered in the interpretation of heading 02.10.[18] It referred in this process

14 Mavroidis, 'No Outsourcing of Law?', at 452.

15 *China – Auto Parts*, Panel, para. 7.663.

16 Horn and Howse, 'European Communities', at 18–19.

17 On this point, the Panel asked the WCO what the rationale was behind the product coverage of the 4-digit heading and the 6-digit heading levels in the Harmonized System. *EC – Chicken Cuts*, Panel Report, Annex C-12.

18 Ibid., para. 7.236.

to 'General Rule 1'[19] and 'General Rule 3'[20] as indicated by the litigants. While the former did not help the Panel in clarifying the meaning of the term 'salted', neither did the Panel attribute weight to General Rule 3, which addresses situations where goods are prima facie classifiable under two headings.

The claimants appealed against this finding, arguing that the Panel incorrectly found that the parties were in agreement that General Rule 3 was inapplicable in this case. Brazil in this context asked the Appellate Body to complete the analyses and find that the products at issue were classifiable under heading 02.10 by virtue of General Rule 3(a) or 3(c).[21] However, the Appellate Body did not decide whether General Rule 3 was applicable, finding that the primary task of the Panel was to determine first the meaning and scope of the concession contained in heading 02.10 of the EC Schedule and only thereafter to decide on the question of whether the products at issue were prima facie classifiable under two or more headings.[22] Since, according to the Appellate Body, General Rule 3 was to be considered in a second step, it did not find it necessary to apply this rule at all.[23]

The situation was quite different in *China – Auto Parts*. The GIR became relevant in determining whether China's tariff provisions for motor vehicles should include auto parts imported separately in multiple shipments for domestic assembly, if such parts would have had the essential character of a motor vehicle had they been imported in a single shipment.[24] It was in this step that the Panel sought guidance from GIR 1[25] and GIR 2(a)[26]

19 Rule 1 reads: 'The titles of Sections, Chapters and sub-Chapters are provided for ease of reference only; for legal purposes, classification shall be determined according to the terms of the headings and any relative Section or Chapter Notes and, provided such headings or Notes do not otherwise require, according to the following provisions . . . '.

20 Rule 3 states in its pertinent parts that 'When by application of Rule 2(b) or for any other reason, goods are prima facie, classifiable under two or more headings, classification shall be effected as follows: (a) The heading which provides the most specific description shall be preferred to headings providing a more general description. However, when two or more headings each refer to part only of the materials or substances contained in mixed or composite goods or to part only of the items in a set put up for retail sale, those headings are to be regarded as equally specific in relation to those goods, even if one of them gives a more complete or precise description of the goods . . . (c) When goods cannot be classified by reference to 3(a) and 3(b), they shall be classified under the heading which occurs last in numerical order among those which equally merit consideration.'

21 *EC – Chicken Cuts*, ABR, para. 232. 22 Ibid., para. 234. 23 Ibid.

24 *China – Auto Parts*, Panel, paras. 7.387–7.397. 25 Above n. 19.

26 General Rule 2 (a) reads: 'Any reference in a heading to an article shall be taken to include a reference to that article incomplete or unfinished, provided that, as presented, the

regarding the HS, which it considered as 'context'. After having found that both rules were relevant for the interpretation of the term 'motor vehicles', the Panel proceeded to the interpretation of the term 'as presented' found in GIR 2(a). The Panel concluded that China's measures had the effect of imposing ordinary customs duties in excess of concessions contained in its Schedules.[27] This issue was appealed, but, regrettably, the Appellate Body did not make findings on this point; this was also a missed opportunity to elaborate on the way the Panel had used various interpretative sources external to the WTO system.

C. *Decisions by the WCO HS Committee*

An important statement was made in the *EC – Chicken Cuts* case in relation to the value of WCO HS Committee decisions as subsequent practice under VCLT Article 31(3)(b). The Panel considered that decisions of the HS Committee of the WCO, even if not binding, could well be a useful source of information on the subsequent practice of WTO members, a large proportion of whom are signatories to the HS Convention and thus are members of the HS Committee.[28] In spite of this statement, the Panel ultimately found that there was no WCO decision applicable to heading 02.10 of the HS for it to consider in the case at hand and so did not use any such decision in its interpretation process.

Reference to these instruments re-emerged in *China – Auto Parts*, where the HS Committee Decision concerning GIR 2(a) was found relevant to the interpretation of the term 'as presented' contained therein. As in *EC – Chicken Cuts*, the Panel noted that the HS Committee Decisions were not 'binding' on the HS contracting parties; as they did not reflect a consensus of the WCO membership they were to be accorded less weight in the interpretative hierarchy of the HS, after the GIR, Section and Chapter Notes and Explanatory Notes.[29] Another interesting clarification was that HS decisions not codified in the texts or Explanatory Notes of

incomplete or unfinished article has the essential character of the complete or finished article. It shall also be taken to include a reference to that article complete or finished (or failing to be classified as complete or finished by virtue of this rule), presented unassembled or disassembled.'

27 *China – Auto Parts*, Panel, para. 7.523.

28 Panel Report on *EC – Chicken Cuts*, para. 7.298.

29 *China – Auto Parts*, Panel Report, para. 7.428. Note that HS Committee Decisions can be deemed to be approved by the WCO if no member objects to its adoption under Art. 8 of the HS Convention.

the HS do not have as much weight as GIR itself or decisions that have been codified. The Panel said that the relevant decision could nevertheless provide guidance on the interpretation of GIR 2(a).[30]

D. The HS Explanatory Notes

Referring to *EC – Computer Equipment*, the complainants in *EC – Chicken Cuts* urged the Panel to give the Explanatory Notes to the HS the same interpretative weight as that attributed to the HS, even though they were not formally listed as part of the HS.[31] Although the EC agreed that the Explanatory Notes should be attributed weight, it contended that these documents 'provide non-authoritative guidance and should not be treated the same way as treaty provisions'.[32] The WCO clarified on this point that 'the classification of products under the HS is based on the wording of the legal texts, that is, the terms of the headings and any relative Section, Chapter and Subheading Notes and the General Rules of the HS'.[33] Not being part of this list, the Explanatory Notes were described by the WCO as the 'official interpretation of the HS, which are taken into consideration in conjunction with the legal texts'.[34] The Panel examined the allegedly relevant Explanatory Notes (to heading 02.10 and Chapter 2 of the HS), and noted that they did not form part of the HS and were not binding; moreover they were not particularly helpful in interpreting the term at issue.[35]

On the other hand, in *China – Auto Parts*, reference to Explanatory Notes was found relevant by the Panel in examining the 'multiple shipments' argument, namely in reinforcing its finding that both GIR 1 and GIR 2(a) form part of the 'context' for the interpreted term.[36] This further shaped the interpretative exercise of the Panel, which read and interpreted the two rules in conjunction. The Notes were again referred to by the Panel in examining the 'essential character' test imposed by the Chinese measure. The use of the Notes helped the Panel in arriving at the conclusion that this test was not in conformity with China's concessions. Conversely, Explanatory Note (VII) to GIR 2(a) was referred to by the Panel in another interpretative step, where it actually found China's classification of 'completely knocked-down kits' (CKD) and 'semi-knocked-down kits' (SKD)

30 Ibid., paras. 7.418–7.423. 31 *EC – Chicken Cuts*, Panel Report, para. 206.0.
32 Ibid., para. 207.0. 33 Ibid., para. 218.0. See the WCO's reply to Panel question No. 1.
34 Ibid. 35 Ibid., para. 7.223.
36 *China – Auto Parts*, Panel Report, paras. 7.389–7.391.

in conformity with the Working Party Report from China's WTO accession and therefore with Article II (b) of GATT 1994.[37]

E. The WCO Secretariat's opinions and information

The *EC – Chicken Cuts* Panel also examined two WCO letters of advice provided by its Secretariat (which amount to opinions of the Secretariat) to Cypriot and Bulgarian authorities in response to their specific inquiries on matters relating to classification of goods. With respect to the value of the Cypriot letter, Brazil noted that it merely expressed the technical opinion of one individual or possibly more, which did not bind WCO members in any way and had no legal value.[38]

The Panel concluded that WCO letters of advice that are directed at individual customs authorities, which have no legally binding effect, cannot be construed as constituting 'concordant, subsequent practice common to all [WTO members]' for the purposes of Article 31(3)(b) of the Vienna Convention. As a result, the letters in questions were not considered by the Panel.[39]

Unlike the letters of advice mentioned above, the information submitted by the WCO Secretariat to the Panel was particularly useful in *EC – Chicken Cuts* in examining how the 'object and purpose' of the Agreement, set out in VCLT Article 31(1), helped to clarify the term 'salted'.[40] The claimants argued that with respect to the application of Article II of GATT 1994, the decisive criterion for characterization of the product was the objective assessment of the product at the time of importation.[41] The

37 Ibid., paras. 7.738–7.741.

38 *EC – Chicken Cuts*, Panel Report, para. 7.291.

39 Ibid., para. 7.299. The Panel ultimately found that the only relevant subsequent practice pertained to the practice of the EC in classifying the products in question under 02.10 prior to the year 2002. This allowed it to conclude that the products in question were indeed covered by this tariff item (Panel, para. 7.303). The Appellate Body reversed this reasoning on the grounds that the practice of only one or even a few parties to a multilateral treaty, such as the WTO Agreement, does not establish a 'concordant, common and discernable pattern' (ABR, para. 259).

40 VCLT Art. 31(1) reads 'A treaty shall be interpreted in good faith in accordance with the ordinary meaning to be given to the terms of the treaty in their context and in the light of its object and purpose.'

41 *EC – Chicken Cuts*, Panel Report, para. 7.304. This approach represents a departure from the GATT case law on customs classification issues, where the Panel was more inclined towards the consideration of the legitimate expectations of the Members above the technicalities of the 'objective assessment' at the time of importation. See Davide Rovetta, Juhi Sud and Edwin Vermulst, 'WTO Dispute Settlement with Respect to Customs Matters', (2009) 4(4) *Global Trade and Customs Journal* 105.

correctness of this statement was confirmed by the WCO in the information provided to the Panel. In this context, the WCO submitted that laboratory analyses might be required to determine whether a product could be regarded as 'salted' within the meaning of heading 02.10 of the HS.[42]

The Panel alleged that the EC had not provided it with any clear idea of what was meant by 'long-term preservation' in practice and how the customs officer at the border responsible for classification was to determine whether the product had been preserved for the long term, and if so, whether it was as a result of salting, freezing or a combination thereof.[43] Considering the arguments of the parties and the WCO information, the Panel concluded that the difficulty for customs officers in classifying products signified that the outcome was hard to predict and that this caused the defendant to violate the WTO provisions, resulting in the rejection of the EC position.[44]

In *China – Auto Parts* an opinion of the WCO Secretariat was considered in interpreting the term 'as presented' found in GIR 2(a). The opinion was found to be relevant when the Panel was actually examining whether an HS Committee Decision was pertinent to its interpretative purpose. The WCO's opinion thus helped the Panel to make its ultimate finding on the non-compliance of the Chinese measure with the WTO obligations.[45]

IV. Evaluation

The analyses of *EC – Chicken Cuts* and *China – Auto Parts* are essential in this study for an understanding of the degree of the WTO panels' or Appellate Body's sensitivity towards other international institutions. As illustrated above, in its interpretation process the panel referred to various clarifications and relevant acts adopted by the WCO. One essential point revealed by the analysis is that, despite soliciting advice from the WCO in the interpretation process, neither the panel nor the Appellate Body suggested that the WTO dispute settlement organs should, as a matter of law, defer to the WCO interpretations or practice with respect to the HS classifications. This approach is consistent with the Appellate Body's earlier jurisprudence on related matters, where the WTO members' Schedules of Concessions were considered as forming an integral part of

42 *EC – Chicken Cuts*, Panel Report, para. 7.321.

43 Ibid., para. 7.322.

44 Ibid., para. 7.323.

45 *China – Auto Parts*, Panel Report, para. 7.442. See also below subsection A.

the Single Undertaking. This point was made in support of the view that the terminology of the Schedules should be interpreted and applied as if one is interpreting and applying the GATT itself or any other treaty part of the Single Undertaking.[46]

A. *The weight of the WCO instruments*

The effects of classification under the relevant VCLT rules of interpretation have been discussed in Chapter 3 above. This concluded with the contention that the attribution of extraneous interpretative material to the primary rules of interpretation under the VCLT is a manifestation of high institutional sensitivity on the part of the WTO judiciary towards the host international organization.[47] Thus by attributing the HS Convention to the 'context' in the cases examined above, the Panel showed a high degree of sensitivity towards the WCO. Horn and Howse make a very important observation in this respect, noting that

> [I]t is true that not all Members of the WTO are bound by the WCO treaty or are members of the World Customs Organization (WCO); however, all WTO Members have used the HS of the WCO in tariff negotiations and the resultant schedules, which are bound under the GATT. Would it not be the common expectation of all WTO Members,[. . .], that the meaning of the schedule in question be decided through the application of rules governing the HS itself and the practice of the international organization that is the guardian of the HS? The Panel accepts that the HS rules and related WCO practice are relevant to resolving the disputes but for some reason refuses to provide a clear legal theory as to why they are relevant, refusing to indicate whether the HS is 'context' within the meaning of 31(2)(b) of the VCLT or rather a relevant rule of international law 'applicable between the parties' within the meaning of 31(3)(c).[48]

Although the Panel report indeed does not reveal an elaborate legal theory behind its choice to attribute the HS to context, something which was corrected by the Appellate Body,[49] there is still some indication therein

46 Horn and Howse, 'European Communities', at 10, referring to *EC – Computer Equipment*, ABR, para. 84.

47 See above Chapter 3, section III.

48 Horn and Howse, 'European Communities', at 21–2.

49 *EC – Chicken Cuts*, ABR, para. 199: 'The above circumstances confirm that, prior to, during, as well as after the Uruguay Round negotiations, there was broad consensus among the GATT Contracting Parties to *use* the Harmonized System as the basis for their WTO Schedules, notably with respect to agricultural products. In our view, this consensus constitutes an "agreement" between WTO Members "relating to" the *WTO Agreement* that

that the HS Convention has been considered as context.[50] Without going into the debate on whether the HS should be attributed to context or other rules of interpretation,[51] one needs to note that the HS is ascribed significant weight as long as it is considered under the primary rules of treaty interpretation. In this respect, such attribution reveals great institutional sensitivity on behalf of the WTO Panel.

The GIR were regarded by the Panel, and rightly so, as an integral part thereof and, as such, their legal value as 'context' was also undisputed. This is because the HS comprises the General Rules for the Interpretation of the System, Sections and Chapter Notes, including Subheading Notes, and a list of headings arranged in systematic order and, where appropriate, subdivided into subheadings.[52]

With reference to the Appellate Body in *EC – Computer Equipment*, the *EC – Chicken Cuts* Panel considered WCO HS Committee Decisions to be relevant as 'subsequent practice' where they existed and to have the value of a non-binding act. In fact, in this case the Panel did not dwell further on the relevance of these documents, given that there were no relevant decisions applicable to the HS heading at issue. Conversely, the *China – Auto Parts* Panel referred to the HS Committee Decision concerning GIR 2(a) providing important guidance on the legal value of these WCO documents, which complements prior jurisprudence. The Panel clarified that materials issued by the HS Committee such as Explanatory Notes, Classification Opinions or other advice prepared as guides to the interpretation of the HS have to be approved by the WCO. This takes place automatically if no contracting party to the HS notifies the Secretary-General of its request that such matter be referred to the WCO Council. This means that any materials issued by the HS Committee, even when specifically approved by the Council pursuant to Article 8 of the HS Convention,

was "made in connection with the conclusion of" that Agreement, within the meaning of Art. 31(2)(a) of the *Vienna Convention*. As such, this agreement is "context" under Article 31(2)(a) for the purpose of interpreting the WTO agreements, of which the EC Schedule is an integral part. In this light, we consider that the Harmonized System is relevant for purposes of interpreting tariff commitments in the WTO Members' Schedules' (emphasis in original).

50 *EC – Chicken Cuts*, Panel, para. 7.189: 'Therefore, we will treat the HS as if it qualifies as "context" under Article 31(2), recalling that the Appellate Body in *EC – Computer Equipment* indicated that the HS should be taken into consideration for the interpretation of a Member's schedule.'

51 See above Chapter 3, section III.B.1 for the discussion on why the HS should not be attributed to 'context'.

52 See above n. 33. See also HS Convention Art. 3.1.

'are advisory rather than conventional in nature'.[53] With this in mind and finding that the Explanatory Notes invoked in the cases were not relevant, the *EC – Chicken Cuts* Panel discarded this material from the list of interpretative elements.

Having agreed with the legal weight previously attributed to HS Explanatory Notes, the *China – Auto Parts* Panel also referred to these documents. First, they were cited in order for the Panel to reinforce its finding that not just one but two GIRs warranted consideration in conjunction with the case.[54] Although the Panel ultimately found that none of the GIRs justified China's approach to classification and tariff differentiation between auto parts and motor vehicles, the Explanatory Notes were referred to once more, but with the opposite effect. They were found relevant in determining that China's CDKs and SDKs tariff lines were in conformity with its obligations to the WTO.

In both cases the Explanatory Notes were seen as context of the elements primarily considered as 'context' by virtue of VCLT Article 31. Naturally, they were not formally identified as 'context', but the degree of relevance of the Notes suggests that quite a weighty role was attributed to them, despite their being non-binding instruments. It might be worth exploring Explanatory Notes under 'subsequent practice' of VCLT Article 31. If this fails to meet all the prerequisites for such identification as described above in Chapter 3, the Notes can always be considered in the examination of supplementary means of interpretation, hopefully for elucidation rather than confirmatory purposes.[55]

Finally, the WCO also played an important role by providing information and opinions in the above cases. Essentially, in *EC – Chicken Cuts* this exercise shaped the Panel's conclusion that the decisive criterion for characterization of the product is its 'objective assessment' at the time of importation – a crucial construct in the outcome of the case. In *China – Auto Parts*, the Panel, too, relied on the WCO's opinion in reaching one of its major findings. These examples demonstrate how important it is for the Panel to be advised by the WCO. Given the complexity of the

53 *China – Auto Parts*, Panel Report, para. 7.420.

54 Indeed, the litigants were in disaccord as to whether both GIR rules applied. In China's view, GIR 2(a) 'allows parts imported in multiple shipments and assembled later into a motor vehicle to be classified as a motor vehicle if they have the essential character of a motor vehicle'. In response, the complainants asserted that GIR 2(a) can be relevant only after applying GIR 1. See *China – Auto Parts*, Panel Report, paras. 7.383–7.384.

55 For the implications arising out of the use of the supplementary means for elucidation rather than confirmatory purposes see above Chapter 3, section III.G.

HS classification exercise and the fact that these issues are specifically addressed by the WCO, it is logical that it steps in and participates actively in the clarification of these issues before WTO panels. This result will be consistent with our proposal for more institutional sensitivity by the WTO adjudicator towards other international organizations.

B. Some issues in the consideration of HS-related instruments

The outcome of the cases still raises some issues with respect to consideration of some HS-related instruments by the panel. The first issue arises from the consideration of the GIR in *EC – Chicken Cuts*. In the decision not to apply GIR 3,[56] which deals with situations when goods are prima facie classifiable under two or more HS headings, the Panel seemed to have read into the term 'prima facie' a requirement for a shared perception of the situation among parties, which was not the intention of this rule.[57] Such a reading would significantly reduce the ambit and scope of this rule, since parties most likely would only rarely agree in respect of its application. This interpretation also would imply effectively removing it from the arsenal of instruments for resolving a conflict over goods classification issues.[58] What is more striking here is the logic applied by the Appellate Body to the Panel's reasoning regarding non-application of this rule. Strangely, although accepting the possibility that it might be applicable, the Appellate Body did not fault the Panel for not proceeding to the next logical step in ascertaining whether to apply it. While this author shares the approach of the Appellate Body in finding that the rule might have been applicable, there is some incoherence or contradiction in its failure to correct the Panel for not taking all necessary steps to determine whether the conditions for applying the rule existed.[59] An examination of the rule in this dispute would have meant paying due recognition to the 'epistemic superiority' of the WCO in matters of customs classification of goods – an approach compatible with this proposal for institutional sensitivity of the WTO adjudicator. To this effect, the *China – Auto Parts* Panel was more scrupulous in analysing which GIR was applicable and providing sound argumentation for its decision that GIR 1 and GIR 2(a) should be read in conjunction as 'context' for the interpreted term.

56 See above n. 20 for the language of General Rule 3.
57 Horn and Howse, 'European Communities', at 21.
58 Ibid. 59 See also ibid., at 22.

A second issue has been raised in the literature in relation to the attribution of the HS Committee Decisions to subsequent practice in *EC – Chicken Cuts*.[60] The problem is that with this approach the Appellate Body signals that it does not believe that Article 31(3)(b) requires subsequent practice to be established by parties to a treaty within the institutional context of that treaty. This approach is to be praised, however, since it represents a way for the WTO adjudicator to show considerable sensitivity towards other international institutions. However, despite the Appellate Body's high level of sensitivity towards the WCO instruments in this instance, neither of the two WTO disputes elaborates on why subsequent practice of another regime should be considered relevant under the WTO. Van Damme, for example, is of the view that a decision of the HS Committee can be subsequent practice under the HS Convention, but not the WTO-covered agreements.[61] She argues that

> The WTO adjudicator could have relied on the decision of the HS Committee as context for interpreting Schedule LXXX. The interpretation by the HS Committee could also have given a 'special meaning' to a term in Schedule LXXX on the basis that WTO Members (not necessarily all of them) had in practice applied this interpretation. The Appellate Body's approach towards decisions by HS Committee is in sharp contrast to the high standard of scrutiny that it applies when examining decisions of WTO bodies as subsequent practice.[62]

While it is not disputed that a decision of the WCO may be identified under other Article 31 VCLT methods, the argument that the Appellate Body has not set a consistent approach towards the decisions of the WTO bodies should not discourage the consideration of the practice emerging from other international regimes, where relevant.[63] The streamlining of the approach by the Appellate Body will certainly serve the proposal for greater institutional sensitivity by the WTO adjudicator advocated in this study.[64]

C. *The relevance of WCO dispute settlement*

The importance of the classification disputes discussed above goes beyond clarifications about the legal value of WCO instruments in the WTO

60 Van Damme, *Treaty Interpretation*, at 342. 61 Ibid. 62 Ibid.

63 The issue here is not only the high standard but also the inconsistent approach by the WTO adjudicator.

64 On the role of consistency of judicial interpretation in the WTO and its linkage to institutional sensitivity, see above Chapter 4, section II.C.

disputes settlement procedure. *EC – Chicken Cuts* in particular raises important institutional questions, such as, for example, the suitability of the WTO or WCO as forums for the adjudication of classification disputes. This issue is elicited from the WCO's statement on the case that the dispute concerned a classification question involving several contracting parties to the HS Convention, and therefore had to be referred to the Harmonized System Committee for settlement.[65] While the WCO had suggested the need to use the HS dispute settlement before going to the WTO, the Panel concluded that there was no possibility of it declining jurisdiction, even temporarily, under the DSU.[66]

Commentators have argued that with respect to a genuine uncertainty concerning classification, and to the extent that a matter could be resolved on technical grounds, the WCO could have a more prominent role to play.[67] Although, in a case of opportunistic behaviour of a party acting in bad faith, this would be better dealt with under the DSU. This role of the WCO could be supported by the existence of a compulsory dispute settlement clause in the WCO treaties. There is no indication that during the Uruguay Round trade negotiations the parties had intended to exclude the application of WCO mechanisms relating to HS classification. As already noted, the customs nomenclature is a highly specialized technical vocabulary for which canons of interpretation exist in the WCO which are different from those of the Vienna Convention.[68] The Vienna Convention rules of interpretation themselves contemplate the possibility of assigning special meaning to the words of the treaty, if the parties so intended.[69] In this context, Horn and Howse note that

> The Panel and the Appellate Body ought to have considered the possibility that the WCO Convention, including its compulsory dispute settlement clause to which almost all WTO Members are parties (and certainly all parties to the dispute), indicates a common intention that the meaning attributed to HS classification be that which has been established in the WCO [text omitted] . . . On this view, a WTO Member would discharge its obligations under Art. II GATT if its decision to apply an HS classification to a particular product is consistent with WCO. In a case like this one, where no previous clear WCO ruling exists on the matter at hand, the practical consequence of this view is that, in order to make their case before the WTO Panel, the complainants will need to go first to the WCO to establish that the defendant has interpreted the classification in question in a manner that is impermissible in the WCO system.[70]

65 *EC – Chicken Cuts*, Panel Report, para. 7.53. 66 Ibid., paras. 7.56–7.59.
67 Horn and Howse, 'European Communities', at 33. 68 Ibid., at 34.
69 VCLT, Art. 31(4). 70 Horn and Howse, 'European Communities', at 34–6.

But the authors themselves question the above proposition, asking whether the sole adhesion of the parties to the WCO Convention, and the arguably related absence of any code on customs classification in the WTO, indicate the expectation or assumption that problems of interpretation of HS would be dealt with at the WCO.[71] They note that one constraint regarding this approach is that not *all* WTO members are WCO members, which may result in non-uniform application of GATT Article II to different members. While this is true (but less of a problem with the increasingly overlapping membership of the two international organizations), another issue is the possibility of submitting the same issue to the WCO after a finding had been made under the WTO. Since the WCO is not required in any way to give weight to such WTO decisions, the largely overlapping membership might generate conflicting obligations. In a final assessment, the development of WTO case law on this subject, largely autonomous from decisions of the WCO, is a recipe for conflict and uncertainty.[72] This suggests that to the extent that relevant classification decisions exist in the WCO, with a view to avoiding conflicts, the WTO adjudicator should attribute considerable weight to those decisions.[73] Thus the use of the WCO HS dispute settlement mechanism on classification issues by WTO members does not necessarily bring about coherence between the two institutions.

V. Conclusions

The WTO–WCO interface is realized mostly through the choice of the WTO members to rely on the HS Convention administered by the WCO for scheduling their tariff headings. As the WTO jurisprudence reveals, this choice resulted in some difficulties on the part of the panels in dealing with complex HS classification issues. This is all the more the case considering that the HS Convention on which the WTO classification of goods is based is an evolving legal instrument which may have a bearing on the commitments of the WTO members. These evolutionary elements

71 The WCO Convention Art. 3(e) states that one of the functions of the WCO Council is 'to make recommendations, in a conciliatory capacity, for the settlement of disputes concerning the interpretation or application of the Conventions referred to in paragraph (d) above in accordance with the provisions of those Conventions; the parties in dispute may agree in advance to accept the recommendations of the Council as binding'. Note that the Convention in paragraph (d) includes also the Nomenclature for the Classification of Goods in Customs Tariffs.

72 Horn and Howse, 'European Communities', at 36–7.

73 Rovetta et al., 'WTO Dispute Settlement', at 111.

turn out to be of great importance in clarifying commitments undertaken under the WTO and in the securing of tariff concessions undertaken by virtue of GATT Article II. The above situation was confirmed in *EC – Chicken Cuts* and *China – Auto Parts*, the relevant parts of which were analysed.

Interactions with the WCO will not, however, be limited to classification disputes. Specific mention of the WCO in a number of WTO provisions, in the context of customs valuation and rules of origin issues,[74] suggests that WCO practice may turn out to be useful in future WTO disputes dealing with this other subject matter. The case law on this is scarce and the evolution of such interactions may be observed only in the future.

74 E.g. Art. 18(2) and Annex II of the Agreement on Implementation of GATT Article VII; Arts. 4(2), 9(1, 2) and Annex I of the Agreement on Rules of Origin.

9

The World Health Organization and the Codex Alimentarius Commission

I. Introduction

Unlike most domestic law regimes, where it is presumed that the administration has competence and must be given a certain margin of discretion, international adjudication, including WTO dispute settlement, does not acknowledge the principle of judicial restraint in highly technical cases.[1] Since there is no separation of powers at the international level, and no administration as such, it is a difficult task for international tribunals to decide to whom to assign fact-finding in these disputes. Given these limitations, the successful resolution of disputes (or decision making in general) is determined by the ability of each international organization or tribunal to relate to 'outsiders' in matters requiring a narrow and specific expertise. The WTO adjudicator is no exception in this sense. The best example of the use made of such assistance in WTO adjudication arises in the context of health disputes.

With this in mind, this chapter explores the role and interaction of the WTO panels with WHO and the Codex Alimentarius Commission (the Codex) as arising from the relevant WTO case law. *Thailand – Cigarettes* demonstrates such interactions with WHO in a controversy over tobacco trading (section II), while *EC – Hormones* and *US/Canada – Continued Suspension* (section III) bring to light a far more complex relationship with the Codex. The choice of these two actors and disputes is not accidental.[2] There has been heated debate over the adjudication of health-related disputes in the WTO, and their outcome has been widely scrutinized by the civil society. In this context, the role of other actors, *in casu* other

1 See generally Oesch, *Standards of Review*. But cf. recent developments in the *US/Canada – Continued Suspension* case, where the Appellate Body reversed the Panel on a number of points, including on its chosen standard of review. For a discussion see Gruszczynski, *Regulating Health*, at 3–16.

2 The two SPS hormones disputes have been selected for a detailed analysis. References are made, however, to many other relevant SPS cases. See section IV below.

international organizations in this process, becomes important, as their input may determine the course of the dispute.

The selected case law analysis emphasizes the grounds and nature of interactions with the selected international organizations. This is followed by an evaluation of their role in WTO dispute settlement and some suggestions on how their contribution in this process could be enhanced to the benefit of the WTO dispute settlement system (section IV), culminating in conclusions (section V).

II. The role of science in the WTO

Before moving into the core analysis of the relevant jurisprudence and how specific international organizations play out in these disputes, it is important to provide some general insight into the role of science in the WTO – a subject which is woven all through the analysis in this chapter.

GATT 1947 made no reference to science and did not embody any express requirement with regard to the consultation of scientific experts. It basically urged the contracting parties to implement health measures with due consideration for the 'most favoured nation' principle, national treatment and a general prohibition on quantitative restrictions. Under GATT Article XX, contracting parties were allowed to depart from these imperatives provided the 'necessity' requirement was respected and that the measures were not a disguised and unjustifiable restriction on trade.

During the Tokyo Round, the so-called 'Standards Code' emerged regulating government specifications for industrial and agricultural products in order to protect human health, the environment and other values.[3] But the Code did not provide for a clear role for science.[4] On completion of the Uruguay Round negotiations, some science-based disciplines emerged in the WTO to govern regulatory measures in the area of public health.[5] These disciplines are at the core of the current WTO SPS Agreement, which requires that sanitary and phytosanitary measures must be 'based on scientific principles and . . . not maintained without sufficient scientific evidence'.[6] Under the SPS Agreement, national measures that conform to

3 See above Chapter 2, section III.B.1 for a more comprehensive account of the Standards Code.

4 The operation of the Standards Code is generally perceived as a failure, see Victor, 'Sanitary and Phytosanitary Agreement'.

5 For an insightful book on the law and science interface, see R. Feldman, *The Role of Science in Law* (Oxford University Press, 2009).

6 SPS Agreement, Art. 2.2.

international standards, such as those established by the Codex Alimentarius Commission,[7] the OIE and the IPPC are presumed to be compatible with WTO requirements.[8] The WTO members may adopt measures that are more stringent than these international standards, provided they are supported by 'a scientific justification'.[9] The non-fulfilment of these conditions by a WTO member triggers the obligation to remove or correct the non-compliant measure. These developments at the WTO have thus contributed to assigning the relevant standard-setting organizations quite a prominent role in the trade forum.[10]

A. *The need for scientific experts*

Explicit reference to scientific experts is found in the SPS Agreement which bases the legality of sanitary and phytosanitary measures on the existence of sufficient scientific evidence for that measure to be maintained. The need for scientific expertise does not, however, arise only in the application of the SPS Agreement. Health and environmental scientific expertise may also be necessary in the adjudication of other provisions, chiefly GATT Article XX exceptions (e.g. *Thailand – Cigarettes, US – Shrimp*). The judicial practice reveals, however, that scientific expertise is called on more frequently in the SPS disputes. This is because whenever SPS measures are challenged by WTO members, it is for the panels to apply the explicit science standard set out in the SPS Agreement. Collecting relevant factual and scientific information may be difficult for trade dispute

7 *Understanding the Codex.* For an overview of Codex-related literature see above Chapter 5, n. 20.

8 SPS Agreement Art. 3(1) obliges members to base their SPS measures on international standards, guidelines and recommendations 'where they exist'. The SPS Agreement in Annex A specifically defines 'international standards, guidelines or recommendations' as those established by the Codex, IPPC, or OIE. Art. 3(2) states that SPS measures of WTO members that are in conformity with international standards, guidelines or recommendations shall be 'presumed to be consistent with the relevant provisions of this Agreement'.

9 SPS Agreement, Art. 3.3. However, the latter permits members to maintain higher standards than the international norm as established by international standards, guidelines and recommendations if a member's measures are based on science or if such measures are the 'consequence of the level of sanitary or phytosanitary protection a Member determines to be appropriate in accordance with paragraphs 1 through 8 of Article 5'. SPS Art. 5(1–3) requires WTO members to base their SPS measures upon risk assessments.

10 Although see above Chapter 5, where some deficiencies in the activity of the Codex are perceived to affect the judicial willingness to ascribe a greater role to this institution in the adjudication of trade disputes.

settlement panels, which have limited fact-finding capabilities and no subpoena power. Moreover, the ad hoc panellists are lay rather than technical experts trained in the scientific disciplines relevant to a particular dispute. Thus panellists do not always possess the necessary knowledge and expertise to assess and evaluate the substance of scientific evidence underlying particular national SPS measures.[11] This is why resorting to scientific experts in these cases is indispensable and is fully justified by the need to avoid situations in which a tribunal of non-scientists might substitute its own judgment for that of scientific professionals.[12]

In WTO dispute settlement, scientific experts have played an important role in several disputes, such as *US – Shrimp*, *EC – Hormones*, *Australia – Salmon*, *Japan – Apples*, *EC – Asbestos*, *EC – Biotech* and *US/Canada – Continued Suspension*. The experts have assisted the panels by explaining the known literature and evaluating the 'risk assessments' presented by the parties involved. *EC – Hormones* is a case where the Panel relied heavily on the advice of its scientific experts.[13] This is testified to by Thomas Cottier, who served as chair in this dispute, noting that 'The Panels strongly relied upon expert views, and could not have rendered their assessment and recommendation without such independent advice of individual experts.'[14] *US/Canada – Continued Suspension* continued the tradition but with significant departures from the approach of the Panel or Appellate Body in *EC – Hormones*. These two cases are analysed in more detail in section IV below.

11 Oesch, *Standards of Review*, at 57.

12 See David A. Wirth, 'The Role of Science in the Uruguay Round and NAFTA Trade Disciplines', (1994) 27 *Cornell International Law Journal* 817, at 858. See also Christoforou, 'Settlement', at 622.

13 Panel Report, para. 8.127: 'All of the scientific studies outlined above came to the conclusion that the use of the hormones at issue (all but MGA, for which no evidence was submitted) for growth promotion purposes is safe . . . We note that this conclusion has also been confirmed by the scientific experts advising the Panel.' See also para. 8.136: 'the scientific experts advising the Panel were of the view that this evidence, as it stands today, does not invalidate or contradict the scientific conclusions reached in the other studies invoked by the European Communities'; para. 8.137: 'all scientific experts advising the Panel confirmed this conclusion and stated that, as of today, no scientific evidence is available which concludes that an identifiable risk arises from the use of any of the hormones at issue for growth promotion purposes in accordance with good practice'; para. 8.114: 'the scientists advising the Panel seemed to consider these reports, from a scientific and technical point of view, to be risk assessments'.

14 Thomas Cottier, 'Risk Management Experience in WTO Dispute Settlement', in David Robertson and Aynsley Kellow (eds.), *Globalization and the Environment: Risk Assessment and the WTO* (Cheltenham: Edward Elgar, 2001), 41–62, at 51.

B. Complexity in dealing with scientific expertise

Some observers have argued that the rules on scientific expertise are not well developed in WTO law and that this may cause a number of problems. This situation implies a certain risk that gaps in WTO law will be filled by panels and the Appellate Body, notwithstanding the principle that the WTO dispute settlement system cannot add to or diminish rights and obligations of members.[15] Thus even if the WTO panellists are supported by scientific experts, they still need to decide how to interpret their responses, how to assess and choose between the conflicting views, what kind of inferences to make on the basis of such opinions, how much weight to attach to particular observations, and so on.[16] In fact, more than once a WTO panel has shown confusion regarding the appropriate role for scientific expertise.[17] This obviously leaves a considerable margin of discretion for the panels, which, aside from illegitimately filling gaps in WTO law, increases the probability of making assessment errors, the costs of which are considerably higher in health-related disputes than in other trade controversies.[18] Gruszczynski, for example, observes this difficulty for the Panel in *US/Canada – Continued Suspension*, from questions it posed during one of the meetings with the experts, as summarized here:

> In the context of discussion on the very complicated issue of genotoxic potential of oestradiol-17β, the panel asked a number of elementary questions concerning the basis of toxicology. One may only wonder how it was ultimately possible for the panel to make a complex factual judgment on, for instance, the existence of threshold in a dose-response relationship of oestradiol-17β, without possessing adequate literacy in scientific matters.[19]

The adjudication of scientific questions has therefore become the subject of considerable controversy and disagreement. Consistent with what

15 Wirth, 'Role of Science', at 858.

16 See also Perez, *Ecological Sensitivity*, 98, noting that the incorporation of experts into the legal process does not guarantee that the information they will provide will be properly interpreted.

17 See John McGinnis and Mark Movsesian, 'The World Trade Constitution', (2000) 114 *Harvard Law Review* 511, at 594; Terence P. Stewart and Amy A. Karpel, 'Review of the Dispute Settlement Understanding: Operation of Panels', (2000) 31 *Law and Policy in International Business* 593.

18 See e.g. Alessandra Arcuri and Giuseppe Dari-Mattiacci, 'Centralization versus Decentralization as a Risk-Return Trade-off', Amsterdam Center for Law & Economics Working Paper No. 2007–06.

19 Gruszczynski, *Regulating Health.*

has been noted above, some authors find that, in an environmental or public health context, the adjudication of 'scientific facts' may be particularly difficult precisely because of the complexity of establishing from a scientific point of view whether an environmental contaminant or pollutant is safe or has no effect.[20]

The difficulty in dealing with scientific standards is to some degree acknowledged in SPS Article 11(2), according to which the panels 'should' seek advice from experts as opposed to 'may' in DSU Article 13(2). The former also sets out the discretion of the panel to establish an advisory technical experts group, or consult the 'relevant international organizations' at the request of either party to the dispute or on its own initiative.

C. *The discretion of the panels to appoint experts*

The discretion of the panels to appoint experts arises from several WTO provisions, such as Article 13 of the DSU, Article 11(2) of the SPS Agreement, Articles 14(2) and 14(3) of the TBT Agreement, Article 19(3) and (4) of, and Annex II to, the Agreement on Customs Valuation; and Articles 4(5) and 24(3) of the SCM Agreement.[21] With minor differences and very few adaptations, the second and third sentences of Article 13(2) of the DSU follow the example of Articles 14(9) and 14(10), in conjunction with Article 14(17), of the Tokyo Round TBT Agreement.[22] Although the number of these provisions in the WTO legal texts is relatively high, the provisions themselves are rather rudimentary, as they fail to assign a clearly defined role to the panel when adjudicating scientific trade disputes.[23]

In dispute settlement the panels are guided by several other provisions, including the imperative of the 'objective assessment of the matter' before them according to DSU Article 11. Other important guidance comes from practice established by the panels and the Appellate Body in case law. For example, in *Argentina – Textiles and Apparel* the Appellate

20 Wirth, 'Role of Science', at 845, citing John Stonehouse and John Mumford, 'Science, Risk Analysis and Environmental Policy Decisions', United Nations Environmental Programme Environment and Trade Series, 1994.

21 See above Chapter 2 on the relevant norms. An important practice emerges, however, from the case law which adds to these norms – e.g. the appointment of individual experts as opposed to expert review groups.

22 A short summary on the history of these provisions is provided in Christoforou, 'Settlement', at 628.

23 Ibid., at 626–7, noting that lack of experience in adjudicating scientific-based disputes under GATT might also have influenced a rather passive approach of the members on the need to lay down more detailed procedural rules.

Body acknowledged that Article 13 of the DSU enables panels to seek information or technical advice as it deems appropriate in a particular case; a panel, however, may not (with the help of its experts) make the case for one or other party (*Japan – Agricultural Products II*).[24] The experts can be appointed by a panel at the request of the parties (*EC – Hormones*) or appointed without such a specific request (*US – Shrimp*). Even if the parties have requested the panel to appoint experts, the panel has full discretion as to whether it accedes to this request. This discretion is somewhat limited by Article 11(2) of the SPS Agreement, which states that the panel 'should seek advice from experts chosen by the Panel'. This explains why in all SPS cases scientific experts have been appointed.

The rules set out in Appendix 4 to the DSU (copied in Annex 2 to the TBT Agreement) provide for the selection procedure of the experts by WTO panels. Although these rules actually require the creation of expert review groups, the panels have always opted for the consultation of individual experts. Thus DSU Appendix 4 rules are applied to the selection of individual experts. In this process panels select 'persons of professional standing and expertise in the field in question', who should act in their 'individual capacities' (para. 2). The citizens of the parties to the dispute shall not serve as experts in that dispute without the joint agreement of the parties 'except in exceptional circumstances when the Panels consider that the need for specialized scientific expertise cannot be fulfilled otherwise' (para. 3). Similarly, government officials of parties to the dispute shall not serve on an expert review group (or as individual experts). The Rules of Conduct for the DSU that apply to panel and Appellate Body members also apply to the experts, requiring that they are 'independent and impartial and shall avoid direct or indirect conflicts of interest and shall respect the confidentiality of proceedings of bodies'.[25]

III. WHO in *Thailand – Cigarettes*

Thailand – Cigarettes was the first case where WHO provided some input into the settlement of a health-related trade dispute. WHO's provision of scientific evidence in this case was a novel situation for the GATT dispute settlement system, operating without solid provisions on the role of science. The case arose in connection with the approval of the 1966 Tobacco Act by Thailand, prohibiting the importation of cigarettes

24 *Japan – Apples*, Panel Report, para. 129.
25 Rule II, Governing Principles, WTO doc. WT/DSB/RC/1, 11 December 1996.

and other tobacco preparations. In 1989 the United States complained to the GATT that the import restrictions were inconsistent with GATT Article XI and considered that they were not justified by either exceptions to the elimination of quantitative restrictions, or the general GATT exception pertaining to measures necessary for the protection of human life or health (Art. XX(b)). Thailand invoked this latter exception with the argument that chemicals and other additives contained in US cigarettes made them more harmful to human health compared with Thai cigarettes.

Thailand requested the Panel to *consult* with WHO[26] experts about recent experience in countries which had opened their markets to cigarettes, in order to evaluate the impact of this liberalization on public health.[27] Following this request the Panel asked WHO to present its conclusions on the health effects of cigarette use and consumption, and on related issues for which WHO was competent.[28] The Panel did not refer to any GATT provision in support of its authority to seek such advice from an international organization.[29]

The WHO experts explained that cigarette smoking was found to be the leading cause of preventable death and disease in developed nations. With respect to Thailand, the WHO representative stated that it did not reveal as high a number of smoking-related cancers as many other developing countries; however, 'an increase in cigarette smoking would lead to an increase in mortality due to lung cancer and hypertension, which was

26 Although there is no formal agreement between WHO and the WTO, WHO has observer status in the SPS and TBT Committees, and it has ad hoc observer status in the TRIPS and GATS Councils. There is extensive collaboration between the two secretariats relating to health and sanitary and phytosanitary measures, and continuing joint efforts to bring attention to the need for policy coherence between trade and health matters at both the global and national level. WTO, www.wto.org/english/thewto_e/coher_e/WTO_who_e.htm.

27 Ibid., para. 27.

28 Ibid., para. 50.

29 With the advent of the WTO, panels usually refer to DSU Art. 13 in support of their decision to seek advice from other international bodies or individual experts. Under GATT – as appears from this case – the panels were not necessarily concerned with providing such references. For an interesting note on this see James Cameron and Stephen J. Orava, 'GATT/WTO Panels between Recording and Finding Facts: Issues of Due Process, Evidence, Burden of Proof, and Standard of Review in GATT/WTO Dispute Settlement', in Friedl Weiss (ed.), *Improving WTO Dispute Settlement Procedures: Issues and Lessons from the Practice of Other International Courts and Tribunals* (London: Cameron May, 2000), 195–242, at 195, noting that 'the working parties did not have formal procedures for the collection and assessment of factual evidence or for the interpretation of legal issues'.

already rising because of the increase in cigarette consumption which had occurred 10 to 20 years ago'.[30]

Having taken note of this evidence, the Panel noted that GATT Article XX(b) requires that the measure be 'necessary'. In their view, a health measure could not be considered as such if a reasonable alternative that would not conflict with free trade rules could be employed.[31] According to the Panel, since Thailand could have achieved its public health objective through internal measures consistent with the GATT, the measure was not 'necessary' within the meaning of Article XX(b).[32] Thus, based on evidence offered by WHO that restrictions on advertising could reduce cigarette consumption, it suggested an alternative means of curbing consumption of cigarettes which could have taken the form of a general ban on tobacco advertising by both foreign and domestic tobacco companies.[33] With this reasoning the Panel rejected Thailand's justification.

A. *The WHO resolution and recommendations*

The WHO submissions to the Panel confirmed differences between cigarettes manufactured in developing countries, such as Thailand, and those in developed countries, which contained more additives and flavouring to make them easier to smoke. The more sophisticated techniques and flavourings of the American brands gave the impression that they were safer to smoke than the Thai cigarettes. As a result, the Thai smokers were stopping smoking home-produced cigarettes and replacing them with American brands. In WHO's view, as a result of these cigarettes entering into the Thai market, their consumption and, in turn, the death and disease attributable to smoking would increase.[34] WHO stated that the use of additives in American cigarettes had increased greatly during the 1970s with the introduction of low-tar cigarettes; however, it did not find any *scientific evidence* to show that one type of cigarette was more harmful to health than another.[35]

WHO further brought data showing a decline in the consumption of cigarettes in Thailand, and argued that this was due to the adoption of WHO smoking control policies, in particular WHO Resolution 43.16.[36] This instrument secured the passage of domestic legislation prohibiting all forms of tobacco advertising, including a ban on events sponsorship,

30 *Thailand – Cigarettes*, Panel Report, para. 51. 31 Ibid., Panel Report, para. 74.
32 Ibid., paras. 74–75. 33 Ibid., para. 78. 34 Ibid., para. 52.
35 Ibid., para. 53. 36 Ibid.

and requiring forceful warning labels on packages. The Resolution urged member states

> [t]o consider including in their tobacco control strategies plans for legislation or other effective measures at the appropriate government level providing for: . . . (c) progressive restriction and concerted actions to eliminate eventually all direct and indirect advertising, promotion and sponsorship concerning tobacco.[37]

WHO further noted that Thailand had implemented the recommendations of the WHO Expert Committee on 'Smoking Control Strategies in Developing Countries', which urged countries to prohibit all advertising and promotion of tobacco products, including through the sponsorship of sporting events. These instruments prescribed that where tobacco was a commercial crop, its role should be reduced in the economy through the alternative use of land and labour for which the assistance of organizations within the UN system, such as the FAO and the World Bank, could be sought.[38]

Assessing Thailand's compliance with these instruments, WHO submitted that Thailand had put some effort into complying with these new policies, but the poorly financed health policies of Thailand would be unable to compete with the promotion budgets of Western cigarette companies, as had been the case in other Asian countries which had opened up their markets.[39]

The Panel ultimately singled out WHO's statement that 'the demand for cigarettes, in particular the initial demand for cigarettes by the young, was influenced by cigarette advertisements and that bans on the advertisements could therefore curb such demand'.[40] Relying on this assertion, the Panel concluded that Thailand could have introduced a ban on advertising – a measure which would have been justified under GATT Article XX.[41] Despite WHO's positive assessment of Thailand's compliance with the relevant WHO instruments, in reaching this conclusion the Panel referred repeatedly to the WHO Resolution that directly prescribed this policy for WHO members.

B. WHO economic data

Apart from representations on the health impact of smoking, WHO presented economic data which revealed that the opening of closed cigarette

37 Ibid., para. 55. 38 Ibid., para. 56. 39 Ibid., para. 52.
40 Ibid., para. 78. 41 Ibid.

markets in some Latin American and Asian countries dominated by a state tobacco company (as in Thailand) resulted in an increase in smoking. WHO contended that 'A study carried out in developing countries indicated that price elasticity of smoking was higher in developing countries than in the developed ones, thus making measures that raise the price of cigarettes, such as excise taxes, effective public health policy tools.'[42] The United States, however, took issue with this statement as it considered that WHO had no competence on this matter, and it urged the Panel to limit its questions to WHO to those authorized in the memorandum of understanding agreed by both litigants.[43] The United States argued that the economic data presented by WHO was not accurate because the experience of cigarette market opening provided different results in different countries. It also believed that there was no evidence showing that advertising and promotion increased the level of tobacco consumption.[44]

C. Evaluation

The analysis of *Thailand – Cigarettes* and of WHO's input into this dispute warrants emphasizing a few points. First, the Panel report indicates that an expert from WHO provided information and documentation to the Panel, but it does not enlarge much on the procedures employed in this process or on why WHO had been selected for this exercise. In principle, GATT panels could have referred to GATT Article XXIII(2) or the Understanding regarding Notification, Consultation, Dispute Settlement and Surveillance in 1979, which mirrors the provisions of DSU Article 13.[45] Providing the legal basis for the consultation with WHO and some reasons behind its selection as an expert in this dispute could have proved useful, especially in dealing with the US argument that the organization was not competent to provide answers to some questions.[46]

Second, the Panel explicitly referred to WHO Resolution 43.16 to stress that this instrument contained GATT-consistent measures which could have been implemented by Thailand in pursuit of its public health objectives. The Panel noted that the health measures recommended by WHO in these resolutions were non-discriminatory and concerned all, not just

42 Ibid., para. 57. 43 Ibid., paras. 57–58. 44 Ibid., para. 60.

45 See Chapter 1, n. 45.

46 For an overview of the assessment of competency and credibility of international organizations in the WTO see above Chapter 5.

imported, cigarettes.[47] In this context one could claim, at least on the face of it, that this reference to WHO stands as an example of institutional sensitivity of the WTO adjudicator vis-à-vis another international regime. However, the fact that the Panel did not defer to WHO's positive evaluation of Thailand's compliance with these instruments evidences the opposite.

1. The disregard of WHO's expertise

Some observers have also noted the failure by the *Thailand – Cigarettes* Panel to show sensitivity towards the expertise provided by WHO. According to Howse, for example, the Panel practically ignored evidence from WHO that opening up markets to American cigarettes in a number of Latin American and Asian countries had led to an increase in smoking.[48] Moreover, with regard to available alternative measures, the WHO data showed that, in the real world of developing countries, the US multinationals had the resources to circumvent advertising bans, either finding loopholes in the laws or evading compliance efforts. Furthermore, the experience of the WHO in the region showed that the opening up of a closed cigarette market dominated by a state tobacco monopoly, as was the case in Thailand, resulted in an increase in smoking.[49] With the disregarding by the Panel of this evidence from WHO, it has been claimed that this case illustrates not only one dimension of institutional insensitivity but two, one relating to the competence of WHO, and the other to the local knowledge of the Thai regulators, attempting to achieve regulatory goals in a real world environment known intimately to them, but not known at all to the Panel.[50]

An opposite view is expressed by Kinnon, who investigated the effects of the Panel's decision. He notes that the outcome of the case indeed adversely affected national tobacco control programmes in some developing countries,[51] but 'this was not the case of Thailand, that had wisely offset the potential impact by taking appropriate public health measures based on the WHO's recommendations for comprehensive tobacco control'.[52] In this process, it had implemented a number of alternative (less restrictive) measures which included increased sales

47 The Panel also examined the report of a WHO Expert Committee to find that a common consequence of import restrictions was the promotion of domestic production, hence this was not a solution. See *Thailand – Cigarettes*, Panel Report, para. 80.

48 Howse, 'Legitimacy', at 392.

49 *Thailand – Cigarettes*, Panel Report, para. 55.

50 Howse, 'Legitimacy', at 392.

51 Kinnon, 'World Trade', at 403.

52 Ibid.

taxes, smoking bans in public buildings, disclosure of ingredients and requirements for prominent health warnings on cigarette packages.

Although challenges over the effective control of smoking certainly remain in developing countries, a joint WHO–WTO study also showed that, in the aftermath of the dispute, smoking prevalence in Thailand declined in the mid and late 1990s.[53] This suggests that the outcome of the dispute should not be subjected to criticism. What can be criticized, however, is the level of the Panel's sensitivity towards the expertise and experience of WHO over the implementation of tobacco control policies in different parts of the world. This should have been attributed greater weight in the dispute.

2. Future WTO–WHO interactions on tobacco control policies

The linkage of the WTO with WHO is elicited from the granting of discretion to WTO members to introduce health measures under a number of GATT/WTO provisions, but also in relation to health services under the GATS. The World Health Assembly recognized the significance of the trade–health linkage in a May 2006 Resolution on International Trade and Health, in which the Assembly called for foreign, trade and health ministries to move towards coherence in formulating national policies on trade and health. To this end, the Assembly tasked WHO with collaborating with other international organizations to generate and share evidence on ways to align trade and health.[54] An important product of this co-operation – the WHO–WTO joint study – stressed that the *Thailand – Cigarettes* case illustrated the relevance of the GATT/WTO, as it affected taxes, prohibitions and human health-related exceptions to trade rules in a tobacco dispute.[55] Thus future interfaces could be expected between the two organizations in this area.

The WHO policies on tobacco control were strengthened with the emergence in 2003 of the WHO Framework Convention on Tobacco Control (FCTC).[56] The parties to the FCTC agreed that the elimination

53 WTO, 'WTO Agreements and Public Health: A Joint Study by the WHO and WTO Secretariat', 2002, www.wto.org/english/res_e/booksp_e/who_wto_e.pdf (visited 20 April 2009), at 73, para. 132.

54 For other co-operation activities between the WTO and WHO see WTO, www.wto.org/english/thewto_e/coher_e/wto_who_e.htm (visited July 2009).

55 Above n. 53.

56 On 21 May 2003, at the 56th World Health Assembly, WHO's 192 member states unanimously adopted the FCTC. As of June 2008, there were 157 parties to the

of all forms of illicit trade in tobacco products, including smuggling and counterfeiting, constituted the core of tobacco controls. Under the mandate of Article 15 of the FCTC, the parties have started to develop a protocol to this agreement which deals with illicit trade in tobacco.[57] This instrument gives countries a range of policy instruments to achieve the goals of the elimination of illicit trade. With the emergence of the FCTC as a binding instrument and its proposed protocols, the WTO adjudicating bodies will have to take it into account in their interpretation process.[58]

Thus, given the emergence of the FCTC, the scrutiny of the process of health and trade reconciliation is now more intense. This binding instrument is hard law which cannot be easily disregarded by the WTO panels.[59] Some concrete challenges still remain in relation to obligations falling under specific WTO Agreements, such as the GATS, concerning the FCTC advertising ban provisions.[60] But since WTO jurisprudence has developed in the direction of accepting the use of other international treaties (although with some limitations) in the interpretation of WTO obligations, there is no reason to believe that this new instrument will not be taken into account in future disputes.[61]

FCTC, representing about 80 per cent of the world population, www.who.int/fctc/text_download/en/index.html (visited 30 April 2009).

57 The WHO FCTC Conference of Parties decided to establish an intergovernmental negotiating body (INB) open to all parties to draft and negotiate a protocol on illicit trade in tobacco products, which would build upon and complement the provisions of FCTC Art. 15 on illicit trade in tobacco products.

58 But see Lin, 'Exploring a Modest Balance', at 314, refuting this idea and attributing it to the restrictive reading of the VCLT rules in *EC – Biotech*, where the Panel declined to take into account such rules unless they were accepted not only by the parties, but by all the members alike. But this approach has been widely criticized in the literature; see Chapter 1, n. 60.

59 See generally Joseph N. Eckhardt, 'Balancing Interests in Free Trade and Health: How the WHO's Framework Convention on Tobacco Control Can Withstand WTO Scrutiny', (2002) 12 *Duke Journal of Comparative & International Law* 197, at www.law.duke.edu/shell/cite.pl?12. See also Sungjoon Cho, 'How to Reconcile Trade and Non-trade Value under the WTO: A Judicial Dimension', in Federico Ortino and Sergey Ripinsky (eds.), *WTO Law and Process: The Proceedings of the 2005 and 2006 Annual WTO Conferences* (London: British Institute of International and Comparative Law, 2007) 42, at 42.

60 Tsai-yu Lin, 'Addressing the Issue of Trade in Services and Public Health in the Case of Tobacco – Are the FCTC Restrictions on Tobacco Advertising Inconsistent with the GATS?', (2006) 7 *Journal of World Investment & Trade* 545.

61 See generally Thomas Cottier, Cintia Busse and Anna Jevtic, 'Is a Legally Binding Ban on Internet Sales of Tobacco Products Compatible with WTO Obligations?', Legal Opinion Submitted to the Secretariat of the World Health Organization WHO, 23 February 2008 (on file with the author).

Another issue concerning this interface relates to the role of WHO as an expert in the settlement of tobacco-related trade disputes. There is no doubt that WHO would be qualified to provide expert advice, including scientific advice, on tobacco-related health disputes at the WTO. But, as revealed by *Thailand – Cigarettes*, there is one remaining question – whether this could extend to include economic expertise. The Panel accepted the US approach, which argued against the acceptance of such input, without attributing significant weight to a number of WHO's economic studies. Yet with the consolidation of the tobacco regime in the FCTC and the setting of a comprehensive co-ordinating anti-tobacco programme by WHO, today such an argument would be difficult to make. These developments give definite impetus to WHO's claim of economic expertise in the field of tobacco control.[62] In this exercise, the WTO panel will have to consider, however, the special claim of economic expertise on tobacco control by other international organizations such as the World Bank, which completed parallel studies on this topic.[63] The absence of a health bias in the studies carried out by an economic and development agency such as the World Bank would enhance the legitimacy of the decision by the WTO adjudicator.

IV. The Codex Alimentarius Commission in SPS disputes

The issues arising in connection with the role of the Codex in WTO disputes pertain to the SPS area and are far more complex. This is explained by the novelty and complexity of the SPS standards for the trade community.[64] For the panels to apply scientific principles is not an

62 In pursuit of its health objectives, WHO, for example, launched the Tobacco Free Initiative – a cabinet project to provide global leadership and to mobilize national and international action for preventing and reducing tobacco use. Moreover, an ad hoc Interagency Task Force on Tobacco Control, chaired by WHO, initiated studies on the economic implications of tobacco reduction, employment issues related to tobacco control, smoke-free policies, smuggling, trade issues related to the framework convention, economic analysis of tobacco control that focuses on demand-side issues, and privatization and illicit trade. See Gian Luca Burci and Claude-Henri Vignes, *World Health Organization* (The Hague, London and Boston, MA: Kluwer Law International, 2004), 343–5.

63 See for example, World Bank, 'Economics of Tobacco Control: Chapter 5, Measures to Reduce the Supply of Tobacco', 2000, at http://www1.worldbank.org/tobacco/book/pdf/06-Tobacco-Chap5.pdf (visited July 2009). See also Allyn Taylor et al., 'The Impact of Trade Liberalization on Tobacco Consumption', in Prabhat Jha and Frank J. Chaloupka (eds.), *Tobacco Control in Developing Countries* (Oxford University Press, 2000), 343, http://www1. worldbank.org/tobacco/tcdc/343TO364.PDF.

64 See above Chapter 2, section III.B.1, for a description of the relevant SPS provisions.

easy task and external expertise is needed in this process. This stems from the fact-finding mandate entrusted to a panel by DSU Article 11, which instructs it to make an objective assessment of the matter before it and the applicability of and conformity with the relevant covered agreements. These complexities are illustrated in more detail below as they emerge in the adjudication of specific WTO disputes.

A. *EC – Hormones*

EC – Hormones represents a benchmark case in the WTO's judicial practice of using of scientific experts.[65] This case launched the generation of science and international trade scholarship, analysing the strengths and weaknesses of the newly established system.[66] The dispute originated from the EC's prohibition in 1988 on the importation from the United States and Canada of beef injected with natural and synthetic growth hormones. The measure was successfully challenged by these two countries, which claimed that the use of hormones in beef for growth promotion purposes was safe and posed no threat to human health. According to them, the ban was scientifically unfounded and was designed to protect EC beef producers from competition, and thus was inconsistent with a number of SPS Agreement provisions (including Articles 3(1) and 3(3)).[67] The EC countered that the hormones might threaten human health and that science supported its policy. The ban was found by a WTO panel to be based on neither international standards (as they existed under the Codex) nor on a risk assessment – a result upheld by the WTO Appellate Body.[68]

In *EC – Hormones*, following consultation with the parties, 'the Panel decided to seek scientific and technical advice as foreseen in paragraph 1 and 2, first sentence, of Article 13 of the DSU, and pursuant to paragraph

65 For an overview of this long-standing case see, e.g., Marco M. Slotboom, 'The Hormones Case: An Increased Risk of Illegality of Sanitary and Phytosanitary Measures', (1999) 36 *Common Market Law Review* 471; Daniel Wüger, 'The Implementation Phase in the Dispute between the EC and the United States on Hormone-Treated Beef', (2002) 33 *Law and Policy in International Business* 777, and for a follow-up of the case see Alberto Alemanno, 'Judicial Enforcement of the WTO Hormones ruling within the European Community: Toward an EC Liability for the Non-implementation of WTO Dispute Settlement Decisions', (2004) 45 *Harvard International Law Journal* 547.

66 For an overview see Jeffrey Atik and David A. Wirth, 'Science and International Trade – Third Generation Scholarship', (2003) 26 *Boston College International & Comparative Law Review* 171.

67 *EC – Hormones*, Panel Report, para. 8.239.

68 Ibid., ABR, para. 253.

2, first sentence, of Article 11 of the SPS Agreement'.[69] The EC proposed that the Panel should seek advice from an expert review group as set out in Appendix 4 to the DSU. The United States, however, believed that consultation with experts was not necessary but that if the Panel were to resort to experts, this had to be done in accordance with the DSU – that is, by setting out an expert review group. The Panel ultimately decided to seek scientific advice from individual experts – a practice that has been followed thereafter in all the WTO scientific disputes.[70] Already by the time of *Japan – Apples* there was a clear indication that the WTO was attempting to standardize this practice. The *EC – Biotech* case is also a testimony to this.[71]

The issue as to whether the panels should seek advice from an expert review group as opposed to individual experts is controversial, and encourages the use of the former.[72] At the same time, this is pivotal in determining the level of scientific involvement requested from the WTO judicial bodies in the case.[73]

1. The provision of information and expert advice by the Codex

The *EC – Hormones* Panel turned to the Codex in order to seek information on a number of questions relating to the substance of the case. Moreover, the Panel chose to select an expert from the Codex Secretariat to assist it.[74] The Secretariat explained to the Panel the relevant Codex terminology, clarifying such concepts as 'acceptable daily

69 *EC – Hormones*, Panel Report, paras. 7.1–7.10.

70 See *EC – Hormones*, Panel Report, para. 6.10; *Australia – Salmon*, Panel Report, para. 6.6; *Australia – Salmon* (Art. 21.5 – Canada), Panel Report, para. 6.5; *Japan – Agricultural Products II*, Panel Report, para. 6.4; *Japan – Apples*, Panel Report, para. 6.4; *Japan – Apples* (Art. 21.4 – Canada), Panel Report, para. 6.2; *EC – Biotech*, Panel Report, para. 7.25; *US – Continued Suspension*, Panel Report, para. 7.86.

71 *EC – Biotech Products*, above n. 70.

72 Alberto Alemanno, *Trade in Food: Regulatory and Judicial Approaches to Food Risks in the EC and the WTO* (London: Cameron May, 2007), 350; Alberto Alemanno, 'Risk Assessment under WTO Law: Workable Requirement or Probatio Diabolica?', Working Paper prepared for the 3rd ESIL Research Forum Science and International Law, Helsinki, 2–3 October 2009; Theofanis Christoforou, 'Law and Precaution in Dispute Resolution on Health and Environmental Protection: What Role for Scientific Experts?', in J. Bourrinet and S. Maljean-Dubois (eds.), *Le Commerce International des Organismes Génétiquement Modifiés* (Paris: Panthéon-Assas, 2003), 255; Christoforou, 'Settlement', at 628–9.

73 Alemanno, *Trade in Food.* See also generally Oesch, *Standards of Review.* For a detailed account of this topic see below subsection C.3.

74 *EC – Hormones*, Panel Report, para. 8.8.

intake', 'maximum residue level', 'veterinary drugs' and 'good veterinary practices'.[75] The expert explained, for example, that 'the terms "good veterinary practice" and "good veterinary and husbandry practice", when used in JECFA reports, are synonyms for GPVD [Good Practice in the Use of Veterinary Drugs]'.[76] All these definitions were set out either by the Codex or by the JECFA – a FAO–WHO Joint Expert Committee on Food Additives,[77] helping the Panel to elucidate the question whether the EC measure was based on international standards pursuant to SPS Article 3.[78]

Having determined that there were Codex standards for the five hormones at issue, the Panel examined their definition and scope of application with a view to determining whether they applied to the EC measures.[79] In this context, the Codex expert provided important information concerning the activity of the Codex and the JECFA on the hormones at issue and the application of the above standards to the EC measures. From the responses provided to the Panel, it seems that the Codex expert also provided answers on scientific aspects of the matter. In this respect, the expert elaborated on some questions addressed to the Codex Secretariat, such as 'the relationship between the acceptable daily intake and the maximum residue limit and whether or not these are measures of the acceptable risk'.[80] Since the Panel relied on these clarifications,[81] it is interesting to note that it assigned the Codex expert

75 See Annex to Panel Report, ibid., Transcript of the Joint Meeting with Experts, held on 17 and 18 February 1997, para. 26.

76 Panel Report, ibid., para. 8.60.

77 While not officially part of the Codex Alimentarius Commission structure, the Joint FAO/WHO Expert Committee on Food Additives provides independent scientific expert advice to the Commission and its specialist committees. The FAO and WHO maintain separate websites highlighting the work of the Committee from the points of view of the two parent organizations: www.codexalimentarius.net/web/jecfa.jsp (visited June 2009).

78 *EC – Hormones*, Panel Report, para. 8.45.

79 Ibid., para. 8.58.

80 Ibid., para. 7.76.

81 Ibid., para. 128 and n. 337: 'we further note that, according to the scientific experts advising the Panel, the data and studies contained in these Monographs with respect to the carcinogenic potential of the hormones in dispute have been fully taken into account in the 1988 and 1989 JECFA Reports which, at several occasions, explicitly refer to these Monographs'; Para 8.132: 'we further note that, according to the Codex expert advising the Panel, most of the evidence contained in these articles and opinions and the potential risks addressed therein were already evaluated and taken into account in the 1988 and 1989 JECFA Reports [footnote omitted]'.

to the pool of scientific experts, referring to his opinion in the report.[82] The report does not reveal, however, whether the Panel understood the implications of this differentiation – that is, between that of the Codex expert acting as a technical expert whose mandate is limited to providing expertise regarding the operation and scope of the Codex standards, and that of a scientific expert entrusted with scientific evaluations.[83] It did not refer to the fact that asking for scientific evaluations from the Codex expert might raise concerns with those member states which, during the negotiations of the SPS Agreement, had been trying to limit the role of these organizations as they feared partisan opinions entering WTO adjudication.[84]

2. The selection of scientific experts

Since the WTO Agreements do not set out rules regarding the selection of individual scientific experts, the panels found guidance in the rules of Appendix 4 to the DSU regarding the functioning of expert review groups – but not without encountering some procedural and substantive issues. One of the fundamental issues in the selection of the scientific experts concerned the *sources* from which the panel should draw them. The Panel ultimately decided to seek the assistance of the Secretariat of the Codex in identifying suitable candidate experts on the subject matter under consideration. Of those proposed by the Codex, the Panel decided to choose two. The Panel also decided to seek names from the International Agency for Research on Cancer (IARC), selecting one expert proposed by this institution.[85] As already mentioned above, the Codex Alimentarius Secretariat was also asked to appoint a technical expert, to provide the Panel with technical information about the Codex's rules and procedures and clarifications of the nature and scope of its

82 See ibid., para. 2.8 for evidence that the Panel was actually distinguishing between two categories of experts (scientific and technical): 'The Panel consulted scientific and technical experts on 17–18 February 1997 in a meeting held jointly with the panel proceeding brought by Canada on the same EC measures.'

83 See above Chapter 2 section V.A.1 for an account of this distinction.

84 For an account see Doaa Abdel Motaal, 'The "Multilateral Scientific Consensus" and the World Trade Organization', (2004) 38 *Journal of World Trade* 855.

85 *EC–Hormones*, Panel Report, para. 7.6. The International Agency for Research on Cancer (IARC) is part of the World Health Organization. The IARC's mission is to co-ordinate and conduct research into the causes of human cancer and the mechanisms of carcinogenesis, and to develop scientific strategies for cancer prevention and control. See www.iarc.fr (visited June 2009).

standards.[86] The parties to the dispute were given an opportunity to comment on these potential experts on the basis of their curricula vitae, and in particular to state any compelling objections they might have with regard to any particular individual. In parallel to the procedure for the selection of experts, the secretary of the Panel (who is a member of the WTO Secretariat, frequently from the division responsible for the subject matter of the dispute) prepared a list of written questions that were submitted to the parties for comments. The Panel established the final list of questions and submitted it to each expert individually.[87]

Thus when it came to the identification of experts the *EC – Hormones* Panel turned to the Codex, justifying such a request with reference to 'the relevant international organizations' enshrined in the SPS Agreement (as well as turning to the IARC, without any such justification).[88] Note should be taken that three of the five selected scientists were regular participants in Codex scientific committees and one even acted as a rapporteur in the risk assessment undertaken by the Codex on the hormones in question in the dispute. This issue was attributed high significance by the EC, which objected to the Panel's method of choosing the experts and considered this to be a serious procedural error, bringing it up for appeal. The main concern of the EC was the impartiality of the selected experts, given their links with the Codex. The EC argued that this error of the Panel encroached on the right to a fair hearing – a general principle of law recognized by civilized nations – that should be taken into account in the interpretation of the notion of an 'objective assessment of the matter' as set out in Article 11 of the DSU.[89] Unfortunately, the Appellate Body did not discuss this point in detail, but seemed implicitly to have rejected it.[90] Exactly the same issue re-emerged in *US/Canada – Continued Suspension*, but this time it was considered by the Appellate Body as relevant, with proper elaboration on this point.[91]

86 See previous section discussing the implications of having a Codex expert advising the Panel.

87 *EC – Hormones*, Panel Report, Para 7.8. For a summary on expert selection in this case see also Christoforou, 'Settlement', at 629–31.

88 See the Preamble to the SPS Agreement: 'on the basis of international standards, guidelines and recommendations developed by the relevant international organizations, including the Codex Alimentarius Commission, the International Office of Epizootics, and the relevant international and regional organizations operating within the framework of the International Plant Protection Convention'.

89 *EC – Hormones*, ABR, para. 133.

90 Ibid., para. 148.

91 *US – Continued Suspension*, ABR, para. 484.

B. *US/Canada – Continued Suspension*

US/Canada – Continued Suspension has a long history, beginning with *EC – Hormones*. It was the latest in a string of WTO cases dealing with the SPS Agreement involving scientific advice. Unlike other scientific trade disputes, it did not begin as a case requiring scientific review, but instead raised purely procedural questions as to the United States' and Canada's continued suspension of the concessions granted to the EC.

The case arose out of an EC measure adopting a Directive in 2003 which maintained the EC's permanent prohibition on meat and meat products from animals treated with hormones until 'more complete scientific information' could be collected with regard to the risks of those hormones to consumers.[92] With the approval of the Directive, which was based on a number of scientific studies, the EC claimed that it had fully complied with the ruling in *EC – Hormones*. It therefore argued that the United States' and Canada's suspension of concessions, under which they refused to lift the import and *ad valorem* duties on the EC products, were no longer justified.

In its report, the Panel considered the adequacy of the new EC legislation in meeting the EC's obligations under the SPS Agreement, and ruled that the EC had not shown that the new measures were consistent with its obligations.[93] On appeal, the Appellate Body found that the Panel had erred in several respects in reviewing the EC's risk assessment and the sufficiency of the Directive under the SPS Agreement. It therefore reversed the Panel's decision that the Directive was not based on a risk assessment under the SPS Agreement.[94] Finding, however, that it lacked sufficient information to complete the analysis itself, the Appellate Body recommended that the parties initiate new proceedings to determine whether the Directive complied with the EC's obligations under the SPS Agreement.[95]

As in *EC – Hormones*, the Panel sought information not only from the selected experts but also from three other relevant international entities: the Codex, JECFA and IARC.[96] The information provided 'focused on institutional and procedural issues as well as definitions relevant to the case'.[97] Moreover, in accordance with the WTO Experts Working

92 Ibid., Panel Report, para. 1.1. 93 Ibid., paras. 7.579, 7.835 and 7.847.
94 *US – Continued Suspension*, ABR, para. 736. 95 Ibid., para. 737.
96 Ibid., Panel Report, para. 7.78. 97 Ibid.

Procedures, the Panel solicited suggestions for names of scientific experts from the secretariats of these organizations.[98]

The main issue in this case, relevant to the present discussion, relates to the fact that two of the six selected scientific experts had previous affiliation to JECFA– a body that provides the independent scientific advice on which the work of the Codex is based. The Codex in turn had adopted the standards for five out of the six hormones at issue. As illustrated in subsection C below, the Appellate Body's findings on this point qualify not only the practice of selecting the scientific experts but also the scope of contribution from the relevant international organizations to the settlement of the WTO disputes.

1. The inclusion of JECFA's affiliated experts

As in *EC – Hormones*, the Panel decided not to establish an expert review group as had been suggested by the EC, but to consult experts on an individual basis. In the selection process, the EC objected to the inclusion of experts who had participated in JECFA's risk assessment work, which according to them was at the heart of the controversy in the case. In their view, the inclusion of these experts would have amounted to asking them to review and criticize their own work.[99] Despite this objection, the Panel decided to select these two experts, justifying its choice as follows:

> The Panel chose not to exclude *a priori* experts who had participated in the preparation and drafting of JECFA's risk assessments because this would deprive the Panel and the parties of the benefit of the contribution of internationally recognized specialists and because the Panel was of the opinion that experts familiar with the JECFA reports would be well-placed to assist the Panel in understanding the work of JECFA extensively referred to by the parties in their submissions, in particular by the European Communities.[100]

The Panel further buttressed its decision with a few other arguments, for example that it planned to ask these two experts only for information relating to JECFA's work and insight on international standards on the hormones at issue, not for scientific evaluations.[101] Besides, it noted that JECFA was the body that provided the independent scientific advice

98 Ibid., para. 7.79.

99 Ibid., ABR, para. 417. The European Communities asked the Panel to reconsider its decision with respect to two experts, Dr Jacques Boisseau and Dr Alan Boobis, arguing that 'these experts had real or perceived conflicts of interests that should disqualify them from assisting the Panel'. Ibid., para. 420.

100 Ibid., para. 419.

101 Ibid., paras. 420 and 422.

on which the work of the Codex was based, and the latter was expressly recognized by the SPS Agreement as having responsibilities for the establishment of international 'standards, guidelines and recommendations'.[102] According to the Panel, the opinions provided by the two experts would not be their own but would represent the consensual view of the JECFA on the matter at issue.[103]

Notably, the impact of the said experts on the outcome of this case was far from negligible; not only did the Panel rely on their input but they dominated the entire scientific examination. Since the EC believed that the Panel's decision to rely on these two experts infringed its due process rights and impaired the objective assessment of the matter, they brought the issue to appeal.[104]

2. The examination of the issue on appeal

In addressing this issue on appeal, the Appellate Body noted that 'the standard to be applied by Panels when selecting experts is whether there is an objective basis to conclude that an expert's independence or impartiality is likely to be affected or there are justifiable doubts about that expert's independence or impartiality'.[105] According to this view, the Appellate Body considered that the Panel should have examined closer the institutional links with JECFA of the two experts at issue and determined whether they complied with the above standard.[106]

Examining the type of input presented by the two experts, the Appellate Body noted that the Panel had not limited its consultation with the experts to the 'work of JECFA', as alleged, but had asked them to make scientific evaluations providing opinions on the adequacy of the EC's risk assessment.[107] According to the Appellate Body, this was problematic because the risk assessment examined in the case 'called into question the validity of JECFA's evaluation and explicitly stated that it would not follow them'. In this context, the Appellate Body's key concern was with the 'direct involvement [of the two experts] in the risk assessments performed by JECFA for the hormones at issue and . . . the particular role that JECFA's risk assessments, and the Codex standards adopted on the

102 Ibid., para. 421. 103 Ibid., para. 422. 104 Ibid., para. 425.
105 Ibid., para. 454. 106 Ibid., para. 457.
107 Ibid., paras. 462–463. See also para. 464, where the Appellate Body pointed to another such question: whether the EC's risk assessment examined the risk arising specifically from the consumption of meat from cattle treated with the six hormones at issue; and para. 468, where the two experts were asked the question about the sufficiency of evidence under Art. 5.7 of the SPS Agreement.

basis of those risk assessments, had in this case'.[108] This was due to the fact that the scientific experts had played a decisive role in complex WTO scientific disputes, and could have significantly influenced the outcome of a dispute. Thus the Appellate Body believed that the Panels had to ensure that the scientific experts were independent and impartial in order not to compromise the fairness of the proceedings. Against this backdrop, the Appellate Body noted that there was an objective basis for it to conclude that the affiliation of the two experts with JECFA in the evaluation of the six hormones 'was likely to give rise to justifiable doubts as to their independence and impartiality'.[109] On these grounds, it finally found that the Panel had infringed the due process right of the EC and failed to make an 'objective assessment of the matter' as required by Article 11 DSU.[110]

C. Evaluation

Drawing on the case law analysis above, and with due consideration of other relevant disputes, this subsection first evaluates the issues arising from the consultation of the WTO panels with the Codex in the settlement of scientific disputes. Second, given the complexity of these cases, it enquires whether the Codex could in some further way contribute to the objective assessment of the matter by the WTO panels in such disputes.

1. Consultation with the relevant international organizations

The first section of this chapter singled out some of the challenges faced by the WTO panels when adjudicating complex scientific matters. It is clear that there is a certain level of confusion on their part when deciding to whom to assign the fact-finding function in these cases. What aids the panels in this process is their entitlement to seek information and expert advice from any relevant source pursuant to Article 13 of the DSU, which includes international organizations. This discretion is supported more specifically by the language of Article 11(2) of the SPS Agreement, prescribing that, in matters involving technical and scientific issues, the panel may consult the relevant international organizations.

a. The identification of experts. There is a reference, but no explicit WTO rule, assigning a function to international organizations in the identification of scientific experts. However, the case law reveals that it has already become practice to consult other international organizations on this issue.

108 Ibid., para. 479. 109 Ibid., para. 481. 110 Ibid.

Thus the Codex would provide this type of service to the panels when the arguments in a dispute related to food safety. The other two sister organizations would play the same role in cases involving animal health (e.g. the OIE in *Australia – Salmon*) and plant health (e.g. the IPPC in *Japan – Apples*). A number of other international organizations have been involved in this process. For example, in *EC – Asbestos*, the Panel solicited assistance in identification of experts from both government and non-governmental organizations such as WHO, the ILO, the International Programme on Chemical Safety (IPCS), the IARC and the International Organization for Standardization (ISO).[111] In *EC – Biotech*, international institutions such as the Convention on Biological Diversity (CBD) and the FAO were also involved in the identification of scientific experts.[112]

With the exception of reference to the three SPS standard-setting organizations, one of the difficulties faced by panels in making expert selection arises from the lack of guidance regarding the institutions to be approached for this purpose (see e.g. *EC – Asbestos*). On the other hand, international organizations may be indispensable in this process, since the ad hoc WTO panels composed of laypersons (i.e. non-judges) may not possess knowledge of existing scientific experts sufficiently well versed in the subject at issue and cannot only rely on the parties to make this choice.[113] As rightly noted by Pauwelyn, the relevant international organizations should bring together the best scientists into working groups and special committees, as they are the ones possessing the best knowledge regarding the independent scientists, those working for public authorities, universities or private research institutions.[114]

Some commentators, however, have shown reluctance to accord such a function to international organizations. According to Christoforou, the reference in the SPS Agreement to 'relevant international organizations' does not mean that names of possible scientific experts should also come from these organizations, as there is the risk thereby of scientific bias favouring the maintenance of the standards and recommendations set by them.[115] This can be countered with the argument that nothing in the WTO texts suggests that the outcome of such consultation with an international organization is mandatory on the panels. If Article 11(2) of

111 *EC – Asbestos*, Panel Report, para. 5.8.

112 For a more detailed account of *EC – Biotech* see above Chapter 1, section III.B.1.

113 It was only in *EC – Hormones* that the Panel allowed parties to nominate scientific experts.

114 Pauwelyn, 'Use of Experts', at 343.

115 Christoforou, 'Settlement', at 630. Alemanno, *Trade in Food*, 352.

the SPS Agreement is invoked to cover such consultation, the use of 'may' in its second sentence suggests that such consultation is not mandatory, much less binding.[116] All the panel has to do in this process is to select the names of the experts from a list offered by the relevant international organizations. In principle, if none of the experts passes the impartiality test, the panel can request submission of additional names from these institutions until it assures itself of their impartiality and so on.

b. The provision of information and expert advice. The input of international organizations in WTO scientific disputes is not limited to the identification of experts. The Codex Secretariat has provided other information in the form of specific written answers to questions addressed by the Panel. As evidenced in *EC – Hormones*, this was uniquely combined with the provision of an expert from the Codex to advise the Panel in his individual capacity, together with other individual scientific experts advising the Panel.[117] Following *EC – Hormones* the practice of seeking information languished for a while until it re-emerged in *EC – Biotech*, where the Panel approached the Secretariats of several organizations such as the Codex, the FAO, the IPPC Secretariat, WHO, the OIE, the CBD Secretariat and the United Nations Environment Programme (UNEP). These institutions were asked 'to identify materials (reference works, glossaries, official documents of the relevant international organizations, including conventions, standards and guidelines, etc.) that might aid the Panel in determining the ordinary meaning of certain terms used in the definitions provided in Annex A to the SPS Agreement'.[118] These materials were 'taken into account . . . as appropriate'.[119] Thus, as in *US – Shrimp*, the recourse to external sources was perceived as legitimate to the extent that these external sources were informative – subject to the ultimate discretion of the treaty's interpreter.[120] As illustrated in Chapter 3 above under the analysis of the 'ordinary meaning', these materials were considered by the Panel as 'evidence' rather than as 'legal rules'.[121]

116 Tarullo, 'Relationship of WTO Obligations', at 165.

117 But in *Australia – Salmon*, although the Panel recognized the need for an expert in the OIE procedures, this organization was not asked to provide an in-house expert for this purpose.

118 *EC – Biotech*, Panel Report, para. 7.31.

119 Ibid., para. 7.96.

120 Ibid., paras. 7.92–7.93.

121 Ibid., para. 7.92. See also the discussion above in Chapter 3, section III.A. For an account of the possible reasons for attributing a limited role to these institutions in WTO dispute settlement see above Chapter 5.

According to Alemanno, the reference by the Appellate Body to these sources 'proves that Article 5.1 [of the SPS Agreement], by referring to the "risk assessment techniques developed" by the international standard-setting organizations, may prove to be a useful legal basis for the WTO judicial bodies to rely upon in order to find some guidance when reviewing complex science-based measures'.[122] This permits the WTO adjudicator to draw from the risk assessment standards elaborated by the standard-setting organizations which aim to promote commonalities of approach for different sectors. This is the right approach towards reducing the involvement of the court in the review of scientific data – a role which is not so appropriate for the laypersons of whom the WTO panel is composed.[123]

Aside from the concerns expressed in relation to the decision making of some SPS standard-setting organizations,[124] this proposition has also to be squared with the concerns expressed by negotiators of the SPS Agreement about their possible involvement in the adjudication of disputes at the WTO.[125] It should be noted that Article 11 of the SPS Agreement mandating the consultation of experts and international organizations by the panels was drafted with substantial disagreements. For example, the Cairns group of agriculture-producing WTO members wished to ensure that any consultation with experts on such cases was done in their personal capacity, as it wanted to minimize the role of international standardizing bodies in dispute settlement.[126]

While, after *US/Canada – Suspension*, having in-house experts from or affiliated to international organizations advising the panels is a challengeable option,[127] the mere provision of information by these organizations should not, in the view of this author, raise particular concerns. Therefore the practice should certainly continue. The written explanations provided by the Codex Secretariat supplement the clarifications obtained from the experts selected by the panel on each dispute and contribute to an objective assessment of the matter as set out by the DSU.

122 Alemanno, *Trade in Food*, 371.

123 Ibid. See also *US – Continued Suspension*, Panel Report, paras. 7.380–7.386 and ABR, paras. 585–616, where the issue of the applicable standard of review was widely discussed. For a recent academic contribution discussing this aspect see Gruszczynski, *Regulating Health*.

124 See above Chapter 5, section III.

125 Christoforou, 'Settlement'.

126 See Motaal, '"Multilateral Scientific Consensus"', at 864, and citations therein.

127 See below subsection 2.b for more detailed analysis of the issue.

2. The Codex and the 'objective assessment of the matter'

The Appellate Body in *EC – Poultry* recognized that failing to conduct an 'objective assessment of the matter' by the Panel was a serious allegation which went to the very core of the integrity of the WTO dispute settlement process.[128] In spite of this finding, after *EC – Hormones* the WTO members continued, although unsuccessfully, to make such claims on grounds of erroneous interpretation of the scientific evidence by the Panels. In the appeal of *Australia – Salmon*, for example, the respondent claimed that the Panel had ignored the relevant evidence placed before it, or had misrepresented evidence, and that this egregious error amounted to an error of law.[129] This related to the consideration by the Panel of scientific studies which, according to Australia, were either not relevant or too general to answer the questions. The Appellate Body explained that in past cases (such as *EC – Hormones* and *EC – Poultry*) it had followed the approach that the determination of the 'credibility' and 'weight' to be ascribed to certain facts is the province of the panel, and it is not normally for the Appellate Body to intervene in that process or to 'second guess' the panel's conclusions.[130] The Appellate Body can intervene in the panel's assessment only if the factual evaluation was so flawed as to amount to a failure to conduct an objective assessment, contrary to DSU Article 11.[131] But in order for such a claim to prevail, the panel would have to be responsible for a *serious and wilful abuse* of discretion.[132]

Some have rightly pointed out that the Appellate Body's standard of the wilful error is too high, noting that it 'basically requires that the appellant alleges bad faith on the part of the Panel. That would be such an extreme allegation that it would almost never be appropriate.'[133] The Appellate

128 The Appellate Body in *EC – Poultry* noted that 'an allegation that a panel has failed to conduct the "objective assessment of the matter before it" required by Article 11 of the DSU is a *very serious allegation*. Such an allegation goes to the very core of the integrity of the WTO dispute settlement process itself'. *EC – Poultry*, ABR, para. 133 (emphasis added). Claims on these grounds have been brought in a number of other subsequent cases, such as *Australia – Salmon, Japan – Apples*, and *EC – Asbestos*. See for example in *Japan – Apples*, ABR, para. 140: 'Japan contends that there was a lack of proper examination of evidence by the Panel, that the Panel cited the views of the experts in an arbitrary manner and that the Panel's evaluation of the evidence was contradictory'.

129 *Australia – Salmon*, ABR, Sec. B.II.

130 Ibid., ABR, paras. 264–267. See also *Japan – Apples*, ABR, para. 98.

131 *Australia – Salmon*, ABR, para. 267.

132 Ibid., ABR, para. 266.

133 See Bronckers and McNelis, 'Fact and Law', at 323; also Christoforou, 'Settlement', at 645.

Body should not, however, let a manifest error of fact stand where that error was critical to the resolution of the dispute, as this undermines the credibility and the legitimacy of WTO dispute settlement.[134] As illustrated below, *US/Canada – Continued Suspension* represents a positive departure from this trend, in the sense that the Appellate Body did examine a claim of unobjective assessment of the matter pursuant to DSU Article 11.

The proper involvement of the Codex (as well as other SPS standard-setting organizations) in the adjudication of scientific disputes can enhance the objectivity of such assessments by the panel and reduce, if not eliminate, such claims with the Appellate Body in the future. A situation in which a contribution by the Codex could have made a difference is well exemplified in *EC – Hormones*, as illustrated below.

a. ***EC – Hormones.*** Although WTO panels are mandated to use outside experts, the problem arises with the fact that the panels are not sufficiently comfortable with the scientific principles applicable in the SPS disputes. The scientific responses of the experts are not easy to interpret and making inferences on such grounds is not an easy task either.[135] This is well attested in *EC – Hormones*, where the EC claimed that the alleged manifest distortion of the views of two scientific experts by the Panel was inconsistent with the 'objective assessment of the matter' set out in DSU Article 11.[136] After having read the statements of the experts carefully, the Appellate Body found that the *EC – Hormones* Panel did not, in fact, represent their opinions accurately. Nonetheless, according to the Appellate Body, this did not 'constitute a *deliberate* disregard of evidence or *gross* negligence amounting to bad faith', which would have been the standard applied by the Appellate Body.[137] This outcome, however, does not rule out the possibility that a panel may make serious mistakes in evaluating and weighing scientific evidence, whether in good faith or as a result of an egregious error or wilful distortion.[138]

A remedy suggested in this context is to intensify the assistance of the relevant international organization, *in casu* the Codex, in the reading of

134 Bronckers and McNelis, 'Fact and Law'.

135 See above section II.A for an account.

136 The two scientific experts referred to the views of Dr Lucier (Environmental Toxicology Programme, National Institute of Environmental Health Sciences, United States) and Dr André (Laboratoire des dosages hormonaux, France). *EC – Hormones*, ABR, para. 17.

137 Ibid., para. 141 (emphasis in original).

138 As illustrated in the previous subsection, the standard established by the Appellate Body in *EC – Hormones* has been met with criticism for being too high. See Bronckers and McNelis, 'Fact and Law', at 323; Christoforou, 'Settlement', at 645.

scientific data presented to the panels by individual scientific experts. The Codex expert in *EC – Hormones* could have been entrusted with this task. Alternatively, the accuracy of the Panel's understanding of the pertinent scientific data could have been corroborated in an informal setting with the Codex Secretariat. This would have facilitated the Panel's review, which is far more detailed when it is advised by individual scientific experts (as compared with expert review groups), where different scientific views have to be reconciled by the panellists. The proposal for the WTO panels to turn to the Codex in this context does not suggest allowing this institution to engage in scientific reviews itself or take a position on the scientific views submitted by the individual experts. The role of the Codex should rather be limited to verifying whether the panel's understanding of the data submitted by independent scientific experts is accurate.

b. *US/Canada – Continued Suspension.* The above emphasis on the limits of the role of the Codex in the settlement of WTO disputes is not accidental. The Appellate Body's analysis in the *US/Canada – Continued Suspension* case reveals a cautious approach towards possible influences of the standard-setting organizations in the settlement of WTO disputes. As illustrated above, the EC claimed that by selecting two experts previously affiliated with JECFA, the Panel had infringed its due process rights and failed to make an objective assessment pursuant to DSU Article 11. Following this claim, the Appellate Body examined the issue of the degree of affiliation of the proposed experts to the relevant institutions and their direct involvement in the risk assessment of the hormones (or other elements) at issue. The Appellate Body found that both experts in question had been directly involved in JECFA's evaluations of the six hormones. One of them had been a member of JECFA when it evaluated all six hormones, while the other had participated in the evaluation of four of the six hormones. The Appellate Body contended that, given their former positions, these experts would have been expected to have played a significant role in the discussions.[139] Against this background, the Appellate Body invalidated the experts' input in the dispute and the reliance thereon of the Panel's findings.[140]

While the vigilant approach of the Appellate Body to the question of the experts' impartiality is fully shared here, the mere participation of experts in the activity of the relevant bodies, without direct involvement in the decision making concerning the adjudicated subject matter, should not

139 See *US – Continued Suspension*, ABR, para. 460.

140 Ibid., ABR, para. 484.

prevent Panels from selecting them. It would probably be bizarre to prefer experts who do not participate in the scientific committees of the Codex (or JECFA for that matter), given that such involvement would indubitably be a testimony to their expertise, credentials and reputation.[141]

3. The use of expert review groups

Another residual factor which is presumed to bear on the ability of the panels to make an objective assessment of the matter in SPS disputes relates to their practice of appointing individual experts rather than expert review groups. The use of expert review groups would not only enhance the objectivity of assessment by the panels but would enable them to benefit more easily from the input of the relevant international organizations in this process.

Despite the existence of clear WTO rules on the appointment of expert review groups by a panel, the case law reveals that panels have preferred to consult individual experts in science-based disputes. The panels have argued on this score that WTO law does not prevent them from using individual experts and that, moreover, they prefer to listen to the opinion of each expert individually rather than having a report reflecting the lowest common denominator. Furthermore, panellists have feared that a group of experts could never reach agreement and find consensus, which might block the adjuducation process.[142] The Appellate Body has approved this approach by the panels with reference to the word 'may' and the general clauses concerning the 'right to seek information from any source' enshrined in Article 13(1) DSU and Article 11(2) of the SPS Agreement.[143]

Given the difficulty of the task of selecting experts, this approach is not necessarily conducive to an 'objective assessment of the matter' by the panel.[144] The DSU offers a better provision for this purpose, which is the

141 See also ibid., para. 459 where the Appellate Body notes that 'Membership of JECFA, in our view, reflects international recognition of the expertise of a particular scientist.'

142 Comment by Thomas Cottier, who served as Chairman in *EC – Hormones*. WTI, Berne, December 2009.

143 DSU Art. 13.2 states that for factual issues concerning scientific or other technical matters the panel 'may' request an advisory report in writing from an expert review group. A similar provision is found in SPS Art. 11.2.

144 For a confirmation see *US – Continued Suspension*, ABR, para. 480: 'We understand that panels often face practical difficulties in selecting experts who have the required level of expertise and whose selection is not objected to by the parties. [footnote omitted] We do not wish to make the expert selection process more difficult than it may already be.' See also section I above.

use of expert review groups. This is prescribed in DSU Article 13(2) and Appendix 4. The use of expert review groups is also supported in some academic works. Alemanno, for example, describes their advantages:

> [T]he appointment of an expert review group, though apparently more time-consuming, may potentially simplify the scientific task that judges are increasingly called upon to accomplish. Being entrusted with the duty of coming up with a written report, the expert group would be forced to either find common ground on the different specific scientific issues at stake or, at least, to genuinely represent the whole spectrum of scientific opinions (i.e. majority and minority) existing in the current scientific state-of-the-art research on that controversial issue. In fact, adherents to different schools of thought should be represented among the experts. By borrowing the Appellate Body's language [*EC – Hormones*, para. 194], the expert review group may set out, according to this model, 'both the prevailing view representing the mainstream opinion, as well as the opinions of scientists taking a divergent view'.[145]

Moreover, according to DSU Article 13(2), expert review groups may consult and seek information and technical advice from any source they deem appropriate (Appendix 4, para. 4). These sources of information could be any source, such as governments, international organizations, other experts or NGOs.[146] It is not clear whether the individual scientific experts preferred by the panels have the discretion to seek information from all these sources and if so, how exactly this should be carried out. Thus it is not at all obvious that the wide discretion of the groups to seek information from other sources is easily transferable to individual experts. In all likelihood, an individual expert would not have the same authority before the targeted bodies (national or international). The governments, for example, might easily refuse to co-operate on a specific matter with an individual expert, whereas they might be more hesitant to do so in relation to an expert review group entrusted with such authority by virtue of explicit rules enshrined in the WTO Dispute Settlement Understanding. This also holds true with regard to experts' interactions with other international organizations. The complexity of individual experts seeking advice from other international organizations is testified to by the fact that the panels have always done so on their own initiative.

The appropriateness of expert review groups would also be indicated in a situation where, in the course of a dispute, the panel realizes that it

145 Alemanno, 'Risk Assessment', at 32.
146 See above Chapter 2, section V.B for an overview.

had not identified all the areas where expertise was required *ab initio*. As a consequence, in such situations it might receive incomplete information from the relevant source. An issue of this kind, however, is unlikely to arise if expert review groups are the preferred choice. It is more likely that they would know upfront what information or expertise was required in the case and they would have the right, by virtue of the DSU rules, to consult other experts (including the relevant international organizations) on that matter.[147]

Lastly, support for the competence of the expert review groups is found in US domestic practice on expert appointment and consultation by the judge. A brief examination of this practice reveals that this process is not an easy task and therefore comprehensive mechanisms are put in place to address the challenge. Since the *Daubert* case in the United States it has been widely accepted that US judges do not have sufficient knowledge to identify the necessary expertise in specific cases involving health issues.[148] This clearly emerges from the US *Silicone Gel Breast Implant* case, where a selection panel was created by the court in order to identify and recommend scientists to the expert panel, composed of four experts from the areas of rheumatology, immunology, epidemiology and toxicology.[149] The expert panel was directed to establish the degree to which 'existing studies, research, and reported observations provided a reliable and reasonable scientific basis for one to conclude that silicone gel breast implants caused or exacerbated' the auto-immune diseases, symptoms and conditions allegedly associated with breast implants.[150]

In discharging its duties, the expert panel heard testimony from experts selected by counsel representing both sides and selected other experts with a view to presenting research findings and other relevant information. Expert panel members could conduct their own literature searches and 'were neither limited nor obliged to use the documents submitted by counsel on either side'.[151] A commentator notes that *Silicone Gel Breast Implant* 'demonstrated the appropriate use of a scientific advisory

147 DSU, Appendix 4.

148 See *Daubert* v. *Merrell Dow Pharmaceuticals*, 509 US 579 (1993).

149 For an account of the case see Peter Gross, 'Clearing Away the Junk: Court-Appointed Experts, Scientifically Marginal Evidence, and the Silicone Gel Breast Implant Litigation', (2001) 56 *Food Drug Law Journal* 227, at 234.

150 Ibid., at 238.

151 Ibid., at 239, citing Barbara S. Hulka et al., 'Experience of a Scientific Panel Formed to Advise the Federal Judiciary on Silicone Breast Implants', (2000) 342 *New England Journal of Medicine* 812, at 813.

panel'.[152] The current practice of WTO panels in the selection and use of scientific experts is a long way from the US expert selection model. However, this example supports the claim that resorting to expert review groups would offer the WTO panels more chance of selecting the 'right' scientific experts and therefore contribute to the making of an objective assessment of the matter.

V. Conclusions

This chapter has discussed the interplay between the WTO and international organizations responsible for global health governance in WTO dispute settlement.[153] Global health regulation is a multi-actor-driven area, and drawing clear lines between their competences and agendas is not a simple exercise. The linkages of the WTO with WHO have been examined in the context of adjudication of a tobacco-related dispute. This helped to elicit a number of issues and look at the prospects for the future of this relationship. The daily exchanges between the two institutions, however, go beyond the issue of tobacco trading. WHO, for example, plays an active role in the current WTO debates and programmes regarding public-health-related intellectual property matters.[154] Moreover, international trade in health-related services also offers scope for co-operation between the two institutions, and they have undertaken various activities to this end. It would not be surprising therefore if WHO was called on by a WTO panel to provide some input in disputes arising out of these matters. The analysis of the linkage between the two institutions in *Thailand – Cigarettes* therefore provides a good analytical framework for these other topics.

The WTO having stepped onto the scene of health governance and with its consolidated dispute settlement mechanism, the remaining actors have had to reinvent their modes of operation in order properly to respond to the legitimacy quests arising out of the incorporation of their standards

152 See Joseph M. Price and Ellen S. Rosenberg, 'The Silicone Gel Breast Implant Controversy: The Rise of Expert Panels and the Fall of Junk Science', (2000) 93 *Journal of the Royal Society of Medicine* 31, at 1432.

153 The findings in this chapter are certainly valid for the other two sister organizations (OIE and IPPC), although the decision making within these three organizations may pose different legitimacy concerns. For a comprehensive account of this issue see above Chapter 5, section III.

154 See WTO, www.wto.org/english/thewto_e/coher_e/wto_who_e.htm (last visited March 2010).

into the WTO system. This is particularly the case with the standard-setting organizations setting out relevant standards under the SPS and TBT Agreements. As discussed in Chapter 5 above, although significant progress was made by these organizations in revising their modes of operations, there are still some problems in their decision-making process which need to be taken into account if the claim of their greater role in the WTO is to persist.

The role of the SPS standard-setting organizations has been widely debated.[155] Although the WTO adjudicator showed institutional openness towards these actors by allowing their engagement in the process, the judicial practice reveals that there is some uncertainty as to whether they should be consulted only on the selection of experts or on the provision of factual information, or on a wider set of issues.[156] Confining their contribution to consultation, which, as evidenced in *US – Shrimp* and *EC – Biotech*, would amount to the provision of factual information, poses the risk of discarding, ignoring or interpreting away their input.

Regarding the expert role of international organizations, the most recent tendencies are quite clear, in that some major actors want also to avoid ascribing such a role to other international organizations in the dispute settlement process.[157] On the other hand, the standard-setting organizations would definitely be more necessary for the WTO adjudicator in this capacity, as compared with other international organizations. Even if the panels composed of laypersons did not encounter too much difficulty in interpreting an IMF, WIPO or WCO legal instrument, the interpretation of scientific data is a far more complex exercise.

155 See Howse, 'New Device'; Echols, *Food Safety and the WTO* and 'Institutional Cooperation'; Scott, 'Cooperative Regulation'; and Victor, 'Sanitary and Phytosanitary Agreement'. See also Michael A. Livermore, 'Authority and Legitimacy in Global Governance: Deliberation, Institutional Differentiation, and Codex Alimentarius', (2006) 81 *New York University Law Review* 766.

156 See Young, 'Fragmentation or Interaction', at 41.

157 See above Chapter 1, section IV, for a comprehensive account.

CONCLUDING SUMMARY

The objective of this study was to understand how the role of other international organizations could be streamlined and, possibly, enhanced in the WTO dispute settlement process – an outcome which would presumably legitimize the WTO adjudication. The analyses focus on those international organizations that emerged in a selected number of WTO disputes by way of provision of information and expert advice. These include the IMF, WIPO, the WCO, WHO and the SPS standard-setting organizations. The investigation is essential both to understanding the strengths and weaknesses of the role of international organizations in the WTO disputes and to envisioning the future framework of their interface with the WTO. Moreover, the lessons drawn from this exercise may be validly employed in mapping out interfaces with other international organizations in WTO dispute settlement which have not been investigated in this study.

I. The general constraints on institutional sensitivity

Although the WTO judiciary's institutional sensitivity is perceived as a positive phenomenon, Part II of this study has made it clear that the scope of such sensitivity is not unlimited. In exercising greater institutional sensitivity vis-à-vis other international organizations, the WTO judicial institutions are constrained by a number of factors. Apart from a restrictive judicial approach in the use of non-WTO rules, combined with their common attribution to supplementary means, the WTO panels have treated the specific input of international organizations as factual, rarely deferring to their legal or expert opinions. On the other hand, the WTO adjudicating bodies cannot lightly relinquish the interpretative elements residing outside the trade regime when these may be brought to bear on an objective assessment of the matter. Once such external elements are entrenched, for example, in the knowledge or experience of the secretariats of the international organizations, there should be a way to legitimately consider this input in the WTO disputes.

The vigilant approach by the WTO panels or Appellate Body to this material is not, however, just a sign of self-sufficiency of the trade regime, as has been claimed in a number of academic works. In this study, the phenomenon has been attributed to a number of existing constraints rooted in both the WTO and the relevant international organizations. On the part of the WTO, these constraints arise from, but are not limited to, imperfections in the relevant WTO legal framework, inconsistent judicial interpretation of the WTO obligations and, fundamentally, WTO political choices. The last is a determinant factor in this proposition, as it will generally shape the WTO adjudicator's approach towards the weight it can attribute to societal values other than trade.

The external constraints certainly go beyond the political or judicial choices at the WTO, as they are inherent in the functioning of other international organizations. The lack of authoritative interpretation mechanisms in the international organizations, for example, has been found to be one of the major external constraints. On these precise grounds the *EC – Chicken Cuts* Panel discarded the Explanatory Notes to the HS Convention from its consideration. It explicitly stated that these documents were non-authoritative. The lack of recourse to the ICJ by parties to the treaties administered by specific international organizations or other well-functioning internal dispute settlement mechanisms also leaves many international organizations without authoritative judicial practice which can be validly relied on by other courts. Efforts to address these issues should be stressed as a precondition to developing further the international organizations' relationship to WTO law.

In the event of the continued absence of such mechanisms, which would attribute some authority to the judicial decisions taken within these international organizations, the other possible input coming therefrom should not, however, be discarded from the list of interpretative materials when relevant to the case. The analysis of the activity of specific international organizations revealed that many of them are engaged in a prolific norm-creating process. While a relevant, authoritatively adopted international organization decision would most likely be considered as 'subsequent agreement' to the WTO interpreted agreement (VCLT Article 31(3)(a)), the plethora of other non-authoritative acts could still be validly taken into account under, for example, Article 31(1) VCLT, for the purpose of clarifying the 'ordinary meaning' of the interpreted term (as in *US – Shrimp*), or the secondary rules of treaty interpretation as set out in VCLT Article 32. Although, given their contribution solely to factual clarifications, little or no normativity will be ascribed to these international organizations' acts, the use of other VCLT interpretative techniques to consider them achieves an integrative effect of the WTO law with rules emerging in other international regimes, and contributes to more coherence and integration of these different systems.

Moreover, factors like transparency in the decision making and consideration of the interests of developing countries in the relevant international organizations may also leave an imprint on the WTO panels' or Appellate Body's willingness to defer to such material. Finally, the reciprocity with which other international organizations respond to this process is another element which has to be taken into account when proposing greater institutional sensitivity.

Other external constraints which have been identified in this study are somewhat more subjective, for they affect perceptions about the competence and credibility of international organizations. Presumably, the international organizations which are specifically mentioned in the WTO Agreements or other WTO legal texts have a special claim in this respect. The claim is further buttressed if the international organizations at stake are universal, as compared with closed or regional organizations. Although these factors provide some guidance as to how far the sensitivity of the WTO adjudicator can go vis-à-vis international organizations, it should be noted that their competence and credibility should not be assessed by the WTO judiciary. Instead, the WTO panels should rely on evaluations made by the relevant WTO subsidiary bodies and draw accordingly on their conclusions on the subject matter.

II. The Vienna Convention on the Law of Treaties as a framework for analysis

In order to explore fully the impact of other international organizations on WTO dispute settlement, an important part of this study has been dedicated to showing how the various acts emerging from international organizations are taken into account by the panels or the Appellate Body. As the ILC Study Group did in exploring the relationship of specialized regimes to general international law, this study employs the VCLT rules of interpretation, as relied on by the WTO judicial institutions, to create a framework for analysis of institutional interactions and consideration of international organizations' material and expertise in the adjudication process. It is believed that a proper use of these rules in the judicial interpretation allows international tribunals to show institutional sensitivity vis-à-vis other regimes. In fact, the VCLT interpretation rules are widely regarded as a coherence device in international law. This framework provides, therefore, not only a proper methodological approach for the purposes of elucidating how the WTO adjudicator has made use of this material, but also allows inferences to be drawn on how the exercise contributes to the wider debate on fragmentation of international law and institutions.

Following this analytical framework, this study makes a number of important findings with respect to the status of the material of international organizations in WTO dispute settlement (Part I). The legal value of this material in its different forms is qualified by its identification under either the primary or secondary VCLT rules of interpretation. Thus an act of an international organization will be regarded as having a higher normative value, hence a weightier effect on the judicial decision, when it is attributed to the primary rules of interpretation enshrined in VCLT Article 31. Conversely, the identification of this material under the supplementary means of VCLT Article 32 will downplay its legal value and hinder its repeated use.

The role of this classification should not, however, be overstated. In the end, the use of the VCLT primary rules of interpretation – irrespective of the technique used – in order to give weight to the material issued by other international organizations is a manifest sign of the WTO's judicial sensitivity towards the regulatory functions of these institutions. This is the more so considering that the integrative effect of VCLT Article 31(3)(c) would cover only general international law – a category which does not formally include the acts of international organizations unless they have acquired the status of customary law or have evolved into a general principle of international law. Given the infrequency of the latter situation, the arsenal of VCLT techniques which could potentially be used for an interpretation by the WTO harmonizing with the acts or material of other international organizations is rather limited. If this integrative effect can be achieved by clarifying the 'ordinary meaning' under VCLT Article 31(1), as exemplified in *US – Shrimp* and *EC – Biotech*, or through the use of 'subsequent practice' as in *Mexico – Telecoms*, it will be determined on a case-by-case basis by the WTO judiciary, and this is believed to be the right approach.

While there is little likelihood that the panels or the Appellate Body will consider material from international organizations as 'context' under Article 31(2) VCLT (as this has been applied only with respect to multilateral treaties), the 'subsequent agreement' rule is a better candidate in this sense. The WTO *Mexico – Telecoms* case actually sets out important judicial practice applicable in examining whether the material of international organizations can be qualified as such. The specific guidance which can be extracted from this case and should be employed in further WTO jurisprudence is that:

- First, the consideration of international organizations' material as subsequent agreement can be carried out with respect to a binding instrument if both litigants adhered to the proposed instrument.
- Second, non-binding acts (such as recommendations) will be taken into account if disputants as well as a large number of the WTO members are also members of the relevant international organization.

Despite the attractiveness of this VCLT technique for interfacing different sytems, the use of 'subsequent agreement' in this context is affected by unresolved issues, such as how subsequent agreements link to the original treaty. Here, the implementation of the ILC mandate to clarify the issue is much awaited.

The 'subsequent practice' under VCLT Article 31(3)(b) offers yet another option, although in this case, too, the challenges are not inconsiderable. The status of institutional practice at the WTO is far from clear, and there is no clear guidance in the WTO case law on the issue. Aside from the fact that the WTO has not made consistent use of its own institutional practice, the most acute of all issues posed by this interpretative technique is its perceived legitimacy flaws (e.g. to what extent it should incorporate *express state consent*, and whether it should be expressed by all WTO members). Some guidance has been elicited on this from non-WTO jurisprudence, namely the *Texaco* case,[1] which is proposed to deal with the application of extra-regime institutional practice by an international tribunal. Specifically, provided all other requirements of the institutional practice are met (e.g. temporality), the standard suggests that

- First, only the material of international organizations (or provisions thereof) which state the existence of a right on which the generality of the states have expressed agreement should be considered, in contrast to those producing new principles which were rejected by certain groups and having nothing more than a *de lege ferenda* value with the states which adopted them. Thus the WTO judiciary should attribute legal

1 For full citation see Chapter 3, n. 105.

value to material from international organizations under this heading only if it were adopted by a majority vote.

- Second, the majority votes should have been distributed evenly among voting developing and developed countries.

This study found that the value of the materials from international organizations in WTO dispute settlement is diminished with their identification as a supplementary means of interpretation under VCLT Article 32. Moreover, this value is further reduced within supplementary means of interpretation if the relevant material is used for confirmatory purposes only. While the WTO judiciary should try to better explore and make wider use of the other rules of interpretation enshrined in VCLT Article 31, in order not to reduce to redundancy the language of VCLT Article 32, it should employ the material in this category for elucidating rather than confirming the meaning of the interpreted term. This will contribute to the elevation of the value of the material of international organizations within the category of supplementary means of interpretation – although always as a less appealing alternative to the use of primary rules of interpretation.

III. The study of specific international organizations and policy recommendations

The VCLT analytical framework leads to the conclusion that other organizations enjoy somewhat non-uniform treatment by the WTO. An outcome of this exercise is the discovery of a scattered and fragmented landscape of international legal order with different international organizations playing differently defined roles, even within the narrow field of WTO dispute settlement. While the general constraints and solutions on the institutional sensitivity have been addressed in the general parts of this study, a detailed examination of the relevant WTO case law has revealed the nature of such inconsistencies. Following the selected case law analysis, the unique role of the IMF in WTO disputes was noted. WTO panels have ascribed substantial weight to the assessments of this organization both on exchange rate determinations and on the balance of payments assessments of member countries. There is nothing to indicate that the IMF should not maintain its solid authority on this subject matter. In spite of this, the case law also reveals a number of issues which may hamper the strength of the WTO–IMF relationship and, with that, the level of institutional sensitivity of the WTO adjudicator vis-à-vis this institution.

The more inconsistent the case law with respect to the role attributed to the IMF and the material therefrom, the greater will be the hesitation of the WTO adjudicator to ascribe it a due role. The failure to address this inconsistency will only downplay the legitimating force entailed in the option of the WTO panels to show greater sensitivity towards other relevant international institutions. Thus the issues identified in the case law would have to be properly considered along the following lines:

- First, special regard should be given to exploring fully the consultation prerogative of the panels with this institution. The WTO panels should not read restrictively Article XV(2) GATT, which prescribes mandatory consultation, as limiting their discretion to consult the IMF under DSU Article 13 on issues going beyond those enunciated in the former GATT provision.
- Second, in consultation of the IMF on the three matters set out in GATT Article XV, resort to the mandatory language of the latter should be preferred over the discretionary language of DSU Article 13.
- Third, on assessments of balance of payments situations, even if other actors are consulted pursuant to DSU Article 13, the WTO adjudicator should retain the IMF's statement as an authoritative one which could not be qualified by statements of these other actors, be they government or non-governmental organizations. Judicial consistency along this line of interpretation would only assign a proper role to this institution in the settlement of WTO disputes.
- Fourth, given the special status of the IMF in the WTO pursuant to GATT Article XV, and for purposes of judicial economy, the WTO judiciary could defer to the interpretative outcomes of the IMF's law when relevant, without going into such exercises itself.

While WIPO's role is weaker in comparison with that of the IMF, the WTO panels have quite frequently turned to it, mostly for factual information. The case law analyses reveal that in only one (atypical) case did the WTO ask WIPO to make a determination amounting to an interpretative opinion. Although such a contribution from WIPO would not be binding on the WTO adjudicator, simply because such decisions are not backed by an authoritative interpretation system within WIPO, giving weight to such opinions would add credibility to the panel's or Appellate Body's deliberations when interpreting the TRIPS Agreement. The WTO panels have instead frequently used and relied on factual information alone from WIPO. In this process they considered instruments such as guides and reports, briefing documents, publications and model provisions, which have been commonly attributed to VCLT supplementary rules of interpretation. Through reliance on these instruments, the role of WTO-incorporated as well as non-incorporated intellectual property treaties have been clarified.

Unlike with respect to the IMF, the WTO Agreement does not contain a separate provision on consultation with WIPO. The case law analyses, however, allowed some guidance to be elicited with respect to what the role of WIPO's material should be in WTO dispute settlement. Particularly, such a role emerges out of two categories of norms: incorporated and non-incorporated. These norms should be considered in WTO dispute settlement as follows:

- With respect to TRIPS-incorporated treaties, WIPO remains a source of state practice, which should be duly taken into account by the WTO adjudicator, preferably under the VCLT primary rules of interpretation.
- As regards the non-incorporated norms, following the example of *US – Section 110(5) Copyright Act* on the WIPO Copyright Treaty, the WTO adjudicator should properly consider the new intellectual property treaties emerging outside the WTO. This should be done even if the parties to these treaties do not perfectly correspond with WTO members – that is, despite the fact that not *all* WTO members have accepted the new treaties, provided, however, that a large majority of them have accepted them. The soft-law developments should be explored to the extent that they meet the standards specified above in relation to 'subsequent agreement' and 'subsequent practice'. Otherwise, those can also be used for the purposes of clarification of the 'ordinary meaning' or residually as 'supplementary means of interpretation'.

Despite the shift of a significant part of the intellectual property regime to the WTO, WIPO continues to be of significance for the WTO. Its role becomes more prominent today with respect to rule-making, given the negotiation stalemate at the WTO. This elevates its status, and we may witness clearer divisions between the functions of these organizations in the near future. WIPO will work as a norm-elaboration agency, while the WTO will deal with their enforcement. Certainly, there are limits to this, arising from the obligation of WTO members to consent to those new obligations. However, as suggested above, the WTO judiciary could partially compensate for the weakness of its political branch through a somewhat more expansive interpretation of the WTO law in the light of developments emerging within regimes with direct relevance to the system. The legitimacy of the judicial branch of the WTO will only be strengthened by engaging in these compensatory tactics. In the current situation this branch is the main pillar, making the multilateralism of trade relations relevant.

An important role of the WCO in WTO dispute settlement emerges through its position as a guardian of the HS Convention. The Panels have treated this instrument as akin to 'context' under the rules of the VCLT – a situation which is novel in the WTO. The attribution of such elevated status to this instrument suggests that the WCO's institutional practice emerging in relation to the HS has to bear significantly on WTO judicial interpretation. In fact, the relevant case law reveals that a number of HS-related instruments came under the purview of panels. The role of the WCO as an expert has also proved very valuable in clarifying complex language pertaining to HS classification.

The WTO's relationship with the WCO is in many ways similar to that with WIPO, although the HS, unlike the relevant intellectual property rights treaties, has not been incorporated into the WTO. Despite this fact, by attributing the HS to 'context' under the Vienna Convention rules of interpretation, the WTO adjudicator extended to it a treatment akin to those of incorporated treaties. Thus the reliance of the GATT contracting parties on the HS Convention for scheduling their commitments during the Uruguay Round makes a very strong case in favour of high consideration of the WCO's practice in classification matters. As revealed by the case law analysis, the role of such practice may turn out to be very valuable for the WTO panels when examining classification disputes. Moreover, the WCO treaties, including the HS Convention, incorporate compulsory dispute settlement mechanisms which make the referencing by the WTO adjudicator to such outcomes easier. As illustrated above in Chapter 4, the decisions to refer to regimes with a well-functioning dispute settlement system in contrast to those which do not provide for one will be regarded as more legitimate. Finally, while direct resort to the WCO dispute settlement system by the WTO members is viewed as a recipe for fragmentation of international law and institutions, *au contraire*, the attribution of weight to these decisions by the WTO adjudicator is indispensable. In fact, the technicality of the classification disputes would not have been well handled without detailed technical input from the WCO, which has guided the panels through the interpretation process.

The relationship is, however, not without flaws, so that a few issues would still require explicit clarification by the WTO judiciary in future disputes:

- First, the WCO General Rules of Interpretation of the HS should be explored more carefully by the WTO judiciary in resolving trade disputes over the classification of goods. This seems to have been addressed much better in *China – Auto Parts*, which offers the latest guidance on the issue. In this process, the advice of the WCO is very important in providing clarification on the objectives and negotiation history of these rules, as well as on how they have been interpreted in relevant HS-related disputes.
- Second, the attribution of the HS Committee decisions to the VCLT 'subsequent practice' was a very positive development in *EC – Chicken Cuts*. The WTO adjudicator should take a step further and develop the legal theory justifying the use of 'subsequent practice' emerging from other international regimes in WTO dispute settlement. The clarification of what constitutes WTO 'subsequent practice' will be a good start in this direction. The practice of other international tribunals on this issue may be further explored.
- Third, given the technicality of the classification disputes and the need for the panel to rely on an external treaty for interpretative purposes, it is worth exploring whether it would be more feasible to incorporate HS and its *acquis* into WTO law, in the same way as some intellectual property treaties have been incorporated into TRIPS. This will bring more expertise into the WTO on the issue and the panels will be able to deal more easily with these issues with the assistance of the WTO Secretariat. This would help to avoid claims on possible delegation of power to the WCO and lack of objectivity of assessments by WTO adjudicators, given that they have to rely on and interpret a treaty which is administered by another organization. As in the case of WIPO, the WCO will preserve its relevance through elaboration of state practice with respect to the judicial interpretation process in the WTO. Otherwise, the WCO will remain relevant for an important number of technical issues which fall beyond the WTO's ambit.
- Finally, the WTO adjudicator should not disregard the other areas where the WCO could effectively contribute to WTO dispute settlement. These relate in particular to issues concerning rules of origin and customs evaluations enunciated in a number of WTO provisions.

Slightly different patterns of interaction with international organizations arise in the WTO adjudication of health-related cases. This is due to the complexity of these cases, which involve science and hence sophisticated expertise. In a dispute over tobacco trading, the Panel relied extensively on WHO legal instruments. The same cannot be claimed, however, with regard to WHO's role as an expert in the dispute. WHO's scientific expertise concerning the effects of smoking on human health was duly taken into account, but the economic expertise of this organization regarding the effects of liberalization of cigarette markets on consumption was disregarded. This would have to be corrected by future WTO panels or the Appellate Body when dealing with similar issues. The economic expertise of the WHO on these issues should not, however, imperil the consideration of the expertise of other legitimate actors with credible experience in the field, such as the World Bank. Interesting insights into the role of WHO in WTO dispute settlement are expected with the filing of a WTO dispute arising from the Australian plain tobacco packaging issue. The case may not be objectively adjudicated without the use of WHO's expertise and guidance on whether measures like plain tobacco packaging are in line with the WHO legal instruments on tobacco control.

An increased role for the WHO in tobacco-related trade disputes is expected to emerge out of the consolidation of its tobacco control policies under the FCTC – a binding instrument in the form of a Convention. WHO's related subsequent practice will also prove very useful in the adjudication of such disputes and in other areas such as the widely debated topic of access to medicines, where WIPO is also involved. The consolidation of its architecture through a proper authoritative interpretation mechanism provided in relation to these instruments will permit the WTO judiciary to make greater use of such developments and assign them a normative value by reference to the VCLT rules of interpretation.

The role of the Codex Alimentarius Commission (a WHO/FAO body) in WTO dispute settlement is more nuanced, as it is determined by the authority of this organization to adopt standards valid for compliance with obligations established under the SPS Agreement. In this context, the Codex (but also the OIE and the IPPC) traditionally assists the WTO panels in identifying scientific experts, and provides other information as requested. Apart from this, this study identifies other ways in which the Codex can contribute to WTO dispute settlement in a manner which can only add legitimacy to the WTO adjudication system. In this exercise the WTO adjudicator has to manifest proper sensitivity by first acknowledging where and how this organization can contribute to the objective assessment of relevant matter.

First, while caution should be exercised in avoiding receiving advice from in-house or formerly institutionally affiliated scientific experts, the WTO adjudicator can certainly continue with the practice of seeking information from the Codex (and other relevant international organizations) in the scientific expert identification process. While the preoccupation with the affiliation of the scientific experts arises mostly out of impartiality concerns, the hesitation to seek technical advice from the Codex Secretariat is rooted largely in its perceived architectural weaknesses, as illustrated above in Chapters 4 and 5. The readiness to take into account such input in WTO dispute settlement, along with acceptance of the interpretations provided by the Codex, will largely depend on the extent to which these decision-making deficiencies are addressed by this organization.

Second, the proper involvement of the Codex (as well as other SPS standard-setting organizations) in the adjudication of scientific disputes can enhance the objectivity of such assessments by the panels and reduce the frequent number of appeal claims to the contrary. The WTO adjudicator could entrust the Codex experts, for example, with the task of assisting the panels in properly reading the scientific data provided by individual scientific experts appointed on the case.

Third, another practice which is presumed to bear on the ability of the panels to make an objective assessment of the matter in SPS disputes relates to the proposed appointment of expert review groups, which would supplant the procedure of nomination of individual experts. In this way the panels would benefit more easily from the contribution of other international organizations, as the expert review groups would have more authority before such organizations and would exercise their mandate of seeking information more widely.

IV. The contribution to the coherence debate

Finally, it should be stressed that in exploring the question of how and to what extent the WTO should consider the input of other international organizations in the dispute settlement process, this study also has wider implications. It touches on the issue of the fragmentation of international law, where the process of fragmentation of the international organizations takes its share of the blame. Constitutionalist approaches to this issue, which envision integration of international organizations or a hierarchical order among them have not offered effective solutions. Thus a less ambitious but more realistic strategy for avoiding the difficulties of a fragmented institutional order is to establish complementarity arrangements, which means that the institutions need to co-ordinate with and defer to each other.

Although the fragmentary character of the international institutions is not to be easily overcome, by using the example of the WTO dispute settlement system this study has attempted to provide some guidance as to how this institution can position itself vis-à-vis other international organizations in the judicial context. The policy recommendations provided in the above sections with regard to how the WTO adjudicator can – by exploring properly the VCLT interpretative techniques –bring about greater unity in the scattered and fragmented system of international law and institutions provide a contribution to this debate. The implementation of these recommendations will also give effect to the explicit message of the WTO Appellate Body that the WTO should not be read in clinical isolation from other international law.

The choice of dispute settlement as the focus here was not accidental. As the analyses in this study illustrate, this is where institutional interactions take concrete shape and have tangible effects. This is where taking into account the expert opinion of an international organization or deferring to their relevant acts will actually have a bearing on the outcome of the dispute, with all the resulting obligations on the part of the WTO members involved. Of course, the judicial interplay of the WTO with these international organizations is only the 'tip of the tip of the iceberg'. The picture would remain incomplete without a proper examination of the day-to-day activities of the relevant subsidiary WTO bodies where the international organizations participate. This is also valid for the examination of the activity of the political bodies of other international organizations and their possible interactions with the WTO. Elucidation of these elements definitely warrants supplementary investigation, as it will elaborate on the existing interaction patterns and predict their evolution. What can be validly affirmed at this stage, however, is that greater institutional sensitivity of the WTO adjudicator towards these institutions will only serve to add legitimacy to its decision making and benefit the trading system as a whole.

BIBLIOGRAPHY

Abbott, Frederick, 'Distributed Governance at the WTO-WIPO: An Evolving Model for Open-Architecture Integrated Governance', (2000) 3(1) *Journal of International Economic Law* 63

'The Future of the Multilateral Trading System in the Context of TRIPS', (1997) 20 *Hastings International and Comparative Law Review* 661

Abbott, Frederick and Cottier, Thomas, 'Dispute Prevention and Dispute Settlement in the Field of Intellectual Property Rights and Electronic Commerce: US – Section 211 Omnibus Appropriations Act 1998 ("Havana Club") ', in Ernst-Ulrich Petersmann and Mark A. Pollack (eds.), *Transatlantic Economic Disputes – The EU, the US, and the WTO* (Oxford University Press, 2003)

Abbott, Frederick, Cottier, Thomas and Gurry, Francis, *International Intellectual Property System, Commentary and Materials* (The Hague, London and Boston: Kluwer Law International, 1999)

Abbott, Kenneth W., 'US–EU Disputes over Technical Barriers to Trade and the "Hushkits" Dispute', in Ernst-Ulrich Petersmann and Mark A. Pollack (eds.), *Transatlantic Economic Disputes: The EU, the US, and the WTO* (Oxford University Press, 2004)

Abbott, Kenneth W. and Snidal, Duncan, 'Why States Act Through Formal International Organizations', (1998) 42 *Journal of Conflict Resolution* 3

Abi-Saab, Georges, 'Fragmentation or Unification: Some Concluding Remarks', (1999) 31 *New York University Journal of International Law and Policy* 919

Ahn, Dukgeun, 'Linkages between International Financial and Trade Institutions: IMF, World Bank and WTO', (2000) 34(4) *Journal of World Trade* 1

Alemanno, Alberto, 'Judicial Enforcement of the WTO Hormones Ruling within the European Community: Toward an EC Liability for the Non-implementation of WTO Dispute Settlement Decisions', (2004) 45 *Harvard International Law Journal* 547

'Risk Assessment under WTO Law: Workable Requirement or Probatio Diabolica?', Working Paper prepared for the 3rd ESIL Research Forum Science and International Law, Helsinki, 2–3 October 2009

Trade in Food: Regulatory and Judicial Approaches to Food Risks in the EC and the WTO (London: Cameron May, 2007)

Alexandrowicz, Charles, *The Law-Making Functions of the Specialised Agencies of the United Nations* (Sydney: Angus & Robertson, in association with the Australian Institute of International Affairs, 1973)

Alvarez, José E., 'Constitutional Interpretation in International Organizations', in Jean-Marc Coicaud and Veijo Heiskanen (eds.), *The Legitimacy of International Organizations* (United Nations University Press, 2001)

International Organizations as Lawmakers (Oxford University Press, 2005)

Alvarez, José E. and Leebron, David W., 'Symposium: The Boundaries of the WTO: Linkages', (2002) 96 *American Journal of International Law* 5

Amerasinghe, Chittharanjan F., 'The Advisory Opinion of the International Court of Justice in the WHO Nuclear Weapons Case: A Critique', (1997) 10 *Leiden Journal of International Law*, 525

Jurisdiction of Specific International Tribunals (Leiden: Brill, 2008)

Principles of Institutional Law of International Organisations, 2nd edn (Cambridge University Press, 2005)

Archer, Clive, *International Organization*, 3rd edn (London: Routledge, 2001)

Arcuri, Alessandra and Dari-Mattiacci, Giuseppe, 'Centralization versus Decentralization as a Risk-Return Trade-off', Amsterdam Center for Law & Economics Working Paper No. 2007–06

Atik, Jeffrey and Wirth, David A., 'Science and International Trade – Third Generation Scholarship', (2003) 26 *Boston College International & Comparative Law Review* 171

Aust, Anthony, *Modern Treaty Law and Practice* (Cambridge University Press, 2000)

Ayling, Julie, 'Serving Many Voices: Progressing Calls for an International Environmental Organization', (1997) 9 *Journal of Environmental Law* 243

Baker, Michael G. and Fidler, David P., 'Global Public Health Surveillance under New International Health Regulations', (2005) 12 *Emerging Infectious Diseases* 1058

Barfield, C. E., *Free Trade, Sovereignty, Democracy: The Future of the World Trade Organization* (Washington, DC: American Enterprise Institute Press, 2001)

Barnett, Michael and Finnemore, Martha, *Rules for the World: International Organizations in Global Politics* (Ithaca: Cornell University Press, 2004)

Beetham, D., *The Legitimation of Power* (Basingstoke: Macmillan Education, 1991)

Benedek, Wolfgang, 'Relations of the WTO with Other International Organizations and NGOs', in Friedl Weiss, Erik Denters and Paul de Waart (eds.), *International Economic Law with a Human Face* (The Hague, Dordrecht and London: Kluwer Law International, 1998)

Bernhardt, Rudolf, 'Interpretation in International Law', in Bernhardt, Rudolf (ed.), *Encyclopedia of Public International Law* (Amsterdam, New York and Oxford: North-Holland Publishing Company, 1981), Book 7 [Instalment 1]

Bhala, Raj, 'The Myth about Stare Decisis in International Trade Law (Part One of a Trilogy)', (1999) 14 *American University International Law Review* 845

'The Power of the Past: Towards De Jure Stare Decisis in WTO Adjudication', (2001) *George Washington International Law Review* 873

'The Precedent Setters: De Facto Stare Decisis in WTO Adjudication (Part Two of a Trilogy)', (1999) 9 *Florida State University Journal of Transnational Law and Policy* 1

Biermann, Frank and Bauer, Steffen (eds.), *A World Environment Organization: Solution or Threat for Effective International Environmental Governance?* (Aldershot: Ashgate, 2005)

Bilder, Richard B., 'The Fact/Law Distinction in International Adjudication', in Richard B. Lillich (ed.), *Fact-Finding Before International Tribunals* (Ardsley, NY: Transnational Publishers, 1992)

Bloche, Gregg M., 'WTO Deference to National Health Policy: Toward an Interpretive Principle', (2002) 5 *Journal of International Economic Law* 825

Bodansky, Daniel, 'The Legitimacy of International Governance: A Coming Challenge for International Environmental Law', (1999) 93 *American Journal of International Law* 596

Bonzon, Yves et al., 'Reflections on Modes of Decision-Making in the World Trade Organization', in Thomas Cottier and Panagiotis Delimatsis (eds.), *The Prospects of International Trade Regulation – From Fragmentation to Coherence* (Cambridge University Press, 2010)

Bowett, D.W., *The Law of International Institutions* (London: Praeger, 1970)

The Law of International Institutions, 4th edn (London: Stevens & Sons, 1981)

Brennan, David J., 'The Three-Step Test Frenzy – Why the TRIPS Panel Decision Might be Considered Per Incuriam', (2002) 2 *Intellectual Property Quarterly* 212

Brewer, Scott, 'Scientific Expert Testimony and Intellectual Due Process', (1988) 107 *Yale Law Journal* 1535

Bronckers, Marco C. E. J., 'More Power to the WTO?', (2001) 4 *Journal of International Economic Law* 41

Bronckers, Marco C. E. J. and McNelis, Natalie, 'Fact and Law in Pleadings before the WTO Appellate Body', in Friedl Weiss (ed.), *Improving WTO Dispute Settlement Procedures: Issues and Lessons from the Practice of Other International Courts and Tribunals* (London: Cameron May, 2000)

Broude, Tomer, *International Governance in the WTO: Judicial Boundaries and Political Capitulation* (London: Cameron May, 2004)

'Principles of Normative Integration and the Allocation of International Authority: The WTO, the Vienna Convention on the Law of Treaties, and the Rio Declaration', (2008) 6 *Loyola University of Chicago School of Law Review* 173

'Taking "Trade and Culture" Seriously: Geographical Indications and Cultural Protection in WTO Law', (2005) 26 *University of Pennsylvania Journal of International Economic Law* 623

Brownlie, Ian, *Principles of Public International Law*, 3rd edn (Oxford: Clarendon Press, 1979)

Burci, Gian Luca and Vignes, Claude-Henri, *World Health Organization* (The Hague, London and Boston, MA: Kluwer Law International, 2004)

Büthe, Tim, 'Agent Selection in International Delegation: The Delegation of Regulatory Authority in the SPS Agreement of the WTO', paper prepared for presentation at the international conference on 'Trade-And-? The World Trade Organization's Fuzzy Borders', Graduate Institute of International and Development Studies, Geneva, 5–6 February 2009

Cameron, James and Gray, Kevin R., 'Principles of International Law in the WTO Dispute Settlement Body', (2001) 50 *International and Comparative Law Quarterly* 248

Cameron, James and Orava, Stephen J., 'GATT/WTO Panels Between Recording and Finding Facts: Issues of Due Process, Evidence, Burden of Proof, and Standard of Review in GATT/WTO Dispute Settlement', in Friedl Weiss (ed.), *Improving WTO Dispute Settlement Procedures: Issues and Lessons from the Practice of Other International Courts and Tribunals* (London: Cameron May, 2000)

Cass, Deborah Z., 'The "Constitutionalization" of International Trade Law: Judicial Norm-Generation as the Engine of Constitutional Development in International Trade', (2001) 12 *European Journal of International Law* 39

Cassese, Sabino, *When Legal Orders Collide: The Role of Courts* (Seville: Global Law Press – Editorial Derecho Global Seville, 2010)

Chakravarthi, Raghavan, 'WTO Concerned over Human Rights Appraisal Report', Geneva, 27 August 2000, available at www.twnside.org.sg/title/appraisal.htm (last visited April 2010)

Chantal, Thomas, 'Balance-of-Payments Crises in the Developing World: Balancing Trade, Finance and Development in the New Economic Order', (2000) 15 *American University International Law Review* 1249

Charnovitz, Steve, 'Triangulating the World Trade Organization', (2002) 96(1) *American Journal of International Law* 28

'A World Environment Organization', (2002) 27 *Columbia Journal of Environmental Law* 323

Chinkin, Christine, *Third Parties in International Law* (Oxford: Clarendon Press; New York: Oxford University Press, 1993)

Cho, Sungjoon, 'How to Reconcile Trade and Non-Trade Value under the WTO: A Judicial Dimension', in Federico Ortino and Sergey Ripinsky (eds.), *WTO Law and Process, The Proceedings of the 2005 and 2006 Annual WTO Conferences* (London: British Institute of International and Comparative Law, 2007)

Christakos, Helen A., 'WTO Panel Report on Section 110(5) of the US Copyright Act', (2002) 17 *Berkeley Technology Law Journal* 595

Christoforou, Theofanis, 'Law and Precaution in Dispute Resolution on Health and Environmental Protection: What Role for Scientific Experts?', in J. Bourrinet and S. Maljean-Dubois (eds.), *Le Commerce International des Organismes Génétiquement Modifiés* (Paris: Panthéon-Assas, 2003)

'Settlement of Science-Based Trade Disputes in the WTO: A Critical Review of the Developing Case Law in the Face of Scientific Uncertainty', (2000) 8 *New York University Environmental Law Journal* 622

Codex Alimentarius Commission, *Understanding the Codex Alimentarius*, 3rd edn (Rome: FAO)

Cordray, Monique L., 'GATT v. WIPO', (1994) 76 *Journal of the Patent and Trademark Office Society* 122

Cottier, Thomas, 'The Agreement on Trade-Related Aspects of Intellectual Property Rights', in P. F. J. Macrory, A. E. Appleton and M. G. Plummer (eds.), *The World Trade Organization: Legal and Political Analysis*, vol. 1 (New York: Springer, 2005)

'Dispute Settlement in the World Trade Organization: Characteristics and Structural Implications for the European Union', (1998) 35 *Common Market Law Review* 325

'Limits to International Trade: The Constitutional Challenge', in American Society of International Law (ed.), *International Law in Ferment: A New Vision for Theory and Practice*, Proceedings of the 94th Annual Meeting of the American Society of International Law, Washington, DC, 5–8 April 2000

'Risk Management Experience in WTO Dispute Settlement', in David Robertson and Aynsley Kellow (eds.), *Globalization and the Environment: Risk Assessment and the WTO* (Cheltenham: Edward Elgar, 2001)

'The WTO Dispute Settlement System: New Horizons', (1998) *Proceedings of the 92nd Annual Meeting of the American Society of International Law* 86

Cottier, Thomas and Delimatsis, Panagiotis (eds.), *The Prospects of International Trade Regulation – From Fragmentation to Coherence* (Cambridge University Press, 2010)

Cottier, Thomas and Nadakavukaren Schefer, Krista, 'Good Faith and the Protection of Legitimate Expectations in the WTO', in Marco Bronckers and Reinhard Quick (eds.), *New Directions in International Law, Essays in Honour of John H. Jackson* (The Hague, London and Boston, MA: Kluwer Law International, 2000)

Cottier, Thomas and Oesch, Matthias, 'WTO Law, Precedents and Legal Change', (2001) 3 *Turku Law Journal* 27

Cottier, Thomas and Oesch, Matthias, *International Trade Regulation: Law and Policy in the WTO, the European Union and Switzerland* (London: Cameron May, 2005)

Cottier, Thomas, Busse, Cintia and Jevtic, Anna, 'Is a Legally Binding Ban on Internet Sales of Tobacco Products Compatible with WTO Obligations?',

Legal Opinion Submitted to the Secretariat of the World Health Organization, 23 February 2008

Dass, D. K., 'Intellectual Property Rights and the Doha Round', (2005) 8 *Journal of World Intellectual Property* 33

De Bievre, Dirk, 'Forum Shopping in the Global Intellectual Property Rights Regime', paper presented at the conference 'Trade-And? The World Trade Organization's Fuzzy Borders', Geneva, 5–6 February 2009, http://graduateinstitute.ch/webdav/site/ctei/shared/CTEI/3413/Fuzzy-Borders-DeBievre-Thomann.pdf

De Giovan Battista, Ileana, 'Acuerdos entre el gablerno argentine y el Fondo Monetario Internacional (Aspectos Juridicos)', *La Ley* (Buenos Aires), 13 February 1990

Dernbach, John C., 'Achieving Sustainable Development: The Centrality and Multiple Facets of Integrated Decision-Making', (2003) 10 *Indiana Journal of Global Legal Studies* 247

Dreyfuss, Rochelle C. and Lowenfeld, Andreas F., 'Two Achievements of the Uruguay Round: Putting TRIPS and Dispute Settlement Together', (1997) 37 *Virginia Journal of International Law* 275

Dunoff, Jeffrey, 'Constitutional Conceits: The WTO's "Constitution" and the Discipline of International Law', (2006) 17 *European Journal of International Law* 647

'The WTO in Transition: Of Constituents, Competence and Coherence', (2001) 33 *George Washington International Law Review* 979

Echols, Marsha A., *Food Safety and the WTO: The Interplay of Culture, Science and Technology* (London: Kluwer Law International, 2001)

'Institutional Cooperation and Norm Creation in International Organizations: The FAO–WHO Codex Alimentarius', Commentary on Victor Mosoti, in Thomas Cottier, Joost Pauwelyn and Elisabeth Buergi Bonanomi (eds.), *Human Rights and International Trade* (Oxford University Press, 2005)

Eckhardt, Joseph N., 'Balancing Interests in Free Trade and Health: How the WHO's Framework Convention on Tobacco Control Can Withstand WTO Scrutiny', (2002) 12 *Duke Journal of Comparative & International Law* 197

Edwards, Richard, *International Monetary Collaboration* (New York: Transnational Publishers, 1985)

Ehlermann, Claus-Dieter, 'Some Personal Experiences as Member of the Appellate Body of the WTO', Policy Paper RSC No. 02/9, Robert Schuman Centre's Policy Paper Series, 2002

Eichengreen, Barry, *Globalizing Capital: A History of the International Monetary System* (Princeton University Press, 1996)

Elias, Olufemi A. and Lim, Chin L., *The Paradox of Consensualism in International Law* (The Hague and Boston, MA: Kluwer Law International, 1998)

European Commission, Report to the Committee Established under Article 7 of Council Regulation (EC) No 3286/94 (Trade Barriers Regulation), Examination Procedure Regarding the Licensing of Music Works in the United States of America, LE.3/JVE D(98), Brussels, 23 February 1996

Evans, Gail E., 'Intellectual Property as a Trade Issue – The Making of the Agreement on Trade-Related Aspects of Intellectual Property Rights', (1994) 18(2) *World Competition, Law and Economics Review* 137

FAO/WHO, Report of the Evaluation of the Codex Alimentarius and Other FAO and WHO Food Standards Work (2002)

Falk, Richard A. et al., *The United Nations and a Just World Order* (Boulder, CO: Westview Press, 1991)

Farrar, John H. and Dugdale, Anthony M., *Introduction to Legal Method*, 2nd edn (London: Sweet & Maxwell, 1984)

Feldman, R., *The Role of Science in Law* (Oxford University Press, 2009)

Ficsor, Mihaly, 'Copyright in the Digital Era: the WIPO "Internet" Treaties', (1997) 21 *Columbia Journal of Law and the Arts* 8

The Law of Copyright and the Internet (Oxford University Press, 2002)

Fidler, David P., 'The Future of the World Health Organization: What Role for International Law?', (1998) 31 *Vanderbilt Journal of Transnational Law* 1078

'From International Sanitary Conventions to Global Health Security: The New International Health Regulations', (2005) 4 *Chinese Journal of International Law* 325

'Return of the Fourth Horseman: *Emerging Infectious Diseases* and International Law', (1997) 81 *Minnesota Law Review* 771

Fisher-Lescano, Andreas and Teubner, Günther, 'Regime-Collisions: The Vain Search for Legal Unity in the Fragmentation of Global Law', (2004) 25 *Michigan Journal of International Law* 999

Fitzmaurice, Gerald, 'The Law and Procedure of the International Court of Justice: Treaty Interpretation and Certain Other Treaty Points', (1951) 28 *British Yearbook of International Law* 1

Footer, Mary E., *An Institutional and Normative Analysis of the World Trade Organization* (Boston, MA: Martinus Nijhoff Publishers, 2006)

'The (Re)turn to "Soft Law" in Reconciling the Antinomies of WTO Law', (2010) 11 *Melbourne Journal of International Law* 241

Gaffney, John P., 'Due Process in the World Trade Organization: The Need for Procedural Justice in the Dispute Settlement System', (1999) 14 *American University International Law Review* 1173

Gardiner, Richard K., *Treaty Interpretation* (Oxford University Press, 2008)

Gardner, Richard N., 'The Bretton Woods–GATT System After Fifty Years: A Balance Sheet of Success and Failure', in Orin Kirshner (ed.), *The Bretton Woods–GATT System: Retrospect and Prospect After 50 Years* (New York: M.E. Sharpe, 1996)

Geping, Rao, 'The Law Applied by World Trade Organization Panels', (2003) 17 *Temple International and Comparative Law Journal* 137

Gervais, Daniel J., 'Towards a New Core International Copyright Norm: The Reverse Three-Step Test', (2005) 9 *Marquette Intellectual Property Law Review* 1

The TRIPS Agreement, Drafting History and Analysis, 2nd edn (London: Sweet & Maxwell, 2003)

Ginsburg, Jane C., 'Toward Supranational Copyright Law? The WTO Panel Decision and the "Three-Step Test" for Copyright Exceptions', (2001) 187 *Revue Internationale du Droit d'Auteur*

Gold, Joseph, *The Fund Agreement in the Courts III* (International Monetary Fund, 1986)

Interpretation: The IMF and International Law (London: Kluwer, 1996)

Grando, Michelle T., 'Allocating the Burden of Proof in WTO Disputes: A Critical Analysis', (2006) 9 *Journal of International Economic Law* 615

Gross, Leo, *Essays on International Law and Organization*, vol. 2 (Leiden: Brill, 1984)

Gross, Peter, 'Clearing Away the Junk: Court-Appointed Experts, Scientifically Marginal Evidence, and the Silicone Gel Breast Implant Litigation', (2001) 56 *Food Drug Law Journal* 227

Grossman, Gene and Mavroidis, Petros, 'Dispute Settlement Corner: United States – Section 110(5) of the US Copyright Act, Recourse to Arbitration under Article 25 of the DSU: Would've or Should've? Impaired Benefits due to Copyright Infringement', (2003) 2 *World Trade Review* 233

Gruszczynski, Lukasz, *Regulating Health and Environmental Risks under WTO Law: A Critical Analysis of the SPS Agreement* (Oxford University Press, 2010)

Haas, Ernst B., *Beyond the Nation-State: Functionalism and International Organization* (Stanford University Press, 1964)

Hafner, Gerhard, 'Risks Ensuing from the Fragmentation of International Law', in *Report of the International Law Commission on the Work of its Fifty-Second Session*, 2000 (A/55/10)

Haraszti, Gyoergy, *Some Fundamental Problems of the Law of Treaties* (Budapest: Akademiai Kiado, 1973)

Hart, Herbert L. A., *The Concept of Law* (Oxford University Press, 1961)

Helfer, Laurence, 'Adjudicating Copyright Claims under the TRIPS Agreement: The Case for a European Human Rights Analogy', (1998) 39 *Harvard International Law Journal* 357

'Regime Shifting: The TRIPS Agreement and New Dynamics of Intellectual Property Lawmaking', (2004) 29 *Yale Journal of International Law* 26.

'World Music on a US Stage: An Analysis of the Section 110(5) WTO Dispute', (2001) 6 *International Intellectual Property Law and Policy*

'World Music on a US Stage: A Berne/TRIPS and Economic Analysis of the Fairness in Music Licensing Act', (2000) 80 *Boston University Law Review* 93

Helfer, Laurence and Slaughter, Anne-Marie, 'Toward a Theory of Effective Supranational Adjudication', (1997) 107 *Yale Law Journal* 273

Hilf, Meinhard, 'Power, Rules and Principles – Which Orientation for WTO/GATT Law?', (2001) 4 *Journal of International Economic Law* 111

'The Role of National Courts in International Trade Relations', (1997) 18 *Michigan Journal of International Law* 321

Horn, Henrik and Howse, Robert L., 'European Communities – Customs Classification of Frozen Boneless Chicken Cuts', (2008) 7 *World Trade Review* 9

Howse, Robert, 'Adjudicative Legitimacy and Treaty Interpretation in International Trade Law: The Early Years of WTO Jurisprudence', in Joseph H. H. Weiler (ed.), *The EU, the WTO, and the NAFTA: Towards a Common Law of Economic Integration?* (Oxford University Press, 2000)

'The Legitimacy of the World Trade Organization', in Jean-Marc Coicaud and Veijo Heiskanen (eds.), *The Legitimacy of International Organizations* (Tokyo: United Nations, 2001)

'A New Device for Creating International Normativity: The WTO Technical Barriers to Trade Agreement and "International Standards"', in Christian Joerges and Ernst-Ulrich Petersmann (eds.), *Constitutionalism, Multilevel Trade Governance and Social Regulation* (Oxford: Hart Publishing, 2006)

'The Use and Abuse of Other "Relevant Rules of International Law" in Treaty Interpretation: Insight from WTO Trade/Environment Litigations', Institute for International Law and Justice Working Paper 2007/1

Howse, Robert and Horn, Henrik, 'European Communities – Measures Affecting the Approval and Marketing of Biotech Products', (2009) 8(1) *World Trade Review* 49

Howse, Robert and Neven, Damien, 'United States – Section 211 Omnibus Appropriation Act of 1998 (WT/DS176/Appellate Body/R; DSR 2002:II, 589, DSR 2002:II, 683): A Comment', in Henrik Horn and Petros C. Mavroidis, *The WTO Case Law of 2002: The American Law Institute Reporters' Studies* (Cambridge University Press, 2005)

Howse, Robert and Nicolaidis, Kalypso, 'Legitimacy through "Higher Law"? Why Constitutionalizing the WTO is a Step Too Far', in Thomas Cottier and Petros C. Mavroidis (eds.), *The Role of the Judge in International Trade Regulation: Experience and Lessons for the WTO*, vol. 4 (Ann Arbor: University of Michigan Press, 2003)

Hrbatá, Veronika, 'No International Organization is an Island . . . the WTO's Relationship with the WIPO: A Model of Governance of Trade Linkage Areas?', (2010) 44 *Journal of World Trade* 1

Hudec, Robert E., *Enforcing International Trade Law: The Evolution of the Modern GATT Legal System* (Salem: Butterworth Legal Publishers, 1993)

'Free Trade, Sovereignty, Democracy: the Future of the World Trade Organization', (2002) 1 *World Trade Review* 211

Hulka, Barbara S. et al., 'Experience of a Scientific Panel Formed to Advise the Federal Judiciary on Silicone Breast Implants', (2000) 342 *New England Journal of Medicine* 812

ICTSD, 'Mixed Ruling on China IP Enforcement', *ICTSD News and Analysis*, March 2009, http://ictsd.net/i/news/bridges/44213

Idleman, Scott C., 'A Prudential Theory of Judicial Candor', (1995) 73 *Texas Law Review* 1307

International Law Commission (ILC), 'Fragmentation of International Law: Difficulties Arising from the Diversification and Expansion of International Law: Conclusions', Report of the Study Group, A/CN.4/L.702, 18 July 2006

Ishikawa, Yoshimichi, 'The Burden of Proof in WTO Dispute Settlement', draft doctoral thesis, World Trade Institute, University of Berne, 2010 (on file with the author)

Jackson, John H., 'Dispute Settlement and the WTO: Emerging Problems', (1998) 1 *Journal of International Economic Law* 329

World Trade and the Law of GATT (Indianapolis: Bobbs-Merrill Company, 1969)

The World Trade Organization: Constitution and Jurisprudence (London: Pinder/RIIA, 1998)

Jacobson, Harold K., *Networks of Interdependence*, 2nd edn (New York: Knopf, 1984)

Jenks, Clarence W., 'Coordination in International Organization: An Introductory Survey', (1951) 28 *British Year Book of International Law* 29

'The Legal Personality Of International Organizations', (1945) 28 *British Yearbook of International Law* 267

The Proper Law of International Organisations (London: Stevens, 1962)

'Some Constitutional Problems of International Organization', (1945) 22 *British Yearbook of International Law*

Jennings, Robert and Watts, Arthur (eds.), *Oppenheim's International Law, Volume I: Peace*, 9th edn (Harlow: Longman, 1996)

Kapur, Devesh, 'Processes of Change in International Organizations', in Nayyar, Deepak (ed.), *Governing Globalization: Issues and Institutions* (Oxford University Press, 2002)

Kazazi, Mojtaba, *Burden of Proof and Related Issues: A Study on Evidence before International Tribunals* (The Hague, London and Boston, MA: Kluwer Law International, 1996)

Kelly, Claire R., 'Power, Linkage and Accommodation: The WTO as an International Actor and its Influence on Other Actors and Regimes', (2006) 24 *Berkeley Journal of International Law* 79

Keohane, Robert O., *After Hegemony: Cooperation and Discord in the World Political Economy* (Princeton, NJ: Princeton University Press, 1984)

Khlestov, Nikolai, 'WTO–WIPO Co-operation: Does It Have a Future?', 10 *European Intellectual Property Review* 560 (1997)

Kimmerling, Stephen J., 'Havana Club: A Case Summary and an Analysis of Selected Legal Issues', *Papers and Proceedings of the Ninth Annual Meeting of the Association for the Study of the Cuban Economy (ASCE), Cuba in Transition, 12–14 August 1999*, vol. 9, http://lanic.utexas.edu/la/cb/cuba/asce/cuba9/kimmerlg.pdf (visited April 2008)

Kinnon, Collette,'World Trade: Bringing Health into the Picture', (1998) 19 *World Health Forum* 397

Kirgis, Federic L., *International Organizations in their Legal Setting* (St. Paul, MN: West Publishing Co., 1993)

'Specialized Law-Making Processes', in Christopher C. Joyner (ed.), *The United Nations and International Law* (Cambridge University Press, 1997)

Klabbers, Jan, 'Constitutionalism Lite', (2004) 1 *International Organizations Law Review* 31

'Reluctant *Grundnormen*: Article 31(3)(c) and 42 of the Vienna Convention of the Law of Treaties and the Fragmentation of International Law', in M. Craven, M. Fitzmaurice and M. Vogiatzi (eds.), *Time, History and International Law* (Leiden: Martinus Nijhoff, 2007)

Koelman, Kamiel J., 'Fixing the Three-Step Test', (2006) 28 *European Intellectual Property Review* 407

Koh, Tommy T. B., 'A Constitution for the Oceans', Remarks made by the President of the Third United Nations Conference on the Law of the Sea, in Official Text of the United Nations Convention on the Law of the Sea with Annexes and Index (1983), E 83V5

Krasner, Stephen, 'Structural Causes and Regime Consequences: Regimes as Intervening Variables', in Stephen D. Krasner (ed.), *International Regimes* (Ithaca: Cornell University Press, 1983)

Ku, Charlotte, *Global Governance and the Changing Face of International Law*, Acuns Reports and Papers 2 (New Haven, CT: ACUNS, 2001), available at www.reformwatch.net/fitxers/22.pdf.

Kuijper, Pieter J., 'The Appellate Body and the Facts', in Marco Bronckers and Reinhard Quick (eds.), *New Directions in International Economic Law: Essays in Honour of John H. Jackson* (The Hague, London and Boston, MA: Kluwer Law International, 2000)

'Some Institutional Issues Presently before the WTO', in Daniel Kennedy and James Southwick (eds.), *The Political Economy of International Trade Law: Essays in Honor of Robert E Hudec* (Cambridge University Press, 2002)

Kwakwa, Edward, 'Some Comments on Rulemaking at the World Intellectual Property Organization', (2002) 12 *Duke Journal of Comparative & International Law* 179

Lamy, Pascal, 'The Place of the WTO and its Law in the International Legal Order', (2006) 17 *European Journal of International Law* 969

'The WTO in the Archipelago of *Global Governance*', Speech at The Institute of International Studies, Geneva, 14 March 2006, www.WTO.org/english/news_e/sppl_e/sppl20_e.htm (visited June 2008)

Lauterpacht, Elihu, *Aspects of Administration of International Justice* (Cambridge University Press, 1991)

Lauterpacht, Hersch, *The Development of International Law by the International Court*, rev. edn (London: Stevens & Sons Limited, 1958)

'Some Observations on Preparatory Work in the Interpretation of Treaties', (1935) 48 *Harvard Law Review* 549

Lauwaars, Richard H., 'The Interrelationship between United Nations Law and the Law of Other International Organizations', (1984) 82 *Michigan Law Review* 1604

Leaffer, Marshall, *Understanding Copyright Law*, 2nd edn (New York: Matthew Bender, 1995)

Lee, Roy S., 'Multilateral Treaty-Making and Negotiation Techniques: An Appraisal', in Bin Cheng and Edward D. Brown (eds.), *Contemporary Problems of International Law: Essays in Honour of Georg Schwarzenberger on his Eightieth Birthday* (London: Stevens & Sons Limited, 1988)

Leive, David M., *International Regulatory Regimes: Case Studies in Health, Meteorology and Food*, vol. 1 (Lexington, MA: Lexington Books, 1976)

Lennard, Michael, 'Navigating by the Stars: Interpreting the WTO Agreements', (2002) 5 *Journal of International Economic Law* 17

Levit, Janet K., 'A Bottom-Up Approach to International Lawmaking: The Tale of Three Trade Finance Instruments', (2005) 30 *Yale Journal of International Law* 125

Lin, Tsai-yu, 'Addressing the Issue of Trade in Services and Public Health in the Case of Tobacco – Are the FCTC Restrictions on Tobacco Advertising Inconsistent with the GATS?', (2006) 7(4) *Journal of World Investment & Trade* 545.

Lin, Tsai-yu, 'Exploring a Modest Balance for Trade in Tobacco, Anti-Tobacco Smuggling and Health Concerns in Light of the Dominican Republic-Cigarettes Case', (2008) 3 *Asian Journal of WTO & International Health Law and Policy* 308

Linderfalk, Ulf, *On the Interpretation of Treaties: The Modern International Law as Expressed in the 1969 Vienna Convention on the Law of Treaties* (New York: Springer Verlag AG, 2007)

Lindroos, Anja and Mehling, Michael, 'Dispelling the Chimera of "Self-Contained Regimes" International Law and the WTO', (2005) 16 *European Journal of International Law* 857

Liu, Chuyang, *Maritime Transport Services in the Law of the Sea and the World Trade Organization*, Studies in Global Economic Law (Berne etc.: Peter Lang, 2009)

Livermore, Michael A., 'Authority and Legitimacy in *Global Governance*: Deliberation, Institutional Differentiation, and Codex Alimentarius', (2006) 81 *New York University Law Review* 766

Lloyd, Peter, 'When Should New Areas of Rules Be Added to the WTO?', (2005) 4 *World Trade Review* 275

Lowenfeld, Andreas F., *International Economic Law* (Oxford and New York: Oxford University Press, 2002)

Luard, Evan, *International Agencies: The Emerging Framework of Interdependence* (Dobbs Ferry, NY: Oceana, 1977)

McCluggage, Laura, 'Section 110(5) and The Fairness in Music Licensing Act: Will the WTO Decide the United States Must Pay to Play?', 40 *IDEA: The Journal of Law and Technology* 1 (2000)

McGinnis, John, 'The Appropriate Hierarchy of Global Multilateralism and Customary International Law: The Example of the WTO', 44 *Virginia Journal of International Law* 229 (2003)

McGinnis, John and Movsesian, Mark, 'The World Trade Constitution', 114 *Harvard Law Review* 511 (2000)

McGrady, Benn, 'Fragmentation of International Law or "Systemic Integration" of Treaty Regimes: EC–Biotech and the Proper Interpretation of Article 31(3)(c) of the Vienna Convention on the Law of Treaties', 42(4) *Journal of World Trade* 589 (2008)

McLachlan, Campbell, 'The Principle of Systemic Integration and Article 31(3)(c) of the Vienna Convention' 54(2) *International and Comparative Law Quarterly* 279 (2005)

MacMillan, Fiona, 'International Economic Law and Public International Law: Strangers in the Night', (2004) 10 *International Trade Law and Regulation* 115

McNair, Arnold D., *The Law of Treaties*, 2nd edn (Oxford: Clarendon Press, 1961)

McRae, Donald, 'Claus-Dieter Ehlermann's Presentation on "The Role and Record of Dispute Settlement and the Appellate Body of WTO"' 6(3) *Journal of International Economic Law* 709 (2003)

'The Emerging Appellate Jurisdiction in International Trade Law', in James Cameron and Karen Campbell (eds.), *Dispute Resolution in the World Trade Organization* (London: Cameron May, 1998) 98–110

Magnone, Gerald J., *A Short History of International Organisations* (New York: McGraw-Hill, 1954)

Maki, Peter C., 'Interpreting GATT Using the Vienna Convention on the Law of Treaties: A Method to Increase the Legitimacy of the Dispute Settlement System', (2000) 9 *Minnesota Journal of Global Trade* 343

Marceau, Gabrielle, 'A Call for Coherence in International Law: Praises for the Prohibition against "Clinical Isolation" in WTO Dispute Settlement', (1999) 33(5) *Journal of World Trade* 87

'Dispute Settlement and Human Rights', (2002) 13 *European Journal of International Law* 753

Marceau, Gabrielle and Trachtman, Joel P., 'The Technical Barriers to Trade Agreement, the Sanitary and Phytosanitary Measures Agreement, and the General Agreement on Tariff and Trade, A Map of the World Trade Organization Law of Domestic Regulation of Goods', (2002) 35(5) *Journal of World Trade* 811

Matsushita, Mitsuo, Schoenbaum, Thomas H. and Mavroidis, Petros C., *The World Trade Organization: Law, Practice, and Policy* (Oxford University Press, 2006)

Mattli, Walter, 'International Governance for Voluntary Standards: A Game Theoretic Perspective', in George A. Bermann, Matthias Herdegen and Peter L. Lindseth (eds.), *Transatlantic Regulatory Cooperation: Legal Problems and Political Prospects* (Oxford University Press, 2000)

Mavroidis, Petros C., 'No Outsourcing of Law? WTO Law as Practiced by WTO Courts', (2008) 102 *American Journal of International Law* 421

May, Christopher, *The World Intellectual Property Organization: Resurgence and the Development Agenda* (London: Routledge, 2007)

Mendelson, Maurice, 'Comment on "May Preparatory Work be Used to Correct Rather than Confirm the 'Clear' Meaning of a Treaty Provision?"', (2005) 2(5) *Transnational Dispute Management*, www.transnational-dispute-management.com.

Mendenhall, James, 'WTO Panel Report on Consistency of Chinese Intellectual Property Standards', (2009) 13 *ASIL Insight* 4

Menescal, Andréa K., 'Changing the WIPO's Ways? The 2004 Development Agenda in Historical Perspective', (2005) 8 *Journal of World Intellectual Property* 761

Mitchell, Andrew D. and Heaton, David, 'The Inherent Jurisdiction of WTO Tribunals: The Select Application of Public International Law Required by the Judicial Function', (2010) 31 *Michigan Journal of International Law* 561

Mitchell, Andrew D. and Sheargold, Elizabeth, 'GATT Art. XV: Exchange Arrangements', in Rüdiger Wolfrum and Peter-Tobias Stoll (eds.), *Max Planck Commentaries on World Trade Law, WTO – Trade in Goods*, vol.5 (Leiden: Koninklijke Brill NV, 2010)

Mitrany, David, *A Working Peace System* (London: Royal Institute of International Affairs, 1943)

Moravcsik, Andrew, 'Is there a "Democratic Deficit" in World Politics?', (2004) 39 *Government and Opposition* 336

Morgenthau, Hans J., 'Positivism, Functionalism, and International Law', (1940) 34 *American Journal of International Law* 260

Mort, Susan A., 'The WTO, the WIPO and the Internet: Confounding the Borders of Copyright and Neighbouring Rights', (1997) 8 *Fordham Intellectual Property, Media & Entertainment Law Journal* 184

Mosoti, Victor, 'Institutional Cooperation and Norm Creation in International Organizations', in Thomas Cottier, Joost Pauwelyn and Elisabeth Buergi

Bonanomi (eds.), *Human Rights and International Trade* (Oxford University Press, 2005)

Motaal, Doaa Abdel, 'The "Multilateral Scientific Consensus" and the World Trade Organization', (2004) 38 *Journal of World Trade* 855

Müller, Jörg P. and Wildhaber, Luzius, *Praxis des Völkerrechts*, 3rd edn (Berne: Stämfli Verlag AG, 2001)

Murray, Craig, 'Implementing the New International Health Regulations: The Role of the WTO's Sanitary and Phytosanitary Agreement', (2009) 40 *Georgetown Journal of International Law* 625

Nichols, Philip M., 'GATT Doctrine', (1996) 36 *Virginia Journal of International Law* 379

Oberthür, Sebastian and Gehring, Thomas, 'Reforming International Environmental Governance: An Institutionalist Critique of the Proposal for a World Environment Organization', (2004) 4 *International Environmental Agreements: Politics, Law and Economics* 359

O'Connell, Daniel P., *International Law*, 2nd edn, vol. 1 (London: Stevens & Sons, 1970)

OECD, 'Arrangement on Officially Supported Export Credits' (2008 revision), OECD Trade and Agriculture Directorate TAD/PG(2007)28/FINAL, www.oecd.org/

Oesch, Matthias, 'The Jurisprudence of WTO Dispute Resolution', (2006) 16 *Revue suisse de droit international et de droit europeen/Schweizerische zeitschrift für internationales und europäisches recht* 501

Standards of Review in WTO Dispute Resolution (Oxford University Press, 2003)

Okediji, Ruth L., 'Becoming WIPO', draft paper presented at the Fordham University Law School Symposium, When Worlds Collide: Intellectual Property at the Interface between Systems of Knowledge Creation, 31 October–1 November 2008

'TRIPS Dispute Settlement and the Sources of (International) Copyright Law', (2002) 49 *Journal of the Copyright Society* 585

'WIPO–WTO Relations and the Future of Global Intellectual Property Norms', (2008) 39 *Netherlands Yearbook of International Law* 69

Oloka-Onyango, Joseph and Udagama, Deepika, 'The Realization of Economic, Social and Cultural Rights: Globalization and its Impact on the Full Enjoyment of Human Rights' (Preliminary Report), Sub-Commission on the Promotion and Protection of Human Rights, 15 June 2000, www.unhchr.ch/huridocda/huridoca.nsf/2848af408d01ec0ac1256609004e770b/21a92d3d0425a0cec125693500484d2f?OpenDocument&Highlight=2, Oloka-Onyango (last visited March 2010)

Orakhelashvili, Alexander, *The Interpretation of Acts and Rules in Public International Law* (Oxford University Press, 2008)

Orellana, Marcos, 'The EU and Chile Suspend the Swordfish Case Proceedings at the WTO and the International Tribunal for the Law of the Sea', *ASIL Insights*, February 2001

'The Swordfish Dispute between the EU and Chile at the ITLOS and the WTO', (2002) 71 *Nordic Journal of International Law* 55

Ortino, Federico, 'Treaty Interpretation and the WTO Appellate Body Report in US – Gambling: A Critique', (2006) 9 *Journal of International Economic Law* 117

Ostry, Sylvia, 'Reinforcing the WTO', Occasional Paper 56, Group of Thirty, 1998, www.utoronto.ca/cis/ostry/

Palmeter, David and Mavroidis, Petros C., *Dispute Settlement in the World Trade Organization: Practice and Procedure* (The Hague, London and Boston, MA: Kluwer Law International, 1999)

'The WTO Legal System: Sources of Law', (1998) 92 *American Journal of International Law* 398

Panizzon, Marion, *Good Faith in the Jurisprudence of the WTO, The Protection of Legitimate Expectations, Good Faith Interpretation and Fair Dispute Settlement* (Oxford: Hart Publishing, 2006)

Passell, Peter, 'Loading the Trade Agenda with Diverse Issues Could Backfire', *New York Times*, 9 October 1997

Pauwelyn, Joost, *Conflict of Norms in Public International Law: How WTO Law Relates to Other Rules of International Law* (Cambridge University Press, 2003)

'Dispute Settlement: How to Win a WTO Dispute Based on Non-WTO Law? Questions of Jurisdictions and Merits', (2003) 37 *Journal of World Trade* 997

'Evidence, Proof and Persuasion in WTO Dispute Settlement: Who Bears the Burden?', (1998) 1 *Journal of International Economic Law* 227

'The Role of Public International Law in the WTO: How Far Can We Go?', (2001) 95 *American Journal of International Law* 535

'The Sutherland Report: A Missed Opportunity for Genuine Debate on Trade, Globalization and Reforming the WTO', (2005) 8 *Journal of International Economic Law* 329

'Unity and Fragmentation in International Law', Introductory Report on the World Trade Organization, Palma Workshop, 20–21 May 2005, http://eprints.law.duke.edu

'The Use of Experts in WTO Dispute Settlement', (2002) 51 *International and Comparative Law Quarterly* 325

Perez, Oren, *Ecological Sensitivity and Global Legal Pluralism* (Oxford: Hart, 2004)

Pescatore, Pierre, Davey, William J. and Lowenfeld, Andreas F., *Handbook of the WTO/GATT Dispute Settlement* (Irvington-on-Hudson: Transnational Publishers Inc., 1998)

Peters, Anne, 'Compensatory Constitutionalism', (2006) 19 *Leiden Journal of International Law* 597

'Membership in the Global Constitutional Community', in Jan Klabbers, Anne Peters and Geir Ulfstein (eds.), *The Constitutionalization of International Law* (Oxford University Press, 2009)

Petersmann, Ernst-Ulrich, 'Constitutionalism and International Organizations', (1997) 17 *Northwestern Journal of International Law & Business* 398

'How to Promote the International Rule of Law? Contributions by the World Trade Organization Appellate Review System', (1998) 1 *Journal of International Economic Law* 25

'Time for a United Nations "Global Compact" for Integrating Human Rights into the Law of Worldwide Organizations: Lessons from European Integration', (2000) 13 *European Journal of International Law* 612

Poli, Sara, 'The Adoption of International Food Safety Standards', (2004) 10 *European Law Journal* 615

Price, Joseph M. and Rosenberg, Ellen S., 'The Silicone Gel Breast Implant Controversy: The Rise of Expert Panels and the Fall of Junk Science', (2000) 93 *Journal of the Royal Society of Medicine* 31

Public Citizen, '"WTO – Shrink or Sink!" – The Turnaround Agenda International Civil Society Sign-on Letter', www.citizen.org/trade/WTO/shrink_sink/articles.cfm?ID=1569 (last visited April 2008)

Qureshi, Asif H., *Interpreting WTO Agreements: Problems and Perspectives* (Cambridge University Press, 2006)

Rayfuse, Rosemary, 'The Future of Compulsory Dispute Settlement under the Law of the Sea Convention', (2005) 36 *Victoria University of Wellington Law Journal* 28

Rehnquist, James C., 'Taking Comity Seriously: How to Neutralize the Abstention Doctrine', (1994) 46 *Stanford Law Review* 1049

Reininke, Wolfgang and Witte, Jan Martin, 'Interdependence, Globalization and Sovereignty: The Role of Non-Binding International Legal Accords', in Dinah Shelton (ed.), *Commitment and Compliance: The Role of Non-Binding Norms in the International Legal System* (New York: Oxford University Press, 2000)

Ricketson, Sam, *The Berne Convention for the Protection of Literary and Artistic Works: 1886–1986* (London: Queen Mary College – University of London, 1987)

Ricuppero, R., 'Rebuilding Confidence in the Multilateral Trading System: Closing the "Legitimacy Gap"', in G. P. Sampson (ed.), *The Role of the World Trade Organization in Global Governance* (Tokyo: United Nations University Press, 2001)

Riggs, Robert F. and Plano, Jack C., *The United Nations: International Organization and World Politics*, 2nd edn (Belmont, CA: Wadsworth Publishing, 1994)

Roessler, Frieder, 'The Institutional Balance between the Judicial and the Political Organs of the WTO', in Marco Bronckers and Reinhard Quick (eds.), *New Directions in International Law: Essays in Honour of John H. Jackson* (The Hague, London and Boston, MA: Kluwer Law International, 2000)

'The Relationship between the World Trade Order and the International Monetary System', in Ernst-Ulrich Petersmann and Meinhard Hilf (eds.), *The New GATT Round of Multilateral Trade Negotiations: Legal and Economic Problems – Studies in Transnational Law*, 2nd edn (Deventer: Kluwer, 1991)

Rovetta, Davide, Sud, Juhi and Vermulst, Edwin, 'WTO Dispute Settlement with Respect to Customs Matters', (2009) 4(4) *Global Trade and Customs Journal* 105

Sacerdoti, Giorgio, 'The Dispute Settlement System of the WTO: Structure and Function in the Perspective of the First 10 Years', (2006) 5 *Law & Practice of International Courts and Tribunals* 49

Sands, Philippe, 'Treaty, Custom and the Cross-Fertilization of International Law', (1998) 1 *Yale Human Rights and Development Law Journal* 85

Sands, Philippe and Klein, Pierre, *Bowett's Law of International Institutions*, 5th edn (London: Sweet & Maxwell, 2001)

Sarooshi, Danesh, *The United Nations and the Development of Collective Security: The Delegation by the UN Security Council of its Chapter VII Powers* (Oxford University Press, 1999)

Schepel, Harm, *The Constitution of Private Governance: Product Standards in the Regulation of Integrating Markets* (Oxford: Hart Publishing, 2005)

Schermers, Henry G., *International Institutional Law*, vols. 1 and 2 (Leiden: Sijthoff, 1972)

'The International Organizations', in Mohammed Bedjaoui (ed.), *International Law: Achievements and Prospects* (Paris and Dordrecht: UNESCO and Martinus Nijhoff, 1991)

Schermers, Henry G. and Blokker, Niels M., *International Institutional Law: Unity Within Diversity*, 4th edn (The Hague and Boston, MA: Martinus Nijhoff, 2003)

Schorr, David, 'Healthy Fisheries, Sustainable Trade: Crafting New Rules on Fishing Subsidies in the World Trade Organization', WWF Position Paper, 2004

Schreuer, Christoph H., 'Diversity and Harmonization of Treaty Interpretation in Investment Arbitration', (2006) 3(2) *Transnational Dispute Management* 1

Schropp, Simon A. B., *Trade Policy Flexibility and Enforcement in the WTO: A Law and Economics Analysis* (Cambridge University Press, 2009)

Schwarzenberger, Georg, 'The Principles and Standards of International Economic Law', (1966/I) 117 *Recueil des Cours d'Academie de Droit International* 1

Schwebel, Stephen M., 'May Preparatory Work Be Used to Correct Rather than Confirm the "Clear" Meaning of a Treaty Provision?', in Jerzy Makarczyk (ed.), *Theory of International Law at the Threshold of the 21st Century: Essays in Honour of Krzystof Skubiszewski*' (London: Kluwer Law International, 1966)

Scott, Joanne, 'Cooperative Regulation in the WTO: The SPS Committee', New York University, Global Law Working Paper 03/06, 2006

The WTO Agreement on Sanitary and Phytosanitary Measures: A Commentary (Oxford University Press, 2007)

Shamsey, John, 'ITLOS vs. Goliath: The International Tribunal for the Law of the Sea Stands Tall with the Appellate Body in the Chilean–EU Swordfish Dispute', (2002) 12 *Transnational Law and Contemporary Problems* 513

Shany, Yuval, *The Competing Jurisdictions of International Courts and Tribunals* (Oxford University Press, 2003)

'One Law to Rule Them All: Should International Courts Be Viewed as Guardians of Procedural Order and Legal Uniformity?', paper presented at the Conference on Unity or Fragmentation of International Law – the Role of International and National Tribunals, Oslo, 14–15 May 2009 (on file with the author)

Shaw, Sabrina and Schwartz, Risa, 'Trade and Environment in the WTO: State of Play', (2002) 36 *Journal of World Trade* 129

Shell, Richard, 'Trade Legalism and International Relations Theory: An Analysis of World Trade Organization', (1995) 44 *Duke Law Journal* 829, repr. in Robert Howse (ed.), *The World Trading System: Critical Perspectives on the World Economy*, vol. 2, *Dispute Settlement* (London and New York: Routledge, 1998)

Shihata, Ibrahim F. I., *The World Bank in a Changing World: Selected Essays* (The Hague: Nijhoff, 1991)

Siegel, Deborah E., 'Legal Aspects of the IMF/WTO Relationship: The Fund's Articles of Agreement and the WTO Agreements', (2002) 96 *American Journal of International Law* 569

Simma, Bruno, 'Self-Contained Regimes', (1985) 16 *Netherlands Yearbook of International Law* 111

Sinclair, Ian M., *The Vienna Convention on the Law of Treaties* (Manchester University Press, 1973)

Singh, Someshwar, 'UN Human Rights Commissioner Responds to the WTO', Geneva, 29 August 2000, www.twnside.org.sg/title/responds.htm (last visited April 2010)

Slotboom, Marco M., 'The Hormones Case: An Increased Risk of Illegality of Sanitary and Phytosanitary Measures', (1999) 36 *Common Market Law Review* 471

Smith, Roger and Wynne, Brian, *Expert Evidence: Interpreting Science in the Law* (London: Routledge, 1989)

Steele, David B., 'The Case for Global Economic Management and UN System Reform', (1985) 39 *International Organization* 561

Steger, Debra P., 'Amicus Curiae: Participant or Friend? The WTO and NAFTA Experience', in Armin von Bogdandy, Petros C. Mavroidis and Yves Mény (eds.), *European Integration and International Co-ordination: Studies in Transnational Economic Law in Honour of Claus-Dieter Ehlermann* (The Hague, London and New York: Kluwer Law International, 2002)

Steger, Debra P., 'Book Review (of *Free Trade, Sovereignty, Democracy: The Future of the World Trade Organization* by C.E. Barfield)', (2002) 5 *Journal of International Economic Law* 565

'The Rule of Law or the Rule of Lawyers', (2002) 3 *Journal of World Investment* 769

Stewart, Terence P. and Johanson, David S., 'The SPS Agreement of the World Trade Organization and International Organization: The Roles of the Codex Alimentarius Commission, the International Plant Protection Convention, and International Office of Epizootics', (1998) 26 *Syracuse Journal of International Law and Commerce* 27

Stewart, Terence P. and Karpel, Amy A., 'Review of the Dispute Settlement Understanding: Operation of Panels', (2000) 31 *Law and Policy in International Business* 593

Stonehouse, John and Mumford, John, 'Science, Risk Analysis and Environmental Policy Decisions', United Nations Environmental Programme Environment and Trade Series, 1994

Sturm, Susan P., 'A Normative Theory of Public Law Remedies', (1991) 79 *Georgetown Law Journal* 1357

Swan, Alan C., 'Havana Club in the WTO: Herein of International Law and American Power', Cuba in Transition: Volume 12, Papers and Proceedings of the Twelfth Annual Meeting of the Association for the Study of the Cuban Economy (ASCE), 1–3 August 2002

Swan, Alan C. and Murphy, John F., *Cases and Materials on the Regulation of International Business and Economic Relations: Documents Supplement* (New York: Matthew Bender, 2001)

Tarullo, Daniel K., 'The Relationship of WTO Obligations to Other International Arrangements', in Marco Bronckers and Reinhard Quick (eds.), *New Directions in International Law: Essays in Honour of John H. Jackson* (The Hague, London and Boston, MA: Kluwer Law International, 2000)

Taylor, Allyn et al., 'The Impact of Trade Liberalization on Tobacco Consumption', in Prabhat Jha and Frank J. Chaloupka (eds.), *Tobacco Control in Developing Countries* (Oxford University Press, 2000)

Thirlway, Hugh W. A., 'Evidence before International Courts and Tribunals', in Rudolf Bernhardt (ed.), *Encyclopedia of Public International Law* (Amsterdam, New York and Oxford: North-Holland Publishing Company, 1981), Book 1 [Instalment 1]

Torres, Hector R., 'Reforming the International Monetary Fund – Why Its Legitimacy Is At Stake', (2007) 14 *Journal of International Economic Law* 237

Trachtman, Joel, 'The Domain of WTO Dispute Resolution', (1999) 40 *Harvard International Law Journal* 333

Trebilcock, Michael J. and Howse, Robert, *The Regulation of International Trade*, 3rd edn (London: Routledge, 2005)

Ulfstein, Geir, 'Institutions and Competences', in Jan Klabbers, Anne Peters and Geir Ulfstein (eds.), *The Constitutionalization of International Law* (Oxford University Press, 2009)

UN Economic and Social Commission for Asia and the Pacific (ESCAP), 'What is Good Governance?', http://www.unescap.org/pdd/prs/ProjectActivities/Ongoing/gg/governance.pdf (visited 22 May 2009)

UN Sub-Commission on the Promotion and Protection of Human Rights, 'Globalization and its Impact on the Full Enjoyment of All Human Rights' (Resolution 2001/5), 25th meeting, 15 August 2001, http://attac.org/nonewround/doc/doc08.htm

Van Damme, Isabelle, *Treaty Interpretation by the WTO Appellate Body* (Oxford University Press, 2009)

Veggeland, Frode and Borgen, Svein O., 'Negotiating International Food Standards: The World Trade Organization's Impact on the Codex Alimentarius Commission', (2005) 18 *Governance: An International Journal of Policy, Administration, and Institutions* 675

Victor, David G., 'The Sanitary and Phytosanitary Agreement of the World Trade Organization: An Assessment after Five Years', (1999–2000) 32 *New York University Journal of International Law & Politics* 874

Villiger, Mark E., *Commentary on the 1969 Vienna Convention on the Law of Treaties* (Leiden: Martinus Nijhoff Publishers, 2009)

Vines, David, 'The WTO in Relation to the Fund and the Bank: Competences, Agendas, and Linkages', in Anne O. Krueger (ed.), *The WTO as an International Organization* (Chicago: University of Chicago Press, 1998)

Viterbo, Annamaria, 'Monetary Measures Affecting Trade and Investments: The Overlapping Jurisdictions of the IMF, WTO and the ICSID', SIEL Online Proceedings Working Paper No. 34/08 (2008), published in *Transnational Dispute Management*, January 2009

Vivas-Eugui, David, 'What Agenda for the Review of TRIPS? A Sustainable Development Perspective', Center for International Environmental Law TEP 2–3 (Summer 2002), www.ciel.org/Publications/AgendaTRIPS_Summer02.pdf (visited 20 March 2009)

Voitovich, Sergei A., *International Economic Organizations in the International Legal Process* (Boston, MA: Martinus Nijhoff Publishers, 1995)

Voon, Tania, 'UNESCO and the WTO: A Clash of Cultures', (2006) 55 *International and Comparative Law Quarterly* 635

Wade, William, and Forsyth, Christopher, *Administrative Law* (Oxford University Press, 1994)

Waincymer, Jeffrey, 'Reformulated Gasoline under Reformulated WTO Dispute Settlement Procedures: Pulling Pandora out of a Chapeau?', (1996) 18 *Michigan Journal of International Law* 141

WTO Litigation: Procedural Aspects of Formal Dispute Settlement (London: Cameron May, 2002)

Wauters, Jasper and Vandenbus Sche, Hylke, 'China – Measures Affecting Imports of Automobile Parts', (2010) 9 *World Trade Review* 201

Weiss, Friedl, 'The WTO and the Progressive Development of International Trade Law', (1988) 29 *Netherlands Yearbook of International Law* 71

White, Nigel D., *The Law of International Organisations* (Manchester University Press, 2005)

Wind, Izaak, 'HS 2007: What's It All About?', (2007) 2 *Global Trade and Customs Journal* 79

Winter, Ryan L., 'Reconciling the GATT and WTO with Multilateral Environmental Agreements: Can We Have Our Cake and Eat It Too?', (2000) 11 *Colorado Journal of International Environmental Law & Policy* 223

WIPO, *The WIPO Arbitration and Mediation Center: Dispute Resolution for the 21st Century*, WIPO Publication No. 779E, www.wipo.int/freepublications/en/arbitration/779/wipo_pub_779.pdf

WIPO International Bureau, 'Implication of the TRIPS Agreement on Treaties Administered by WIPO', *International Review of Industrial Property & Copyright Law* 164 (May 1996)

Wirth, David A., 'The Role of Science in the Uruguay Round and NAFTA Trade Disciplines', (1994) 27 *Cornell International Law Journal* 817

Wolfrum, Rüdiger, Stoll, Peter-Tobias and Kaiser, Karen, *WTO: Institutions and Dispute Settlement – Max Planck Commentaries on World Trade Law* (Boston, MA: Martinus Nijhoff Publishers, 2006)

Woods, Ngaire, 'The Challenge of Good Governance for the IMF and the World Bank Themselves', (2000) 28 *World Development* 823

'Good Governance in International Organizations', (1999) 5 *Global Governance* 39

Woolf, Harry, Jowell, Jeffrey L., De Smith, Stanley A. and Le Sueur, Andrew P., *De Smith, Woolf & Jowell's Principles of Judicial Review* (London: Sweet & Maxwell, 1999)

World Bank, 'Economics of Tobacco Control: Chapter 5, Measures to Reduce the Supply of Tobacco', 2000, http://www1.worldbank.org/tobacco/book/pdf/06-Tobacco-Chap5.pdf

World Commission on the Social Dimension of Globalization, 'A Fair Globalization: Creating Opportunities for All', March 2004, at www.ilo.org/public/english/wcsdg/docs/report.pdf

WTO, 'The Future of the WTO', Report by the Consultative Board to the Director-General Supachai Panitchpakdi (2004), www.WTO.org/english/thewto_e/10anniv_e/future_WTO_e.htm (visited March 2008)

'WTO Agreements and Public Health', a joint study by the WHO and WTO Secretariat, 2002, www.WTO.org/english/res_e/booksp_e/who_WTO_e.pdf (visited 20 April 2009)

Wüger, Daniel, 'The Implementation Phase in the Dispute between the EC and the United States on Hormone-Treated Beef', (2002) *Law and Policy in International Business* 777

Yasseen, Mustafa K., 'L'interprétation des traités d'après la convention de Vienne sur le droit des traités', (1976/III) 151 *Recueil des Cours d'Academie de Droit International* 3

Yemin, Edward, *Legislative Powers in the United Nations and Specialized Agencies* (Leyden: A. W. Sijthoff, 1969)

Young, Margaret A., 'Fragmentation or Interaction: The WTO, Fisheries Subsidies and International Law', (2009) 8 *World Trade Review* 477

'The WTO's Use of Relevant Rules of International Law: An Analysis of the Biotech Case', (2007) 56 *International and Comparative Law Quarterly* 907

Zamora, Stephen, 'Economic Relations and Development', in Christopher C. Joyner (ed.), *The United Nations and International Law* (Cambridge: American Society of International Law and University of Cambridge, 1997)

Ziegler, Andreas, 'Scope and Function of the WTO Appellate System: What Future after the Millennium Round?', (1999) 3 *Max Planck Yearbook of United Nations Law* 439

Zimmermann, Claus D., *Fundamental Exchange Rate Misalignment and International Law* (University of Oxford and International Monetary Fund, 2008)

'Jurisdictional Competition between the IMF and the WTO and its Impact on the Prevention of Monetary Protectionism', Society of International Economic Law (SIEL) Inaugural Conference 2008, Paper 16/08, 26 June 2008

Zimmern, Alfred E., *The League of Nations and the Rule of Law* (London: Macmillan, 1939)

Zleptnig, Stefan, *Non-Economic Objectives in WTO Law: Justification Provisions of GATT, GATS, SPS and TBT Agreements* (The Hague: Martinus Nijhoff Publishers, 2010)

INDEX